CHANGE IN THE INTERNATIONAL SYSTEM

Other Titles of Interest

About the Book and Editors

Change in the International System
edited by Ole R. Holsti,
Randolph M. Siverson,
and Alexander L. George

Unlike most texts on the international system, which stress continuities, this volume focuses on changes — what has caused them, where they will stop, and perhaps most important, where they will take us. Designed to initiate and structure inquiry into the dynamics of international change, the book is organized to reflect three main dimensions of system transformation: its nature, its sources, and its limits. The fourteen distinguished authors enable both teachers and students to derive new and more meaningful insights into the workings of the international system and global politics.

Ole R. Holsti is chairman of the Political Science Department and George V. Allen Professor at Duke University. Randolph M. Siverson is associate professor of political science at the University of California, Davis. Alexander L. George is Graham H. Stuart Professor of International Relations at Stanford University.

CHANGE
IN THE
INTERNATIONAL
SYSTEM

edited by
Ole R. Holsti
Randolph M. Siverson
Alexander L. George

Westview Press / Boulder, Colorado

© 1980 by Westview Press (Chapter 10 © 1980 Alexander L. George)

Published in 1980 in the United States of America by
  Westview Press, Inc.
  5500 Central Avenue
  Boulder, Colorado 80301
  Frederick A. Praeger, Publisher

Library of Congress Cataloging in Publication Data
Main entry under title:
Change in the international system.
  1. International relations—Addresses, essays, lectures. I. Holsti, Ole R. II. Siverson, Randolph M. III. George, Alexander L.
JX1395.C465   327.1'01   80-11913
ISBN 0-89158-846-9
ISBN 0-89158-895-7 (pbk.)

Printed and bound in the United States of America

For a friend and colleague, gentleman and scholar:

ROBERT C. NORTH

Contents

Part 1
Change in the International System

Part 2
Sources of Change in the International System

ix

Part 3
Constraints upon Change in the International System

Figures and Tables

Figures

Tables

Preface

Even a casual reader of the chapters that follow will note that our understanding of important questions about international system change, imperfect as it is, has been significantly illuminated by the theories and research of several pioneering scholars, including Quincy Wright, Karl Deutsch, Ernst Haas, Joseph Nye, and Robert C. North.

As this volume goes to press, Bob North approaches a landmark birthday that normally mandates retirement from the faculty at Stanford University. To describe him as a pioneer in the study of international systems is a statement that is as accurate as it is incomplete. His published work ranges from a political novel written while he was a graduate student to major works on Chinese communism, and from pathfinding inquiries into international crises to the work that has engaged much of his time during the past dozen years — on the sources and nature of system change as well as on the type of preferred international system toward which we might all strive.

Of the fourteen authors represented in this book, eight have engaged in graduate studies with Bob North (Choucri, Genco, both Holstis, Hopmann, Rittberger, Siverson, and Zinnes). A ninth (Hermann) spent a summer at Stanford during his graduate studies, while preparing to write a dissertation on crisis decisionmaking. Two others (George and Keohane) are among his faculty colleagues at Stanford, and still another (Rosenau) has maintained close personal and professional ties with him. The remaining authors — King and Mason — although less closely associated with Bob North, have nevertheless been influenced by his work, as has an entire generation of international relations scholars. Thus, in our various capacities we have been privileged to know Bob North, a dedicated scholar whose mind is always open to new ideas and fresh insights, a warm friend, and truly a gentleman. We dedicate this book to him.

Several other persons who have been associated with Bob North furnished us with assistance at various stages of this project. They include Richard Ashley, Edward Azar, Richard Brody, David Clarke, David

Dewitt, Arlee Ellis, Richard Fagen, Michael Haas, Howard Koch, Daniel Tretiak, Jan Triska, and Kim Woodard. In order to maintain the thematic unity of the book we have not included essays by them but we wish to record here our gratitude for their willingness to join us in honoring Bob North. We also wish to thank Vicki Zinner and Brenda Peterson for typing final drafts of the tables. Jeanne Remington, Lynne C. Rienner, and others at Westview Press have been pleasant and helpful at every stage of the production process.

Ole R. Holsti
Randolph M. Siverson
Alexander L. George

Introduction

The international system has undergone profound changes since World War II. Relationships of conflict and cooperation have been altered or blurred, the cold war has given way to an uneasy détente, and the major postwar alliances have been eroded in both size and cohesiveness. Previously weak, dependent nations are undertaking bold courses of national development, frequently with increases in national influence unimaginable fifteen years ago. The most prominent examples of this are, of course, the oil-producing nations of the Middle East. Concomitantly, the prospects of a system dominated by a Soviet-U.S. condominium have eroded significantly, as neither superpower has been able to maintain hegemonic power across all issue areas in its own "bloc," much less among more peripheral, once quiescent, client states. These and other changes are having a deep, and probably lasting, impact upon the international system. There is, however, less agreement about what caused these changes, where they will stop, or perhaps most importantly, where they will take us. Lack of understanding in this area is in part a consequence of undue attention upon the statics of particular types of international systems, to the neglect of the dynamics of system change.

In one sense, however, the observation that the international system is changing is as trivial as it is true, for the system is constantly changing. Whether our purpose is description or forecasting, theory-building or policymaking, we need to pose and answer a series of more precise questions if we are to gain some better understanding of this ubiquitous phenomenon.

First, we need to describe more precisely the nature of the change in the international system and, not quite the same question, the international system as perceived, evaluated, and supported by different national and transnational actors. What is the *direction* of various types of change in the international system? How are the essential structures of the system changing? What changes have taken place in the objectives of the leading national actors? Are their goals becoming more or less compatible? How are the means used to achieve goals changing? What is the *magnitude* of change? Is it occurring within a given system (for example, shifts within a balance-of-power system), or is the system itself being transformed (for example, from a tight bipolar structure, in which most of the units are aligned with one of two competing coalitions, toward a balance-of-power system)? What is the *pace* of change? Does it take place gradually and incrementally, as might be the case with the creation and nurturing of new international institutions, or does it occur in sharp and abrupt transformations such as with the signing of the Nazi-Soviet Pact in 1939? Finally, are the changes *reversible* or are they likely to be irreversible? Shifts in alignments among political units illustrate a reversible change (the Nazi-Soviet Pact lasted less than two years), whereas the destruction of an essential actor in the system is much less so.

A second cluster of questions concerns the sources of system change. We do not lack candidates. At one end of the spectrum are found "great man" theories of history that emphasize the unique; for example, those which locate the explanation for system change in the ambitions and political skills of a specific leader such as Caesar, Charlemagne, Louis XIV, Napoleon, Wilson, Lenin, Hitler, Stalin, or Roosevelt. At the other end of the spectrum are teleological explanations in which history is viewed as the ineluctable unfolding of some grand design; examples include various Marxist theories.

Between these poles may be found a series of other explanations in which specific variables are identified as the sources of systemic change. But success in such endeavors has often proved to be elusive. Even some of the more plausible efforts of this type have fallen short when put to the test of predictive validity. Two examples, both involving skilled perceptive political analysts, illustrate this point.

Early in the atomic age, John Herz predicted that the introduction of nuclear weapons would bring about the demise of the nation-state, clearly a systemic transformation of major proportions.[1] His prediction was based on the perceived parallels between the impact of gunpowder on the feudal system and the likely consequences of atomic weaponry on the nation-state system. Because gunpowder and the cannon permitted the walls of the feudal manor to be breached with little difficulty, the feudal lord could no longer maintain his end of the feudal bargain — guaranteeing the physical safety of his subjects. Hence the decline of the feudal system and the consolidation of authority in a larger unit — the nation-state — that was capable of providing that safety. He went on to argue that because no nation, not even the most powerful, could provide safety in an age of nuclear weapons and almost instantaneous means of delivery across continents, the raison d'être of the nation-state was disappearing. Alternative forms of political organization would thus come into being. At least to this point, there is little evidence to bear out this prediction.

A second example emerges from theories of international integration, pioneered by Ernst Haas, wherein cooperative undertakings in one sector (for example, coal and steel in postwar Western Europe) were thought to have high potential for "spilling over" into other sectors, ultimately paving the way for far-reaching integration.[2] Once more, the experiences of recent decades have not provided substantial evidence in support of the predicted systemic changes.

That these predictions have not been borne out is not unusual. Indeed, what is most noteworthy about them is not that they have thus far proved incorrect but, rather, that their authors have subsequently undertaken further analyses of why their predictions failed.[3]

A third cluster of questions centers upon constraints to international system change. Given the fact that during this century war has resulted in the loss of over fifty million lives (a figure that might well be matched within the first few hours of any future world war), why have we been unable to create and sustain the structures and rules governing the patterns of interaction among nations — rules that are necessary for a more peaceful international system? It is not as if many statesmen and revolutionaries, philosophers and reformers had not provided us with blueprints for how one ought to proceed. Unless one is simply prepared to ascribe conflict and war to man's inherent perversity or to original sin (in which case one is left with an answer that is as simple as it is unsatisfactory to those who believe that even limited progress is both possible and worthwhile), the question of constraints upon system change is a vital concern.

These, then, are some of the questions addressed in the essays that follow.

Part 1, including chapters by Dina A. Zinnes, Kal J. Holsti, and Stephen J. Genco, considers several general issues about international system change. Although the three chapters were written from quite different perspectives, they contain a common theme and each of them concludes that much of our current understanding of change in the international system is deficient.

In a rather sober appraisal of the current literature on the topic, Zinnes identifies four questions to which students of international systems should be able to provide satisfactory answers:

1. What does the term "international system" mean and how do we identify specific variants of international systems?
2. How are the relevant system variables operationally defined?

3. What are the processes by which systems are transformed?
4. Why should we be vitally interested in the problem of international system change?

She then proceeds to demonstrate that the existing theories and explanations of change in the international system often fall short with respect to each of these four questions. In this opening chapter Zinnes thus establishes an agenda of important theoretical issues, and she concludes her essay with some prescriptions for remedying several of the more glaring problems.

In Chapter 2, K. J. Holsti reiterates Zinnes's point that such key terms as integration, independence, and nationalism are imprecisely and inconsistently defined. The main theme of his essay, however, is that the existing literature exhibits a strong bias toward interdependence and integration and an inadequate appreciation of modern nationalism as a force for *dis*-integration and fragmentation in the contemporary international system. Technology and other factors may be creating a shrinking world or, as some have put it, a "global village," but it is hardly a village marked by unanimous applause for internationalism, consensus on the benefits of interdependence, or uniform movement toward integration. Holsti points out that the recognition of a shrinking world may in fact lead some members of the international system to undertake significant efforts aimed at protecting or extending their autonomy. In short, the centripetal forces have by no means been universally replaced by centrifugal tendencies. Holsti illustrates his thesis with several examples. Canadian-U.S. relations during the past decade reflect a widespread sentiment north of the forty-ninth parallel that interdependence between the two North American nations may leave the smaller partner in a position of political, economic, and cultural dependence upon the United States. The case of Burma illustrates even more dramatically the extent to which a nation may go to protect itself from foreign penetration and asymmetrical interdependence; the Burmese response has been extensive withdrawal from the international system. Finally, Holsti identifies the plethora of secessionist movements — by no means confined to the often artificial nation-states that emerged from the disintegration of colonial empires in Africa and elsewhere — that suggest further Balkanization rather than integration in the international system.

In the concluding chapter of Part 1, Stephen J. Genco, elaborating on one of the themes in the Zinnes essay, observes that difficulties in explaining change in the international system are in fact part of a larger problem: All social sciences have been notably more successful in developing taxonomies (statics) than in explaining change (dynamics).

Following a detailed critique of integration theory, Genco draws upon the work of Lindberg, Scheingold, Almond, and others to develop a framework to examine the important case of system change in Western Europe following World War II. In light of the popularity of many teleological theories of system change (for example, Marxist theories, "spillover" theories, and others), one of the more interesting conclusions in the Genco essay is that what comes out of a system transformation episode is not necessarily predictable from what goes in.[4] Clearly that conclusion is of more than passing interest to both the theoretician and the policymaker.

Any comprehensive list of factors that have at one time or another been identified as sources of change in the international system would run for many pages. A shorter, more discriminating list would almost certainly include scientific/technological innovation and diffusion, international economic transactions, international crises, and war. The six chapters that constitute Part 2 focus upon these four potential sources of change.

Much of the literature on technology and international system change has been directed at the impact of military technology. There is thus a vast literature on how the development of this weapon or that — be it the crossbow, gunpowder, the ironclad ship, or the machine gun — has made possible (or constrained) new types of relationships and interactions among nations. The most familiar recent examples center around putative consequences arising from the development and diffusion of nuclear weaponry. Will nuclear weapons result in the demise of the nation-state (John Herz)? Or the obsolescence of alliances (Charles DeGaulle)? Will their proliferation have a significant (Stanley Hoffmann) or relatively insignificant (Kenneth Waltz) impact on the international system?[5]

Of more recent interest have been the links between science and technology, economic development, and change in the international system. Much of the emphasis has been on the potentially beneficial impact of science and technology for narrowing the gap between the rich and poor nations of the world. In the lead chapter of Part 2, Volker Rittberger emphasizes that science and technology constitute a two-edged sword — that they can exacerbate as well as eradicate significant social problems. Treading what he calls the "realist" path, rather than that of the "optimist" or "pessimist," Rittberger discusses the diffusion of science and technology in the context of international development strategies in the United Nations. Expanding a theme that appeared earlier in K. J. Holsti's chapter, Rittberger points out that science and technology transfers may create new forms of dependencies among nations. An understated theme in Chapter 4, but one that ought not to be overlooked, is the possible *unforeseen* consequences of science and technology transfers. For example, with how much confidence can we foresee the long-range consequences for the international system of increasing diffusion of, and dependence upon, nuclear energy plants?

A venerable intellectual tradition has linked the growth of international commerce to a most significant type of international system transformation—a system in which war would no longer play a role in resolving international disputes. This line of reasoning may have reached its apogee during the decades immediately preceding World War I, when many came to accept and propagate the thesis that because war had become such an economic liability (it would disrupt the mutually beneficial system of international trade), nations would no longer engage in it. In short, because it did not "pay," it would not occur. The calamity of World War I may have discredited some of the more optimistic visions about the systemic consequences of international trade, but it did not mark the end of efforts to develop a fuller understanding of the complex relationship between international politics and economics. Events of the 1970s have provided substantial impetus in this direction. Interest in "international political economy" is no longer the virtual monopoly of those working from Marxist premises.

Chapters 5 and 6 focus upon international economics and system change. Nazli Choucri and Robert O. Keohane demonstrate the importance of a multidisciplinary perspective on change in the international system, a perspective that also goes well beyond the premise of a single path of causality from economics to politics, or vice versa.

The underlying theme of Choucri's chapter on theories of international relations that stress economic or political factors is that neither of them is sufficient and that both of them are necessary if we wish to understand system change. Her essay suggests that, despite the often-proclaimed need to approach complex social phenomena from an interdisciplinary perspective, the well-traveled roads are not filled with those whose thinking is equally informed by economic and political theory and who are comfortable working in the interstices of the two disciplines. In her conclusion Choucri suggests some of the links between the two disciplines that should be of special interest to students of international system change.

Keohane's essay tests the theory that a concentration of power—more specifically, the existence of a hegemonic power—is necessary to maintain strong economic "regimes," defined as patterned and regularized ways of conducting relations in a specific issue area. Keohane examines in some detail developments during the 1967–1977 decade in three such regimes: trade in manufactured goods, international monetary relations, and petroleum trade. The evidence provides substantial support for the theory, although it is not of equal magnitude for each of the three issue areas. It is strongest for petroleum trade and weakest for trade in manufactured goods.

Chapters 7 and 8 are concerned with crises as sources of change in the international system. In the first of the two essays, P. Terrence Hopmann and Timothy D. King test the proposition that the missile crisis of 1962, the most severe confrontation to date between the United States and the Soviet Union, served as a major turning point in the relations between the two superpowers. Their systematic analysis includes data drawn from action of the United States and the Soviet Union over a twenty-two-year period, as well as from the negotiations leading up to the Nuclear Test Ban Treaty of 1963. The findings generally support the more impressionistic conclusions of such observers as Arthur M. Schlesinger, Jr., that the sobering experience of the missile crisis did indeed provide an important impetus toward efforts to defuse some of the more dangerous aspects of relations between Washington and Moscow.

The Hopmann-King essay provides us with a useful reminder that crises may in fact provide *opportunities* for benign system changes. The next chapter, by Charles F. Hermann and Robert E. Mason, is an equally cogent reminder of the *dangers* inherent in crises as agents of international system change.

The final essay in Part 2 examines the relationship between war and system change. At first glance, the impact of war on the international system would appear to be so obvious as to require little further discussion. For example, is not World War I a necessary part of any explanation for the emergence of Nazi Germany and Soviet Russia and the powerful challenges they have represented to the existing world order? But perhaps two additional points are worth making. First, we know relatively little about why some wars have profound systemic consequences and others do not. Second, there is a school of thought that downplays the role of war, suggesting that its impact is limited to the short run. In a recent study, Organski and Kugler provide evidence that even as cataclysmic a conflict as World War II had little long-term effect on the international system.[6]

Randolph M. Siverson's essay in Chapter 9 challenges the Organski-Kugler thesis on the grounds that the global distribution of economic power — the primary measure upon which Organski and Kugler rely to support their thesis — is too narrow a base for definitive judgments about change, or lack thereof, in the international system. Siverson examines such other possible consequences of war participation as impact on elite attitudes, internal political stability, and regime change, as well as the international distribution of power. His findings indicate that war does indeed have an impact on the system. Left unanswered, however, is the question: Why do some wars have significant systemic consequences whereas others have virtually none?

The chapters in Part 3 focus upon constraints on change in the international system. That there are multiple sources of constraint is a point that requires little elaboration, although it is a point that has not always been sufficiently appreciated by the many philosophers, reformers, and statesmen who have drawn up blueprints for perpetual peace, world government, or other dramatic transformations of the international system.

The two chapters included in Part 3 do not consider the whole range, or even a representative sample, of these constraints. Rather, both of them center upon the domestic factors within a single nation (the United States) during a relatively narrow period of time (since the outbreak of World War II).

In Chapter 10, Alexander L. George discusses the requirement of "foreign policy legitimacy" for a nation seeking changes in the international system. After developing an analytical framework that includes the "grand design," strategies, and tactics, as well as the cognitive beliefs that support each, he examines two cases in which the United States attempted to develop cooperative relations with the Soviet Union. The first case involves Franklin D. Roosevelt's efforts during World War II to develop a postwar international security system in which Soviet-U.S. collaboration was to play a critical role (the "Four Policemen" also included Great Britain and China, but their roles were clearly less crucial). George's second case examines efforts by President Richard Nixon and Secretary of State Henry Kissinger to steer Soviet-U.S. relations toward a complex network of relationships that would secure a more stable and constructive relationship between Moscow and Washington. The central concept in George's analysis of both the Roosevelt and Nixon-Kissinger cases is "policy legitimacy." Only an administration that is able to persuade relevant persons and groups within and outside government that its "grand design," strategy, and tactics are both feasible and acceptable will find sufficient domestic support to enable it to pursue such major external undertakings as creating a new international order in a coherent and consistent manner. George demonstrates how and why both the Roosevelt and Nixon-Kissinger efforts ultimately failed to achieve policy legitimacy.

The concluding chapter analyzes the state of leadership beliefs in the United States following the Vietnam War. Drawing upon the responses of over two thousand U.S. leaders—including political figures, military officers, foreign service officers, media persons, labor officials, clergy, business executives, educators, and others—Ole R. Holsti and James N. Rosenau find substantial evidence of deep cleavages. The data point to the existence of three quite distinct, almost mutually exclusive, sets of beliefs about the nature of the international system and proper goals, strategies, and tactics that the United States should pursue in its external relations. As there are relatively few beliefs shared by the "cold war internationalists," "post-cold war internationalists," and "isolationists," the prospects for an early domestic consensus—barring some unifying international calamity—seem sufficiently remote that U.S. administrations may, in the near future, have considerable difficulty in pursuing ambitious undertakings aimed at creating new international regimes.

At this point the reader will probably have discerned that this enterprise does not lead directly to a single, parsimonious theory of international system change. That is an accurate conclusion. Indeed, if there is a single powerful theme that runs through most of the essays that follow, it is this: Whether as theorists, reformers, or policymakers, we should approach questions of stability and change in the international system with an acute sensitivity to complexity. This is *not* a plea for expanding our categories and variables ad infinitum; a mindless inductive approach will ultimately result in paralysis for both the theorist and the actor. Rather, we have in mind three closely related points.

First, the international system—as well as major regional subsystems—is characterized by sufficient diversity and complexity to confound most deterministic or teleological theories of system change. For example, expectations that, even within such relatively homogenous regions as Western Europe or North America, the forces of regional integration would follow a single course have been confounded. Clearly, one should be all the more sensitive to crosscurrents and countervailing pressures for and against change when attempting to analyze the international system as a whole.

Second, identifying potentially important sources of system change may be a relatively easy task but because many of them can give rise to a diversity of outcomes, tracing out their actual consequences is not. This is, of course, merely another way of saying that it is easier to deal with social statics than with social dynamics. Thus, one should be skeptical of theories and policies that posit single (and simple) paths of causation. Expectations that international economic networks, diffusion of science and technology, or even crises and conflicts, will give rise to easily predictable systemic outcomes are challenged repeatedly in these essays. Sensitivity to potentially unforeseen systemic outcomes is useful to the theorist, reformer, and policymaker.

The role of leadership constitutes a third source of complexity. Leadership is a notoriously difficult concept, especially when compared to some of the more readily measured indices of international interactions. As a consequence, leadership variables are often treated as a residual category, at best reserved for deviant case analysis. Yet, as indicated in several of the essays, the nature of leadership often belongs at the center rather than at the periphery of our purview. For example, whether nationalism serves as a constraint upon integration or as a force for dis-integration often depends upon the willingness and ability of leaders to define it and to use it in those terms. Whether a major national actor is successful in an undertaking aimed at significant system change often depends upon his intellectual and political skills in developing "grand designs" that are both internationally feasible and domestically acceptable.

Ole R. Holsti
Randolph M. Siverson
Alexander L. George

Notes

1. John H. Herz, "Rise and Demise of the Territorial State," *World Politics* 9 (1957):473–493.

2. Ernst B. Haas, *The Uniting of Europe: Political, Social and Economic Forces, 1950–1957* (Stanford, Calif.: Stanford University Press, 1958).

3. John H. Herz, "The Territorial State Revisited: Reflections on the Future of the Nation-State," *Polity* 1 (1968):12–34; and Ernst B. Haas, *The Obsolescence of Regional Integration Theory*, Institute of International Studies, Research Series, no. 25 (Berkeley: University of California Press, 1975).

4. This important point also emerges in Chapter 8 by Hermann and Mason.

5. John H. Herz, "Rise and Demise of the Territorial State"; Stanley Hoffmann, *Primary or World Order: American Foreign Policy Since the Second World War* (New York: McGraw-Hill Book Co., 1978); and Kenneth N. Waltz, "The Stability of a Bipolar World," *Daedalus* 93 (1964):881–909.

6. A.F.K. Organski and Jacek Kugler, "The Costs of Major Wars," *American Political Science Review* 71 (1977):1347–1366.

The Contributors

Nazli Choucri, professor of political science at M.I.T., worked extensively on aspects of international political economy. She is author of *Population Dynamics and International Violence* (1974), coauthor with Robert C. North of *Nations in Conflict* (1975), and author of *International Politics of Energy Interdependence: The Case of Petroleum* (1976). The M.I.T. Press is publishing her new book, *International Energy Policy: A Simulation of Oil Prices, Trade, and Payments* (1980).

Stephen J. Genco is a Ph.D. candidate in political science at Stanford University. His chapter in this volume is based upon his dissertation, "Explaining International System Transformation: Bargaining, Institutionalization, and Integration in Western Europe." He has also written, with Gabriel Almond, "Clouds, Clocks, and the Study of Politics," *World Politics.*

Alexander L. George is the Graham H. Stuart Professor of International Relations at Stanford University. He is the author of *Woodrow Wilson and Colonel House*, written with his wife, Juliette L. George; *Deterrence in American Foreign Policy* (coauthored with Richard Smoke), which won the Bancroft Prize in 1975; and several other books and articles. His most recent book is *Presidential Decisionmaking in Foreign Policy* (Westview Press, 1980). Professor George has been a fellow at the Center for Advanced Study in the Behavioral Sciences and served as president of the International Studies Association in 1973-1974. He was elected a fellow of the American Academy of Arts and Sciences in 1975.

Charles F. Hermann is director of the Mershon Center and professor of political science at Ohio State University. He received his Ph.D. from Northwestern University and during that period of graduate training spent a summer at Stanford University with Robert North with the Conflict and Integration Project. In addition to the study of crisis, he is interested in the comparative study of foreign policy and in collective decisionmaking. These interests are reflected in *International Crisis* and *Why Nations Act,* to which he was a contributor as well as editor.

K. J. Holsti is professor and head of the Department of Political Science at the University of British Columbia, Vancouver, Canada. Former editor of the *International Studies Quarterly* and current editor of the *Canadian Journal of Political Science*, Professor Holsti is the author of *International Politics: A Framework for Analysis* and books on Finnish foreign policy and foreign policy restructuring, as well as numerous articles.

Ole R. Holsti is the George V. Allen Professor and chairman of the Department of Political Science at Duke University. He is the author of *Crisis, Escalation, War; Content Analysis for the Social Sciences and Humanities;* and several other books and articles. He has been a fellow at the Center for Advanced Study in the Behavioral Sciences and served as president of the International Studies Association in 1979–1980.

P. Terrence Hopmann, professor of political science and director of the Harold Scott Quigley Center of International Studies in the Hubert H. Humphrey Institute of Public Affairs at the University of Minnesota, received his Ph.D. from Stanford University in 1969. He is a coauthor of *Unity and Disintegration in International Alliances* and has written extensively on bargaining in arms control negotiations. Currently he is an editor of the *International Studies Quarterly*.

Robert O. Keohane is professor of political science at Stanford University. He is the author, with Joseph S. Nye, of *Power and Interdependence: World Politics in Transition* (1977). His current work constitutes an attempt to understand the international politics of modern capitalism through an analysis of how and why international regimes change and the effects that regimes, and changes in regimes, have on the world political economy.

Timothy D. King is a research associate at the Mershon Center for Research and Education in National Security and the Policy Sciences at Ohio State University. He received his Ph.D. in political science from the University of Minnesota in 1977 and held a John Parker Compton postdoctoral fellowship at the Woodrow Wilson School of Public and International Affairs at Princeton University in 1978. His research has focused primarily on arms control negotiations and the United Nations Special Session on Disarmament.

Robert E. Mason is a graduate student in political science at Ohio State University where he is writing his dissertation on "Foreign Policies of the Post Industrial Nations."

Volker Rittberger studied law and political science at the Universities of Frieburg im Breisgau and Geneva as well as at Stanford University. He holds a Ph.D. degree from Stanford (1972). He has been a professor of political science at the University of Tubingen/Germany since 1973 and a special fellow of the United Nations Institute for Training and Research (UNITAR) since 1978. One focus of his research interests is on the role of international organizations in change in the international system. His publications include *Evolution and International Organization* (1973) and several articles, papers, and reviews on related topics.

James N. Rosenau is director of the Institute for Transnational Studies at the University of Southern California. His recent publications include *The Dramas of Political Life* (1980), *The Scientific Study of Foreign Policy* (revised ed., 1980), and *The Study of Global Interdependence* (1980). He is also editor of *In Search of Global Patterns* (1976).

Randolph M. Siverson is associate professor of political science at the University of California, Davis. His research interests are in the areas of war and international alliances. His articles have appeared in the *International Studies Quarterly, International Interactions, The Journal of Conflict Resolution, International Organization, The Western Political Quarterly,* and *The American Journal of Political Science.* In 1974–1975 he was visiting professor and Senior Fulbright Lecturer at El Colegio de Mexico.

Dina A. Zinnes is the Merriam Professor of Political Science at the University of Illinois. She is the recipient of several National Science Foundation grants. Her research interests include international crises and arms race modeling. In addition to many articles she has published *Contemporary Research in International Politics: A Perspective and Critical Appraisal; Quantitative International Politics: An Appraisal* (coeditor); and *Mathematical Models in International Relations* (coeditor). Her extensive professional service includes the presidency of the International Studies Association (1980–1981).

Acronyms

AP	Associated Press
BPA	Bargaining Process Analysis
CARIFTA	Caribbean Free Trade Association
CIA	Central Intelligence Agency
COMECON	Council for Mutual Economic Assistance
CREON	Comparative Research on the Events of Nations
C.S.S.R.	Czechoslovakia
DMZ	Demilitarized Zone
ECSC	European Coal and Steel Community
EDC	European Defense Community
EEC	European Economic Community
ENDC	Eighteen Nation Disarmament Conference
Euratom	European Atomic Energy Community
FBI	Federal Bureau of Investigation
GATT	General Agreement on Tariffs and Trade
GDP	Gross Domestic Product
GNP	Gross National Product
IEA	International Energy Association
IMF	International Monetary Fund
ISA	International Studies Association
LDC	Less Developed Country
LINK	International Linkages in Economic Systems
MFA	Multifiber Agreement
MNC	Multi-National Corporation
NATO	North Atlantic Treaty Organization
NORAD	North American Air Defense
OECD	Organization for Economic Cooperation and Development
OPEC	Organization of Petroleum Exporting Countries
R&D	Research and Development
RA	Relative Advantage
RCMP	Royal Canadian Mounted Police
SALT	Strategic Arms Limitation Talks
SDRs	Special Drawing Rights

TCDC	United Nations Conference on Technical Cooperation Among Developing Countries
UNCSTD	United Nations Conference on Science and Technology for Development
UNITAR	United Nations Institute for Training and Research
UN/UNDP	United Nations Development Program
UPI	United Press International
WEIS	World Events/Interaction Survey

Change in the International System

1

DINA A. ZINNES

Prerequisites for the Study of System Transformation

The literature on international systems has two intriguing characteristics. First, the number of studies that analyze international systems is relatively small. Although the area contains a core of devoted scholars, the number of books that have appeared in the last ten years can almost be counted on both hands, and the number of articles is not much greater. Second, those studies that have appeared, with only a few exceptions, are largely static. Most studies of international systems concentrate on identifying and describing types of systems.

One interpretation of these two characteristics is that the field is young. Fledgling areas of inquiry often begin with static descriptions by a few scholars. But such an interpretation cannot account for the sporadic and essentially noncumulative appearance of analyses of international systems over the course of the last twenty-five years. Of interest is how separated in time are some of the major works in this field (Kaplan appeared in 1957, Rosecrance in 1963, Luard in 1976) and even more surprising is the fact that there is so little reference from one study to another, as if each writer were working in a vacuum. If international systems is a blossoming new field one would anticipate a greater concentration of studies in time and considerably more interaction and building from one to another. Perhaps then the two characteristics should be interpreted differently.

The limited attention to, and largely static treatment of, international systems could indicate a basic lack of clarity within the subject matter. Ambiguities in concepts and the absence of explicit research questions could well deter analysts from devoting time to an area of inquiry. Thus the sparse treatment of system transformation may be the consequence of a fuzziness in the use of concepts and the posing of research questions. This is the problem that will be explored in the following pages. What *are* the prerequisites for studying system transformation, to what extent does the literature meet these requirements, and what needs to be done to enhance the development of this area of research?

How Do We Know One When We See One?
The Unit-of-Analysis Problem

Clearly the first prerequisite for the study of system transformation is the ability to identify an international system. What is the meaning of the concept "international system"? The term has appeared frequently in the literature and a number of analysts have presented definitions. Unfortunately, however, these are of rather little help. It is not that analysts do not know what the word "international" means. The difficulty lies in the concept "system" and its coupling with the word "international." Consider a few excerpts from key writers in the field. Kaplan proposes:

> The materials of politics are treated in terms of systems of action. A system of action is a set of variables so related, in contradistinction to its environment, that describable behavioral regularities characterize the internal relationships of the variables to each other and the external relationships of the set of individual variables to combinations of external variables.[1]

And later and a bit more simply: "The study of systems involves the study of relationships between variables."[2] This definition suggests that systems are distinguishable from environments so that presumably if "environment" were understood it would be possible to know what was not a system. Beyond that, however, the definition only specifies that systems are relationships between variables that describe "internal" behavioral regularities. What is meant by "internal," what kind of variables describe internal behavioral regularities, and what kind of relationships are implied?

In McClelland's volume on *Theory and the International System* an initial, somewhat more explicit, definition is given: "The conception of the international system is an expanded version of the notion of two-actors-in-interaction. A view of the whole phenomenon is involved."[3] But this emerging clarity becomes clouded as we read further:

> A system of whatever kind is an ensemble of parts or subsystems capable of changing from one state to another state. It is the ability to change that is interesting to the observer and that allows the ensemble to be considered a system. Any system is a structure that is perceived by its observers to have elements in interaction or relationships and some identifiable boundaries that separate it from its environment.[4]

Apparently an international system requires two nations, an important first clue. But what is "interaction"? To define a system in terms of subsystems is somewhat circular while to define it in terms of something that is "capable of changing" presents an almost infinite range of possibilities.

Finally Rosecrance proposes "the subdivision of international relations into distinctive patterns, each enduring for a limited period of time and demarcated by significant changes in diplomatic style. . . . In this sense international relations might be conceived in terms of separate 'systems.'"[5] Obviously this definition requires yet another to be useful: we need to know how "distinctive patterns" are to be identified.

The above definitions by no means exhaust the range that can be found in the literature, but they are sufficient to illustrate the fact that the literature has not been very helpful in identifying the unit of analysis. If it is not possible to unambiguously identify what it is that is being studied is it surprising that there have been so few studies devoted to this topic? Yet the fact is that there have been some studies of international systems. Despite the above attempts to provide an analytic definition, researchers *have* proceeded to study the attributes and consequences of international systems. Clearly then, while we cannot precisely define the unit of analysis, we do seem to have an intuitive feel for what is and is not an international system.

In February 1979 China invaded Vietnam. This single event can be seen from two totally different perspectives: (1) the so-called nation-state or decisionmaking focus in which the unit of analysis is the nation-state or (2) the systems perspective in which the unit of analysis is an international system. It is interesting to contrast the two perspectives within the context of this event. The analyst working at the nation-state level would observe that in 1978 there had been a surging interest within China for a major economic drive forward. Manifestations would include the sending of emissaries abroad to develop ties throughout Asia, Africa, and the Middle East, the signing of a trade agreement with France, a treaty with Japan and a willingness to look the other way with respect to Taiwan to permit normalization of relations with the United States. Coincident with this campaign of "outreach" to obtain resources and expertise there was evidence that all was not well within the Chinese capital. The China wall-poster campaign suggested internal dissatisfaction and there were signs that a power struggle might be in the making. Putting these pieces together the analyst might draw an analogy with a new company seeking extensive economic backing. Cambodia had been an ally. China had to show that it was a viable international entity, a nation that could not be ignored and with whom cooperation and exchange was both possible and profitable. "China felt that Vietnam had threatened its credibility as a great power and that it had to prove it was no paper tiger."[6] An explanation for China's behavior was largely sought *within* the Chinese nation-state: The desire of the Chinese leaders to achieve dramatic internal economic development led — according to this explanation — to China's move into Vietnam.

Consider now a second analyst who looks not only at China, but also at the relationships between China, Japan, Vietnam, Cambodia, and the Soviet Union. China and Japan signed a historic peace treaty on 23 October 1978 that contained a clause stating that both countries opposed hegemony in Asia by any country. China insisted on the clause as a signal against Soviet moves in Asia; Japan agreed, but with some misgivings as it had no desire to be pulled into the Sino-Soviet contest. The clause infuriated the Soviet Union. Shortly after this treaty was signed the Soviets signed a treaty with Vietnam and military aid flowed into Vietnam. Not long after, Vietnam invaded Cambodia. The Pol Pot regime in Cambodia was backed by China. If the Soviet-backed Vietnamese could invade Chinese-backed Cambodia with impunity then China would loose several points of credibility in its worldwide struggle with the Soviet Union. A quick "surgical" expedition into Vietnam would show the Soviets that China would not stand idly by while its allies were overrun. It would also show other Soviet-backed powers the true meaning of Soviet friendship since the Chinese believed that the Soviets would not interfere if China engaged in a punitive expedition without taking territory. In this case the explanation for the Chinese invasion was found through an examination of the *relationships* between a set of nations; thus the implicit unit of analysis is a system (or subsystem).

The contrast between these two examples illustrates that on purely intuitive grounds it is possible to classify studies into those which do and those which do not focus on an international system. Furthermore, a relationship can be seen between the definitions cited previously and the contrast between the two explanations of the Chinese invasion. McClelland's criterion that there be two nation-state units is certainly one characteristic that distinguishes the first from the second explanation. And if "relationships between variables" corresponds to "ensembles of parts capable of change" and "distinctive patterns" then these characterizations of another attribute of an international system can be seen in the brief sketch of the relationships, and the dynamics of those relationships, between the five nation-states considered. In short, although there currently does not exist a completely satisfactory analytic definition of "international system," this problem is not paralyzing.

Given the above discussion, three criteria can be used to define the unit of analysis. Studies of international systems must consider *nations,* these studies must focus on at least *two* entities, and the analyses and questions must concentrate on *relationships* between the units. However, implicit in these three defining criteria are two further questions. First, is an international system considered a system only if there are two or more nations? Given McClelland's definition and the contrast developed between the two studies of the Chinese invasion the answer would be yes. Yet an affirmative answer is not entirely satisfactory. It suggests, for example, that the Holy Roman Empire could not be considered an international system, a somewhat strange conclusion. Furthermore, it belies the description of two of Kaplan's international systems. In the hierarchical system "the national actors will lose their primary role function of transmitting the rules of the national systems. National actors will be territorial subdivisions of the international system rather than independent political systems."[7] While less integrated than the hierarchical system the universal system would also appear to be something of a single unit system: "With respect to some functions, it will determine the jurisdictional boundaries of its members . . . [although it] . . . is unlikely to do this for all decisionmaking functions."[8] When there are two national units it is reasonable to identify an international system. The question is whether the existence of a single unit implies that there is no international system. What is needed is a criterion that permits a distinction between a nation-state, like China, and an entity like the Holy Roman Empire.

The second question concerns the word "relations." What exactly does it mean to say that the study of an international system is a study of *relations* between two or more units? The Chinese example suggests that when we examine alliance ties, or, more generally, bonds of hostility and friendship, we are looking at a system. The implication is that systems are definable only in terms of bonds or directed behaviors. Yet discussions of specific international systems like the balance of power or the bipolar system consider more than ties or bonds. A key characteristic of either a balance of power or bipolar system is the distribution of power over the members of the system. Thus the concept "relations" requires additional clarification.

The literature helps us to identify two broad classes of variables that capture different connotations of the term "relations." The first set of variables might be termed *configurational*. These variables define systems in terms of the ties, or directed behaviors, between nations. The degree of polarity and the tightness or looseness of the poles are examples of configurational variables. They reflect levels of interaction between units. *Composite* variables, on the other hand, characterize international systems by summarizing the attributes of the nations. The concentration of power in a few or across many nations is an example of a composite relational variable and is obtained by aggregating the attributes of the nation units.

Waltz would strongly disagree with our working definition of an international system. Although he speaks of both the systems *approach* and the study of an *international system* it is possible to see that his definition of an international system differs from that given above: "Any approach to theory if it is rightly termed 'systemic' must show how the systems level or structure is distinct from the level of interacting units. . . . Definitions of structure must omit the attributes and the relations of units."[9] But if configurational or composite variables are not to be used in identifying an international system, then how, in concrete operational terms, are we to know a system when we see one? The difficulty is compounded by a statement made later in the volume. To discriminate between types of change in a system Waltz provides a three-part definition of structure, the last of which proposes: "Structures are defined, third, by the distribution of capabilities across units."[10] How is it possible to consider the distribution of capabilities distinct from the attributes of the units?

Although the issue of single unit systems remains unresolved it seems reasonable to conclude that the literature offers a plausible basis for meeting the first prerequisite for a study of system transformation. An unambiguous definition of an international system does not yet exist, but a usable working definition can be constructed.

How Do We Distinguish Between International Systems?

Although it may be possible to identify international systems, an analysis of system transformation further requires the discrimination between systems. If an explanation is sought for how system A becomes system B it must be possible to distinguish between systems A and B. This is not a trivial question. Suppose system A contains five nations. Does the addition of a sixth produce a new system? The answer to the question requires three steps.

First, it must be possible to identify the variables along which systems are to be distinguished. Is "number of nations" a variable which will demarcate system A from B? Second, given a set of defining variables it is necessary to postulate thresholds. If "number of nations" is a relevant variable does the addition of each new nation produce another system? Perhaps a new system will occur when moving from 3 to 4 nations but not when moving from 100 to 101 nations. The third issue concerns the independence of the variables and is partially a component of the threshold question. If "number of nations" and "power distribution" are two variables to be used in defining an international system, does the change from 3 to 4 nations produce a new system regardless of the way in which the power is distributed over the units? Where does the literature take us with respect to each of these issues?

There are encouraging signs with respect to the first issue. From the works of Luard,[11] Holsti,[12] Rosecrance,[13] and Kaplan,[14] it is possible to construct a reasonable list of agreed upon variables that would allow one to discriminate between systems. Using the distinction made earlier, four "composite" and three "configurational" variables can be found.

Of the four composite variables the two most important are the number of nations within the system and the distribution of power over those nations. It has often been argued that large systems must differ from small ones; the dynamics of systems like the Greek city-state system that at one point contained over a hundred units must differ from the Italian city-state system of roughly a half dozen units. Theorists have contended that the natural balancing dynamics of a balance-of-power system can only operate when there are a limited number of major-power states; there have been debates over whether this ideal size is as few as five or as many as eight. Deutsch and Singer[15] put forth the plausible argument that as the size of the system increases the number of possible relations between pairs of nations increases and this in turn makes polarization less possible. Since polarization into two major hostile groupings is often a precondition for conflict and war this argument implies a linkage between system size and certain significant events. Thus while theorists may differ with respect to the impact and consequences of system size, it is clear that they believe this variable to be an important attribute of international systems.

Some would argue that the second variable is of even greater importance: the distribution of power over the nations in the system. In the Italian city-state system the units were roughly equal in capabilities while in the ancient Chinese system there were two very strong nations and a number of smaller units. This difference between systems with respect to the distribution of power, some contend, accounts for the differences in the frequency and magnitude of war, trade, communications, etc. Theorists have argued that the most dangerous international system is one in which a single nation possesses more power than the sum of the remaining nations. In such a system the will and wishes of the dominant nation cannot be challenged by the combined forces of the remaining nations. Snyder and Diesing propose that an international system composed of two dominant nations and a number of smaller units is inevitably slated for conflict and possibly war: "In bipolarity . . . a power gain for one superpower means a power loss for the other . . . [and] resistance to the opponent's every move, no matter how minor, is . . . the guiding rule of behavior."[16] Waltz sees the situation somewhat differently. Given two major powers it is necessarily obvious who the opponent is and it is clear to both nations that neither can let the other get away with anything. The result is a "constant presence of pressure and the recurrence of crises."[17] But crises act as a safety valve, releasing pent-up steam, so that frequent crises decrease the chance for war: "Rather a large crisis now than a small war later."[18] Again, while there are disagreements as to the consequences, there is a general acceptance that power distribution is an attribute that is relevant in distinguishing between systems.

The remaining two composite variables have received somewhat less attention in the literature. One is the objectives of the nations in the system. Luard, for example, discusses at length how international systems can be distinguished on the basis of the motives of the governing elites and the means that they are willing to employ to achieve those goals. He describes the Chinese multistate system by noting: "the most important single motive was without doubt the search for territory . . ."[19] while in the Greek city-state system the "one major motive was the concern to see governments of a sympathetic ideology in power in neighboring states."[20] In a similar vein Kaplan proposes that national goals play a role in distinguishing between systems. For example, the main goal for nations in a balance-of-power system is to increase power: "Act to increase capabilities but negotiate rather than fight. Fight rather than pass up an opportunity to increase capabilities."[21] In a loose bipolar system national goals are considerably more complex and depend in part upon whether the nation belongs to a bloc. Bloc members are to work to increase the size and capabilities of their bloc and subordinate other objectives to the objectives of their bloc, whereas nonbloc members must coordinate policies with the universal actor, reduce danger of war between blocs and refuse to support the policies of one bloc against those of the other.

The fourth composite variable can be found in both Holsti[22] and Luard:[23] the type of governmental or decisionmaking structure possessed by the units of the system. At times Luard is concerned with where the power resides (who composes the elite), but at other points he is interested in the decision structure (the extent to which decisionmaking is shared or concentrated): "The concentration of decision-making power in a single ruler, which remained the normal situation in China, even if increasingly modified, was almost unknown in Greece after the age of the tyrants. . . . [During the age of the tyrants] . . . policy decisions were the result of discussion among a considerable group."[24] Holsti argues similarly: "We are concerned with the types of governments and administrations political units developed, the role of the average citizen or subject in the political unit's external relations, and the methods by which resources of the unit were mobilized to achieve external objectives."[25] Although neither writer examines the consequences of systems containing different mixes of units with various decision structures the historical examples explored by both make it evident that international systems are indeed discriminable along this dimension.

Each of the four composite variables is a summation or aggregation over the units of the system. The number of units in the system is added, the dispersion of power over the units is calculated with reference to the number of units and the total amount of power, and the frequency with which types of goals or decision structures is represented is counted. In contrast, the three configurational variables distinguish between systems on the basis of the relationships between the nations. Unquestionably the most important of these is what might be termed the "tie" between nations: the friendship and enmity patterns between each pair of nations. Who is aligned with whom and the number of such alignments has been considered a key ingredient for understanding the dynamics of nation-state behavior. The difference between a balance-of-power system in which there are no permanent alliances and a bipolar system in which there are two alliances has frequently been debated. Some argue that the absence of formal commitments in the balance-of-power system produces flexibility and permits the nations to react immediately to aggressive moves by any nation. This enhances the prospects for peace. Others contend that bipolar systems are more likely to be peaceful. Bipolar systems reduce the ambiguities inherent in a balance-of-power system. In a balance-of-power system there is no guarantee that the aggressive move of one nation will be countered by a combined reaction on the part of the remaining nations. This uncertainty encourages some nations to make risky aggressive moves. In a bipolar system, on the other hand, the confrontation that exists between the two blocs makes it more likely that a move on the part of one will be countered by the opposing bloc. The fact that nations can predict more clearly the consequences of aggressive acts in a bipolar system, some argue, constrains the aggressive tendencies of all nations. Thus alignment ties, but more generally patterns of hostility and friendship, are a significant dimension for distinguishing between systems.

The second configurational variable is the set of rules and customs that govern the behavioral interactions of nations. "Any group, however small and temporary, will usually develop accepted modes of interaction. . . . It is thus not surprising that international societies . . . have . . .

evolved rules of mutually acceptable conduct to regulate behavior."[26] "In the Chinese multistate period . . . the rules were designed to express the obligations of feudal lords to their overlord" but were subsequently extended to the relations between states: "Ceremonial rules . . . [became] a part of the customary law of the system: The respects to be paid by one state to another on the death of a ruler or a marriage . . . were among the most clearly established."[27] The rules of the Greek city-state system, on the other hand, originated from religious associations: "One of the earliest rules was the rule of a truce during the celebration of festivals. . . . There were also international rules concerning sanctuary that were again semireligious in character. Anyone who found refuge within a temple was normally given sanctuary."[28] Nicolson's fascinating account of the evolution of diplomacy provides yet another series of examples of the differences between international societies in the treatment and role of national emissaries. Diplomats in the early Greek city-state system were simple town criers, in Roman times they became administrators of territories, and in the Italian period they were spies. Because diplomats provided the linkages between the units of the system, the role that they played was significant in determining the style of interaction between the units.[29] An even clearer historical picture of the difference between systems with respect to their modes of interactions is given in *Politics and Culture in International History* by Adda Bozeman.[30] Although rules of conduct, formal (international law) or informal (custom), are difficult to specify and not always operative over the entire system at all times, analyses by Luard, Holsti, Nicholson, and Bozeman imply that it would be a mistake not to consider them as a basis for distinguishing between systems.

The third configurational variable may well be questioned by some. Its treatment in the literature is more recent and sketchy. Nevertheless such analysts as Organski,[31] Galtung,[32] and Kaplan,[33] and researchers like Singer and Small,[34] and Waltz[35] have suggested a very plausible third dimension: the individual status of nation-states. This variable differs from the power distribution variable because of its perceptual component. It is not simply who has how much power but rather who perceives whom as having how much influence and consequently who is willing to interact with whom. This third variable is more difficult to characterize than any of the previous because its definition by different writers is not uniform. Waltz suggests that the relevant variable is the discrepancy between a nation's *actual capabilities,* as measured by such indicators as gross national product (GNP) or steel production, and its *accorded status,* as measured by the number and level of diplomats sent to that nation by the other members of the system. The difference between actual and recognized power position is the basis for discriminating one system from another.[36]

Galtung's analysis is slightly different. Galtung is less concerned with the difference between actual and perceived and more interested in the "disequilibrium" for a particular nation. For Galtung an international system is "an interaction system [that] is a multidimensional system of stratification, where those who have and those who have not . . . are forced into their positions."[37] Stratification occurs simultaneously along all dimensions and while it is possible that a nation may be at the top on all dimensions this is not necessarily the case. Nations at the same level of stratification will interact with one another as equals while nations at different levels will not. A "disequilibrated nation" occurs if a nation interacts with other nations as an equal with respect to its "high" dimension but as an unequal with respect to the other dimension:

> The disequilibriated TU (a nation having high status on one dimension, top dog, T, and low status on another, underdog, U) will use TT as his reference group even if UU is his membership group, whereas a consistent underdog, UU, may not even dare to think in terms of TT as a reference group. . . . The destabilizing effect of this discrepancy will produce a mobility pressure, and, . . . if there are not open channels of mobility, rectification of the disequilibrium will be carried out by other means.[38]

For Galtung, then, systems would be differentiated with respect to the number of disequilibrated nations and perhaps the intensity of their disequilibrium, regardless of whether a nation's accorded status is in line with its actual capabilities.

It appears that the first step in the outlined procedure for discriminating between international systems has been accomplished. The literature has provided a list of at least seven relevant variables. The second stage of the analysis is to determine thresholds. But can this be done on the basis of the foregoing discussion? The description of the variables in the past few pages is somewhat misleading; the implication is that each of these variables has a precise definition. Unfortunately this is not the case, as becomes abundantly clear when moving to the second stage of distinguishing between systems.

Consider, for example, the variable "distribution of power." Theorists concerned with this variable are interested in the relative differences in power between nations: Are there two very powerful nations and many small ones or are all nations roughly equal in power? Assuming that it is possible to obtain agreement on an operational measure of "power," how does one best measure the concept "relative differences"? A mean power value for the international system would be one approach. But the variance of the power distribution or a Gini index which measures a system's deviation from a purely equal distribution of power also provide measures of power concentration or dispersion. To say that power distribution is an important varible for distinguishing systems is less than half the battle because there are a multitude of ways to formulate or "operationalize" power distribution. Obviously very different systems will emerge depending on the measure chosen. System A may or may not differ from B depending on the choice of a measure.

The configurational variable "alignment," like the power distribution variable, has experienced a variety of operational conceptualizations. One of the more interesting operationalizations is provided in the applications of graph theory by Harary,[39] Hart,[40] and Healy and Stein.[41] Using indices derived from the mathematics of graph theory it is possible to measure the degree of polarization and alignment within a system. A very different approach to measuring alignment can be seen in the works of Russett,[42] Alker and Russett,[43] and Brams.[44] These researchers use factor analysis to group nations on the basis of similarities and thus draw out what might be termed "implicit" alignment patterns. As is true in the instance of the power distribution variable, each of these indices produces a very different conceptualization of "alignment." Again, the differences between systems will depend on this choice.

Or consider the variables "objectives of the units in the system" or "governmental organizations of the units." To say that these are variables along which systems can be differentiated is to imply that it is possible to identify different objectives and governmental types and to classify systems on the basis of these types. Furthermore, to classify systems on the basis of national goals or government types requires decision as to whether the classification is in terms of the diversity of goals (or governments) or the predominance of a particular goal (or government). Is the important characteristic of system A the fact that the predominant, though perhaps not universal, goal is power maximization or is the significant attribute of system A the fact that there *is* an overwhelming predominant goal shared by most nations? Similar problems exist with the variables "rules and customs" and "status." With the possible exception of Holsti and Luard, theorists have not provided guidelines for measuring these variables.

Why is the issue of operationalization important? Is it not sufficient to specify relevant variables in general descriptive terms? The answer is no. Without explicit operational rules it is impossible to specify thresholds. How can system A be discriminated from system B with respect to power distributions unless "power distribution" is measurable. To discriminate between systems it must be possible to postulate that one system exists when a particular index falls between x and y and another comes into existence when the index falls between y and z. Obviously the specification of thresholds is not invariant with respect to the index used. The Gini index will delineate very different systems than those that would result from a variance measure.

Thus we have only moved a small way towards the completion of the first of the three-stage process. We have a list of possible variables but only a vague and general understanding of each. It is not too surprising then to find that no progress has been made with respect to the third stage: a consideration of the interdependency of the variables. There is very little discussion in the literature about how variables combine. Yet they do combine, for systems analysts almost never consider these variables independently. It is not simply the fact that the system contains only five nations that is important. It is this characteristic in *combination* with such variables as the power distribution and alignment pattern that theorists consider important. Five equal nations with no alignment commitments, each trying to maximize its own power, identifies a balance-of-power system. Note how the operational issue pervades the combination problem. Without clear specification of the variables it is next to impossible to consider various combinations of values.

But even assuming that the operational issue can be resolved, the combinatorial problem contains a further issue. Increasing the size of an international system, given one kind of alignment configuration, may well produce a new system, whereas increasing the size of a system in which a different alignment configuration exists may not. Consider the following two systems. System A consists of four nations of equal power and two alliances with two nations belonging to each alliance. System B consists of four nations of equal power and no alliances. It could reasonably be argued that the addition of a fifth nation of equal power value will alter system A but not system B. What the example shows is that the variables do not operate independently. Solving the operational issue will only carry us part of the way towards a delineation of different systems. The combinatorial question will require additional work.

Although we may be able to identify international systems and even list those attributes along which systems might be discriminated it is clear from the foregoing that a far better understanding is needed of measurement, thresholds and attribute combinations. The inability to distinguish between systems necessarily makes impossible a study of system transformation. If systems A and B are not distinguishable what does it mean to study the transformation of A into B? Perhaps this is the source of the problem, the reason for the relatively few and basically static analyses of international systems.

The Study of Transformation Processes

The reader should not draw the conclusion that system analysts have never considered the issue of system transformation. Luard clearly believes that systems change since his entire volume is devoted to a demonstration of how international systems have differed on the various variables described earlier. If there have been different historical systems then, clearly, international systems have undergone change.[45] Rosecrance's analysis is also focused on the way in which systems have differed, but he further suggests factors that might account for system change: the relationship between nation-state actor disturbance, a "regulator" (usually an international institution), and environmental constraints.[46] Kaplan's discussion of the six international systems he identifies contains numerous allusions to the possibility that one system will evolve into another: "The factors responsible for the rise of the loose bipolar system after the breakdown of the 'balance of power' system are well known."[47] "The universal international system conceivably could develop as a consequence of the extension of the functions of a universal actor in a loose bipolar system."[48] "The hierarchical system may be imposed by force upon a bipolar or universal system. . . . It may evolve from a universal system."[49] Organski divides nations into three types: those that have potential power and whose growth rate is negligible, those going through a transitional growth period and whose growth rates are extremely large, and those which have reached maturity and whose growth rates have declined.[50] Systems differ with respect to the numbers of nations possessing each of the three types of power growth rates. In the preindustrial era all nations had negligible growth rates whereas the current era contains nations with all three growth rates. Organski suggests that the force that governs the transitions between systems by affecting national growth rates is the industrial revolution.

There have indeed been attempts to study system transformation. But these attempts have not gone very far, possibly due to the problems outlined earlier. Suppose, however, that these difficulties did not exist. What are the basic issues that would need to be addressed in a study of system transformation?

Another word for "transformation" is change. Change implies that something is happening through time and that what was true at one time point is different at a subsequent time point. A study of system transformation is therefore an analysis of how differences occur through time. It is a study of time-dependent processes defined over the basic attributes that identify and discriminate between systems. If this is a reasonable characterization of what is meant by system transformation then several issues are implicit in an analysis of system transformation.

One critical question concerns the relationship between the transformational forces and the variables that discriminate between international systems. Although Kaplan does not explicitly describe the forces that govern change, implicit in his analysis is the suggestion that change is *part of the system* itself: "The universal international system conceivably could develop as a consequence of the extension of the functions of a universal actor in a loose bipolar system."[51] In contrast, Organski's analysis suggests that system change is *independent* of the variables that identify the system.[52] If we discriminate between systems on the basis of mixes of nations with various growth rates then another process must be postulated to explain the changes in the growth rates. The differences between the two analysts might be characterized by saying that the first proposes that systems change on the basis of variables that are *endogenous* to the system, the second considers that systems change on the basis of variables that are *exogenous*. Needless to say, transformation could be a function of either or both types of processes.

If the forces making for change are endogenous to the system, then a further distinction is useful. Are the endogenous variables "autoregressive" in character or "interactive"? To say that system change is an autoregressive process is to imply that it is the "growth" in magnitude of a given variable that produces the change. Consider, for example, the variable "power distribution." To say that the transformational process is "autoregressive" implies that changes in the distribution of power are a function of previous distributions of power: There is something about the character of a given power distribution that produces the next power distribution. In contrast, to say that transformation is an interactive process is to suggest that power distributions affect other endogenous variables such as alliance configuration. The interaction between power distribution and alliance configurations produces a new system.

Whether the variables are endogenous or exogenous, discussions of system transformation indicate that there is yet another distinction of significance. Rosecrance's analysis strongly suggests that transformations are discontinuities, discrete events, that produce major upheavals.[53] Yet one could postulate a dynamic for Organski's[54] systems that would be smooth and continuous, a function which would gradually alter national growth rates. The distinction between discrete and continuous processes is a critical ingredient of how transformation processes are conceptualized — whether they represent dramatic system shocks or gradual processes of decay or growth.

Finally, Kaplan's phraseology adds yet another dimension to the discussion: "The universal international system *conceivably could*" or "The hierarchical system *may* be imposed" (italics mine).[55] These phrases suggest that a transformational process may not be completely determined. Although well defined, a process could be stochastic. A transformational process is deterministic if, once the process is described and an initial condition given, the transitional states are completely determined. If the changes in the power distribution of a system of nations was modeled using linear differential equations, then given the initial condition of the system all future systems would be known. It would thus be possible to discern, for example, if particular power distributions would ever occur. This would not be the case if the transformation process was conceptualized as a Markov chain. While the process would be equally explicitly specified, given the initial state of the system it would not be known what the power distribution of the system would be at some subsequent time point. All that would be known would be the probability that the system had a given power distribution at a particular time point.

Theorizing about the transformational processes requires a consideration of whether the variables are exogenous or endogenous, autoregressive or interactive, discrete or continuous, deterministic or stochastic. But these are essentially "mechanical" issues. They specify the alternatives that might be considered in postulating various transformational processes. There is perhaps a more fundamental issue that needs attention before beginning a study of system transformation. This is the question of "why bother?"

Why is it important to chart the change from one system to another? The literature would probably provide two answers to this question. First there are those who would argue that system transformation is itself an important event. These analysts usually view transformation as a discrete exogenous process, a cataclysmic happening like war. System transformation is therefore equivalent to major events and since these major events are of significance, system transformation is worth studying. Transformation = war, war is worth studying, therefore transformations should be analyzed.

A more useful rationale is provided by considering more broadly why systems analysts are concerned with international systems. The goal inherent in the study of most international systems is not simply to describe the attributes of particular systems but to link those attributes to things that transpire within the system. What is the linkage between power distribution and alliance configuration, on the one hand, and the likelihood of war, on the other? If, for example, we take seriously the debate over the relative merits of a balance-of-power versus a bipolar system and if it can be determined that conflict and war are more likely in one than the other, an immediate corollary question concerns the relationship between these two systems. Suppose it could be demonstrated that bipolar systems have a greater prospect for war than do balance-of-power systems. An analysis of the conditions under which bipolar systems become balance-of-power systems, or vice versa, is of immediate interest. More generally, if we are interested in the problem of the likelihood of interstate violence and it is possible to specify which systems contain the most violence, the issue of system transformation becomes a necessary component of the analysis. Knowing the conditions under which one system becomes another provides a partial understanding of internation violence.

Answering the "why bother" question is not just a matter of providing a rationale that will permit researchers to study the topic. It is not simply a question of justifying the existence of system transformation studies. The issue goes more deeply. Above we described various ways systems might be discriminated and noted the fact that operational measures would have to be developed, thresholds demarcated, and combinatorial problems settled. Subsequently we noted that a variety of choices exist in theorizing about the process itself, choices between endogenous, exogenous, discrete, continuous, stochastic, or deterministic. Each of these represents a decision that must be made by an analyst. But how can such decisions be meaningfully made without an initial problem focus? What is the research question that is being asked about system transformation? It is the answer to this basic question that will provide the guidelines for making reasonable choices between the alternatives.

Notes

1. Morton Kaplan, *System and Process in International Politics* (New York: John Wiley & Sons, 1957), p. 4.

2. Ibid., p. 9.

3. Charles A. McClelland, *Theory and the International System* (New York: Macmillan, 1966), p. 20.

4. Ibid.

5. Richard N. Rosecrance, *Action and Reaction in World Politics* (Boston: Little, Brown and Co., 1963), pp. 5-6.

6. *New York Times,* 25 February 1979.

7. Kaplan, *System and Process,* p. 45.

8. Ibid.

9. Kenneth N. Waltz, *Theory of International Politics* (Reading, Mass.: Addison-Wesley Publishing Co., 1979), p. 40.

10. Ibid., p. 101.

11. Evan Luard, *Types of International Society* (New York: Free Press, 1976).

12. Kal J. Holsti, *International Politics: A Framework for Analysis,* 3rd ed. (Englewood Ciffs, N.J.: Prentice-Hall, 1977).

13. Rosecrance, *Action and Reaction.*

14. Kaplan, *System and Process.*

15. Karl W. Deutsch and J. David Singer, "Multipolar Power Systems and International Stability," *World Politics* 16:3 (April 1964):390–406.

16. Glenn H. Snyder and Paul Diesing, *Conflict Among Nations* (Princeton, N.J.: Princeton University Press, 1977), p. 425.

17. Kenneth N. Waltz, "The Stability of a Bipolar World," *Daedalus* 93:3 (Summer 1964):883.

18. Ibid., p. 884.

19. Luard, *Types of International Society,* p. 146.

20. Ibid., p. 149.

21. Kaplan, *System and Process,* p. 23.

22. Holsti, *International Politics.*

23. Luard, *Types of International Society.*

24. Ibid., p. 118.

25. Holsti, *International Politics,* p. 28.

26. Luard, *Types of International Society,* p. 282.

27. Ibid., p. 284.

28. Ibid., p. 288.

29. Harold Nicolson, *The Evolution of Diplomacy* (New York: Collier Books, 1966).

30. Adda B. Bozeman, *Politics and Culture in International History* (Princeton, N.J.: Princeton University Press, 1960).

31. A.F.K. Organski, "The Power Transition," in James N. Rosenau, ed., *International Politics and Foreign Policy* (Glencoe, Ill.: Free Press, 1961), pp. 367–375.

32. Johan Galtung, "A Structural Theory of Aggression," *Journal of Peace Research* 1:2 (1964):96.

33. Kaplan, *System and Process.*

34. J. David Singer and Melvin Small, "The Composition and Status Ordering of the International System, 1815–1940," *World Politics* 18:2 (January 1966): 236–282.

35. Waltz, "Stability of a Bipolar World," 881–909.

36. Waltz, *Theory of International Politics.*

37. Galtung, "Theory of Aggression," p. 96.

38. Ibid., p. 99.

39. Frank Harary, "A Structural Analysis of the Situation in the Middle East," *Journal of Conflict Resolution* 2:2 (1961):167–178.

40. J. Hart, "Symmetry and Polarization in the European International System: 1870–1879," Situational Analysis Project, mimeo, paper no. 3 (Cornell University, 14 January 1972).

41. B. Healy and A. Stein, "The Balance of Power in International History: Theory and Reality, 1870–1881," Situational Analysis Project, mimeo, paper no. 1 (Cornell University, 1 October 1971).

42. Bruce M. Russett, "Delineating International Regions," in J. David Singer, ed., *Quantitative International Politics* (New York: Free Press, 1968), pp. 317–352.

43. Hayward R. Alker, Jr. and Bruce Russett, *World Politics in the General Assembly* (New Haven, Conn.: Yale University Press, 1965).

44. Steven Brams, "The Structure of Influence Relationships in the International System," in James N. Rosenau, ed., *International Politics and Foreign Policy,* rev. ed. (New York: Free Press, 1969), pp. 583–599.

45. Luard, *Types of International Society.*

46. Rosecrance, *Action and Reaction.*

47. Kaplan, *System and Process,* p. 36.

48. Ibid., p. 45.

49. Ibid., p. 48.

50. Organski, "Power Transition."

51. Kaplan, *System and Process,* p. 45.

52. Organski, "Power Transition."

53. Rosecrance, *Action and Reaction.*

54. Organski, "Power Transition."

55. Kaplan, *System and Process.*

2

K. J. HOLSTI

Change in the International System: Interdependence, Integration, and Fragmentation

Observers of contemporary international relations have used a variety of terms to capture the essential characteristics of global interaction and politics. Many have emphasized détente, dependency, neo-colonialism, or the development of multipolarity. Even Luard, in his comparative analysis of historical international systems, calls the 1914–1974 period an "age of ideology," in contrast to most of the nineteenth century, which was an "age of nationalism."[1] But whatever the relations between the major powers, the distribution of power and influence in the international system, or the forces that motivate foreign policy, most would argue that *interdependence* is the most pervasive and fundamental result of rapidly growing *transaction* rates between societies. The development of closer and multidimensional contacts between societies thus constitutes one of the fundamental forms of system change in the twentieth century.

Few have argued that another prominent feature of our world is disintegration and international fragmentation. The dramatic growth of means of transportation, communication, and exchange of goods, money, and ideas has helped bring about an unprecedented "interconnectedness"[2] between societies. It has thus been fashionable for commentators to claim that in these circumstances, the "shrinking world" has superseded nationalism. Nationalism reached its zenith in nineteenth century Europe and in the anticolonial movements of this century; to most observers, it is now declining as an international phenomenon.[3]

This view is largely incorrect either as a description of current reality or as a prediction for the future. Analysts have been so impressed by growing interdependence that they have ignored a simultaneous or parallel process that results in increased international fragmentation. This chapter argues, and provides some evidence, that while transactions

23

between societies have indeed grown dramatically throughout this century, nationalism, separatism, and international dis-integration have also been prominent. Walker Connor may exaggerate when he claims that "the centrifugal forces of national aspirations are growing more powerful than the centripetal forces of transnationalism."[4] Yet, the two trends of integration and dis-integration or fragmentation are taking place concurrently, and in some cases the latter is the consequence of, or reaction to, "too much" interdependence or integration. Both represent different types of system change.

If the concept of nationalism has been surrounded by definitional problems, the notions of interdependence, integration, dis-integration, and fragmentation are no less precise. We begin, then, by outlining some of the behaviors implied by the term *nationalism* and then proceed to analyze the literature of international relations theory to answer the question of why so little attention has been paid to nationalist phenomena in contemporary international politics.

Nationalism can be defined both as attitudinal attributes of individuals — strong primary or exclusive loyalties to the ethnic group, nation, or to its legal embodiment, the state — and also as governmental policies that are designed to control, reduce, or eliminate a wide range of foreign influences and transnational processes on a society.[5] This essay uses the term in the latter sense. Such policies reflect a search for autonomy in a world of interdependence, amalgamation, and homogenization. A government that raises tariffs to protect a particular industry and its employees is not necessarily expressing either mass sentiments of national loyalty or a search for autonomy. Seeking greater economic benefits may be involved in nationalist behavior, but psychological benefits and threat/vulnerability reduction appear more significant. A government that simultaneously imposes barriers to foreign investment, censors incoming publications and films, expels foreign aid advisers, bars a wide range of imports, inculcates a distrust of foreigners, and places restrictions on the activities of foreign firms or diplomats likely does these to minimize or reduce threats it sees emanating from overly profuse links with the outside world. Deliberate and comprehensive reduction of transactions between any pair of states results in international fragmentation. In cases where two political units have achieved a high level of formal political or economic integration[6] and one subsequently attempts to establish increased autonomy, dis-integration is the result. In both cases, the transaction "distance" between societies has been increased, resulting, presumably, in a decline of interdependence or, in asymmetrical dyads, of dependence. Further, as will be shown below, fragmentation or dis-integration may occur at the national as well as international level.

Before exploring the relationship between interdependence, and fragmentation or dis-integration, we must raise the question why processes and policies that make the headlines almost every day somehow escape the attention of many international relations scholars. To my knowledge, no major approach to international relations theory has emphasized the prominence of nationalist behavior as an important characteristic of the contemporary international system. And only a few have examined the nature and sources of autonomy-seeking behavior at the foreign policy level.[7] The glitter and dazzle of growing interdependence have caused a degree of myopia in both academic speculation and diplomatic rhetoric. When we examine the popular contemporary portraits of the international system, it becomes easier to understand why nationalist phenomena have received so little attention. There is insufficient space to provide a full analysis of all current characterizations of the international system; hence, the systems image will be reviewed only briefly, with more elaborate explorations of the literature on interdependence and integration.

The World as a System of Transnational Relations

Many authors have rejected the image of international politics as a game played by sovereign, impermeable states. They argue that the archaic conception of power politics does not take into account the fundamental consequences of modern technology, the close interconnection between domestic and foreign policy, and the permeability of societies to outside forces. To accommodate the new facts of international life, the world must be seen as a system of patterned interaction in which the main units of action are individuals and a variety of functional groups, as well as national and subnational government units. All these actors "process" issues; somehow political and economic outcomes feed back and create new "states" of the system. The world, then, looks like millions of spider webs superimposed on each other, with individual filaments symbolizing various types of transaction flows.[8] For a system to survive, adaptation to new technological, political, and economic trends is necessary. This view seems based on an assumption that as interactive processes grow and expand, as people increasingly interact across state frontiers, they will be more prone to adjust their differences rather than resort to lethal violence which might destroy the system. A further assumption holds that as technology increases the opportunities (some imply necessity, rather than opportunity) for interaction, people, groups, and states will want to take advantage of them and will seldom suffer losses from so doing. Interactions, transactions, networks, nodes — all of these terms apply to processes going on in a genuine international community.

The systems metaphor has the advantage of placing the state in a setting that is broader than the traditional one in which only diplomats, heads of state, and military forces interact. We are alerted to the importance of subnational foreign policies, to the influence of international organizations, and to the role of transnational groups that have an impact on states and societies. Multinational corporations (MNCs) and terrorist groups are obvious examples. But except for studies on the economic and political impacts of MNCs on developing countries, little attention has been directed to the efforts of many governments to control, reduce, and sometimes even to eliminate the influence of transnational groups and processes on their societies and politics. While the growth of transnational organizations may appear inevitable, it is by no means inevitable that governments will merely "adapt" to them. Some will perceive them as threats to a variety of national values and will deal with them accordingly, even at considerable economic cost. Attempts to enlarge autonomy, to reduce external penetration, and to control transnational organization may involve the construction of national "moats." To date, however, the systems image has promoted more research and writing on international interconnections than on the efforts to control or reduce them.

The World of Interdependence

Interdependence, of course, is not an approach, framework for analysis, or metaphor distinct from those discussed above; indeed, the image of a global system, in which profuse transnational relations take place, implies a high degree of interconnectedness among a variety of units. If there is no connection, there is no system. Global interconnectedness has certain sources (technology, transportation, and communication), it can be measured by looking at transactions, and it leads to sensitivity and vulnerability, where conditions in country A become critically influenced by decisions, trends, and events in countries B . . . X. As Cooper defines it economically, "interdependence, by joining national markets, erodes the effectiveness of [domestic] policies and hence threatens national autonomy in the determination and pursuit of economic objectives."[9] Interconnectedness often, but not necessarily, creates interdependence. Much of the early literature on interdependence measured growth or fluctuations in transaction flows without exploring the problem of sensitivity and vulnerability, that is, interdependence. Confining their analyses primarily to statistics from industrial countries, the authors often assumed that growth in transaction flows had approximately equal consequences for all those engaged in the transactions.[10] Only recently have studies begun to explore the consequences of varying transaction flows on the international system and the foreign policies of countries. Among the more important consequences noted or hypothesized by some authors are the following:

1. An increased national sensitivity and vulnerability to decisions, trends, and events abroad — that is, increased interdependence — evolves.
2. More cooperative endeavors and common problem solving occurs, which increases gains for all involved. No single nation can regulate any system characterized by rich transaction flows, and efforts to make decisions purely in terms of short-run national advantages — increasing national autonomy — will result in trade wars, currency instability, decline of investment, unemployment, and ultimately recession or depression.[11]
3. The latitude of choice of governments in fashioning domestic economic and welfare programs is reduced.[12]
4. Governments are growing incapable of effectively controlling transnational activities.
5. "Complex interdependence" grows, tantamount to a new type of international politics. It is characterized by the importance of nonstate actors in setting the international agenda and determining bargaining and conflict outcomes, no permanent hierarchy of issues on the agenda, and the irrelevance of military power and threats in issue processing and bargaining outcomes.[13]
6. At the system level, status hierarchy declines as interdependence grows. The relatively weak tend to obtain more favorable outcomes and the major powers are less able to attain desired ends. They increasingly have to lead by example and persuasion rather than by dictation or coercion.[14]
7. As international communications develop and spread out, knowledge and information of others increases, which in turn augments mutual understanding and tolerance. Reduced levels of international conflict are a likely outcome of international exchange.

Most of these hypothesized consequences are undoubtedly correct in many contexts. But some need to be subjected to scrutiny and not accepted uncritically. For example, because it measures aggregate transaction flows, the literature implies that interconnectedness is a condition affecting equally all parties involved. Thus, we often hear that the *world* is increasingly interdependent, as if growing interconnectedness affected everyone the same way. Once we begin looking at pairs of states rather than at regional or global trends, however, the realities of great differentials in vulnerability, dependency, influence, and coercive capacity become much more apparent. The world may indeed be more interdependent, but that fact has not radically altered the position of, for example, Czechoslovakia or Chile when they attempted to break away from the hegemony of the Soviet Union and the United States. If anything, the extensive interconnection between the client states and their mentors prevented the former from achieving policymaking autonomy and generated conflict, not mutual tolerance or empathy.

Statements such as "the world is increasingly interdependent" are generally nonilluminating except in the banal sense that what people do today has greater impact on others abroad than was the case six centuries ago. Even if the comment contains some face validity, it can be applied with complete accuracy only to the relations between the industrial countries and possibly between them and members of the Organization of Petroleum Exporting Countries (OPEC). The fact is that important transaction flows are not growing at equal rates across different regions. The proportion of less developed countries (LDCs) exports to total world exports, for example, continues to decline. Except for the OPEC countries, there is virtually no investment from the LDCs into the industrial countries, and only a limited amount from a few communist countries into the West. What Tanzania does economically has little or no impact on economic fortunes in Kenya, Uganda, or England. Except for contacts through international organizations, the relations between most Latin American and Southeast Asian countries are virtually nonexistent.

The argument that increased interdependence is likely to reduce international conflict is also open to serious question.[15] As diplomatic relations in Africa have grown more complex, the number of diplomatic quarrels appears to have increased. It would be well to recall also that the marked growth of European interconnectedness and interdependence throughout the nineteenth and twentieth centuries did not prevent the outbreak of the two most destructive wars in human history. To sum up: the fact of increasing interconnectedness is undoubtedly correct. Its consequences remain problematical, however. Increased transaction flows can lead to dependency, exploitation, conflict, and violence as well as to more collaboration and mutual knowledge. To find out the actual consequences of interconnectedness, one must examine pairs of states and avoid the ecological fallacy of arguing that a system property pervades the relationships in all dyads.[16] The *patterns* and *qualities* of transactions are more important than quantities and growth rates. Nationalist policies, secession, and international fragmentation and/or dis-integration are likely to occur exactly in situations typified by asymmetrical patterns of sensitivity and vulnerability, unequal exchange, unidirectional flows, and attempts by the strong to penetrate the political, economic, and cultural life of the weak.

The World of Integration

Few postwar diplomatic developments have excited as much intellectual enthusiasm as has the regional integration of Western Europe. Unlike systems approaches to the study of international politics (whose main contribution has been to look at old phenomena in new ways or to expand the list of phenomena that ought to be investigated), integration theorists have undertaken a massive cumulative effort to explain why formerly independent units come together to create supranational bodies. While the movement for European unification gave the impetus to the inquiry, most of the theories and models of integration have been developed with an eye to universal application. This body of literature has sought to identify necessary and sufficient conditions for integration, has developed techniques for measuring degrees of integration, and has speculated at great length on which variables explain what aspects of the integration process.

What types of independent variables are relevant? Virtually any condition between proximate societies has been mentioned. In some of Deutsch's work, transaction flows, mutual responsiveness, shared values, and the like are posited as necessary conditions for the creation of "security communities."[17] As in the interdependence literature, communication between societies is also essential. Yet in later work, Deutsch speaks of transaction flows as *indicators* of integration or political cohesion — that is, as dependent rather than independent variables.[18] The dependent variable — integration — has caused no less confusion. To some, public attitudinal support for supranational bodies is tantamount to successful integration. For others, supranational policymaking is the critical indicator. At the other end of the spectrum, a mere willingness to enter into transactions appears sufficient to indicate a high degree of community.[19]

Debates on methodological questions have prompted investigators to examine many of their assumptions, develop better techniques of measurement, and come to understand that a consensus on definitions of independent and dependent variables is unlikely to be achieved. Yet, many of the normative proclivities of authors have remained immune from scrutiny. While research on integration has generally followed many canons of scientific inquiry, there is little question that authors have been "for" integration — hence the problem has been approached in a particular way, namely locating the necessary and sufficient conditions for *successful* integration. Conditions militating *against* integration — particularly political opposition to integration — have received little attention.

Why the great concern — or hope — for political amalgamation? Most authors implicitly, and sometimes explicitly, assume that integration reduces international conflict. Hence, to study integration is to study the conditions of peace. Although this notion borders on a tautology, it is ultimately the search for peace that has justified the extensive intellectual endeavor. Deutsch's earliest formulations on integration were motivated by a desire to explore the fundamental problem of international politics and organization, "the creation of conditions under which stable peaceful relations among nation states are possible and likely."[20] According to the early Deutsch, "if the entire world were integrated into a security community, wars would eventually be eliminated."[21] To Amitai Etzioni, "The most compelling appeal of regionalism is that the rise of regional communities may provide a stepping-stone on the way from a world of a hundred-odd states to a world of a stable and just peace. Such an achievement seems to require the establishment of a world political community."[22] Although Etzioni approaches the subject of integration from a scientific perspective, his values are clearly revealed in his disappointment, for example, that the Scandinavians have not taken the final step into full political amalgamation. Integration, however defined, is thus the ultimate answer to the problem of war. Why should we assume that decreasing the number of sovereignties decreases the incidence of lethal violence?

The most obvious answer is that people who share a common identity and political loyalties do not quarrel as often or as lethally as those who are separated by language, ethnic, religious, and political frontiers. In the work of Deutsch and his colleagues, for example, transaction flows assume central importance as a foundation for successful integration. As people communicate, they become salient to each other. Mutually rewarding transactions help develop mutual trust, confidence, and similar perceptions of international problems. While Deutsch more recently has acknowledged in passing that communication and interpersonal contacts can be "negative,"[23] most of the literature posits a causal relationship between increasing transactions, integrations, and ultimately, less conflict. Integration theory rests squarely upon the old idea that the better people know each other the more they will like each other. This "birds of a feather flock together" thesis is a critical normative dimension in much of the literature, one which is more often assumed than demonstrated.

Many authors have criticized early writings on integration for their air of inevitability and universality. In particular, they have pointed out that conditions in the developing countries today are so different from those in Europe during the 1950s and 1960s that the successful European Economic Community (EEC) experience can provide few clues to the possibilities of success in other geographic contexts. If one had to wait for the richness of transaction flows found in Europe, even prior to the Rome Treaty, to be duplicated in the LDCs, the chances of successful integration in the Third World would be virtually nil today. Transaction flows within most Third World regions have not yet even reached the levels found in Europe in the nineteenth century.

But it is more than a question of comparative transaction flows, or even the economic gains that can be achieved by the creation of large markets. Conditions in Europe after World War II were unique in ways other than those that can be easily quantified. To what extent were these conditions important in helping make the EEC a success? If the judgment is that they were important, or critical, then we must ask whether or not their absence in other regional settings would preclude successful integration. First, on the eve of economic rationalization in Western Europe, the region had just emerged from the most destructive war in human history. One of the prime lessons of that experience was that the ancient Franco-German enmity must be resolved. One way to accomplish the task was to create institutions—the European Coal and Steel Community (ECSC)—that would lock the two economies into a system of mutual dependence. Second, a real pan-European movement, particularly appealing to the young, developed in part to underline Europe's separate identity from the United States. The emotional commitment to "Europe" was an important part of the milieu in which plans for the Common Market were launched. Third, many accounts give considerable personal credit to Jean Monnet and Maurice Schuman for developing the blueprints for the ECSC and for their many years of lobbying to sell the conceptions to the various national capitals. Fourth, nationalism throughout Europe in the late 1940s and early 1950s was probably at its historical nadir—a condition that exists in few other regions today and one that has changed even in Europe in the past decade. Finally, part of the motivation for the Common Market was to decrease dependence upon the United States and to create economic institutions that could compete effectively with U.S. enterprises and exports. To a certain extent, then, the Europeans accepted integration in order to dis-integrate (or at least to create more equality) from a hegemon.

With the exception of the last condition — which has been a relevant consideration in the formation of economic groupings such as the Andean Pact — the others have not been duplicated elsewhere. This is not to argue that customs unions and common markets in Southeast Asia, Africa, and Latin America are doomed to failure, but we must be aware that success in Europe could not be predicted *solely* from the growth of pro-European public opinion or from broadening transaction flows. Much of the theoretical literature, in its attempts to operationalize variables that can be both measured and compared, by necessity overlooks unique historical circumstances, some of which may be critical. For example, the ephemeral phenomenon — leaders' political will — is crucial to integration. If there is no desire to amalgamate, then it does not matter how much mail, trade, tourism, telephone calls, student exchanges and compatibility of values flourish. The examples of Canada–United States, Australia–New Zealand, and Scandinavia should make this clear.

Political or economic integration should not be expected to occur, moreover, where there is a basic asymmetry in the pattern of transactions and in expected economic gains between the parties. Asymmetrical "interconnectedness" between two societies or groups is likely to lead the smaller and weaker to perceive threats to its national identity and possibly to cultural survival. There may be only a fine line between integration and absorption. The 1972 Norwegian vote against ratifying membership in the EEC was in part based on widespread fears that economic integration would lead to the destruction of traditional small farming and fishing sectors. Promises of future economic gains were insufficient to offset fears that certain lifestyles would be destroyed through decisions taken by Eurocrats who had little or no knowledge of Norwegian traditions and social values. A significant portion of British opponents of EEC membership argued along the same lines. Yet, the literature has mostly ignored the phenomenon of opposition to integration.[24] If authors explored the issue, perhaps they would not so easily dismiss nationalism as some declining relic of previous centuries. By asking the fundamental question, "Why, or under what conditions, does integration succeed?" commonalities are likely to be emphasized. Were researchers to approach the subject in terms of "Why has there been no movement to integrate in areas characterized by rich transaction flows and cultural similarities?" or "Why didn't integration fail in Europe?" they would focus on different phenomena, including the peculiar conjunction of circumstances that led many Europeans *not* to fear absorption. Why didn't the opponents of integration prevail? Perhaps it is, as Caporaso has put it, "because the new community system has . . . made it possible for Europeans to enjoy the fruits of a large market and customs union while at the same time sacrificing neither cultural identity nor political autonomy."[25] But in many other areas of the world, where transactions and other types of relationships are characterized by asymmetry, vulnerability, and conflict, amalgamation would be perceived as a threat to a variety of national values. In their longing for successful integration, and hence peace, many academics have easily slipped into the position of seeing Europe not as an exception to the course of history and the near-universal persistence of nationalism, but as a harbinger of the future and as a model for others to emulate.

These comments are not meant to imply that all integration schemes will stop short of political amalgamation. Yet we should not accept any process as inevitable. While there are forces creating demands for more integration (and interdependence) there are also those that are pushing in the direction of dis-integration, resisting further integration, and promoting international fragmentation. Ours is still an age of nationalism despite technology—and sometimes because of it.

Others have made the observation that processes leading to increased interdependence and fragmentation may occur simultaneously.[26] But is there a connection between the two processes? My argument is that in some cases, dis-integration and fragmentation are *responses* to asymmetrical integration and to certain profiles of transactions in dependent and interdependent relationships. They are the reactions of those who see greater interconnectedness not in terms of greater opportunities or benefits, but rather as resulting in inequitable distribution of rewards or as posing threats to national, ethnic, language, or religious identity. In brief, the "shrinking world" may result not in greater consensus and internationalism, but in heightened nationalism and drives to extend or protect autonomy.

Five general types of policies resulting in international dis-integration or fragmentation can be outlined. Governments or groups claiming governmental status may:

1. Terminate practices of joint policymaking, problem solving, or policy coordination; they may also withdraw from, or reduce participation in, institutions having supranational characteristics.
2. Construct mechanisms systematically to reduce or terminate the free flow of goods, people, funds, and ideas between two or more societies. Those fearing absorption or loss of autonomy attempt to reduce external penetration of their government, economy, and society by building walls to reduce access. In its extreme form, it can be termed isolationism.

3. Alter asymmetrical relationships by significantly diversifying external contacts, building regional coalitions, or entering into regional integration schemes as a way of escaping domination by a hegemon.
4. Organize, at the national level, a secessionist movement which seeks to secure or protect autonomy by establishing independent statehood.
5. Resist further integration but not seek to dis-integrate or secede. This would be a marginal category.

As we will see in the two illustrations, governments may pursue several of the policies simultaneously. Whether singly or in combination, the underlying objective is to create more distance between governments and societies and/or to gain national control over transnational processes. In the brief outline of the nationalist behaviors in Canada and Burma in recent years, we will see that the results of greater transaction flows and increased interdependence (or dependency) were not those predicted in most of the literature. The inexorable forces of interdependence in these cases did not result in more integration, more mutual empathy and understanding, or less international conflict. If anything, the reverse was the case.

Canada–United States

No two separate societies in the world better fulfill the assumed necessary conditions to amalgamate politically than do those of the United States and Canada. For most of this century these two countries have constituted a pluralistic security community, where no military forces have been arrayed against each other and where no government has contemplated the use of force to resolve bilateral conflicts. Using some of Deutsch's variables in which high rankings on indicators of social assimilation predict successful integration, Canada and the United States could have been expected to amalgamate long ago.

Proximity. Not only are Canada and the United Sates neighbors, but they have the longest unguarded frontier in the world. Moreover, approximately 90 percent of Canada's population lives within 100 miles of the border, a distribution which is unique among the territorially large states of the world.

Social Homogeneity. With the exception of Quebec's six million French-speaking residents, and the 11 percent Negro population in the United States, the composition of these two countries' populations are similar in terms of ethnic background (predominantly English, Scots, and Irish), language, social mobility, educational level, literacy, and political and social values.

Transactions. The transaction indicators clearly reveal that there are more transactions annually between these two societies than any others in the world. It is not possible to obtain separate figures on mail flows and telephone calls between the two countries because Canada and the United States already constitute a fully integrated communications network with the border having no practical impact on flows. In the early 1970s, Canadians and Americans annually made an average of 12 million visits to each other's country; no other pair of nations begins to approach such magnitudes of personal exchange. Seventy percent of Canada's exports go to the United States, a figure which constitutes approximately 22 percent of Canada's GNP, while the United States provides nearly that figure as a source of imports. While U.S. trade with Canada constitutes a much lower percentage of its total trade, Canada is still the largest single foreign market and source of supplies for the United States.

Money flows freely across the border as well. Until the mid-1960s, Americans had invested more funds in Canada than in Latin America and Europe combined. Likewise, virtually all of Canadian foreign investment was directed to the United States. Until petrodollars began flowing into the United States, Canadians owned more of the U.S. economy—although the percentage of total economic activity was miniscule—than did any other national group. In addition to these figures we could cite the fact that throughout the 1950s and 1960s Canadians watched more U.S.- than Canadian-originating television programs, a large proportion of Canadian university graduates went to the United States for graduate studies, and there was almost unrestricted migration between the two countries.

Mutual Knowledge. Here asymmetry is the rule: Canadians know a great deal about the United States—indeed some Canadians know much more about U.S. politics and history than they do about their own country. Americans, while on the whole perceiving Canadians with strong positive regard,[27] have little substantive knowledge of the country.

Previous Integrative Experience. Through enterprises such as agreements on trade in farm implements, the St. Lawrence Seaway, North American Air Defense (NORAD), the North American Automotive Product Trade Agreement—all of which contain integrated characteristics—both countries have gained appreciably. These schemes have applied criteria of economic and security rationality in order to maximize joint gains, and for the most part have succeeded. The Automotive Product Trade Agreement of 1965, for example, has made North America a single production and marketing zone. This has vastly increased Cana-

dian production of cars, provided substantial employment and tax benefits for Canada, and slightly reduced price differentials of cars between
the United States and Canada. The Defense Production Sharing Agreement has created free trade in arms bidding and manufacturing, thereby
sustaining a Canadian defense industry which would not be viable if its
market were confined to the small Canadian armed forces. [28] NORAD
has created an early warning and antibomber defense sysem that would
have cost much more and been less effective had each country proceeded
on its own.

Integration of Policymaking Institutions. There are some nineteen permanent joint U.S.-Canadian institutions. Most of them meet occasionally for discussions and consultation, but a few of them have some of the
characteristics of supranational authority. Perhaps equally important is
the vast network of transgovernmental relations, where elements of the
two countries' bureaucracies deal directly with each other, far removed
from central control. The manner in which government business was
conducted between Ottawa and Washington almost suggested the irrelevance of the international border. In some policy areas, collaboration
and coordination reached very high levels (e.g., between the U.S. Federal
Bureau of Investigation [FBI] and the Royal Canadian Mounted Police
[RCMP], or between the defense establishments), if not total integration.
While Canada and the United States would not score as high on Nye's
integration indicators[29] as would the EEC members, by the mid-1960s
the two countries indulged in considerable policy consultation and coordination. One could argue that if the trends of the 1950s and 1960s had
been allowed to continue, a fully integrated continental economy would
have emerged by the 1980s or 1990s, and if the spillover hypothesis was
correct, this would subsequently lead to political integration.

Such predictions were, of course, the problem. By the mid-1960s,
many Canadians were becoming increasingly concerned that if natural
market forces were allowed to continue between the two countries,
Canada eventually would be *absorbed* by the United States. Although
the scope and breadth of transactions between the two societies was unparalleled in the world, the flows were basically asymmetrical. Hence,
many Canadians came to regard them as threatening to Canadian culture
and identity, and ultimately to political autonomy. What a neutral observer (particularly a theorist of integration) might see as an extraordi-
narily rich relationship in terms of empathy, shared values and transactions, many Canadians came to see as overextensive U.S. penetration
into Canadian society.[30]

Whether or not one sympathizes with various manifestations of Canadian nationalism, it is not difficult to understand why a negative

response to asymmetrical transaction structures would arise. For example, on the average during the 1960s, Americans owned or controlled 55 percent of Canada's manufacturing capacity, constituting more than 20 percent of Canada's GNP; over 90 percent of the theaters (which refused to show Canadian films); and virtually the entire retail trade industry. In the same period, more than 70 percent of unionized Canadians belonged to U.S. labor organizations. With a majority of the Canadians living within the broadcast range of U.S. television stations, most Canadians were watching U.S. material most of the time. The Canadian entertainment industry, with its market only 10 percent that of the United States, could not compete successfully. Although Canadian newspapers and magazines were locally owned, virtually all news of the outside world came via United Press International (UPI) and Associated Press (AP), or from *Time* magazine. Finally, in many Canadian universities, some departments were heavily staffed by Americans, and in more than one instance U.S. department heads would hire fellow nationals without even looking for qualified Canadians.

Under these circumstances — as well as the Canadians' view of the Vietnam War and domestic disturbances in the United States — Canadian nationalists were able to select from a wide menu of issues and argue that if trends in economics, communication, education, and culture were allowed to continue, Canada would eventually lose what remained of its political autonomy. While public opinion polls of the period clearly showed a rising concern about the problem of U.S. investment and influence in the country, at the leadership levels many prominent figures of all political persuasions united to express demands for placing controls on the free flow of goods and investment between the two countries.

Between 1968 and 1973 the Canadian federal government — reacting to, rather than leading, public opinion — instituted a variety of measures to alter the pattern or structure of transactions and to halt certain integrative trends. This included a notable decline in the use of some of the many Canadian-U.S. institutions for policy coordination. At the cultural level, the Canadian Radio and Television Commission imposed minimum Canadian content requirements on all broadcasting facilities; developed a set of regulations forcing advertisers to produce their commercials in Canada rather than importing them from the United States; and required Canadian broadcasting companies to divest themselves of U.S. ownership to the 20 percent level. The Canadian secretary of state's office placed considerable pressure on U.S.-owned theater chains to show Canadian films. It also acted several times to prevent U.S. firms from buying out Canadian publishers. After years of debate the Canadian federal government also set up a foreign investment review board with the task of assuring that foreign investment and takeover bids of existing Canadian companies would bring "significant benefits" to Canada.

Starting in 1972 the government also reorganized its policymaking procedures with the United States. Its general philosophy was to create a more "arms length" approach, to accept higher levels of conflict with the United States, and to impose more central control over transgovernmental relations.[31] The days of the "special relationship" and "good partner" diplomacy came to an end. Moreover, the Canadian government politely turned down U.S. proposals to establish more institutions for policy coordination and joint problem solving. The political atmosphere in Ottawa and the country was such that any proposals smacking of "continentalism" (the Canadian expression for arrangements containing integrationist characteristics) were quietly rejected. A detailed Economic Council of Canada study on trade between the two countries, which emphasized the economic gains accruing to the country from a free trade arrangement, never saw the light of public or parliamentary debate.

At the level of foreign policy, the Canadian government set out to diversify its diplomatic and trade contacts as a means of reducing Canada's vulnerability to U.S. economic decisions, such as Nixon's import surcharge and dollar devaluation in August 1971. The major thrust of the program was to use the EEC and Japan as counterweights to the overwhelming trade reliance upon the United States.

Measures to reduce penetration and to reverse integrationist arrangements were not confined to the federal government level. Many provincial governments passed legislation prohibiting the sale of crown lands to nonresidents and a few even considered banning sales of private property to foreigners. The Canadian trade union movement began systematically untying itself from U.S. organizations: by the mid-1970s more than one-half of Canada's unionized labor belonged to independent Canadian unions; a decade earlier the figure had been only 30 percent. The universities agreed upon regulations requiring all academic positions to be advertised in Canada, and a number of departments unofficially began to give preference to Canadian applicants.

Taken together, all these policies were designed, sector by sector, to monitor and control, or alter the profile of Canadian-U.S. transactions, to build up local institutions more effectively to compete with Americans, and to erect filters or screens on some forms of U.S. penetration such as private investment. Programs were also designed to create more distance in diplomacy, to turn the border into a reality as far as cultural relations were concerned, and in a few cases to abandon or modify certain Canadian-U.S. arrangements and institutions that contained integrated characteristics. The policies represent a combination of types 1,

2, 3, and 5 listed earlier. The Canadian case shows clearly the linkage between increased transaction flows, interdependence (or dependence), and the rise of nationalism. Although the United States and Canada share many attributes and still engage in unparalleled quantities of transactions, there is undeniably greater "distance" between the two countries today than there was a decade ago.

Burma

Burma is an example of an even more extreme reaction to foreign penetration and asymmetrical interdependence. From 1963 to 1966, the Burmese government constructed an extensive set of mechanisms to reduce foreign penetration and to establish a greater degree of policy-making autonomy.[32]

The U Nu government, from 1948 until its overthrow in 1962 by the military, generally opened up the country to a number of foreign influences and adopted the typical strategy of development through foreign tutelage, learning from others, seeking foreign investment and aid, and importing modern technology.

The military regime under General Ne Win adopted exactly the opposite approach: total autarchy and isolation, with development achieved through self-reliance. Burma is an extreme case, of course, but it does illustrate how the typical postcolonial pattern of contacts between industrial and developing countries can lead to a fear of being overly penetrated and ultimately losing all cultural and political autonomy.

The Ne Win government systematically began expelling foreigners in 1963: missionaries; foreign professors teaching at the University of Rangoon; all foreign researchers, from agricultural specialists to anthropologists; and medical personnel. Cultural exchange programs such as Fulbright, Ford Foundation, and British Council were terminated, aid programs were not renewed, and foreign travelers were provided with only twenty-four-hour visas, thus ending tourism. The government imposed strict censorship on foreign books, films and magazines – not so much to control political thought as to prevent the "pollution" of Burmese culture from "degenerate" foreign materials. Foreign advisors, who in the U Nu days had been operating at all levels of society from small villages throughout the bureaucracy to assisting cabinet ministers, had all departed by 1964. The country had become effectively sealed off from foreign penetration within two years after the coup.

In its foreign policies, the Ne Win government also shunned external contacts. It scrupulously avoided any involvement in Southeast Asian regional economic and technical undertakings. Its delegates, once active in United Nations affairs, were prominent primarily by their absence or by the number of times they abstained from voting. Once a leader of the nonaligned movement, by the 1960s and 1970s Burma attended only in a perfunctory capacity. And in the Geneva disarmament committee, the Burmese delegate — supposedly a representative of the nonaligned states — stopped attending.

Ne Win's attempt to turn Burma into a hermit nation was motivated in part by security considerations — relations with China and the problem of domestic rebellions — but also by the judgment that Burma would eventually lose its autonomy if it continued the U Nu strategy of development through foreign tutelage. Important sectors of the Burmese elites wanted to end a situation that they defined as one of foreign penetration and domination, where the country was in effect run by outsiders who knew little about Burmese history and culture. Interdependence, if that meant slavishly copying foreigners and indiscriminately adopting their cultural habits, was, in the government's view, a condition that could only lead to the destruction of all that was good, pure, and moral in the Burmese culture. Modern communications, transportation, and publications, because they were primarily running in one direction — into Burma, but not from Burma abroad — would eventually turn the Burmans into second-rate carbon copies of Westerners — just as Burmese civil servants had become under British colonial rule. In Ne Win's judgment, Burma could not achieve true independence if Burmese politicians and civil servants took their political (cold war) cues, their consumption habits, their cultural values, and their life aspirations from others. Interdependence (or as the Burmese would define it, overdependence) thus led to an extreme, almost xenophobic response. Isolationism seeks not just to create greater "arm's length" from a former or actual hegemon, but to reduce *all* contacts with the outside world to a bare minimum.

Many have argued that isolationism is no longer feasible in today's interdependent world. Indeed, if growth in national wealth is the criterion of national success or failure, isolationism in most cases — including Burma — leads to economic decay. But as theorists of interdependence and integration seldom acknowledge, economics is not everything. Other values — in the Burmese case, national pride and fear of loss of autonomy — are also relevant. Economic gains may be forsaken in order to maximize other values.

Some may object that the Burmese case is so atypical that it hardly constitutes evidence for the assertion that processes of fragmentation resulting from "too much" interdependence and/or integration constitute an important trend in the *system*. How much of any phenomenon is required in order to establish a trend is of course an arbitrary matter. With the exception of the EEC there has not been much successful economic integration in other regions of the world, and virtually no political amalgamation anywhere. Yet, if measured by trade, investment, and communications, interconnectedness has dramatically increased since World War II.

On a highly judgmental basis — since there are no reliable data — we can list those countries which in the past decade or so have built significant walls around them to reduce foreign penetration, have taken steps to undo integrationist programs or institutions, or, in the marginal case, have resisted attempts to create more integrated mechanisms. The list would include Albania, Bhutan, Burma, Canada, Chile (1971-1973), Cambodia, Iran, Iraq, Norway, Peru, Tanzania, some Council for Mutual Economic Assistance (COMECON) members, and perhaps others. In each of these cases, governments sought by various means to fundamentally alter the interdependent — or dependent — relationships they had become enmeshed in during the 1950s and 1960s.

Secessionist Movements
and International Fragmentation

International fragmentation may result also from the myriad of contemporary secessionist movements. There are no collected longitudinal data on the incidence of secessionist movements during this century, so it is not possible to determine whether or not there are trends. Nevertheless, ethnically based nationalism is highly visible today and is not confined to the developing nations. Table 2.1, which is not exhaustive, illustrates the pervasiveness of nationalism at the substate level, and suggests that desire for group independence persists strongly in our age of interdependence.

If increased interdependence is supposed to create bonds of community between peoples and societies, why does the search for autonomy and separateness continue at the national and international levels? Several hypotheses might be advanced.[33]

The necessary condition for most secessionist movements is the existence of more than one ethnic language or religious community occupying the same state territory. This condition exists in a majority of the world's states. Connor writes that of 132 states (in the late 1960s), only 12, or 9 percent, can be described as basically homogenous in ethnic makeup. In 32 states, the largest single ethnic group does not comprise even 50 percent of the population, and in 53 states, the population is divided into more than five significant groups.[34] In such nations in-

TABLE 2.1
Active Secessionist Movements, 1973-1980

Movement	Location
Movements employing violence on a significant scale:	
Basques	(Spain)
Canary Islands	(Spain)
Corsica	(France)
Eritrea	(Ethiopia)
Kachins	(Burma)
Kurds	(Iraq, Iran)
Muslims	(Philippines)
Nagas	(India)
Ogaden Somalis	(Ethiopia)
Polisario	(Morocco, Mauritania)
Shaba	(Congo)
Shans	(Burma)
South Moluccans	(Indonesia)
Ustashi	(Yugoslavia)
Active, non-violent secessionist movements:	
Azores and Madeira	(Portugal)
Bretons	(France)
Catalonia	(Spain)
Karens	(Burma)
Nepalese	(Bhutan)
Pushtoos	(Pakistan)
Quebec	(Canada)
Scottish National Party	(United Kingdom)
Transylvania Magyars	(Romania)

creased communications between ethnic, language, or religious groups may underline uniqueness, cause greater group solidarity, promote stereotypic thinking, and ultimately increase intergroup cleavages. Connor[35] has argued that the optimistic predictions about the results of increasing social communication are taken from the U.S. or European nineteenth century experience and are not borne out in other milieus. In many developing countries, the first extensive contacts between minority groups and central government authorities or the dominant cultural communities lead to conflict, not assimilation. Leaders of many secessionist movements are not those who have remained isolated; on the contrary, most have had considerable experience with the majority population and central government agents.[36] They have rejected offers to assimilate and even to share political power, and chosen the path of armed struggle for independence. Increased communication has fostered separatism, not integration. Contrary to much popular thinking on interdependence and political development, we might hypothesize that the faster the rate of growth of communication between distinct social groups or societies, the greater the probability that autonomy-preserving or -seeking behavior will result.[37]

A second avenue for exploration would focus on the *profile of social transactions* between groups or states. Our examples suggest that where transactions are highly asymmetrical and contacts between societies involve unidirectional penetration, perceptions of nonmilitary threats (e.g., threats to autonomy, continued independence, cultural survival, religious purity, and the like) are likely to arise, resulting in demands for controlling international transactions and instituting policies to establish greater "distance" between groups within a state, or between states. When some see their community or society has become highly penetrated by outsiders—even by good friends—common knowledge, broad communication, and empathy are not likely to prevent demands from protecting or reestablishing autonomy. The Quebec independence movement grew apace as French-speaking Canadians were required to speak English in English-Canadian firms, as the flow of non-French-speaking European immigrants into the province continued to rise, and as the birth rate of French-Canadians continued to decline. The nationalists drew the obvious conclusions from these trends: if allowed to continue, French language and culture in North America would no longer exist after several generations. Few in Quebec could ignore these facts, even if they were bilingual, felt national loyalty to Canada, conducted extensive transactions with English-Canadians, and "understood" them. Quebecois have argued that the flow of transactions and communications, increasing throughout the 1960s, was predominantly in one direction: from English-Canada into Quebec. While Anglophone Canadians were worrying about the U.S. "threat," Quebecois were worrying, not about Yankees, but about Anglophone Canadians. The parallel in each language group's concern with autonomy and cultural preservation is striking.

If we combine the variables of communication growth rates and degrees of transaction asymmetry, the probabilities of autonomy-seeking behavior as an outcome might appear more like an inverted U than linear. Robert Keohane has suggested that as very high levels of communication increase, combined with great asymmetry in transaction flows, autonomy is extremely difficult to achieve. The small state or nationalist group in all probability has been successfully absorbed or thoroughly dominated by the hegemon. He points out, for example, that anticolonial movements were much more vigorous in Indo-China than among the small weak states of Francophone Africa. Similarly, nationalist policies in Argentina, Chile, Brazil, and Mexico are significantly more prominent than in Nicaragua, Guatemala, and Honduras, where asymmetrical ties and fast-growing communications with the United States are particularly pronounced.[38]

A third line of explanation would emphasize hardheaded economic calculations: dis-integrative and secessionist movements are likely to arise when certain groups perceive that they are not receiving an adequate and/or fair share of economic gains, resulting from interdependence, or are paying an inequitable share of government or supranational burdens. The East African Community dissolved in 1977 over disagreements on both costs and rewards.[39] Small secessionist movements in western Canada argue that Alberta and British Columbia pay taxes to the federal government way out of proportion to the services they receive from Ottawa.[40] Finally, Chile withdrew from the Andean Pact after 1974 because the Pinochet regime did not want to apply the restrictions on foreign investment called for in the treaty.

Fourth, demands for dis-integration or secession may arise where loss of decisionmaking autonomy has become intolerable. Interdependence and integration exact a high cost in freedom of choice. The reasons for collaboratve undertakings and integration are no doubt compelling—particularly maximizing joint gains—but frequently some are going to believe that supranational policymaking bodies do not take into account sufficiently the unique needs of certain partners. The Canadian attempt to return to a more classical diplomatic relationship with the United States was in part formulated on the grounds that use of joint institutions locked Canada into agendas set in the United States and induced a presumption of collaborative behavior that mitigated against the vigorous pursuit of Canadian national objectives.

Finally, the doctrine of self-determination, a genuine transnational ideology or value, has become one of the most important sources of political legitimacy, the most potent propaganda symbol used to raise the consciousness (and conscience) of both nationals and foreign audiences. A national liberation movement, no matter how authoritarian its leadership and bloody its tactics, can obtain significant international attention, sympathy, and occasionally material support by portraying itself as fighting a colonial regime or seeking to obtain independence for a distinct ethnic, language, or religious group. In the early twentieth century, the notion of self-determination was closely linked to democratic principles. Its application to the defeated powers after World War I was based on the assumption that the new states would adopt reasonably pluralist political institutions. Today, in constrast, a national liberation movement does not have to establish democratic credentials in order to claim legitimacy. Merely to speak in the name of a minority is usually sufficient. Thus, as long as there are states whose boundaries do not coincide with ethnic divisions, we can expect to see the continued development of secessionist movements, invoking the doctrine of self-determination to justify their struggles.

Consequences

If we acknowledge that nationalism continues to be a potent force in national and international politics, and that increased interdependence may foster nationalism and instability as well as integration and harmony, what consequences can we expect in terms of the structure and processes of the international system? At first glance, the prevalence of secessionist movements might suggest that the number of sovereign units in the system will continue growing, with perhaps as many as 200 members in the United Nations by the end of the century. If such were to be the case, the system would be numerically one of the largest since the early spring and autumn period during the Chou dynasty in China of the eighth century B.C. Many of the microstates would be highly dependent upon outsiders for economic and defense support, but they would still possess voting power in international organizations. Since many of the new states would come from the developing areas, we would expect them to lend additional weight to the LDCs on north-south issues. The industrial countries would thereby become an even smaller minority in global organizations, maintaining influence primarily by the size of their financial contributions rather than by their numbers. We could predict as well that if the number of violent secessionist movements continues to grow, new arenas of international conflict would appear, as the major powers would likely involve themselves either to promote the forces of national liberation or to protect the territorial integrity of the mother nation — as the Soviets and the French have done in Ethiopia and the Congo.

Numerous predictions about the consequences of increasing the size of the international system by about 25 percent over the next decades could be made, but for such an exercise to be worthwhile there must be a reasonable probability that the predicted trend will in fact occur. Despite the universal popularity of the self-determination principle and the widespread sympathy secessionist movements manage to generate abroad, experience of the past suggests that many of the movements will not succeed in obtaining full independence. Whatever their sympathies, most governments have opted for the principle of territorial integrity over minority independence when confronted with the choice.[41] The ethnic rebellions in Burma have been continuing for almost three decades, with little probability of ultimate success, and with little outside support. In Biafra, the Congo, the Ogaden, and elsewhere, most foreign governments have ended up on the side of the central authorities in their contests with secessionist movements.[42] In the United Nations, members have voted consistently to emphasize that the principle of self-determination applies to territories and not to peoples. For example, during the fifteenth session of the General Assembly the members strongly supported a resolution that stated: "Any attempt at the partial or total disruption of the national unity and territorial integrity of a country is incompatible with the purposes and principles of the United Nations Charter."[43]

With the possible exception of Quebec, secessionist movements in the industrial countries seem to have few possibilities for obtaining full independence. Both local arrangements involving greater autonomy and protection of ethnic, language, or religious traditions, and/or repression seem more likely outcomes. In brief, the probabilities of a significant increase — say 25 percent — in the number of new states are quite low. This is not to say that the number of secessionist movements is likely to decline, however. If increased communication in multiethnic societies results in greater conflict, as often seems to be the case, we could expect continued fragmentation, particularly in the developing countries where many central governments are only beginning to foment "crises of penetration" as they seek to establish jurisdiction and economic programs in the hinterlands. Domestic instability and occasional insurrection remain distinct possibilities, but dramatic increases in the rate of international fragmentation appear unlikely.

The incidence of international dis-integration or more "moat-building" foreign policies in the future remain problematic. Weak and vulnerable societies involved in highly asymmetrical relationships no doubt find strategies of self-sufficiency and autarchy politically, if not economically, appealing, if only to break down dependency and to reduce foreign penetration of their institutions. On the other hand, development strategies such as those pursued by Saudi Arabia and the shah's Iran, where extensive foreign investment and penetration are accepted, may have greater appeal because of the visible and rapid economic results. The lack of research on isolationist and autarchic impulses makes it difficult to predict which types of societies, under which sorts of domestic and international conditions, will attempt to disengage themselves by turning inward.

Certainly the Canadian relationship vis-à-vis the United States finds few counterparts in Western Europe. There, the small members of the EEC appear content with their lot, and new members will join the organization soon. Even though we may expect to find considerable opposition to *major* moves in the direction of political unification the Norwegian vote must be interpreted as an aberration rather than as a symptom of general European malaise about protecting cultural identity or political autonomy. In Eastern Europe dis-integration takes the form of our marginal category, that is, resistance to further integration. Compared to the North Atlantic Treaty Organization (NATO), the Warsaw Treaty Organization has achieved more integration, particularly in standardization of weapons and command structure. But there has been little evidence of "spillover" from security arrangements to other spheres, and Soviet attempts to establish a permanent economic division of labor in the region have been resisted. While there has been some movement toward establishing integrated institutions, the centrifugal forces in Eastern Europe remain vigorous.[44]

In the remainder of the world, regional economic integration schemes enjoy varying fortunes. Some, like the Central American Common Market, have significantly increased regional trade, but serious problems of benefit distribution remain. The Andean Pact, on the other hand, has failed to enhance the mutual trade of the signatories, and Chile has withdrawn from the organization. The Caribbean Free Trade Association (CARIFTA) has barely succeeded in reducing its members' dependency on the United States and Britain, and also faces problems of benefit distribution and the distrust of the smaller members toward Jamaica and Guyana.[45] Some of the regional organizations in Africa rest on similarly shaky foundations. The East African Community, probably the most advanced integrative scheme in the developing world, with prospects of even greater successes in the future, collapsed in 1977.

Conclusion

This excursion into the international ramifications of modern nationalism has been undertaken in an attempt to compensate for some of the distortions found in contemporary conceptions of the international system, as well as in much current diplomatic rhetoric. Themes such as a "shrinking world," "growing interdependence," "regionalism," or "international system" often imply inevitable processes leading to desirable outcomes, affecting all equally. While there are undoubted benefits accruing to human societies from their greater interconnectedness, there are costs that must be considered as well. Concerned about the impact that U.S. military presence in Iceland has had on the local culture, Sigurdur Magnusson has written:

> Nationalism is not the most highly regarded sentiment in this age which has been accustomed at least to think that international cooperation and understanding are worthy ends. But there are various kinds of nationalism, and for tiny nations like Iceland nationalism is in reality a pre-condition for the continuous growth of native culture and the preservation of political independence.[46]

Weak, vulnerable societies and communities are not likely to favor schemes of economic or political integration if they predict that their implementation will lead to extensive foreign penetration, inequitable distribution of costs and rewards, and submerging of local lifestyles. To argue abstractly that integration increases the possibilities of peace is not likely to make much impact on those who see their language, religion, customs, or occupations threatened by foreign penetration.

The statistics demonstrating increased transaction flows throughout most of the world cannot be denied. But as this essay has sought to underline, this growth can have numerous consequences, not all of which contribute to international peace and stability or integration. An accumulating body of evidence suggests that in many instances as interconnectedness increases, so does nationalism (in the sense of more "moat-building"), and interethnic and international conflict. If our conceptions of the international system are to be reasonably consistent with realities, we must not confuse the European with a universal experience, assume that the consequences of increased communications are always positive, or argue that processes that are developing primarily among the industrial states extend to other areas of the world as well. This is not to argue that the manifestations of nationalism outlined previously lead to desirable consequences either. Ultimately the costs and gains of integration or fragmentation can only be assessed according to one's value preferences. But before that debate can be launched, the international relations scholarly community must at least recognize that nationalism is a persisting phenomenon, one that has not been done in by the advent of supersonic aircraft, large trade volumes, and international television.

Does the continuation of fragmentation constitute a fundamental trend or a step-level change in one property of the international system? Does it meet some of the criteria of system transformation outlined in the chapter by Dina Zinnes? In brief, is the number of actors in a system a key identifying variable? Taking a long-range historical perspective, we are not seeing qualitative system change so much as the playing out of European-originated nationalism to its logical conclusion. Our international system has grown from 23 members in the Napoleonic period to more than 150 today. The increase in numbers has occurred in fits and starts (the addition of the Latin American republics during the early nineteenth century was as much a quantum leap in the size of the international system of the time as was the addition of more than 30 African states in the 1950s and 1960s), but the trend line is clear. And the forces which helped create the new nation-states of the nineteenth century are basically similar to those that still operate today: the drive to establish the state on the basis of a distinct ethnic, language, or religious group. As the cursory list of secessionist movements indicates, that drive is not confined to the Third World. We cannot conclude, if the forces and manifestations of change remain basically similar, that we have observed in the past decades fundamental system change. We could, however, adopt the Hegelian proposition that, ultimately, changes in quantity lead to new qualities, but to say that we have one type of system when it was comprised of 46 members in 1945 and another one when there will be 200 would be purely arbitrary unless we could demonstrate that such cutoff points make significant differences in other properties of the system, such as the incidence of major war, fundamentally new transaction profiles, or new patterns of dominance and subordination.

What is new — or at least unexpected — is the continuation or resurgence of nationalism in areas where considerable integration (defined as the existence of a "security community," vast transaction flows, or institutionalization of bilateral diplomatic and technical relationships) has already occurred. North America, Scandinavia, Australia–New Zealand, Eastern Europe, and perhaps Latin America do not represent change as much as they are living demonstrations that growing transaction flows and mutual empathy do not result inevitably in integration. The balance between the search for continued autonomy and efforts to create supranational institutions clearly lies on the side of the former.

Acknowledgments

I am grateful for the many useful comments and suggestions offered by Peter Busch, David Haglund, Ole Holsti, Roff Johannson, Robert Keohane, Saadia Touval, and John Wood.

Notes

1. Evan Luard, *Types of International Society* (New York: Free Press, 1976).
2. Alex Inkeles uses the term to signify transactions and interactions between

societies in "The Emerging Social Structure of the World," *World Politics* 27 (July 1975):467–495.

3. Walker Connor, "Self-Determination: The New Phase," *World Politics* 20 (October 1967):45; Zbigniew Brzezinski, *Between Two Ages* (New York: Viking Press, 1970), esp. p. 275. A notable exception to this view is Robert O. Keohane and Joseph S. Nye, Jr., *Power and Interdependence: World Politics in Transition* (Boston: Little, Brown and Co., 1977), esp. p. 4.

4. Connor, "Self-Determination: The New Phase," p. 46.

5. Nationalism translated into foreign policy has also been viewed as involving aggressive behavior, embodied in imperialism or efforts to expand territorially. This essay does not use the term in this sense.

6. There are numerous definitions of integration and the phenonemon has been measured in many different ways. For a review of the various conceptualizations, see Joseph S. Nye, Jr., *Peace in Parts: Integration and Conflict in Regional Organizations* (Boston: Little, Brown and Co., 1971), chap. 2.

7. Richard Cooper, "Economic Interdependence and Foreign Policy in the Seventies," *World Politics* 24 (January 1972):159–181; Connor, "Self-Determination: The New Phase"; Arnfinn Jorgensen-Dahl, "Forces of Fragmentation in the International System: The Case of Ethno-nationalism," *Orbis* 19 (Summer 1975): 652–674; and the argument that interdependence is now giving way to a new mercantilism, Gregory Schmid, "Interdependence Has its Limits," *Foreign Policy* 21 (Winter 1975–1976):188–197.

8. John Burton uses the metaphor in his *Systems, States, Diplomacy and Rules* (Cambridge: Cambridge University Press, 1968), p. 8.

9. Cooper, "Economic Interdependence," p. 164. Modern authors on interdependence are certainly not the first to predict that transaction flows can lead to loss of national autonomy. Lenin observed that international capitalism "breaks down national barriers, obliterates national distinctions, and assimilates nations." Lenin, *Collected Works*, vol. 20 (Moscow: Progress Publishers, 1960–1972), p. 28.

10. K. J. Holsti, "A New International Politics? Diplomacy in Complex Interdependence," *International Organization* 32 (Spring 1978):517.

11. Cooper, "Economic Interdependence." He acknowledges that some small states can flout the system and get away with it. Examples include countries granting flags of convenience and tax havens.

12. Edward L. Morse, "Crisis Diplomacy, Interdependence, and the Politics of International Economic Relations," in Raymond Tanter and Richard H. Ullman, eds., *Theory and Policy in International Relations* (Princeton, N.J.: Princeton University Press, 1972), pp. 123–150.

13. Robert O. Keohane and Joseph S. Nye, Jr., *Power and Interdependence: World Politics in Transition* (Boston: Little, Brown and Co., 1977), chap. 2.

14. Ibid., esp. chap. 8.

15. Morse, "Crisis Diplomacy." He predicts increased incidence of crises and conflict resulting from interdependence. Other newer writings on interdependence also acknowledge that interdependence and conflict do not necessarily vary

in the same direction. See Keohane and Nye, *Power and Interdependence*, chap. 5, pp. 8–11.

16. Holsti, "A New International Politics?" p. 520.

17. Karl W. Deutsch et al., *Political Community and the North Atlantic Area: International Organization in the Light of Historical Experience* (Princeton, N.J.: Princeton University Press, 1957), esp. pp. 70–78.

18. Karl W. Deutsch, "Transaction Flows as Indicators of Political Cohesion," in Philip E. Jacob and James V. Toscano, eds., *The Integration of Political Communities* (Philadelphia: J. B. Lippincott Co., 1964), chap. 3.

19. For example, Roger W. Cobb and Charles Elder, *International Community: A Regional and Global Study* (New York: Holt, Rinehart and Winston, 1970).

20. Deutsch et al., *Political Community and the North Atlantic Area*, p. 5.

21. Seventeen years later, however, Deutsch wrote: "This notion that groups that do not integrate must destroy each other is a widespread but false belief. Luckily it is not true." "Between Sovereignty and Integration: Conclusion," in Ghita Ionescu, ed., *Between Sovereignty and Integration* (London: Croom Helm, 1974), p. 181.

22. Amitai Etzioni, *Political Unification* (New York: Holt, Rinehart and Winston, 1965), p. x. Ernst B. Haas stated forcefully that the search for peace justified the intellectual pursuit in "The Study of Regional Integration," *International Organization* 24 (Autumn 1970):608–609.

23. Deutsch, "Communication Theory and Political Integration," in *The Integration of Political Communities*, p. 67.

24. The importance of preserving autonomy while accepting regional policy coordination and some economic free trade arrangements in Scandinavia is discussed in Toivo Miljan, *The Reluctant Europeans: The Attitudes of the Nordic Countries Toward European Integration* (Montreal: McGill–Queen's University Press, 1977). This is one of the few studies that seriously examines opposition to integration.

25. James Caporaso, "Theory and Method in the Study of International Integration," *International Organization* 25 (Spring 1971):231.

26. See Geoffrey Goodwin, "The Erosion of External Sovereignty," in *Between Sovereignty and Integration*. Robert Gilpin has discussed the causal relationship between increased integration and the rise of economic nationalism in the smaller party in "Integration and Disintegration in the North American Continent," *International Organization* 28 (Autumn 1974):851–874. Anti-integrationist tendencies are acknowledged in Ernst B. Haas, "Turbulent Fields and the Theory of Regional Integration," *International Organization* 30 (Summer 1976):185, 195–196.

27. See John H. Sigler and Dennis Goresky, "Public Opinion on United States–Canadian Relations," in Annette B. Fox, Alfred O. Hero, and Joseph S. Nye, Jr., eds., *Canada and the United States: Transnational and Transgovernmental Relations* (New York: Columbia University Press, 1974), pp. 45–47.

28. For a discussion of the economic gains accruing to Canada from the auto-

motive and defense arrangements, see Canada, Standing Senate Committee on Foreign Affairs, *Canada–United States Relations, Vol. II: Canada's Trade with the United States* (Ottawa: Queen's Printer, 1978), pp. 89–107. More recent academic evaluations have suggested net trade losses for Canada, however.

29. Nye, *Peace in Parts*, chaps. 2, 3.

30. The increase of Canadians' perceptions of threat emanating from U.S. presence — particularly economic — in Canada is clearly revealed in public opinion polls. For example, in 1964, 46 percent of the respondents believed there was enough U.S. investment in the country. In 1978, the figure had risen to 69 percent. See *Vancouver Sun*, 12 August 1978, p. D–1. Responding to the question, "Do you think the Canadian way of life is, or is not being too much influenced by the United States?" 39 percent replied in the affirmative in 1961, and 53 percent in 1966. See Sigler and Goresky, "Public Opinion," pp. 64–65.

31. The most comprehensive treatment of Canadian policy formulation to alter the pattern of Canadian-U.S. relations is by John Kirton, *The Conduct and Co-ordinaton of Canadian Government Decisionmaking Towards the United States* (Ph.D. diss., The Johns Hopkins University, 1977).

32. A detailed description of Burma's isolationist strategy and an attempt to explain the reasons it was chosen is in K. J. Holsti, *Why Nations Realign: Foreign Policy Re-structuring in the Postwar World*, forthcoming, chap. 7.

33. A thorough discussion of the preconditions and necessary conditions for the rise of secessionist movements is in John R. Wood, "Toward A Theory of Secession" (Paper presented to the American Political Science Association meetings, New York, September 1978). Only a few of the conditions that are relevant both to secession and international dis-integration are discussed here. Multiethnicity is an important source of dis-integration only at the national level.

34. Walker Connor, "Nation-building or Nation-destroying?" *World Politics* 24 (April 1972):320–321.

35. Ibid., pp. 346–348.

36. Jorgensen-Dahl, "Forces of Fragmentation," p. 664.

37. In a statistical study of secessionist movements, Church and his colleagues demonstrate a positive relationship between degrees of social mobilization and separatism. Social mobilization, of course, involves a notable increase in communication flows. Roderick Church et al., "Ethnoregional Minorities and Separatism: A Cross-National Analysis," mimeo (1978), pp. 20–21.

38. Correspondence with the author, 27 November 1978.

39. See Nye, *Peace in Parts*, p. 33.

40. The Quebec government has used data to demonstrate that the province has done poorly in terms of taxes and government benefits under confederation. This argument rationalizes separation and is not a cause of it.

41. Various considerations underlying external powers' generally conservative stance regarding support for secessionist movements are discussed in Wood, "Toward a Theory of Secession," pp. 26–27.

42. The successful breakaway of East Pakistan, with Indian assistance, is the significant exception to the generalization.

43. Cited in Jorgensen-Dahl, "Forces of Fragmentation," p. 669.

44. Cf. Paul Marer, "Prospects for Integration in Eastern Europe: The Council for Mutual Economic Assistance," in Jan F. Triska and Paul M. Cocks, eds., *Political Development in Eastern Europe* (New York: Praeger Publishers, 1977), pp. 256–274.

45. R. S. Milne, "Impulses and Obstacles in Caribbean Political Integration: Academic Theory and Guyana's Experience," *International Studies Quarterly* 18 (September 1974):291–316.

46. Sigurdur A. Magnusson, "Iceland and the American Presence," *Queen's Quarterly* 85 (Spring 1978):83.

3

STEPHEN J. GENCO

Integration Theory and System Change in Western Europe: The Neglected Role of Systems Transformation Episodes

Introduction

Explaining change has always been a difficult task for the social sciences. As Leon Lindberg has observed, "It seems to be widely agreed by economists, sociologists, and political scientists alike that their respective disciplines have either neglected the study of change or have not dealt with it satisfactorily."[1] Political science is probably the worst offender of the three. Sociologists "have regularly bemoaned their lack of knowledge concerning social change," says Samuel Huntington, but "compared with past neglect of the theory of political change in political science, sociology is rich with works on the theory of social change."[2]

International relations has not fared much better than its parent discipline. Indeed, most specialists would be quick to agree with Smoke and George that "empirical theory in international affairs so far has made little headway with the problems of understanding how the international system changes over time."[3]

While there are some exceptions to this static bias in international relations, perhaps none has been so enduring as the study of regional integration. This area of research has exhibited an unswerving interest in the processes of international change since the mid-1950s when Ernst Haas and Karl Deutsch published their pathfinding studies *The Uniting of Europe* and *Political Community and the North Atlantic Area*, respectively.[4] These works gave birth to a vigorous and cumulative body of literature dedicated to the explanation of integrative change both in Europe and elsewhere. As this literature evolved through the 1960s, the original theories of Haas and Deutsch were subjected to many criticisms and suggested modifications, but the overall commitment to explaining outcomes in terms of underlying change processes remained. Subsequently, in the early 1970s, these criticisms led to the formulation of several "revisionist" theories of integration. Among the most important of these were the theories put forward by Joseph Nye and by Leon Lindberg and Stuart Scheingold.[5]

More recently—and somewhat ironically—the study of regional integration has tended to be swallowed up by the study of international interdependence and system change, which are more broadly conceived.[6] As Haas himself has argued,

> Events in the world and conceptual developments in social science have conspired to suggest that the name of the game has changed, and that more interesting themes [than integration] ought to be explored. These themes—grossly captured by the terms *interdependence* and *systems change*—can profit from incorporation of aspects of the theory of regional integration. But they are sufficiently different in scope and portent from integration as to suggest that theorizing about it is no longer profitable as a distinct and self-conscious pursuit.[7]

In one sense, this shift represents a broadening or generalizing of integration theory; in Haas's words, the notion of integration should now be seen to refer to "*institutionalized procedures devised by governments for coping with the condition of interdependence.*"[8] In another sense, however, it signals a clear retreat from theorizing about integration processes per se. With an apparent slowdown, if not complete halt, in the progress of European integration in the early 1970s, the contributions of Nye and Lindberg and Scheingold have come to be seen not as important steps to a more realistic and explanatory theory of integration, but as "epitaphs" to an approach that has been falsified by historical experience. The next step toward a more adequate theory of integration, therefore, has yet to be taken.[9]

The problem of explaining regional integration in Western Europe is important—both theoretically and substantively—and still far from solved. I agree with Haas and others that integration theory has so far failed to carry the full burden of explaining this complex course of change. On the other hand, I believe that integration theory can still carry a significant part of this burden—it is more "incomplete" than "incorrect." Given this view, the key question becomes: "How can we augment integration theory so as to improve its explanatory capacity?" Again following Haas's lead, I argue that European integration—not only in the 1970s (as Haas maintains) but also in the 1940s, 1950s, and 1960s—must be accounted for within the context of a theory of system change that is more broadly construed. This means that we must conceptualize the evolution of international relations in Western Europe since the end of World War II as an emergent outcome over time of at least three basic kinds of change processes: environmental changes, process-level changes within the system, and structure-level changes of the system, or systems transformations.

Integration theory offers a very useful explanation of process-level changes within the system, as well as some hypotheses concerning the environmental sources of system change. Systems transformations, however, have generally been neglected by integration theory, and are not particularly amenable to its incremental logic of explanation. As a consequence, they must be explained differently; primarily through the analysis of interstate bargaining in "system transformation episodes." In order to improve the explanatory capacity of integration theory, therefore, it will have to be augmented with an account of the processes and outcomes of these transformation episodes. Only in this way can one begin to construct an adequate explanation of the *overall* course of system change in Western Europe.

Integration Theory: Conjectures, Criticisms, and Revisions

Integration theory can be seen as having passed through three stages of development. Following a typology put forward by Huntington (although with reference to a different context), these can be called "comparative statics," "teleological," and "explanatory" stages.[10] The earliest "federalist" approaches, for example, were primarily first-stage exercises in comparative statics. As Charles Pentland has observed, "The older federalists have been more or less content to describe the 'before' and 'after' characteristics of the system, comparing the Hobbesian anarchy of the former with the domestic harmony of the latter. . . . These writers have not concerned themselves in much depth with the causes and dynamics of the integration process itself."[11]

The first process-oriented approaches, in contrast, tended to be rather deterministic or teleological in their representations of the processes and outcomes of integrative change. This was true of both the "transactional" approach developed by Deutsch and the "neo-functional" approach developed by Haas. In the former case, integrative change was seen to be derived primarily from increases in the volume and frequency of communications and transactions between states. Increases in communications and transactions, in turn, were seen to lead to greater mutual trust and confidence, which led to further increases in communications and transactions, which led to still greater trust and confidence, and so on in a sort of endless positive feedback loop. Eventually, this process was seen to reach a "takeoff" point at which it became self-maintaining. It is not difficult to see the deterministic tendencies inherent in this conceptualization of integrative change.

The neo-functional approach put forward by Haas differed from Deutsch's approach in that it saw integrative change to be dependent upon the prior establishment of a supranational organization among a group of states. Given such an organization, integration was seen to be a cumulative and expansive process through which the organization would slowly extend its sphere of authority so as to encompass a wider and wider range of decisionmaking activities. The motivating force underlying this expansion of authority was described in terms of the concept of "functional spillover." This concept referred to a process "in which a given action, related to a specific goal, creates a situation in which the original goal can be assured only by taking further actions, which in turn create a further condition and a need for more action, and so forth."[12] Haas used this notion to argue that the integration of a strategically located economic sector—say, coal and steel—would lead "inevitably" to the integration of related sectors, and ultimately to political integration as well.[13] This process was seen to be more or less inevitable because it was not necessarily *purposive*. As Haas has noted more recently, "neofunctionalists rely on the primacy of incremental decisionmaking over grand designs, arguing that most political actors are incapable of long-range purposive behavior because they stumble from one set of decisions into the next as a result of not having been able to foresee many of the implications and consequences of the earlier decisions."[14] Embracing this incremental conception of decisionmaking, Haas was able to argue that an integrating system would "be transformed into some species of political union even if some of the members are far from enthusiastic about the prospect when it is argued in purely political terms."[15]

Throughout the 1960s these second-stage formulations were subjected to sustained criticism, part of which we will review in a moment. As a consequence of this criticism, the 1970s saw the emergence of several third-stage theories of integration. These third-stage theories—most notably those of Nye and Lindberg and Scheingold—attempted to correct the deterministic and teleological biases of their predecessors by emphasizing the need to explain the *multiplicity* of directions and outcomes that the integration process could manifest. The approach taken by Lindberg and Scheingold will be examined later in this section.

What went wrong with integration theory? In the case of the transactional approach, the most often heard criticism was quite basic and straightforward: it was not explanatory. This conclusion did not derive merely from the banal observation that correlation is not causation; instead, it stemmed from the realization that the logic of explanation hypothesized by the approach was circular. As Pentland has summarized this view, "some of the variables which Deutsch and others use to indicate a state of integration serve also to define the process and this makes it difficult to determine cause and effect. For example, is a high level of trade between two countries to be seen as a factor favouring further integration, or as evidence that some integration has already occurred? If it is taken to be both, then a circular process is postulated, the causal dynamics of which it is still incumbent on the theorist to explain."[16] As a consequence of this criticism, transaction analysts have now come to see their approach more as a rigorous quantitative description of the communication and transactional changes that accompany integration, rather than as an explanation of integration.[17]

In the case of the neo-functional approach, the basic problem was not that it failed to provide an explanation—it obviously did—but rather that the theory's explanation of how the integration process was supposed to unfold in Western Europe proved to be incompatible with the actual course of events in the region. This was the key point stressed by Haas in what might be regarded as his "funeral oration" to neo-functional theory. "The theories we have developed for describing, explaining, and predicting regional integration," wrote Haas, "have a tendency not to predict very accurately the events which come about, and not to explain very convincingly why events which are predicted did come about in fact."[18]

The criticisms and suggested modifications of integration theory that were put forward during the 1960s tended to focus upon three errors or mistakes in the Haasian formulation that caused it to misread the evolving situation in Western Europe.[19] First, the critics argued, integration theory had not adequately taken into account the role of *leadership*— especially as exercised by national policymakers—in guiding and/or diverting the integration process. Second, integration theory had not adequately taken into account the effects of *external actors and circumstances* on the course of integration. And third, integration theory had been overly dependent upon *incremental conception of system change* that caused it to underestimate the influence of more dramatic types of change on the integration process.

Haas originally saw the crucial actors in European integration to be the integrationist-technocrats who manned the supranational organization and the interest groups they served. National policymakers, in contrast, "were assumed to be economic incrementalists and responsive to the economic logic of integration. It was thought that the technocrat-politicians would be able to bypass the electoral or support politicians and directly forge links to an ever stronger regional organization."[20] The rise of Charles de Gaulle in France put an end to this benign view of national politicians. As a consequence of de Gaulle's actions in the early 1960s (his 1963 veto of the British bid to join the European Economic Community and his 1965 boycott of the Community's institutions), Haas revised his assessment of actors by including in the theory what he called actors with "dramatic-political" aims.[21] The effect of this revision was more than simply to add a new variable to the theory; it implied that the presumably automatic process of spillover could in fact be upset by an adequately motivated and powerful leader, and therefore that the process could no longer be seen as necessarily cumulative and unidirectional.

It is interesting to note that leadership, particularly as exercised by highly motivated national policymakers, has always been recognized as a crucial ingredient in the *initiation* of integration schemes, if not in their later maintenance and growth. As Lindberg and Scheingold put it, "All the great formative events in the history of the European Community have seen an active role for such people."[22] It is important to stress, however, that *integration theory, even in its more recent third-stage formulations, does not attempt to explain the origins of an integration process.*[23] Comments about initiation, therefore, usually appear as asides to discussions of other issues. The problem of explaining initiations will be further discussed in the next section.

The lack of concern with external influences on the integration process was another important theme of the 1960s criticisms of integration theory. "The original neo-functionalist formulation," said Nye, "paid insufficient attention to the role of external factors in integration processes — perhaps in reaction to federalist theories which overstressed them, perhaps in the absence of change in the external situation in Europe at the time when the approach was originally formulated."[24] The first criticisms made along these lines tended to focus on the effects of external actors, the global balance of power, and the politics of the Western alliance. Stanley Hoffmann, in one of the most detailed early attacks on integration theory, focused on the importance of the nuclear stalemate between the two superpowers as a factor greatly favoring the early successes of integration in Western Europe.[25]

More recently, critics have begun to emphasize the degree to which trans-regional perceptions, processes, and interdependencies can influence the course of integration. Nye, for example, stresses among his "perceptual conditions" underlying integration the "perceived external cogency" of an integration scheme. In his words, "The way that regional decision-makers perceive the nature of their external situation and their response to it is an important condition determining agreement on further integration."[26] Giving this point a somewhat more contemporary twist, Haas has argued that emerging trans-regional interdependencies in the 1970s have begun to interfere substantially with integration in Western Europe.[27]

Again, as with the role of national leadership, the role of external factors in the *origins* of Western European integration has generally been taken for granted. Nye argues that among the most important elements "needed to account for the creation of a regional economic organization are events in the external environment that impress upon both mass opinion and political legitimizing leaders the political cogency or usefulness of asserting their regional identity in an institutional form."[28] Thus, both the U.S. contribution to the recovery of Europe and the ideological split between Eastern and Western Europe have come to be seen as crucial conditions favoring the initiation of European integration.[29] As noted above, however, these factors are not included in integration theory per se. The theory, even in its third-stage formulations, takes an original commitment to integrate as a given, rather than as something requiring explanation.

The third basic criticism of integration theory in the 1960s had to do with its dependence upon incremental decisionmaking as the chief mechanism of integrative change. Although this criticism was aimed primarily at the neofunctional approach, it was in many ways equally applicable to other approaches as well. As Haas has remarked, "Most theories of regional integration have been anchored in the notion of incrementalism. . . . Functionalists, neo-functionalists, and pluralists (including students of transaction and communication patterns) have been in agreement that the processes of regional integration are best explained by the gradual adjustment of instrumentally motivated actors to relatively small changes in mutual interactions."[30]

The logic of this incremental view of change was first thrown into doubt by the actions of the "dramatic-political" leader Charles de Gaulle. If de Gaulle could so effectively derail the process of incremental change, what did this imply for integration theory's understanding of European system change in general? Clearly, it seemed to imply that the theory not only ignored certain important actors, it also ignored the ways in which those actors could influence the course of integration.

Haas chose to deal with this problem by reemphasizing a distinction he had originally discounted and which had been strongly defended by Hoffmann—the distinction between the "low politics" of incremental decisionmaking in economic and technical sectors and the "high politics" of diplomacy, strategy, and national security. Contrary to his previous formulations, Haas observed in 1967 that "The history of the European unity movement suggests that the relationship between politics and economics remains somewhat elusive."[31] The dynamic of functional spillover, he now argued, could properly be expected to operate only in the latter realm. The extent to which it would flow from economics to politics, on the other hand, he saw as ultimately dependent upon the state of relations in the "high" political sphere: "Pragmatic interests, simply because they are pragmatic and not reinforced with deep ideological or philosophical commitment, are ephemeral. Just because they are weakly held they can be readily scrapped. And a political process which is built and projected from pragmatic interests, is bound to be a frail process, susceptible to reversal."[32]

The basic source of such a reversal was seen to be a deterioration in the consensus among national leaders, either over the methods and goals of integration itself, or over some substantive "high" political issue. By this reformulation, then, integrative progress came to be seen not as self-motivating, but as contingent upon a framework of agreement that was itself subject to change. Such "high" political changes, in turn, seemed to be consequences of processes about which integration theory said nothing, *even though they seemed to have a profound impact on the course of integrative change.* Integration theory, therefore, was beginning to look like a seriously incomplete account of the change processes that had been at work in Western Europe since the end of World War II.

The cumulative effect of these criticisms upon integration theory was substantial. Most fundamentally, they seemed convincingly to falsify the second-stage teleological approaches of both Deutsch and Haas. Whatever change processes *were* operating in Western Europe, it could now be asserted with great confidence that they were neither automatic nor uni-directional in their combined effects. At the same time, these criticisms did not seem to converge toward any obvious successor to the second-stage formulations; rather, they presented integration theorists with a bewildering array of semiautonomous variables, processes, and outcomes. The resulting state of unrest in the field was clearly reflected in a 1970 special issue of the journal *International Organization* devoted to regional integration theory.[33]

The most constructive responses to this problematic situation were the third-stage theories of integration mentioned above.[34] Since the purpose of Nye's theory is to aid in the comparison of integration schemes across regions, whereas Lindberg and Scheingold's is designed to improve the explanation of integrative change in Western Europe itself, only the latter analysis will be examined here.

The theory of system change put forward by Lindberg and Scheingold is a detailed and self-conscious attempt to come to terms with the criticisms of integration theory we have just reviewed. The authors see their goal as the construction of a "theoretical and conceptual framework capable of providing an overall perspective on the often conflicting theories, descriptions, predictions, and evaluations" of integration in Western Europe.[35] In striving for a greater degree of comprehensiveness, they hope to show—in a "spirit of synthesis"—that the earlier formulations were not so much contradictory as they were partial: "By confronting different theories in the context of an overall analytic framework, as applied to a specific concrete example of integration, we hope to demonstrate the extent to which theories which appeared to produce contradictory diagnoses and predictions did so not because of different findings of fact, but because they were focusing on different aspects of a larger whole."[36] A synthetic goal such as this is characteristic of third-stage theories of change.

With respect to actors, Lindberg and Scheingold attempt to take into account not only "dramatic-political" leaders but also a much broader spectrum of other participants than had earlier theories. They treat actors as influencing the course of integration in two different but somewhat overlapping ways; actors are seen both as sources of demands on the system and as sources of leadership in coping with demands. In the first category, actors are classified in terms of their aims and styles (dramatic-political vs. incremental-economic), their scope of responsibility (national vs. subnational), and their interests in integration (whether they see their interests as best served by further integration, by conserving the present level of integration, or by rolling back the integration already achieved). In the second category, "task-oriented" leadership is seen as coming from supranational actors (e.g., the members of the commission and its staff), and "identitive" or "legitimizing" leadership is seen as coming from national actors (e.g., presidents, prime ministers, cabinet members). The two categories are somewhat overlapping in that the same actors can in some circumstances be sources of both demands and leadership.

External actors are not seen as particularly important participants in the integration process by Lindberg and Scheingold, except in the context of "systems transformation," as will be seen below.

With respect to change processes, Lindberg and Scheingold's conceptualization of system change revolves around the notions of commitment and obligation. Ultimately, they see systems as changing because actors commit themselves, or take on new obligations, to behave in ways different from their previous behavior. This focus on actors and commitments, rather than on the unintended consequences of incremental decisionmaking, gives Lindberg and Scheingold's approach a somewhat more voluntaristic emphasis than is found in earlier neo-functional theories. Changes having to do with integration are thus traced to two types of commitments or obligations: a commitment to participate in a joint decisionmaking process (i.e., to *make new policies* within the jurisdiction of the EEC's institutions) or a commitment to implement agreements already arrived at, or to enforce rules already decided upon (i.e., to *administer* a previously accepted area of joint activity).

These two types of obligations can culminate in any of three logically distinct types of outcomes: they can be fulfilled, retracted, or extended. What links each of these obligations, on the one hand, to each of these outcomes, on the other, is a distinct *process of change*. Lindberg and Scheingold's representation of these processes is reproduced in Figure 3.1.[37]

Lindberg and Scheingold argue that each of the models referred to in Figure 3.1 can be seen as characterizing the process of change going on in any given sector or issue-area at any given time. The *forward linkage* model, for example, refers to "a sequence whereby commitment to participate in joint decision-making has initiated a process that has led to a marked increase in the scope of the system and its institutional capacities." In contrast, *output failure* involves "a situation in which such a commitment was accepted but where the system was unable to produce an acceptable set of policies and rules." *Equilibrium* occurs "when an area of activity is routinized or institutionalized. Rules are established and recognized, and there is little need for new intergovernmental bargaining." The *spill-back* model, in turn, identifies "a situation in which there is a withdrawal from a set of specific obligations. Rules are no

FIGURE 3.1
Alternative Change Processes

Obligations	Outcomes		
	Fulfillment	Retraction	Extension
To participate in a joint decisionmaking process (i.e., to make new policy)	Forward-Linkage Model	Output-Failure Model	Systems Transformation Model(s)
To implement agreements, and the routine enforcement of specific rules (i.e., to administer a previously agreed upon area of joint activity)	Equilibribrium Model	Spill-Back Model	

longer regularly enforced or obeyed. The scope of Community action and its institutional capabilities decrease." Finally, *systems transformation* involves "an extension to specific or general obligations that are beyond the bounds of the original treaty commitments, either geographically or functionally. It typically entails a major change in the scope of the Community or in its institutions, that often requires *an entirely new constitutive bargaining process* among the member states, entailing substantial goal redefinition among national political actors."[38]

The theory of system change put forward in *Europe's Would-Be Polity* clearly goes a long way toward correcting the inadequacies associated with earlier theories of integration. Perhaps its main virtue in this regard is that it focuses on system change processes in general, rather than on integrative change alone. Indeed, if we define "integration" in the original Haasian sense — as a process of growth in which progressively more centralized and authoritative regional decisionmaking emerges as a consequence of functional spillover and the creative guidance of supranational leadership — then only the forward linkage model can be said to describe strictly "integrative" change. The other four models refer to quite different but equally important kinds of processes.

Taken together, Lindberg and Scheingold's five process models, and the change dynamics associated with them, provide a much more comprehensive and differentiated view of system change in Western Europe than could be attained from their second-stage progenitors. Lindberg and Scheingold's approach is more comprehensive in that it includes all logically possible directions and outcomes of change, as well as all actors who might influence the course of change. It is more differentiated in that it treats all five process models as analytically equivalent; that is, it goes well beyond treating "nonintegrative change" as a residual category into which everything that fails to qualify as "integration" can conveniently be dumped. It is in these two senses, then, that Lindberg and Scheingold's theory can be classified as a third-stage explanatory theory of system change. This is not to say, of course, that the theory cannot be improved.

Beyond Integration Theory:
The Problem of Systems Transformation

The next step beyond Lindberg and Scheingold's impressive initial foray into third-stage theorizing ought to be concerned with the problem of linking their five process models together within a more general theoretical framework so as to provide a truly evolutionary account of the *overall* course of system change in Western Europe since the end of World War II. The basic problem here is to account for what Lindberg and Scheingold quite correctly call the "very uneven and irregular pulse" of the European Community.[39] Their description of this system-wide course of change is as follows:

> Since the early 1950s [the Community] has known a number of radical ups and downs. Take-off occurred with the ECSC [European Coal and Steel Community] in 1951, and then came the apparent collapse of European integration with the failure of the European Defense Community and the European Political Community in 1954. This was quickly followed by a meeting at Messina in 1955, at which it was agreed to try to "relaunch" Europe; thus began the negotiations that finally led to the EEC [European Economic Community] and Euratom treaties, signed in 1957. The EEC enjoyed steady growth and spectacular successes in its early years, e.g., the "acceleration" of the customs union agreed to in 1960 and the first major agricultural agreements in 1962, but these were interrupted in 1963 by the crisis created by De Gaulle's first veto of British membership in the Community. The year 1964 saw a recovery to new heights with major agricultural agreements, and then an even deeper crisis followed in 1965–66 when France boycotted the Community institutions for six months in a struggle over the role of these institutions in the bargaining process. Another recovery in 1966–67 culminated in further progress in agriculture and in the Kennedy Round negotiations, only to be followed by a new failure in 1967–68 over Britain's renewed membership application.[40]

This "roller coaster" of alternating successes and failures has continued to operate into the 1970s. Following de Gaulle's departure in 1969, the Hague Summit of that year seemed to promise a second "relaunching" of Europe with renewed commitments to intensify the quest for political and economic union. Then in 1973 Great Britain, along with Ireland and Denmark, finally joined the EEC. These successes were soon overshadowed, however, by the EEC's inability to forge a common response to the Arab oil boycott in 1974. There subsequently followed a period of stagnation in European integration, as the system members tried to come to grips — often unilaterally — with problems of massive inflation and monetary instability. More recently, a few positive outcomes have occurred such as the launching of the European Monetary System (although not all members joined), the establishing of direct elections for the European Parliament, and the decision to expand the EEC by offering membership to Spain, Portugal, and Greece.[41]

The basic reason why Lindberg and Scheingold's process models cannot be brought directly to bear upon the explanation of this overall course of change stems from the fact that they are sectorally disaggregated. As they put it, "Our analytic procedure involves 'disaggregating' the Community system, that is, we look at it as a set of more or less discrete or autonomous sectors or decision areas." This procedure, they note, "leaves us with an analytical problem. It is well and good to explain discrete events, but something else again to cumulate these in terms of statements about the system of which they are all a part."[42]

In order to understand and explain the overall course of integration in Western Europe, it seems best to begin with a consideration of the crucial role played by *crises* in that process. Crises have long been recognized as important elements in the "up and down" progress of European system change. As Lindberg and Scheingold put it, "flux and stress, contradiction and crisis are basic conditions of the process of integration."[43]

The kinds of crises that have proven important in the course of European integration are not quite the same as the crises we generally think of as characterizing international relations. In international relations we have tended to define crises functionally; that is, as situations involving high threat to national values, short decision time, and surprise.[44] The crises of importance to integration, in contrast, can be more usefully defined in substantive terms, as they are in the political development literature. In this sense, crises are seen as "situations in which the basic institutional patterns of the political system are challenged and routine response is inadequate."[45] Crises thus involve threats to the institutional integrity or continuity of a system. As a consequence, they often act as sources of fundamental institutional change. In Sidney Verba's words, "crises represent situations in which the society moves in a new direction. They are the major decisional points at which the society is redefined, and are therefore relevant to sequential change."[46] Crises in this substantive sense, rather than in the functional sense stressed in international relations, have been of importance in the course of European integration.

According to Lindberg and Scheingold, the primary role played by crises in the course of European integration has been as *catalysts* of growth-inducing changes. They note, for example, that "it is often the creative manipulation of crisis situations that forces political actors to redefine their goals and their interests in integration so as to make forward linkages or systems transformations possible."[47] It would appear that this catalytic role of crises has been most pronounced in the systems transformation process. This type of change, Lindberg and Scheingold argue, "may not be possible when things are going well but only when some crisis is manifest."[48] This is a strong statement; it implies that crises may not only be helpful adjuncts to the transformation process, they may indeed be necessary antecedents without which transformation could not take place at all.

Given this close association between crises and systems transformations, our attention is naturally drawn to the latter concept. What, precisely, is a systems transformation, and why is it seen to be so closely related to crises?

Lindberg and Scheingold have some difficulty dealing with this concept; they readily admit that "many ambiguities tend to complicate the category of systems transformation." Despite these ambiguities, however, they insist that "the record of the Community indicates that [this process] can be meaningfully distinguished both analytically and empirically from the other outcome patterns."[49] Six basic characteristics of systems transformation distinguish it from the other four change processes, based on Lindberg and Scheingold's discussion.

1. *Systems transformation involves "step-functional" or "step-level" change rather than incremental change.* This is the key distinction that separates transformation from forward linkage. As Lindberg and Scheingold put it, "The essential difference is that incremental growth involves changes in amounts and dimensions that are already established; the changes are quantitative, not qualitative. Incremental change can be predicted by *projecting* well-established trends, whereas this is often not possible with step-functional change, for it may involve large and unexpected variations and the introduction of wholly new variables."[50]

2. *Systems transformation is a system-wide rather than sectoral process of change.* Although, as noted above, Lindberg and Scheingold's "focus is predominantly on change within . . . sectors or issue areas," they stress that it "seems implicit in the concept of systems transformation that what we are talking about is system-wide."[51]

3. *Systems transformation involves the extension of commitments into new areas, and therefore a significant change in the goals or objectives of participating actors.* The spill-back process also involves a change in goals — i.e., the abandonment of a previous commitment — but it does not, like transformation, involve an extension "beyond the bounds of the original treaty commitments, either geographically or functionally."[52] In contrast to these two models, the other three models all assume a constancy or continuity in actors' goals. Haas has recently underscored the extent to which the notion of incremental change is dependent upon such an assumption.[53]

4. *National leadership plays a greater role in systems transformation than it does in the other change processes.* This characteristic follows the fact that transformation involves gaining access to actors currently outside the system. Bringing such actors into the system is the other side of the coin of extending commitments into new areas. National leaders, ac-

cording to Lindberg and Scheingold, are particularly well suited for this task: "In general it is reasonable to believe that national leadership has much more effective access to . . . new groups that must be brought into the system. By access we mean the bargaining leverage which results from socialization, positive feedback, the possibilities for log-rolling and the authority that inheres in control of the national system."[54]

5. *Supranational leadership and functional spillover play a smaller role in systems transformation than they do in the other change processes.* Supranational leadership tends to be weak in precisely those areas where national leadership is strong. Consequently, in systems transformation, "supranational leadership . . . is not in a very strong position."[55] There appear to be two basic reasons for this relative weakness. On the one hand, supranational leaders have few resources at their disposal for influencing the process of transformation. As Lindberg and Scheingold put it, "The problem of the resources of supranational leadership stems directly from the fact that there is no explicit or general commitment to the scheme in question. Accordingly, the executive . . . is not legally authorized to initiate proposals and its official jurisdiction does not extend to the matters in question."[56] On the other hand, the process of functional spillover is "less likely to be effective" in systems transformations.[57] This is especially debilitating to supranational leaders, because the manipulation of functional spillover is probably the most important bargaining tool available to them. "What is perhaps most striking" about the negotiations leading to the creation of the EEC, Lindberg and Scheingold observe, "is the minimal role played by functional spillover in the process of transformation."[58]

6. *External factors play a greater role in systems transformation than they do in the other change processes.* Lindberg and Scheingold seem to be somewhat ambivalent on this issue. At one point, they argue that their analysis "restricts the implication of the external variable."[59] Yet when they examine two cases of systems transformation—the first British bid to join the EEC and the formation of the EEC and Euratom—they note several important external influences. In the first case, beyond the obvious point that the British application was itself an external input into the system, they trace the French veto at least in part to de Gaulle's uneasiness concerning British ties with the United States. They also emphasize Britain's relationship with the Commonwealth as an important factor in the negotiations that preceded the veto. In the second case, Lindberg and Scheingold point to the failure of the European Defense Community (EDC) as a major impetus for the decision to set up a common market. The EDC plan itself, of course, was primarily a response to U.S. demand for West German rearmament; its demise, in turn, was in part a product

of the relative thaw in the cold war that followed the death of Stalin. In addition, Lindberg and Scheingold note that "while the treaties were being negotiated, the Suez Crisis painfully underscored the weakness of a divided Europe," and thereby contributed to the eventual success of the deliberations.[60] In contrast to these references to external factors in the two transformation cases, Lindberg and Scheingold mention very few external influences in their case studies dealing with the other four processes of change.

Three important observations would appear to follow from this list of characteristics. First, *the systems transformation process is clearly quite unlike the other four change processes.* As Lindberg and Scheingold put it, "extension of the European Community was the result of a distinctly different process from advances made within the framework of the original Coal and Steel Community or progress since 1958 in Euratom or the Common Market." Thus, it is not surprising that "the transformation of the European Community cannot be adequately described within the context of the standard neofunctional model with its heavy emphasis on supranational institutions and functional linkages."[61]

Second, *the characteristics that identify systems transformation seem to be just those characteristics that "standard" integration theory was criticized for ignoring throughout the 1960s.* According to the critics, it was the failure to take into account national leadership, external influences, and nonincremental change that caused neo-functional theory to mispredict the course of integration in Western Europe. Given the list of characteristics enumerated here, the critics might just as well have charged that integration theory had failed to account for systems transformations.

Third, *if systems transformation is similar to anything, it is much more like the initiation of integration schemes than it is like the incremental processes of growth, equilibrium, or decline that follow initiation.* The six characteristics of systems transformation are all just as relevant to the change processes that led to the original Coal and Steel Community as they are to the processes that led to the British entry veto or to the formation of the EEC and Euratom. Despite these obvious similarities, however, integration theorists, including Lindberg and Scheingold, still insist upon drawing a qualitative distinction between how an integration plan comes into being and how it evolves afterward. The value of such a distinction is that it emphasizes the degree to which integration involves processes different from those that characterize more traditional types of international interaction. The similarities previously noted between initiation and transformation, on the other hand, emphasize the opposite point; i.e., that integration also involves processes quite similar to those that characterize more traditional international interactions.

Linkages Between Systems Transformations and Incremental Processes of Change

The problem of describing the ways in which the systems transformation process can be linked to the other four change processes is addressed in this section. Clearly, it seems unsatisfactory to describe transformation as simply "standing alongside" the other processes, as being in a sense interchangeable with them. Rather, transformations somehow "hover over" the other processes — occurring at a different level, so to speak. This image brings to mind Haas's and Hoffmann's distinction between the "low politics" of economic exchange and the "high politics" of national pride and security. But that distinction does not seem quite right; transformations do not necessarily involve changes only in the substantive realm of "high politics."

A somewhat similar but analytically more useful distinction has recently been emphasized by Robert Keohane and Joseph Nye. In discussing the complexities of the relationship between international politics and international economics, Keohane and Nye argue that international systems ought to be conceptualized in terms of "two levels of analysis, a 'process-level,' dealing with short-term allocative behavior (i.e., holding institutions, fundamental assumptions, and expectations constant), and a 'structure-level,' having to do with the long-term political and economic determinants of the incentives and constraints within which actors operate." The structure level of a system, Keohane and Nye argue, predominates over the process level in that it sets the parameters or limits within which interactions among the system members can take place. Thus, "At the structural level, we are interested in how institutions, fundamental assumptions, and 'rules of the game' of political systems support or undermine different patterns of allocation for economic activity, as well as the converse — how the nature of economic activity affects the political structure."[62]

This distinction between the structure and process levels of an international system facilitates concise and easily understandable depiction of the basic qualitative difference separating systems transformation from forward linkage, output failure, equilibrium, and spill-back. Put simply, *transformation involves change at the structure level of a system; the other models refer to changes in the processes that go on within the parameters of a given structural configuration.* Transformations thus constitute fundamental "changes of system"; the other processes are best described as "within-system changes."

The structure and process levels of an international system, Keohane and Nye continue, are usually "relatively well insulated from one another. Basic institutions and practices are accepted as legitimate by all major parties." In such circumstances, in other words, changes are occurring only at the process level; structure remains constant. "At other times, however, allocative decisions, and the rules of the game themselves, are called into question by major participants." It is at these times that systems transformations (or attempted transformations) take place. Such changes, unlike process-level changes, are characterized by increases in the controversiality or "politicization" of the system's structure: "attention of top-level decisionmakers is focused on the system, and nonroutine behavior dominates routine behavior." As a consequence, "Insulation between the structure of the system and particular processes breaks down: specific quarrels become linked to macro-level arguments about appropriate institutions and permanent arrangements."[63]

This description of the linkages between changes at the structure and process levels of an international system also describes quite well the linkages between systems transformations and the other four change processes in the overall course of system change in Western Europe. For the most part, these two types of change remain well insulated from one another. Institutions, commitments, treaty obligations, and more generalized "rules of the game" usually provide a relatively unchanging backdrop of constraints within which incremental processes of forward linkage, output failure, equilibrium, and spill-back unfold in specific sectors of activity. The only way in which these within-system process-level changes can have an effect on structure-level change is if they become perceived by influential policymakers as having some sort of relevance to progress or problems at the structural level. Thus, for example, the sectoral successes in the Coal and Steel Community provided a "lesson" that contributed to national leaders' desires to expand the EEC system by creating the Common Market and Euratom.[64] Similarly, but with a more negative consequence, the failure to achieve certain agreements in the agricultural sector was an important impetus for de Gaulle's decision to boycott the EEC's institutions in 1965–1966 and subsequently to demand revisions in the EEC's voting rules as specified in the Treaty of Rome. In both these cases, demands for structure-level changes were generated—at least in part—by national leaders' perceptions of process-level changes which they saw as relevant to the overall structural characteristics of the system.

These examples should not be taken to imply that all demands for systems transformations are necessarily derived from perceptions of successes or failures at the process level of a system. Process-level changes, in fact, are only one of several types of sources that can motivate national leaders to make such demands. The point being made here is that this perceptual link is the primary way in which process-level changes can influence structure-level changes.

The opposite path of influence — i.e., the effects of transformations on within-system processes — tends to be much more dramatic and easily traced. Transformations, after all, are major events in the history of an international system. When the European Common Market came into existence in 1958, for example, the patterns of interaction that had previously characterized the relations of "the Six" (as the EEC members came to be called) underwent radical changes in several sectors of activity. These changes, in turn, were derived from actors' conscious attempts to adapt their behavior to the new commitments, institutions, and rules of the game that had been created by the EEC and Euratom treaties. Such adaptations constitute the primary way in which structure-level changes influence process-level changes: actors recognize the existence of new structural constraints on their behavior and modify their patterns of interaction accordingly.

If systems transformations are thought of as fundamental changes at the structure level of an international system, then it is easy to see why these changes are so closely associated with crises. The structure of a system, as shown earlier, is usually very much in the background of system members' day-to-day activities; it tends to be taken for granted as a legitimate and noncontroversial context within which normal interactions take place. In order for this background to become controversial or politicized, something must happen to cause one or more system members to express significant dissatisfaction with the current structural state of affairs. Such an expression, in turn, almost invariably creates a crisis in the sense described previously by Verba. This is so because a crisis of this type has the interesting attribute of being self-validating; i.e., if one or more system members come to believe, for whatever reasons, that their system's structural configuration is no longer legitimate, then that structure *is* no longer legitimate, and a systemic crisis is at hand. Thus, it could plausibly be argued that crises are not so much a *source* of systems transformation as they are a *defining characteristic* of it.

In addition, the conceptual equivalence of transformations and structure-level changes allows us to see more clearly why transformations share so many characteristics with initiations of integration schemes. Both types of changes are basically changes in structure; initiations are distinctive only in that they involve the *initial* setting up of a supranational institutional arrangement. Transformations, in contrast, involve later modifications of that initial arrangement. The chief difference between the two types of change is therefore chronological, not analytical. This also means that it is not particularly constructive to view initiations as "creations out of the blue." Actors who form a new system do not do so out of a prior state of mutual isolation; their previous interactions must also have taken place within the context of some sort of structural configuration. Thus, even initiations are basically transformations from one type of structure to another, and are therefore as susceptible to theoretical explanation as are any other transformations.

Systems transformations are apparently of such major importance to the course of the evolution of an international system that even *failed* transformation attempts can have a substantial impact on systemic change. Lindberg and Scheingold illustrate this effect in their discussion of the consequences that resulted from de Gaulle's veto of the first British bid to join the EEC.

> The French veto marked the end of the halcyon days of integration and the beginning of a souring of relationships among the six. The resentment engendered by the veto smouldered for two or three years and finally led the Commission to an unfortunate gamble, which resulted in the notorious Gaullist partial boycott of 1965–66. Since then bargaining relationships have degenerated until the earlier Community spirit is only a bittersweet memory. . . . The British negotiations thus resulted in a setback much worse than the coal crisis, in that they set off a chain reaction which amounted to a kind of spill-back in the Community capacity for decision-making.[65]

In this case, it seems, the failure to transform the system through a change in membership led to an unintended structural change of quite a different sort—i.e., an erosion in the legitimacy of the informal rules that had governed bargaining among the system members. This change, in turn, contributed to a second transformation attempt—de Gaulle's boycott and demand for revisions in the EEC Treaty—which has come to be regarded as the most serious structural crisis the system has yet faced.

Not all failed transformation attempts have such negative consequences. As noted above, Lindberg and Scheingold believe that it was the "failure of the European Defense Community" that triggered the efforts that "led to the EEC and Euratom Treaties."[66] This consequence, they argue, came about because the rejection of the EDC "seemed to catalyze the dramatic-political actors" who at that time favored further European unity.[67] In this case, then, as in the French veto case, one transformation attempt was linked to another because the unsuccessful outcome of the first contributed to national leaders' motivation to instigate the second.

In summary, systems transformations and attempted (but unsuccessful) transformations are the primary means by which changes occur at the structure level of an international system. Structure-level changes, in turn, are the signposts by which overall (as opposed to sectoral) system change can be traced. It follows from this that the analysis of systems transformations ought to occupy a central position in any explanation of international system change in Western Europe since the end of World War II. Traditional integration theory, however, has consistently under-estimated the explanatory importance of systems transformations.

Summary and Conclusion

Structure-level systems transformations can be linked to the change processes that go on at the process level of an international system. Although these process-level changes have been the primary focus of traditional integration theory, they are in fact only indirectly relevant to the overall evolution of an international system. The reason their influence is indirect is that they must be perceived and reacted to by national leaders before they can have any impact on the structure-level characteristics of the system. In contrast to traditional integration theory, therefore, systems transformations, not process-level changes, must stand at the center of any adequate explanation of European integration (or dis-integration). The history of international system change in Western Europe can best be understood as a sequence of "systems transformation episodes"—that is, either successful or unsuccessful attempts to change the structure-level characteristics of the system—that have produced an evolving set of structural constraints within which the process-level changes of interest to integration theorists have taken place.

There are very good reasons why change has always been a problem for social explanation. Much more than the explanation of stability or regularity, the explanation of change requires incorporation of aspects of the empirical world such as so-called unique occurrences, chance conjunctions, creativity, and the possibility of altering a course of events in a completely unpredictable way. As Albert Hirschman has observed:

> Most social scientists conceive it as their exclusive task to discover and stress regularities, stable relationships, and uniform sequences. This is obviously an essential search, one in which no thinking person can refrain from participating. But in the social sciences there is a special room for the opposite type of endeavor: to underline the multiplicity and creative disorder of the human adventure, to bring out the uniqueness of a certain occurrence, and to perceive an entirely new way of turning a historical corner.[68]

The ability to combine these two tasks, Hirschman continues, is especially important in the analysis of change:

> The importance of granting equal rights of citizenship in social science to
> the search for general laws and to the search for uniqueness appears particularly in the analysis of social change. One way of dealing with this phenomenon is to look for "laws of change" on the basis of our understanding
> of past historical sequences. But the possibility of encountering genuine
> novelty can never be ruled out—this is indeed one of the principal lessons
> of the past itself. And there is a special justification for the direct search for
> novelty, creativity, and uniqueness: without these attributes, change, at
> least large scale social change, may not be possible at all.[69]

The notion of a systems transformation episode is in effect a theoretical construct designed to help us capture this element of "genuine novelty" in the course of an international system's evolution. Transformation episodes, as we have seen, are historical junctures at which systems can manifest "step-level change" (Lindberg and Scheingold), or at which they can be "redefined" (Verba). Both these characterizations seems to reflect the same basic idea; i.e., that what comes out of a transformation episode is not necessarily predictable from what goes in.

It is this essential unpredictability of systems transformation episodes that makes them appear somewhat suspect as objects of scientific explanation. At the same time, however—if we follow Hirschman's analysis— it is this unpredictability that makes them indispensible for the explanation of "large scale" system change. What we seem to be faced with, therefore, is something of a dilemma: either we engage in "scientific" explanation and ignore change or we explain change and stand accused of being "unscientific." It is not surprising that most social scientists confronted with this dilemma have opted for the first alternative, and that the study of social change has suffered accordingly. But times change as well, and the second alternative no longer looks quite so forbidding as before. To those who would voice the dreaded accusation, can we not simply reply that it is more scientific to explore as best we can the subject matter that interests us than to ignore that subject matter in the name of some arbitrary conception of scientific explanation?

Acknowledgments

The research upon which this chapter is based was made possible through a Dorothy Danforth Compton Fellowship from the Institute for the Study of World Politics. This support is gratefully acknowledged. I would also like to thank Gabriel Almond, Linda Cahn, Alexander George, Ernst Haas, Kal Holsti, Ole Holsti, Robert Keohane, Henry Nau, and Randolph Siverson for helpful comments on earlier versions of this chapter.

Notes

1. Leon Lindberg, "Introduction: Politics and the Future of Industrial Society," in Leon Lindberg, ed., *Politics and the Future of Industrial Society* (New York: David McKay Co., 1976), p. 3.

2. Samuel Huntington, "The Change to Change: Modernization, Development, and Politics," *Comparative Politics* 3 (April 1971):283.

3. Richard Smoke and Alexander L. George, "Theory for Policy in International Affairs," *Policy Sciences* 4 (December 1973):411.

4. Ernst B. Haas, *The Uniting of Europe: Political, Social and Economic Forces, 1950–1957* (Stanford, Calif.: Stanford University Press, 1958); and Karl W. Deutsch et al., *Political Community and the North Atlantic Area: International Organization in the Light of Historical Experience* (Princeton, N.J.: Princeton University Press, 1957).

5. Joseph S. Nye, Jr., *Peace in Parts: Integration and Conflict in Regional Organization* (Boston: Little, Brown and Co., 1971); and Leon Lindberg and Stuart Scheingold, *Europe's Would-Be Polity: Patterns of Change in the European Community* (Englewood Cliffs, N.J.: Prentice-Hall, 1970). Another important revisionist theory was put forward by Philippe Schmitter, "A Revised Theory of Regional Integration," in Leon Lindberg and Stuart Scheingold, eds., *Regional Integration: Theory and Research* (Cambridge, Mass.: Harvard University Press, 1971), pp. 232–264.

6. See, for example, Robert O. Keohane and Joseph S. Nye, Jr., "International Interdependence and Integration," in Fred I. Greenstein and Nelson W. Polsby, eds., *Handbook of Political Science: International Politics*, vol. 8 (Reading, Mass.: Addison-Wesley Publishing Co., 1975), pp. 363–414; Henry R. Nau, "From Integration to Interdependence: Gains, Losses, and Continuing Gaps," *International Organization* 33 (Winter 1979):119–147.

7. Ernst B. Haas, *The Obsolescence of Regional Integration Theory,* Institute of International Studies, Research Series, no. 25 (Berkeley: University of California Press, 1975), p. 1, emphasis in original.

8. Ibid., p. 89, emphasis in original; see also Keohane and Nye, "International Interdependence and Integration," p. 371.

9. Many of the researchers who pioneered in the study of regional integration are currently moving into new areas of research that reflect their continuing interest in international change, if not in the dynamics of European integration. Haas, for example, along with John Ruggie and others, has been studying the problem of how processes of international change can be managed through the creation of technological regimes for coping with various kinds of interdependence. Lindberg

has turned his attention to the problem of how advanced industrialized nations respond to changes and dislocations in their economic, ecological, and technological environments. And Nye, in his latest book with Robert O. Keohane, has addressed the general problem of how and why international regimes change over time. All of these works, and a few others like them, constitute offshoots of an earlier interest in the processes of integrative change. At the same time, they represent the current "state of the art" in the study of international change.

10. Huntington, "The Change to Change."

11. Charles Pentland, *International Theory and European Integration* (London: Faber and Faber, 1973), p. 161.

12. Leon Lindberg, *The Political Dynamics of European Economic Integration* (Stanford, Calif.: Stanford University Press, 1963), p. 10.

13. Ibid.

14. Ernst B. Haas, "The Study of Regional Integration," in Lindberg and Scheingold, eds., *Regional Integration*, p. 23.

15. Ernst B. Haas and Philippe Schmitter, "Economics and Differential Patterns of Political Integration," *International Organization* 18 (Autumn 1964):717.

16. Pentland, *International Theory and European Integration,* pp. 43–44.

17. See Donald J. Puchala, "International Transactions and Regional Integration," in Lindberg and Scheingold, eds., *Regional Integration*, esp. p. 158.

18. Haas, *Obsolescence,* p. 1.

19. The focus here is not on criticisms having to do with the ability to generalize integration theory to other regions, but on those criticisms aimed at the theory's ability to explain the dynamics of change in Western Europe.

20. Nye, *Peace in Parts,* p. 60.

21. Ernst B. Haas, "The Uniting of Europe and the Uniting of Latin America," *Journal of Common Market Studies* 5 (June 1967):315–343.

22. Lindberg and Scheingold, *Europe's Would-Be Polity,* p. 132.

23. See, for example, Nye, *Peace in Parts,* p. 64; and Lindberg and Scheingold, *Europe's Would-Be Polity,* p. v.

24. Nye, *Peace in Parts,* pp. 73–74.

25. Stanley Hoffmann, "Obstinate or Obsolete? The Fate of the Nation-State and the Case of Western Europe," *Daedalus* 95 (Summer 1966):862–915. Critiques similar to Hoffmann's include Karl Kaiser, "The Interaction of Regional Subsystems: Some Preliminary Notes on Recurrent Patterns and the Role of the Superpowers," *World Politics* 21 (October 1968):84; and Roger D. Hansen, "Regional Integration: Reflections on a Decade of Theoretical Efforts," *World Politics* 21 (January 1969):242–271.

26. Nye, *Peace in Parts*, p. 84.

27. According to Haas (*Obsolescence,* p. 9), many problems currently afflicting Western Europe, such as inflation and unemployment, "transcend the space and the jurisdiction of the Community's institutions because they are functions of economic interdependence with trading partners outside of Europe." Such problems tend not to be dealt with by means of self-contained Community policies because these "would incur integration costs which some of the member states are

unwilling to shoulder because of economic benefits now accruing from transactions with nonmembers which they would have to forego. As a result, efforts to cope through collective action are channelled into other international organizations and forums as well as into bilateral agreements."

28. Nye, *Peace in Parts*, p. 64.

29. See, for example, Max Beloff, *The United States and the Unity of Europe* (New York: Vintage, 1963).

30. Haas, *Obsolescence,* p. 12.

31. Haas, "The Uniting of Europe and the Uniting of Latin America," p. 315.

32. Ibid., pp. 327-328.

33. Lindberg and Scheingold, eds., *Regional Integration.* Henry Nau has nicely summarized the conclusions of this volume in "From Integration to Interdependence," pp. 120-121, as follows: "The judgment emerged that integration theory, in order to cope with an increasingly complex and recalcitrant reality, would have to become more and more multidimensional. Independent as well as dependent variables would have to be expanded both to account for the varying background and process conditions of integration in different parts of the world and to include alternative outcomes, even disintegration. The consequence, as critics have noted, was a loss of both parsimony and predictability of regional integration analysis."

34. Not all responses have been theoretically constructive. As Nau argues (ibid., p. 134), many contemporary studies "do not go much beyond the highly disaggregated, steady-state picture of European politics which emerged from the review of integration theory at the end of the 1960s. They help us to describe an increasingly complex reality but they offer few aids to explain this reality, except in unique cases, and nothing that comes close to the explanatory power of regional integration theory applied to the early history of the Common Market."

35. Lindberg and Scheingold, *Europe's Would-Be Polity,* p. v.

36. Ibid.

37. Ibid., p. 136.

38. Ibid., p. 137, emphasis in original.

39. Ibid., p. 103.

40. Ibid.

41. Two useful analyses of these more recent developments are Pierre-Henri Laurent, ed., "The European Community After Twenty Years," *The Annals of the American Academy of Political and Social Science* 440 (November 1978); and the articles collected in "Looking for Europe," *Daedalus* 108 (Winter 1979).

42. Lindberg and Scheingold, *Europe's Would-Be Polity,* pp. 108, 109.

43. Ibid., p. 105.

44. See, for example, Charles Hermann, *International Crises* (New York: Free Press, 1973).

45. Sidney Verba, "Sequences and Development," in Leonard Binder et al., *Crises and Sequences in Political Development* (Princeton, N.J.: Princeton University Press, 1971), p. 302.

46. Ibid., p. 306.

47. Lindberg and Scheingold, *Europe's Would-Be Polity,* p. 219.

48. Ibid., p. 240.

49. Ibid., pp. 221–222.

50. Ibid., pp. 137–138, emphasis in original.

51. Ibid., p. 138.

52. Ibid., p. 137.

53. Haas, *Obsolescence,* p. 15.

54. Lindberg and Scheingold, *Europe's Would-Be Polity,* p. 244.

55. Ibid., p. 222.

56. Ibid.

57. Ibid.

58. Ibid., p. 242.

59. Ibid., p. 226.

60. Ibid., p. 240.

61. Ibid., pp. 243, 244.

62. Robert O. Keohane and Joseph S. Nye, Jr., "World Politics and the International Economic System," in C. Fred Bergsten, ed., *The Future of the International Economic Order: An Agenda for Research* (Lexington, Mass.: Lexington Books, 1973), p. 117.

63. Ibid.

64. In Nye's words (*Peace in Parts*, pp. 53–54): "The creation of the EEC and Euratom in 1957 represented less a 'spillover' effected by the inherent linkages of tasks undertaken by the ECSC than an example of some lessons learned through ECSC being applied with new political initiatives."

65. Lindberg and Scheingold, *Europe's Would-Be Polity,* p. 238.

66. Ibid., p. 298.

67. Ibid., p. 240.

68. Albert Hirschman, *A Bias for Hope* (New Haven, Conn.: Yale University Press, 1971), p. 27.

69. Ibid., p. 28.

PART 2

Sources of Change
in the International System

4

VOLKER RITTBERGER

Science and Technology in the New International Order: Problems Facing an International Development Strategy of the United Nations

The Ideological Uses of Science and Technology

For many, science and technology or, sometimes, Research and Development (R&D) have become magic formulae in today's world: Whenever social problems arise (in the broadest sense) the call for more scientific research and technological know-how is one of the most prominent responses of contemporary ruling elites in many parts of the world.[1] Currently, one prominent, if not dominant, approach to social problem solving through policy planning is the technocratic one.[2] Typically, technocratic "problem solvers," when faced with difficult social problems, resort to an analysis that almost invariably points up the complexity of the situation, which in turn justifies, indeed necessitates, more research as a precondition for successfully grappling with the problems in question. Expert committees are then set up, conferences and symposia convened, new R&D programs initiated, and the role of science and technology as a productive force of prime importance is once again emphasized.

There is no question that science and technology can help solve social problems and have done so in the past.[3] Yet, the bias toward scientism — i.e., that there is a science-based technical solution to every social problem — inherent in the technocratic approach to social problem solving should be scrutinized for its usually unstated political implications. The prominence attributed to science and technology by technocratic elites tends to obscure the possibility that it may be the very technocratic approach which prevents or impedes the solution of urgent social problems because the acceptance of certain solutions of other than a purely technical nature might entail consequences that amount to "rocking the boat," i.e., transform the social status quo.

Take, for example, the case of hunger and malnutrition.[4] Undoubtedly, this constitutes a crucial social problem in many parts of the world. All relevant international statistics, incomplete and inaccurate as they may be in various details, agree that starvation continues to plague a very large proportion of people in developing countries and that there is little prospect for improvement over the next few years. The most prominent solution to which the technocratic "problem solvers" have turned (including those from developing countries) is the call for more R&D in agriculture (and, of course, for an expansion of food aid). What happened, and still happens, is that more R&D in agriculture may lead to increased productivity without necessarily decreasing hunger and malnutrition, for increases in agricultural productivity help eradicate hunger and malnutrition only if the increased output is channeled toward satisfying domestic needs and if the needy can acquire the means to share in this increased output. In fact, the problem of hunger and malnutrition is not necessarily one of agricultural productivity and therefore of insufficient R&D inputs only, as the technocratic "problem solvers" like to see it, but one of a social structure inappropriate to solving the problem of hunger and malnutrition.[5]

The coalition working against a serious consideration of agrarian reform includes the relevant scientific and technological communities in developed countries because their expertise is geared primarily toward large-scale farming, which is more capital- and therefore more technology-intensive than small-scale farming. However, this is not to assert that the scientific and technological communities cannot make a constructive contribution to the development of the agricultural sector in developing countries, i.e., to help the peasant and small farmer to improve food production satisfying domestic needs. Indeed, the improvement of small-scale farming may not be feasible without substantial R&D efforts. Yet, the R&D required here would be of a different kind such as upgrading traditional village technologies, developing the techniques of ecofarming, and the like.[6]

In summary, when entering a discourse about "science and technology for development" it should be made clear that development is not just more — usually measured in aggregate terms — of certain goods and services. To be useful as a category of social science and praxis of the concept of development requires a specification in terms of "who gets what," etc., as a result of marshalling scientific-technological resources for solving critical social problems.

The Role of Science and Technology in the UN International System

Science and technology also play a great role in documents (resolutions, declarations, programs of action, etc.) of the United Nations system of calling for a reshaping of the international system with a view toward improving the well-being of developing countries and of their poorer segments (people and regions) in particular. The principal document for this special emphasis on science and technology as levers for accelerating the development process of developing countries has been the action program of the General Assembly for the Second United Nations Development Decade.[7] Some of the central points in this document are:

- the expansion of the capability of developing countries to apply science and technology to development and to reduce the technological gap (paragraph 60);
- the increase, by developing countries, of their expenditure on research and development averaging 0.5 percent of their GNP per annum (paragraph 61);
- the development of appropriate technologies for developing countries (paragraphs 61–63);
- the strengthening of international cooperation and assistance to promote science and technology in developing countries (paragraphs 62 and 63);
- the establishment of a program for promoting the transfer of technology to developing countries (paragraph 64).

Five years later, in 1975, the General Assembly resolution on Development and International Economic Cooperation[8] devoted a full section to science and technology and reiterated its position that a series of measures needed to be taken to foster progress in developing countries by strengthening their scientific and technological capabilities and by giving them more rapid and wider access to existing productive know-how. In this resolution the General Assembly also recommended that a United Nations Conference on Science and Technology for Development should be convened before the end of the decade.

Aside from this resolution, adopted during the Seventh Special Session of the General Assembly, virtually all major global conferences organized by the United Nations and/or its Specialized Agencies have referred in their final documents to science and technology as important factors in the development process. In a study on such conferences during the 1970s, John Logsdon and Mary Allen discovered the following trends pointing to areas of consensus about the nature and function of science and technology in the development process:

> an emphasis on creating the appropriate balance, for each member state, between the development of indigenous scientific and technological capabilities and access to the scientific and technological resources of other countries;
>
> a growing interest in technology described as "practical," "appropriate," or "intermediate" as a particular focus for United Nations activity;
>
> a constant concern with the migration of trained scientific and technical personnel away from their native countries; an emphasis on the roles developed countries should play on various scientific and technological issues by:
>
> 1. devoting more attention in developed country research and development programmes to problems of concern to developing countries;
> 2. providing access for developing countries on equitable terms to the scientific and technological resources of developed countries;
> 3. providing greater assistance, both on a bilateral basis and through multilateral institutions, to the developing countries in their attempts to develop indigenous scientific and technological capabilities;
>
> increasing emphasis on the importance of technical cooperation among developing countries;
>
> particular emphasis on research, training and information requirements related to achieving basic human needs.[9]

From this brief summary of United Nations statements on science and technology for development, there emerge the contours of a concept which takes a view of science and technology that dispenses with the examination of the social prerequisites, conditions, and consequences of relying on science and technology for solving development problems. Put differently, one cannot escape the conclusion that there is a strong technocratic ring in the United Nations statements.

Alternative Perspectives on the Role of Science and Technology in the Development Process

The role of science and technology in the development process can be conceptualized in summary fashion in terms of three general perspectives: optimism, pessimism, and realism. One might ask which perspective comes closest to the prevailing view in United Nations concepts of a new international order and an international development strategy.[10]

It is suggested that the perspective characterized as scientific-technological optimism best captures the way in which United Nations documents perceive the relationship between science and technology on the one hand, and the development process on the other. It is also the lifeblood of the technocratic approach. This means that they proceed from the assumption that science and technology have played a crucial and in general beneficial role in the development of today's economically advanced countries and regions. Thus, they take the view that the fruits of applying science and technology to development previously enjoyed by a few countries only should be made available to all countries and regions of the world. To this end they propose a two-pronged approach to strengthen the scientific-technological capacities of developing countries and to transfer technology to them as a means of fostering, above all, economic growth.

Quite obviously, the United Nations documents referred to above and the development strategy conceived by them have little, if anything, in common with the pessimistic perspective on the role of science and technology in the development process. This pessimistic view is informed by "a feeling that some of the problems of modern industrialized societies have not emerged in spite of modern technology but *because* of modern technology."[11] It is interesting to note that in developing countries this view appears to have little support among the national elites. Rather, "even where there is scepticism in the Third World about western societies, enthusiasm for western science and technology nevertheless seems to prevail."[12] In summary, then, if scientific-technological pessimism regards scientific-technological change as a, or even the, source of many critical social problems rather than as a means to solve them, then this perspective stands in clear contradiction to what the prevailing United Nations conception of the role of science and technology in the development process is all about.

One might still wonder, however, whether this juxtaposition of the optimistic and pessimistic perspectives is really helpful in critically assessing the conceptions of the role of science and technology in the development process. The following assumptions seem plausible in forming the basis for another — realistic — perspective:

- science and technology play a pervasive role in social dynamics;
- science and technology can help solve social problems and contribute to development;
- the application of science and technology to the solving of social problems may entail unintended consequences that may be detri-

mental to development efforts—this occurs most often when the
social implications of scientific and technological change have
been neglected;
* that science and technology can be, and have been, used for
wasteful and destructive purposes.

The notion of the dialectical nature of scientific-technological change
inherent in the realistic view refers to the historical simultaneity of constructive and destructive qualities in man's labor and interaction. In the
words of a recent publication by the World Council of Churches:

> [Knowledge] is power to create and destroy, power loaded with promises
> and threats. . . . Science through its contribution to understanding liber-
> ates people from many forms of ignorance and superstition. Technology
> liberates them from many physical constraints and insecurities. . . . Yet in
> the face of all these promises, science and technology appear to many peo-
> ple as threats. . . . It is not only destructive human purposes that turn
> science and technology from promise to threat. Even well-intended uses of
> technology have unintended consequences that perplex or frustrate the peo-
> ple who initiated them.[13]

The critical aspect of this evolutionary process today is the need for a
theoretically informed and ethnically grounded social praxis that successfully prevents the destructive qualities of scientific-technological change
from dominating the constructive ones. Admittedly, these ideas will not
be found in the United Nations documents on a new international order
and an international development strategy given the optimistic ring per-
vading all of them. It appears, though, that in other connections—the
issue area of disarmament may be cited as an example—the question of
wasteful and destructive uses of science and technology has been dealt
with in United Nations documents in a very explicit and critical way. For
instance, the fact was criticized that a very large proportion of the
world's scientific-technological resources (financial and human) is absorbed by military R&D work.[14] Nevertheless, this cannot detract from
the more general observation that United Nations documents dealing
with issues of development do not project a coherent, realistic picture of
the nature of scientific-technological change.

Scientific-Technological Dependence
as an Obstacle to Development

The United Nations documents on the establishment of a new international order and development strategy stress the problem-solving role of

science and technology. This focus has an ideological function as well as empirical validity. There exists a very real basis for giving top priority to questions of mobilizing science and technology for development in the structure of international society, particularly as far as the access to, and the equitable distribution of, resources (in the broadest sense) among and within nations are concerned. It is probably safe to state that the quest for a new international order imposed by the developing countries on many international and most United Nations policymaking processes arise from their perception of gaps along a vartiety of dimensions relevant to development – and, of course, from their perception of possessing a modicum of political leverage toward the developed countries, in particular, the countries of the Organization for Economic Cooperation and Development (OECD).

One of the most serious of these gaps is certainly found in science and technology. Even though we have not yet a fully satisfactory data base for determining exactly the distribution of the world's R&D resources, it is nevertheless possible to sketch a global picture without distorting the main features and trends. Jan Annerstedt, who has done pioneering work in the compilation and analysis of R&D data on a worldwide basis, poses the problem as follows: "Today, is the majority of the countries in the world forming a research desert, and can the remaining countries be seen as a small number of R&D oases?"[15] In answering this question he has based his analysis of the international division of labor in science and technology on two indicators: the distribution of world R&D expenditures and of world R&D manpower. His general assessment as of 1973 is summarized in Tables 4.1 and 4.2.[16] They clearly reflect a highly skewed distribution in favor of the developed countries and reveal interesting variations between the two indicators selected, as well as between regions or groups of countries.

Several stark features stand out. First, the developing countries taken as a whole are indeed far behind in the development of R&D capacities. There has been some progress in reducing the gap between developed and developing countries over the last two decades, yet the extent of this change has been comparatively small. The share of developing countries in the world's R&D resources appears to be more sizable when based on the distribution of manpower than on the distribution of expenditures.[17] However, this should not be too surprising given the salary differentials and the differences in investment per scientist/engineer between developed and developing countries. At the same time, the higher share of R&D manpower gives some idea of the important potential that the developing countries already possess. The growth of this potential becomes even clearer when one takes the trends in higher education into consider-

TABLE 4.1
Distribution of World R & D Expenditures Among Major Regions in 1973

	R & D Expenditures in mn U.S. Dollars	in Percent of World Total	Per EAP[a] in U.S. Dollars	in Percent of GNP at Market Prices
World Total	96,418	100.0	66.4	1.97
Developing countries	2,770	2.9	3.0	0.35
Africa (excluding South Africa)	298	0.31	2.8	0.34
South and Middle America	902	0.94	9.0	0.37
Asia (excluding Japan)	1,571	1.63	2.1	0.34
Developed countries	93,648	97.1	182.1	2.29
Eastern Europe (including U.S.S.R.)	29,509	30.6	160.0	3.82
Western Europe (including Turkey)	21,418	22.2	135.1	1.55
North America	33,716	35.0	331.1	2.35
Other (including Japan, Australia)	9,005	9.3	129.8	1.76

Source: Preliminary data from the World R & D Survey (1978). Figures are rounded, but percentages and other data are calculated on the most detailed figures available.

[a] Economically active person

TABLE 4.2
Distribution of Researchers (R & D Scientists and Engineers) Among Major Regions

| | Researchers (R & D Scientists and Engineers) | | |
	Total (000)	in Percent of World Total	Per mn EAP
World Total	2,279	100.0	1,570
Developing countries	288	12.6	307
Africa (excluding South Africa)	28	1.2	271
South and Middle America	46	2.0	461
Asia (excluding Japan)	214	9.4	292
Developed countries	1,990	87.4	3,871
Eastern Europe (including U.S.S.R.)	730	32.0	3,958
Western Europe (including Israel and Turkey)	387	17.0	2,441
North America	548	24.1	5,386
Other (including Japan, Australia)	325	14.3	4,687

Source: Preliminary data from the World R & D Survey (1978). Figures are rounded, but percentages and other data are calculated with the most detailed figures available.

ation; the number of Third World students enrolled in higher education (as a percentage of global higher education enrollment) rose from 15 percent in 1950 to 25 percent in 1972.[18]

A second feature commanding attention is the indication of considerable variations in the scientific-technological capabilities both among developed and developing countries.[19] Within the group of developed countries, it is noticeable that the socialist countries devote a relatively larger proportion of their gross national product to R&D activities than the other developed countries. This is also reflected in the list of the ten most R&D-intensive countries: USSR, German Democratic Republic, Czechoslovakia, the United States, Romania, Federal Republic of Germany, Hungary, Netherlands, Japan, and France. With regard to R&D manpower, the share of the socialist countries is slightly higher than the expenditures would suggest, whereas Western Europe's share is somewhat lower and the share of North America (the United States and Canada) even more so. Comparing Western Europe and North America, it is found that the latter region has twice as many scientists and engineers per economically active person than the former.

In the developing countries, it becomes apparent that the Latin American countries tend to spend three times as much per economically active person as African and Asian nations. Also, Arab, South and Southeast Asian countries commit a lower-than-average share of their gross national product to R&D activities. The stratification pattern of R&D manpower among the developing countries does not change much. Again, the Latin American countries come out on top, closely followed by the Arab countries, while the countries of South and Southeast Asia and those of sub-Saharan Africa lag far, even very far, behind.

However, while analyzing these intragroup variations among both developing and developed countries, the point of departure, i.e., the dramatic gap in scientific-technological capacities between developed and developing countries, should not be lost from sight. It is still the developing countries that rely heavily, if not exclusively, on externally created knowledge and skills, feeding them, more or less uncontrolled, into their educational systems and productive sectors.

Surendra Patel[20] has attempted to indicate the foreign exchange costs that developing countries incur as a result of their technological dependence. He distinguishes between direct, indirect, and other costs.[21] Patel considers it essential for a full understanding of the nature and extent of these costs that one acknowledge the power tendencies toward concentration in the world market(s) for technologies. The owners of technologies are thus provided with a considerable bargaining edge over the buyers of technologies, particularly in developing countries – an asymmetrical relationship strengthened by the already existing lack of adequately equipped and staffed institutions in the field of science and technology.

Direct costs have been estimated to amount to 1.5 billion U.S. dollars in 1968 (usually in foreign convertible currency). This is equal to one-third of the external debt servicing or to two and one-half times the public expenditures on science and technology of developing countries. Indirect costs are held to be many times higher than direct costs to which must be added other types of costs, in particular opportunity costs. "Rough estimates suggest that these costs amount to 2–4 per cent of the national income of developing countries, i.e., 6–12 billion U.S. dollars. In comparison, the amounts spent by developing countries on R&D represent one-tenth to one-twentieth of these costs (about 600 million U.S. dollars)."[22] Patel concludes that developing countries, instead of bearing these costs, should – and could – devote more resources to the creation of indigenous scientific-technological capabilities.

If this analysis seems tenable the following question arises immediately: Are the United Nations conceptions of a new international order and an international development strategy grounded in a valid theory (or theories) of underdevelopment and dependence? Without such a scientifically acceptable foundation, what chance do political efforts stand to accomplish anything in terms of achieving realistically defined goals and avoiding foreseeable pitfalls? At this point, it must suffice to state that the emergence of scientific-technological dependence (and underdevelopment) is part of a more general historical process by which Europe and North America became the centers of the first truly global civilization. The reverse side of this process was represented by an increasingly relative, sometimes even absolute, backwardness of most other regions of the world. Since the sixteenth and seventeenth centuries the world grew apart, with the twentieth century witnessing the wide gap described earlier. This historical process was caused and conditioned by a complex combination and interaction of endogenous and exogenous factors. Today one of the most difficult analytical tasks consists in identifying not only the most potent dependence-generating endogenous and exogenous factors for a given country or region in the Third World but also their relative weight; for without such a thoroughgoing analysis there can only be a shaky basis for devising appropriate development strategies to reduce scientific-technological dependence. It may be considered an open question whether, and to what extent, the United Nations conceptions of a new international order and of an international development strategy fully satisfy this requirement.

Development of Indigenous Scientific-Technological Capabilities in Developing Countries

Given the general mix of dependence-generating factors one of the foremost goals of development strategy leading to a new international order consists in promoting indigenous scientific-technological capabilities both by mobilizing dormant or under-utilized domestic energies and by drawing on external assistance. However, since existing scientific-technological capabilities of developing countries vary greatly according to the level of socioeconomic development already reached individually, this goal needs a great deal of specification to be of operational value in guiding policy for, and within, a given developing country or region.

On one extreme, the goal could be defined as creating viable scientific-technological infrastructures in the very poor countries. This would imply, above all, the setting up of large-scale and differentiated education and training programs for technicians, engineers, and scientists (including social scientists), the initiation of basic institution building, and the fostering of R&D work oriented toward local (and locally defined) needs (which will almost certainly include "basic needs" but must not be restricted to them).

On the other extreme, the general goal of promoting indigenous scientific-technological capabilities could be operationalized by emphasizing *adaptation* and *reorientation* of the existing, relatively advanced scientific-technological institutions and capabilities to contribute to social and economic development which is not simply equated with growing per capita GNP. One important implication of such an operationalization would be the reshaping of national systems of higher learning and of academic research to bring them into closer contact with domestic agricultural and industrial production.[23]

This need for goal operationalization, which also takes into account the differences between developing countries, tends to be neglected by the United Nations conceptions of a new international order and of an international development strategy. Thus, potentially controversial discussions, both at the international and the national level, about the substance of development goals to be served by indigenous scientific-technological capabilities are discouraged rather than encouraged. In line with this avoidance strategy, internationally agreed-upon development targets tend to be defined in purely quantitative terms, thereby ensuring compatibility with differing qualitative policy objectives. In sum, the goal of promoting indigenous scientific-technological capabilities in developing countries, unless specified and operationalized, indicates nothing about its real social and political meaning.[24] It is this social and political meaning, however, that determines the developmental relevance of promoting scientific-technological capabilities, be they indigenous or not.

In additon to discouraging substantive controversies over development goals within the United Nations, the setting of development targets in quantitative terms also facilitates the achievement of spurious consensus between developing and developed countries. One reason is that this consensus does not carry binding force. More importantly, developed countries can more easily agree on helping to strengthen the indigenous scientific-technological capabilities of developing countries as long as the achievement of this goal remains qualitatively undetermined and, thus, leaves them free to exert their influence on developing countries building up their scientific-technological infrastructures. Put differently, most developed countries will express their readiness to contribute to the strengthening of scientific-technological capabilities in developing countries, particularly if this is to follow a pattern that is likely to suit their foreign economic interests and their own scientific-technological aspirations. If assistance from developed countries is sought by developing countries as well as some measure of independent scientific-technological development, then developing countries must engage developed countries in a substantive debate, reaching broad social strata, over goals and processes of development as a means of arriving at authentic consensus. Yet, this is a risky endeavor for any national leadership and therefore is not to be expected on a broad scale. Nevertheless, the possibility for coalition formation across the North-South divide among internationally reformist regimes and movements deserves further exploration.

Dilemmas of Technology Transfer

To overcome technological dependence the United Nations conceived of a new international order and of an international development strategy that calls for a rapid and massive increase in the transfer of technologies from developed to developing countries on more favorable terms. Even though certainly justified, in principle, as a way to counteract the effects of exogenous factors generating or maintaining technological dependence, transfer of technology is beset with ambivalences and loaded with seemingly inescapable contradictions.

Criticizing the assumptions underlying the United Nations conceptions one position holds that, in general, transfer of technology will reproduce, at best, the existing dependency relationships while increasing the differentiation among, and the fragmentation within, developing countries. Johan Galtung views indiscriminate transfer of technology "as a structural and cultural invasion; possibly of much larger significance than colonialism and neo-colonialism."[25] Less sweepingly, Dieter Ernst sees a relationship between increased technology transfer and a "new industrialization scenario . . . which, superficially, may fulfill some of the expectations . . . in some recent declarations of the 'Group of 77,' [but which] may in fact turn out to fulfill nearly all preconditions to increase significantly the technological dependence of these countries, [i.e.] technological dependence on a qualitatively higher level."[26] Thus, calling for an increase in transfer of technologies may well imply, objectively, agreeing to continued technological superiority of the developed countries. Given the importance of their comparative advantages in the field of R&D, developed countries — and the transnational corporations based there, in particular — will resist, or try to thwart, any international action which might endanger their competitiveness in crucial world markets, i.e., those with a high or above average growth potential.[27]

However, it could also be argued that the competition among developed countries and transnational corporations for markets and investment opportunities, both in the extractive and in the manufacturing sectors, in the Third World provides developing countries with a bargaining power, the full and determined use of which would allow them to pursue both goals of increased inflow of know-how and of establishing or retaining control with regard to the appropriateness of imported technology. This argument could be thought of applying best to the major oil exporting and the so-called threshold countries in the Third World. For they appear to satisfy at least some of the conditions that lay the groundwork for "self reliance of judgment"[28] and action in the selection of technologies including the question of importation. It should be noted here that this argument does not presuppose any international action by the United Nations or any other international organization. Rather, it refers to a "natural" process of change, which political intervention can perhaps facilitate but not generate.

While these conflicting views of the possible and probable extent, nature, and effects of increased transfer of technology cannot easily be reconciled — even though both of them have their merits — there remains the question of the relationship between promoting indigenous capabilities and importing technologies. Among transnational corporations surveyed by Business International,[29] none indicated that the transfer of technology on their part was related to the promotion of indigenous technological capabilities in developing countries. Leading government spokesmen in developed countries, however, "believe that technology transfer . . . will contribute to meeting human needs and developing human capacities and to upward mobility through the growth of indigenous technical and managerial skills."[30]

Contrary to these attitudes of indifference or of benevolence, which seem to prevail in business and government circles of major industrialized countries, a growing number of social scientists attempt to probe more deeply into the problem of how to deal with technology transfer while pursuing the goal of scientific-technological autonomy. Ward Morehouse and Jon Sigurdson, seeing a "circle of continued dependence on foreign technology inhibiting the development of an autonomous capacity for technological change," propose that serious consideration be given to the debate on implementing two contradictory measures: (1) declaration of a ten-year moratorium on new transfer of technology from industrialized to developing countries; (2) removal of all constraints on technology transfers including patents and other restrictions on proprietary technology.[31] Adopting a more differentiated approach, Dieter Ernst suggests that the answer to the problem lies in a strategy of "selective technological delinking" after having identified, on the basis of a systematic review of branch- and product-specific patterns of technological dependence, the priority sectors for the implementation of this strategy.[32]

In this connection Ernst warns explicitly against such a strategy "applied indiscriminately to all/most sectors of the economy, [because it] would be bound to fail anyway."[33] Admittedly, these analyses and strategic recommendations concerning the relationship between transfer of technology and scientific-technological autonomy have not yet gone past the stage of substantive controversy. However, there can be little doubt as to the validity of many findings brought out in these critical analyses. Apparently, there is no reflection of this, as yet, in the United Nations conceptions of a new international order and of an international development strategy.

International Scientific-Technological Cooperation and the Problem of Structural Asymmetries

International scientific-technological cooperation, be it bilaterally or multilaterally organized, has spread considerably over the last decades, as shown in a book-length study by Jean Touscoz some years ago.[34] Yet, the evidence suggests that the patterns of cooperation largely reflect, and may even tend to reproduce, the gap in scientific-technological capacities between developed and developing countries referred to earlier. In other words, cooperation among developed countries is not only more frequent than between developing and developed countries, let alone among developing countries themselves; it also appears that the results of such cooperation, i.e., among developed countries, are more equally shared.

United Nations conceptions of a new international order and international development strategy place considerable emphasis upon increasing scientific-technological cooperation between developed and developing countries as well as among developing countries themselves. The latter, at least in part, was the subject of another ad hoc conference organized by the United Nations Development Program (UN/UNDP): United Nations Conference on Technical Cooperation Among Developing Countries (TCDC), Buenos Aires, 30 August–12 September 1978.[35] Again, we must not shy away from asking probing questions: How can we expect that these objectives will be met and, if met, that they will significantly reduce the scientific-technological dependence of developing countries?

If one accepts a notion of cooperation that implies comparability of efforts, commonality of interests, as well as proportionate sharing of costs and benefits, then scientific-technological cooperation among developing countries might hold the greatest prospects for advancing their autonomy in the field of science and technology.[36] However, two obvious problems should not be overlooked. One results from the already mentioned fact that there exist wide discrepancies in scientific-technological capabilities among developing countries. In other words, structural asymmetries may stand in the way of successful cooperation here, too, though at a lower level. The other problem is related to the long held and still widely shared orientation of the scientific-technological communities in developing countries toward the developed countries, sometimes only toward the former colonial power. While it can be expected that this restrictive condition is more easily overcome in the foreseeable future, it is safe to predict that increases in scientific-technological cooperation among developing countries are likely to concentrate on the more advanced ones.

When calling for increases in scientific-technological cooperation between developed and developing countries one should not lose sight of the danger that "cooperation" could turn out to represent "old wine in new bottles," i.e., relationships of domination, paternalism, and exploitation, if the preconditions for cooperation are not present. Cooperation and the persistence of basic structural asymmetries must be considered as mutually exclusive. Therefore, if authentic scientific-technological cooperation is to be promoted one has to look for programs and projects that are capable of satisfying the preconditions for cooperation. To illustrate this, two possibilities come to mind: First, one could focus on areas for scientific-technological cooperation in which developing countries have already reached a sufficient level of competence and expertise. Second, in other areas, cooperative programs and projects would be linked to promotional schemes that provide for raising the level of competence of participating scientists and technologists in developing countries to that of their partners from developed countries in the course of implementing the program or project. Other types of cooperation, properly speaking, should and can be identified. However, if scientific-technological cooperation, particularly between developed and developing countries, is to contribute to development in the Third World, it will do little good to achieve more cooperation without paying much more attention to the social and political contents of such cooperation.

Acknowledgments

The views and conclusions put forward in this chapter are those of the author[37] and do not necessarily reflect the official position of any of the institutions with which he is associated. The author wishes to acknowledge his intellectual indebtedness to his colleagues Jürg Mahner and Ward Morehouse. He also expresses his gratitude to the editors of the present volume for their helpful comments on an earlier draft. However, no one but the author should be held responsible for any shortcoming in this chapter.

Notes

1. The situation referred to is well summarized in a recent newspaper article: "The danger . . . is that in the quest for solutions to what are fundamentally political and social problems, the gusher of interest in science might simply lead to swapping one set of witch doctors for another." Cf. Daniel S. Greenberg, "Science: Society's New Crutch," *International Herald Tribune*, 12 January 1979, p. 4.

2. The most distinctive characteristic of the technocratic approach to social problem solving consists in eliminating the difference between praxis and technique: The knowledge of the requirements and constraints of a hypostatized logic of progress tends to preempt the possibilities of discussing socially valued goals. For an in-depth theoretical analysis of this problem see Jürgen Habermas, *Technik und Wissenschaft als 'Ideologie'* (Frankfurt/M.: Suhrkamp, 1968), pp. 48ff.

3. For an assessment of the potentials and limitations of science and technology in social problem solving see the section in this chapter entitled "Alter-

native Perspectives on the Role of Science and Technology in the Development Process."

4. As indicated, the case of hunger and malnutrition is used for illustrative purposes only. However, it highlights the fallacy of believing in technological fixes for sociopolitical problems—not only hunger, but also unemployment, diseases, energy scarcity, etc.

5. On this point cf. the recent article by Francois de Ravignan, "Le Mythe de la Pénurie Alimentaire," *Le Monde Diplomatique* no. 294 (September 1978):9, where the author summarizes several new publications supporting the argument presented here. This argument has now been recognized by the Secretary General of the special FAO Conference on Agrarian Reform and Rural Development, Hernan Santa Cruz, who writes that the causes of rural poverty include, inter alia, "the inertia of obsolete socio-economic structures and the resistance to change by privileged groups." Cf. his article "Land for the Lost," *Development Forum* 6 (May 1979):1.

6. The preceding observations have been informed by several studies that seem to converge in their critical analyses of many past and contemporary policies to fight hunger and malnutrition: Rudolf Buntzel, "Umriss einer landwirt-schaftlichen Entwicklungsstrategie für Afrika," in Alfred Schmidt, ed., *Strategien gegen Unterentwicklung* (Frankfurt/M.: Campus, 1976), pp. 199–214; Kurt Egger and Bernhard Glaeser, "Ideologiekritik der Grünen Revolution," in *Technologie und Politik*, vol. 1 (Reinbek b. Hamburg: Rowohlt, 1975), pp. 135–155; and Dieter Senghaas, *Weltwirtschaftsordnung und Entwicklungspolitik* (Frankfurt/M.: Suhrkamp, 1977), pp. 189–202.

7. Cf. *International Development Strategy. Action Programme of the General Assembly for the Second United Nations Development Decade* (New York: United Nations, 1970), pp. 15–16.

8. General Assembly Resolution 3362 (S-VII) in *General Assembly Official Records*, 7th Special Session, supplement no. 1 (A/10301), sect. III.

9. John M. Logsdon and Mary M. Allen, *Science and Technology in United Nations Conferences* (A report for the UN office for Science and Technology, Washington, D.C., Graduate Program in Science, Technology and Public Policy, George Washington University, January 1978), pp. 7–8.

10. The concepts of technological optimism and pessimism are adapted from Thomas G. Weiss and Robert S. Jordan, *The World Food Conference and Global Problem Solving* (New York: Praeger Publishers, 1976), pp. 139–140.

11. Johan Galtung, "Towards a New International Technological Order?" (Manuscript, Geneva, 1978), p. 2.

12. Ibid., p. 3.

13. Cf. "Science and Technology—Promises and Threats," in Paul Albrecht, ed., *Faith, Science and the Future* (Geneva: World Council of Churches, 1978), pp. 21–23.

14. See *The Arms Race and Development* (New York: United Nations, 1978), pp. 10–11 and passim. However, the waste of scientific-technological resources inherent in the single-minded efforts by many countries, i.e., their hegemonic sociopolitical strata, to build a vast number of nuclear power plants, as well as the

squandering of R&D resources on space activities, has not yet come under similar critical scutiny in major United Nations organs.

15. Cf. Jan Annerstedt, *Global Resources of Research and Experimental Development. Contributions to the Symposium on the Application of Science and Technology to the Development of Indigenous Potentialities in Connection with the Establishment of the New International Economic Order* (Algiers: 9–12 September 1978), p. 4. For data on R&D expenditures and R&D manpower that deviate slightly from Annerstedt's, but apparently have a less inclusive information base, see the report of the UNCTAD secretariat prepared for UNCTAD V, "Towards the Technological Transformation of the Developing Countries," TD/238, 15 March 1979, p. 29.

16. Cf. Annerstedt, *Global Resources*, p. 8.

17. Ibid., p. 13.

18. Ibid., p. 17 (Table 3). While presenting these data we are aware of the obvious qualifications: More R&D personnel does not automatically translate into higher R&D output and its absorption by the productive sector.

19. This and the following paragraph paraphrase or summarize information spread throughout Annerstedt, *Global Resources*.

20. See Surendra Patel, "Der Preis der Abhängigkeit von der Technologie," in *Technologie und Politik*, vol. 1 (Reinbek b. Hamburg: Rowohlt, 1975), pp. 124–134; also Surendra Patel, "The Technological Dependence of Developing Countries," *Technology and Development*, UNITAR News 6, no. 4 (1974):23–25.

21. Direct costs include payments for patents, licenses, know-how and trademarks as well as for management and other services. Indirect costs refer to "payments for technology embodied in the cost of imported equipment and intermediate goods and in remitted profits." Cf. the report of the UNCTAD secretariat, *Major Issues Arising from the Transfer of Technology to Developing Countries* (New York: United Nations, 1975), pp. 25–27.

22. Cf. Patel, "Der Preis der Abhängigkeit," p. 133 (translation mine).

23. This point has been stressed by Miguel S. Sionczek in his generally provocative article on the preparations for UNCSTD, "Some Questions for the 'World Jamboree,'" *Bulletin of the Atomic Scientists* 30, no. 10 (1977):30.

24. A more elaborate "list of criteria or considerations" which could be guidelines in decisionmaking on building up or strengthening indigenous scientific-technological capabilities is given in Johan Galtung, "Towards a New Order?" p. 16. Adding that there does not yet exist "an adequate generally agreed-upon methodology of selection" (p. 17), he sees his list "as a guide for a better mix of more appropriate technologies operating at the various levels, in different and in the same sectors of goods and services" (p. 18).

25. Ibid., p. 11.

26. Dieter Ernst, "Technological Dependence and Development Strategies" (Manuscript, Hamburg, 1978), esp. pp. 3, 14 ff.

27. See, in this connection, the difficulties of reaching an agreement between developed and developing countries within the framework of UNCTAD, on a Code of Conduct on Transfer of Technology, be it in the form of nonbinding "guidelines" or in that of a legally binding convention. On the most recent state of

deliberations, cf. *Report of the Inter-Governmental Group of Experts on an International Code of Conduct on Transfer of Technology to the United Nations Conference of an International Code of Conduct on Transfer of Technology* (Geneva, 13 July 1978).

28. This phrase is borrowed from Ward Morehouse, *Science, Technology and the Global Equity Crisis: New Directions for United States Policy,* Occasional Paper 16 (Muscatine, Iowa: Stanley Foundation, 1978), p. 19.

29. Cf. Business International, *Transfer of Technology, A Survey of Corporate Reaction to a Proposed Code* (Geneva, 1978), pp. 13–15, where the main reasons for transferring technologies by transnational corporations to developing countries are described. They are, not surprisingly, very mundane indeed.

30. E.g., the deputy to the under-secretary for security assistance, science and technology in the U.S. Department of State, Joseph S. Nye, Jr., "Science and Technology, Technology Transfer Policies," *Department of State Bulletin* 78:2012 (1978):40.

31. See Ward Morehouse and Jon Sigurdson, "Science and Technology and Poverty. Issues Underlying the 1979 UN Conference on Science and Technology for Development," *Bulletin of the Atomic Scientists* 30:10 (1978):26.

32. Cf. Dieter Ernst, "Strengthening the Technological Autonomy of Developing Countries—Some Controversial Hypotheses Concerning UNCSTD" (Manuscript, Hamburg, 1978), p. 7 ff.

33. Dieter Ernst, "Technological Dependence and Development Strategies" (Manuscript, Hamburg, 1978), p. 5.

34. Jean Touscoz, *La Coopération Scientifique Internationale* (Paris: Éditions Techniques et Économiques, 1973).

35. See *Report of the United Nations Conference on Technical Co-operation Among Developing Countries,* Buenos Aires, 30 August–12 September 1978 (New York: United Nations, 1978).

36. A good compilation and analysis of various proposals for enhancing Third World cooperation in science and technology is contained in David W. Chu and Ward Morehouse, "Third World Cooperation in Science and Technology for Development," Science and Technology Working Papers Series, no. 5 (New York: UNITAR, 1979).

37. This chapter was written while the author was codirecting, at UNITAR, a project on the preparations for the United Nations Conference on Science and Technology for Development (UNCSTD), Vienna, 20–31 August 1979. Related papers by the author include "The New International Order and United Nations Conference Politics: Science and Technology as an Issue Area," Science and Technology Working Papers Series, no. 1 (New York: UNITAR, 1978); and "Options for an Institutional Follow-up to the UNCSTD," Science and Technology Working Papers Series, no. 6 (New York: UNITAR, 1979).

5

NAZLI CHOUCRI

International Political Economy:
A Theoretical Perspective

Introduction

The decline of the dollar, worldwide inflation, and the threat of an impending recession are indicative of fundamental changes in economic relations among nations. The increasing economic strength of certain raw material exporters, the inability of the industrial countries to develop coherent international economic policies, and the repeated calls for a new international economic order reflect major changes that are having severe effects on political relations among states.

The thesis of this chapter is that the causes and consequences of these changes cannot be explained solely by economic theory or by theories of international relations. It presents a perspective on system change derived from the insights of both disciplines. Toward this end, it draws upon selected aspects of international relations theory in conjunction with relevant insights and evidence from economic theory, and it outlines integrated theoretical directives for the analysis of system change. International trade and finance are a device — an issue area — for presenting a political economy approach to change and for indicating the linkages between economic theory and political analysis.

Economists and political scientists have fundamentally different explanations for international trade and finance, which give rise to different types of predictions and different policy recommendations. Each discipline tries to explain somewhat different aspects of the flows of goods and payments across national boundaries. Economists are more rigorous in both theory and method, but focus almost exclusively on static or comparatively static relations. Political scientists are, to a large extent, concerned with institutional and historical change, but their theories are generally vague and their methods often lack theoretical foundation.

A political economy perspective on international change entails integrating the insights provided by the two disciplines. The formal deductions of economic theory can provide critical inputs in an interdisciplinary framework for analyzing changes in international relations. Political influences affect economic interactions, particularly in shaping the composition and magnitude of trade in goods and services and in influencing the composition of the balance of payments and its adjustments; conversely, patterns of trade and payments affect the nature of political relations among nations and changes in these relations.

The analysis in the chapter proceeds as follows: first it surveys the main elements of the theories and empirical analyses of international trade and balance of payments that bear directly on the analysis of change in the international system. Then the influence of political variables in determining economic interactions generally, and trade relations specifically, is identified. This is followed by a review of the role of economics in different international relations theories. These sections provide the background for the development of an integrated framework for a political economy approach to international relations. The chapter then focuses on theoretical aspects of change in the international system and concludes with some specific directives for guiding empirical analysis.

International Economics: Clues for Change

The economic theory of international trade is conventionally divided into two branches: the pure theory of international trade and the monetary theory of balance-of-payments adjustments. Each deals with different aspects of trade, focusing on different problems and policy measures. Although both branches of theory are explicitly apolitical in their analyses they refer to processes and policies that are, in many ways, deeply political. A review of the main assumptions and related deductions of the theory of international trade and payments highlights the potential implications for explaining and predicting change in international systems.

Theory of International Trade

The theory of international trade is fundamentally static in nature. Its traditional focus is the explanation of patterns of trade. The modern theory of international trade stems from Adam Smith's critique of the mercantilist view that national wealth can be viewed in terms of the stock of precious metals and trade as a means of increasing that stock. The theory begins with the recognition that patterns of domestic consumption differ from patterns of domestic production, and that, in the absence of trade, domestic relative prices would differ from one country to another. In these circumstances, it is possible for one or both countries to gain by exchanging commodities. Neither country will be made worse off by trade and both will benefit if goods are exchanged at some intermediate price ratio.

The explanation of international price differences has its origin in the Ricardian model stipulating that prices reflect the ratio of labor costs to production, and trade patterns are determined by differences in labor productivity. In this labor theory of value, comparative costs provide the key to trade patterns. The Ricardian theory, based on one factor of production, constant returns to scale, two commodities, and two countries, generates the deduction that each country will export the commodity in which it has comparative advantage in labor productivity.

The modern theory of international trade has a more comprehensive theory of prices and costs, explaining differences in comparative costs as the result of differences in the ratio in which countries are endowed with factors of production. The Heckscher-Ohlin model deduces trade patterns resulting from such differences in factor endowments. It assumes that production functions are similar across nations and consumer tastes are identical everywhere, with two factors of production, two countries, two commodities, and different and nonreversible factor intensities among countries. The theory deduces that countries will export that commodity which makes most intensive use of the country's most abundant factor. Trade encourages resources to move into these productive sectors for which the country has a comparative advantage. As a result of engaging in trade with internal factor mobility, factor prices between two trading countries will, under certain assumptions, tend to equalize. Thus, free trade will tend to equalize factor prices across countries despite the assumption of international factor immobility. If there were complete equalization of factor prices, free trade would be a complete substitute for international mobility of factors. The Heckscher-Ohlin model has also been used to examine a range of comparative-static questions, such as tariff policy and technical change. This entails a comparison of two static conditions; it does not explain the change, but depicts the result of change.

The gains from trade are derived from two processes: gains due to the consumption domestically at prices different from the original home prices; and gains due to the reallocation of domestic resources that shift production and, through trade, raise income, thereby allowing consumption to expand. The benefits may be uneven across countries. It does not address itself to the costs of trade or the internal distribution of the effects of trade.

When a country undertakes trade, it expects international conditions to affect the home market. Since trade influences domestic production, it must affect fundamental aspects of a country's economy. Thus, the internal effects of trade shape a country's international position, and the international effects of trade shape its domestic economic situation.

Free trade under competitive conditions would generate a world distribution of consumption that could not be further changed to improve the welfare of all the trading partners without harming at least one country. In this restricted and aggregate sense, free trade is Pareto (optimally) efficient. Free trade, of course, assumes certain political conditions, both nationally and internationally, as will be noted below.

The contemporary theory of international trade exploits the formal apparatus developed in Samuelson's rigorous extensions of the Heckscher-Ohlin model to analyze a number of specific issues, such as: (1) the conditions of competitive equilibrium with many traded goods and services; (2) the effects of various domestic distortions and imperfections, including monopoly power and fixed factor payments; (3) the effects of distortions such as tariffs and quantitative restrictions; (4) the implications of trade for prices and outputs of nontraded goods; and (5) the implications of customs unions.[1]

There are other, less fully formulated theories of trade than those related to the Heckscher-Ohlin model and its specifications. First are theories that address the reasons for trade among countries with similar tastes.[2] There are the "product cycle" theories, which explain the changing composition of trade as the result of the spread of demand and production capabilities from technologically innovative countries to other countries.[3] Speculative thinking about the effects of overseas corporate activities can be regarded as a type of trade theory that has been expanded into theories of multinational operations.[4] Finally, the view of trade as a "vent for surplus"[5] has its modern counterpart in the theory of export-led growth.

The observations on trade theory indicate the type of explanations that are provided by the pure theory, but they do not explicate the processes by which the change takes place. Although the focus is on static analysis and equilibrium conditions, the implications for *change* in economic relations can, however, be deduced from the explanations proposed for determining the initial trade patterns. The balance of trade is a good indication of changes in relations among nations, and changes in the relative payments positions of nations are, in turn, useful measures of changes in the overall system's structure.

The Theory of Balance of Payments Adjustments

The theory of balance of payments stems initially from concern with the processes by which overall surpluses or deficits in a country's balance of payments are adjusted. This initial focus has broadened to include explanations of adjustments to capital movements and the theory of the determination of foreign exchange rates.

Classical economists resorted to the price specie-flow mechanism to explain internal adjustments to international trade imbalances. The Keynesian adjustment mechanisms emphasized induced import changes due to changes in national income levels. The monetarists expanded the adjustment theory, with the recognition that both domestic income levels and the balance of payments reflect international monetary influences. There are at least three approaches to the balance of payments adjustments in the contemporary literature that provide partial explanations for linkages among nations. The *elasticity approach* specifies the balance as a function of the differential price responsiveness of exports and imports; the *absorption approach* describes the balancing process as the result of changes in income induced by changes in imports and exports; and the *monetary approach* emphasizes the role of foreign reserves, other sources of money creation that influence interest rates and the general price level and, therefore, trade, capital movements, and the foreign exchange rate.

Each view of the balance of payments entails different policy foci. The elasticity approach emphasizes the effect of changes in relative price on imports and exports and, therefore, on the balance of payments. The absorption approach focuses on changes in income that result in changes in the balance of payments. Thus, the policy concerns of the absorption approach deal with the effects of exogenous changes in spending, such as government expenditures, exports, and, in some cases, investment, and their induced effects on income and foreign expenditures. The monetarist approach focuses on changes in the foreign reserves and other assets of the central banking authority, and the implications for domestic money creation and interest rates. These factors, in turn, influence domestic interest rates and the levels of expenditures and income. The balance of trade reacts to these domestic developments, as do the magnitude and composition of international capital movements.

The monetarist approach, which has recently been gaining in popularity, explains inflation by the rate of growth of the money supply.[6] Both the "new" and traditional monetarists are concerned with the international transmission of inflation. Government deficits are regarded as a critical aspect of aggregate demand policy by Keynesians, but are considered by monetarists only as a monetary device. Models of aggregate expectation formation have been developed to describe endogenously the reaction of economic decisions to exogenously imposed and induced changes in monetary and aggregate spending variables. A recent comprehensive study of the sources of balance of payments adjustment processes stresses the complementarity of various theories of adjustment.[7]

The channels by which macroeconomic conditions in one country affect such conditions in other countries are illustrated by the international transmission of the effects of inflation. This transmission is generally viewed as taking place through the channels of the effects of price, demand, liquidity, and international demonstration.[8] The first transmits inflation through the changes in values of traded goods; the second through transmission of demands for foreign goods and services; the third through capital movements and foreign exchange rate adjustments; and the fourth through anticipatory price and wage increases.[9]

There are many implicit references in the economic theories of balance of payments adjustments to the constraints imposed by both domestic and international institutional arrangements and, more fundamentally, by the domestic and international political contexts. But these constraints are seldom, if ever, made explicit, and remain peripheral to the economic theory of the balance of payments, capital flows, and foreign exchange rate adjustments. Unfortunately, the political changes created by economic changes are fully specified by neither economic nor political theories of international relations.

Empirical Models of International Trade and Payments

All economic models of international trade and payments view international economics as a system in which domestically induced changes in one country's income, prices, endowments, and/or productivity influence the economic activities in other nations.[10] In turn, these changes are transmitted back to the country of origin. These influences have direct policy implications because they affect domestic policies and, inevitably, the coordination of economic policies among nations. The economic theories of trade and adjustments have been explored and applied empirically in a number of models, which continue to confine themselves almost exclusively to economic factors. Yet some investigators recognize the significance of political variables.

In the empirical models of international trade, exports and imports are modeled as functions of relative prices, foreign exchange variables, real disposable income, relative resource endowments, industrial production, real changes in investment, relative factor prices, and real GNP—to name the most commonly used explanatory variables.[11] The effects of transportation, distance, and costs are also included. The flow of trade is, with few exceptions, explained and predicted by these economic vari-

ables alone. Political indications of "influence," power, coercion, cooperation, and the like are singularly absent.

The basic representational technique is the trade matrix of imports and
exports by country of origin and source of destination, with rows or columns summing up to total world exports and total world imports—by
commodity and by total value of trade. The representation, commonly
referred to as a transaction matrix, has been used to categorize information not only on commodity flows across national boundaries, but on
payments for trade, services, and capital flows.[12] But it is not the basis
on which to test hypotheses dynamically, or to examine processes underlying trade patterns or changes in these processes.[13]

Approaches similar to trade matrix accounting have been adopted by
political scientists seeking to describe the worldwide network of trade.[14]
These approaches, too, are largely atheoretical and nonpredictive in
nature, yielding information that is mainly descriptive, but in the analysis of international relations they have been tied to theories of integration and community formation.

The models of balance of payments adjustment and international
transmission of changes in levels of domestic activity are more behavioral in nature and more process-oriented than transaction models. The
objective of these models is to identify interconnections between national
economic activity and international economic interactions. These models
have a long history, beginning with interwar analyses of trade flows
sponsored by the League of Nations to the present large scale International Linkages in Economic Systems (LINK) project, described below.
Earlier works focus on the effects of changes in investment,[15] income
and capital flows,[16] investments and changes in prices,[17] and income,
prices, and industrial capacity.[18] The models differ mainly in the manner
in which the determinants of imports and exports are specified.[19]

One of the conventional criticisms raised is that such models are too
deterministic and do not allow for a wide enough range of factors that
influence trade flows, in part due to their highly aggregate character. In
addition, the models only embody trade flows; capital flows, which are
critical to a country's overall economic transactions, are typically treated
as residuals. The general theoretical formulation of international adjustments imbedded in these empirical models has recently been modified
and expanded to take monetary factors and exchange rates into account,
following the later development in adjustment theory. To a considerable
extent, more recent empirical models are extensions of models of domestic activity with trade and payments sectors added. For example, the
LINK models, so prominent among international economists, are a set of
relationships designed to examine the international transmission mecha-

nisms, forumlated with the explicit objectives of connecting the activity and trade levels in a number of countries, explaining the imports of each country, and estimating exports from trade shares.[20]

There are still newer approaches in the construction of empirical models of international trade. For example, Roemer recognizes that although transportation costs were assumed at zero in most trade models, the empirical reality is such that transport costs are important and must be taken into account.[21] He finds that the observed biases in trade patterns cannot be explained solely by distance, but are the outcome of influences that "are not distinctly economic in the narrow sense."[22] In further explaining his results, Roemer concludes that "powerful countries market more of their competitively weak sectors in areas where they have influence, for historical and political reasons, than they would otherwise."[23] He then speculates on the nature of the "sphere of influence" relationship. Parenthetically, Kindleberger is one of the few international economists noted for giving specific attention to these factors.[24]

The Roemer measures and those of similar studies are closely related to the "concentration" indices developed thirty years earlier by Hirschman to determine the power implications of trade.[25] Subsequently, such measures were expanded by both economists and political scientists,[26] but these developments in measurements have had minor effects on the basic economic theory of international trade and only marginal incorporation in any integrated political economy perspective on international relations.

It is fair to conclude that economic analyses of international trade are largely static in nature, focus on flows, specify at times the differential attributes of nations generating differences in trade patterns, stress composition of trade and not direction of flows, and isolate trade from the broader network of economic relations.

Political Factors in International Economic Theory

There is no explicit statement in the conventional economic theory of international trade and payments regarding the influence of political variables. In reviewing both the trade theory and theory of balance of payments adjustments, however, it is clear that there are a number of implicit political factors that should be considered explicitly in a more comprehensive approach.

Recall that the pure theory deduces gains from trade. The concepts of comparative advantage and gains from trade are as critical to the original views expressed by Ricardo and Smith as they are in the more recent theories that focus on differences in factor endowments. The historical case of trade relationships between England and Portugal that centered around the famous Methuen Treaty of 1703 is often used as an illustration of the principle of comparative advantage, both in the earlier Smith and Ricardo works and in the context of the modern line of theory. Ricardo's statement that "under a system of perfectly free commerce, each country naturally devotes its capital and labor to such employments as are most beneficial to each,"[27] while using the example of the factors determining the manufacture of wine in Portugal and cloth in England, has been the classic example of the principle of comparative advantage. The economic theory of international trade has continued to refer to this as an example, and to present the theory of comparative advantage as the primary and only general explanation with predictive power of trade among nations. Yet even within the economic explanations there are implicit assumptions about political influences. Politics and the use of force that have, in many cases, contributed to changes in the fundamental factor endowments have modified the gains from trade and have heavily influenced trade patterns so often characterized by economists as determined simply by comparative advantage.

The classic historical example itself illustrates this broader perspective. A political analysis of the historical case and a parallel analysis by an economist have raised substantial doubts that Portuguese-English trade was mutually beneficial.[28] This historical evidence indicates that free trade between Portugal and England was the result of the extensive use of military coercion and the manipulation by the stronger state of the weaker state's political position. The outcome was a transformation of trade relationships toward the consolidation of what was later called the working out of comparative advantage by Smith and Ricardo.

Many specific assumptions in the economic theory of international trade hide the role of political factors; these assumptions must be relaxed or eliminated completely in order to achieve a more realistic understanding of trade conditions. For example, the conventional theory assumes perfect competition in trade, although important extentions of that theory investigate in detail the significance of monopoly power in setting tariffs and of monopsony power in setting export taxes. However, both the assumptions of perfect competition and full exploitation of monopoly, and of monopsony, power are seldom if ever warranted. There are also constraints determined by international politics on the exercise of monopoly power. The influences of fundamental factor endowments are expressed in economic theory only through markets, and correctly expressed only if those markets are perfectly competitive. However, relative factor payments are heavily influenced by political conditions. Thus, factor endowments in themselves do not determine trade patterns as completely as is asserted by the economic theory of international trade.

The political factors embedded in international economic theory are also related to the determinants of market structure and interactions which reflect the capabilities of national governments, their domestic strength, and the extent to which they can and do make use of the policy instruments available to them. Recently, the interactions between national governments and international economic organizations revealed the stresses and pressures to which a government can be subjected, and the effects of its responses upon the international structure of power relations.[29] Cognizance of the trade-off between inflation and unemployment and of the attendant pressure groups that would be affected by policies designed to influence inflation or unemployment has given rise also to new lines of inquiry.[30] The emphasis, however, has been overwhelmingly on the analysis of domestic politics. The international aspects of the connections between political and economic variables remain for the most part unexamined, as are their implications for change in both the structure and the process of relations among nations.

Economics in Theories of International Relations

With few exceptions, the political analysis of international relations has traditionally focused on problems of governance and of power, examining transactions among nations largely as they bear on these two factors. Among the political philosophers, Hume stands out in his explication of the criticality of the balance of payments to a country's international position.[31] The classical mercantilist view makes a direct connection between power and wealth, and a more recent reassertion of the posture stresses fundamental interconnections between the "pursuit of power and the pursuit of wealth."[32]

The evolution of modern international relations theory—through the idealist-institutional, realist, behavioral, and postbehavioral phases—reveals different degrees of reliance on economic theories and processes. At least three contemporary paradigms in international relations theory have direct relevance to the analysis of international trade: the realist-mercantilist view, the liberal-interdependence perspective, and the radical-Marxist view. Each is predicated on different assumptions about the nature of the state, of political behavior, and of relations among nations, and each draws upon different aspects of economic theory.

The "idealist" posture, which initiated the formal study of international relations as a distinct discipline in the United States, was influenced by

Wilson's Fourteen Points and developed into a focus on institutional arrangements that could contribute to the preservation of international peace.[33] The emphasis was overwhelmingly on legalistic and distributional arrangements. The League of Nations occupied a central position in the analysis of relations among nations. The problem of reparations gained attention after World War I, and economists debated the political as well as economic constraints on Germany meeting the Allies' reparations claim. By contrast, however, political scientists paid relatively less attention to the politics of reparations.

The outbreak of World War II contributed to a realist critique of idealism. The orientation of Morgenthau's *Politics Among Nations* became the dominant view. The relationship between economics and politics was only briefly noted: "It is necessary to distinguish, say, economic policies that are undertaken for their own sake, and economic policies that are instruments of a political policy."[34] The "behavioral" revolution during the 1950s and early 1960s emerged in part as a reaction against the *realpolitik* premise that power, especially military power, is the essential concept in the understanding and analysis of relations among nations.

Major research projects during the 1960s — including the Inter-Nation Simulation, the Stanford Studies in International Conflict and Integration, the Dimensionality of Nations Project, and the Correlates of War Project — took only marginal cognizance of trade and other economic variables as bearing upon relations among nations.[35]

The postbehavioral "revolution" in international relations placed greater emphasis on the unmeasurable factors and on the role of context in interpreting political outcomes. It contributed to a greater appreciation of the complexity of national goals and political objectives by attempting a more explicit conceptualization of the fundamental political processes.[36]

The three contemporary paradigms in international politics that bear directly on a political economy of relations among countries — the realist-mercantilist paradigm, the interdependence school, and the radical-Marxist paradigm — are predicated on different views of the role of the state, the goals of nations, and the interconnections among nations, and each draws upon different aspects of economic theory. The debt to economic theory is not always explicit, but there is, in each case, an observable connection.

The first theoretical paradigm focuses on the power of nations, is explicitly nationalist in orientation, and draws upon the realist school, the mercantilist tradition in economics, and the emphasis on power relations. The orientation is derived from Morgenthau's precept that politics has primacy over economics, is state-centric, focuses on national wealth, and examines the interconnections between the political and economic goals of nations.[37]

The interdependence paradigm draws partly upon neo-classical economics and the earlier integrationist school in political science.[38] The interdependence school emerges as an attempt to understand the context within which nations operate internationally and seeks to understand the extent of mutual leverage that can be exerted.[39] The focus is less on power as such than on the constraints on national behavior, the outcomes that create regimes that regulate interaction in certain issue areas, and the policies that could generate outcomes that can be beneficial, albeit asymmetrically, to all parties in an international exchange.[40] The major concepts are asymmetry, vulnerability, and sensitivity, as three indications of political relations and influence among nations. The logical implications of these maxims have not been fully explored, nor do there exist comprehensive, empirically based models which reveal the predictive strength of the theory or the interconnections between economic and political variables in explaining change.

Trade patterns, analyzed as part of the earlier integrationist school,[41] were used as indicators of community formation and centered around the concept of "relative acceptance" and the development of associated measures. More recently, the use of trade as an indication of asymmetrical relations in an interdependence framework has been undertaken for examining political problems relating to petroleum trade.[42] The focus in both cases is on the inferences to be derived from changes in the direction and magnitude of trade flows. The Deutsch tradition relates flows of trade to broader patterns of communication. The work on petroleum trade seeks to delineate the structure of mutual political leverage created by different patterns of imports and exports of oil and the connection to commodity trade and financial flows.[43]

The third contemporary paradigm in international relations theory has origins in Marxian economics and has recently been extended into the *dependencia* literature and related center-periphery relations.[44] It focuses on the potentially exploitative nature of political and economic relations, and on the domination and control dimensions of international politics.[45]

Theoretical, as opposed to descriptive, analyses of "unequal exchange"[46] have recently been extended to dependency relations. Duvall and colleagues have developed the most rigorous and conceptually rich set of indicators of different aspects of dependency relations.[47] This pretheoretical exercise is important for the development of a more rigorous examination of the *dependencia* arguments. There is a debt to the earlier work of Hirschman and his efforts to measure the concentration of trade and infer the political relationship between trading partners.[48] Hirschman viewed trade as an instrument of control, and the measurement efforts of the Duvall group as a contribution to more rigorous, extensive, and conceptually based measurement of control, penetration, and domination.

In summary, the contributions of contemporary international relations theory to an integrated framework for a political economy approach to system change can be characterized as follows:

- From the realist-mercantilist school there are emphases on the importance of "wealth" in influencing "power," the primacy of political objectives, the use of economic instruments for the pursuit of political goals, and the importance of "power" in influencing "wealth."
- From the interdependence school, the concepts of asymmetrical relations, mutual leverage, shared interests and vulnerability are important additions to the realist-mercantilist orientation, as is consideration of nonstate actors.
- From the radical-Marxist-*dependencia* school, the concepts of domination, relational control, spheres of influence, and unequal exchange are major contributions.

Political Factors in the International Economy

Neither international trade and balance of payments theory, on the one hand, nor international political theory, on the other hand, provides a sufficiently robust framework for describing or explaining relations among nations, although each provides insights into which variables should contribute to a more comprehensive understanding of international relationships. The distribution of power in the international political system, and the nature of that system, provide the institutional framework within which regimes governing economic relations are generated. Over time, shifts in economic activities change the relative productivity of nations and contribute to the transformation of the existing power arrangement and political structure of the international system. These transformations, in turn, create changes in the international economic positions of countries.[49] There is an inevitable interdependence between economic policies and political behavior, and this interdependence serves to shape the range, scope, and type of interactions among nations and the changes that are feasible. There are both potential conflicts and common purposes among the goals of nations, as well as the possible trade-offs between economic and political objectives. For theory-building purposes it is important to appreciate the influence of political variables on international economic behavior, as well as the impacts of economic variables on a nation's political activities.

International payments position affects both a country's own situation and the overall global configuration. It is thus useful to differentiate types of payments position. One distinction pertains to countries that have a chronic trade deficit but where deficits are matched by long-term financial inflows, versus countries that are faced with more short-term difficulties for which immediate intervention is sought. The positions of both types of countries raise political issues pertaining to international power relationships. By the same token, the international political position of surplus countries is affected by the character and magnitude of the surpluses. Justifying surpluses to allies in deficit is one of the major contemporary problems, as evidenced by recent Japanese-U.S. relations. Countries may also be "in balance" when export earnings are equal to import expenditures. The ability to "manage" imbalances is a corollary of power; the inability is a corollary of weakness. The political as well as economic policies and interventions adopted by each of these three types of country will result in different measures to deal with the economic and political constraints, with different consequences for the configuration of global relations.

The fact that a country is in surplus at one time does not, of course, guarantee that it will continue in that position. External commitments in excess of inflows result in a reduction of the surplus and, if continued, in a change of basic economic position. Every action a country takes to change and/or maintain its international economic position will have an effect on itself as well as other countries. For example, if a country devalues its currency in order to make its exports cheaper and more competitive on the world market so as to reduce a trade imbalance, its smaller trading partners may be forced to follow suit so that they do not find themselves in a severely disadvantaged position. The type and nature of these effects will differ according to the polity and to the centrality of the country to the international economy as a whole, as well as to the economies of its trading partners.

In addition to the overall balance of payments and reserve positions, countries differ in the market share of their particular exports and the ease with which their exports can be substituted for by the exports of other countries. The latter condition determines the degree of monopoly power which the exporting country can exercise, but even in the absence of monopoly power a country with a relatively large share of particular export markets has a different impact on international economic conditions than a country with only a small share. There are analogous distinctions with respect to imports. The grant of access to a large import market creates different opportunities than access to small markets. These economic differences, in turn, influence political relations and, in fact, can be used as political instruments.

A country's pattern of international financial transactions, though related to its current balance of payments and trade, will not be completely determined by them. Rather, the history of its previous trade and its current and previous political associations may be as, if not more, important. Participation in each of the major monetary blocs — the sterling, dollar, and franc — reflects the previous, as well as current, trade and balance of payments conditions. Financial relations among advanced and developing countries often follow the relations established during periods of colonialism or more exclusive trading arrangements. While there are economic reasons for this persistence in the concentration of information about trading partners in certain centers, these economic reasons may be reinforced or attenuated by political relationships, and the latter, in turn, are influenced by the financial interactions.

Countries can be characterized in terms of their international political position.[50] The conventional classification of countries is in terms of major powers and a range of lesser powers. The international policies and behavior of countries will be shaped by their capabilities and constraints. For purposes of conceptual and empirical clarity, therefore, one must delineate the economic policies adopted by a nation and how they influence a country's political position.

What a country will do to manage any economic imbalance and how it will do it depend on a number of economic and political factors and the types of domestic and external pressures it faces. Among the main economic variables are the following: the size of the economy; the magnitude of its international economic transactions with other countries; the sensitivity of its imports and exports to price changes; the state of the economies of its trading partners; and its own financial "power," namely its effective influence in international monetary relations.[51]

The choice among economic policy alternatives can have important political implications. "External balance" with respect to trade and capital movements, and "internal balance" in achieving high levels of employment without inflation may not be feasible at the same time. Thus, national leaderships will be confronted with difficult trade-offs. The economic choices will be determined in large part by government preferences and policies. A result of such choices may be the creation of new linkages between domestic and international economic variables. Even in a period of flexible exchange rates, a country's balance of payments and the international distribution of "surplus," "deficit," and "balanced" countries is one of the most revealing indicators of economic and political relations.

The major political variables that determine the choice of economic policies and instruments for economic adjustments are its domestic political orientations, its military capability, and its international political position.[52] The dominant political orientation of the country reflects itself in terms of type of governance, the nature of economic preferences, and the nature of economic institutions.

Economic policies are shaped not only by economic factors, but also, sometimes strongly, by the nature of the polity and government's preferences. Politics often defines the economic problems that are perceived as important, or it can change the nature of the problem as defined initially. Political decisions and values can constrain the choice of instruments, and even provide a preference for some alternative economic policies over other types of measures.[53] Different economic policy options have different implications for political relations among nations, for a nation's capacity to influence other nations, and for the probabilities that it will come into conflict with other nations or, alternatively, increase their cooperation. In a world of increasing interdependence, Clausewitz's famous maxim—that war is a continuation of diplomacy by other means—can be extended to the maxim that under certain conditions, trade can be the manifestation of political influence by other means. The statement that "war is the ultimate protective tariff" points to the interconnections of trade and politics in the extreme case.[54] This insight has not been systematically pursued by anyone examining changes in international relations.

An essential aspect of the relations among nations entails the bargaining power each can exert, given the contextual and structural constraints on their behavior. A critical indicator of a nation's international behavior is its mode of interaction with other nations.[55] The extension of a nation's activities outside national boundaries can be thought of as "lateral" pressure. The mode, or combination of modes, of this pressure is often influenced by the broader international context. Different forms of lateral pressure will change the structure, and even processes, of international relations. For instance, trade, and the terms on which nations engage in it, is one important expression of lateral pressure and the extent of pressure. As nations interact more extensively along this dimension, there are propensities for change in their relations and, by extension, in the system as a whole. This means that any dramatic change in trade patterns—whether among the Scandinavian countries or, as a contrast, between China and the Soviet Union—will result in system change.

The balance of payments registers both the annual and the cumulative effects of a country's overall interactions and commitments. These commitments are an expression of lateral pressure. Trends in current and capital accounts may reveal the *mode* of such pressure.

The payments profiles of nations reveal changes in international economic regimes and indicate changes in economic and political relations. The debates over the new international economic order are, in this context, a global reflection of changing economic and power positions of nations. In sum, trends in payments position reflect macrosystemic adjustments, and they are unmistakable records of system change.

Toward an Integrated Framework of International Political Economy and System Change

This section provides the basis of a general set of relationships to guide theory building and empirical analysis. We draw explicitly upon the insights of economic theory and international relations theory, and stress their interconnections by recognizing the dual imperatives of national behavior: the pursuit of power and the pursuit of income and wealth.

Economic theory allows rigorous deductions regarding the effect of national endowments on trade patterns and financial relations among nations. Over time, patterns of trade and finance contribute to shaping a country's international economic position, measured in terms of market shares, reserves, and similar variables. That position also influences, and is influenced by, a country's diplomatic alliances, military capacity, and power in international relations. In this context, the balance of payments can be viewed as a critical (accounting) measure of international economic transactions, and thus provides an indicator which can be related to other measures of political behavior, influence or strategic factors.

The general framework we propose as the basis for an integrated approach to international political economy is represented in the following propositions:

- Trade patterns (imports and exports of commodity goods) are determined domestically by factor endowments and other variables, and constrained by political factors. International influences on trade patterns include alliance commitments, international political capability and relations, and spheres of influence.
- The international payments position of countries (in terms of the balance of payments and its components) is influenced by internal political and economic policies and by such international political

and economic variables as size of spheres of influence (which may guarantee markets), trade patterns, and military presence overseas.

- Political capability (international capacity for control) is affected by trade patterns and international payments position, as well as by military allocations and activities, size of spheres of influence, and alliance commitments.
- Political behavior (in terms of cooperation and/or conflict) is determined by the political capability of nations and their alliance commitments, and constrained by their international payments position and transactions, as well as by internal political influences and military activities.

Each of the above statements is derived from the theoretical reviews and substantive illustrations of the previous sections. These statements are for purposes of initial theoretical development and, eventually, the derivation of testable hypotheses. They represent jointly dependent variables in which change is implicit. The mechanisms by which the four endogenous variables feed back on and change the domestic and international context within which these interactions take place can be examined empirically. Throughout the system at large, international rearrangements indicate macroadjustments. The political implications of these adjustments create reverberating effects throughout the system as a whole.

Balance of payments profiles are overt records of behavior, but they result from a complicated set of underlying processes. Determining the theoretical directives for delineating these processes and changes in them is, in itself, a major challenge. Specifying the factors that lead to the pattern of a country's current account over time, the trends in the capital account, and the overall effects on payments position entails more than an economic analysis. Each account reflects political purposes and commitments. For instance, allocation to the military overseas, which is a debit in the current account, reflects a drain on resources motivated by political concerns. But the "trace" of these concerns is economic in nature.

Far from being an esoteric issue, the question of theoretical representation is critical to the analysis of system change; characterizing international system change entails a focus on the structure of the system, on the one hand, and a determination of the appropriate analytical representation for delineating change in structure, on the other.

The structure of the international system, determined by differential attributes and capabilities, generates a hierarchy of power relations. That hierarchy is one of domination and control, or, at a minimum, of mutual constraints on national behavior. International relations are, at their core, relations among unequals. How inequalities are ordered in international relations is shaped by the differentials in attributes and capabilities of nations and the effects of these differentials upon decisionmaking.

Changes in capabilities may result in changes in structure.[56] The dynamic elements in a system of relations are represented by the processes that relate different parts and levels of a system. The nature of the processes—in terms of transformation, adaptation, breaks, or variants thereof—will in large part be shaped by the interactions among the relevant entities, by the prevailing regimes, and by the connectives across levels of interaction. Therefore, the process of international change must be kept distinct from the structure that itself might be undergoing change.

Process unfolds over time, of course. Different time perspectives, and intervals, are appropriate for analysis of different situations. There is as yet, however, no theoretical determination of time, or the attendant intervals that are appropriate for the analysis of different aspects of system change. What might appear as a series of rapid permutations might be viewed as a smooth change if the time perspective were extended.[57]

These observations point to the importance of characterizing international systems and changes in terms of multilevel interactions. A multilevel conception includes the conventional connections and constraints of nations as they relate to each other—the domestic influences on international behavior, the inter-state influences (such as alignments or other factors), the transnational influences (such as nonstate actors), and the supranational influences (such as international organizations)—but goes beyond these to incorporate other aspects of interaction.[58]

The extensions involve specifying the interconnections between and within levels of interactions as conventionally defined—and the relative strength of the connections—and recognizing the asymmetries in the strength of various influences on the behavior of nations. For the present purposes this implies acknowledging the interdependencies yet differences between economic and political variables and the mutual constraints and capabilities that each presents to the other.

The rationale of a multilevel view of the international system is to begin with, but go beyond, the conventional unit and level of analysis characterization proposed nineteen years ago,[59] and stress the mutually directed, but possibly asymmetrical, influences exerted by different levels and systems of interaction. It is necessary also to specify theoretically and model explicitly the interdependence between politics and economics. Each can be viewed analytically as a "system" exerting an influence on the overall exchanges and relations among nations.

The concept of "level" must be extended to incorporate and include political and economic interactions that have conventionally been relegated to a separate domain of theoretical discourse and empirical analysis. This conception must be integrated with the conventional view of international systems that still regards the appropriate "levels" to be state-centric or bearing directly and only on the international structure within which nations interact. These propositions incorporate economic and political influences upon national behavior within one framework, use the nation-state as the focus on inquiry, but specifically recognize the impact of domestic and external factors on national behavior. Further, they represent, albeit approximately, interdependence among systems of activity, political and economic, with the nation-state as the arena within which these systems interact.

Conclusion

This chapter has argued that an adequate analysis of system change requires two necessary conditions: first, the development of an integrated theoretical perspective on international systems; and second, a view of the system and of change that entails complex multilevel characteristics. The first condition is critical in international relations because neither economic nor political theories alone can explain system change. The second recognizes the interdependence and asymmetries in political and economic interactions and in their interrelationships. Politics provides the value orientation and institutional context within which economic behavior is undertaken. Economics provides the exchange principles that are expressed within the bounds of politically permissible behavior. The complexity pertaining both to structure and to process of interaction in the international system can best be represented in terms of a multilevel system incorporating these dual influences.

Acknowledgments

The comments and suggestions of several colleagues and graduate students were extremely helpful in the preparation of this chapter. I am particularly indebted to Richard S. Eckaus for a careful review of the sections on international economics. Hayward R. Alker and Lance Taylor commented critically on earlier drafts. Peter Brecke made careful observations. Finally, I am most appreciative of the research assistance of Dale L. Smith, who commented on each draft and made useful observations throughout. My greatest debt, however, is to Robert C. North. Our ongoing collaborative research has contributed to many of the ideas contained in this chapter. The editors of this volume made numerous, and sometimes forceful, suggestions. I would like to thank them for their comments.

Notes

1. A review of selected works is in Richard E. Baldwin and J. David Richardson, eds., *International Trade and Finance* (Boston: Little, Brown and Co., 1974).

2. See Staffan Burenstan-Linder, *Trade and Trade Policy for Development* (New York: Praeger Publishers, 1967).

3. See, for example, Raymond Vernon, "International Investment and International Trade in the Product Cycle," *Quarterly Journal of Economics* 80 (May 1966):190-207; Raymond Vernon, ed., *The Technology Factor in International Trade* (New York: National Bureau of Economic Research and Columbia University Press, 1970); and Louis T. Wells, Jr., "International Trade: The Product Life Cycle Approach," in Louis T. Wells, Jr., ed., *The Product Life Cycle and International Trade* (Boston: Harvard University, 1972), pp. 3-33.

4. See, for example, Charles P. Kindleberger, ed., *The International Corporation* (Cambridge, Mass.: M.I.T. Press, 1970), and an extension of his work by Stephen H. Hymer, *The International Operation of National Firms: A Study of Foreign Investment* (Cambridge, Mass.: M.I.T. Press, 1976).

5. This approach is developed in Richard E. Caves, "Export-led Growth and the New Economic History," in Jagdish N. Baghwati, ed., *Trade, Balance of Payments and Growth: Papers in International Economics in Honor of Charles P. Kindleberger* (Amsterdam: North-Holland Publishing Co., 1971), pp. 403-442.

6. Examples of this approach include Milton Friedman, "The Role of Monetary Policy," *American Economic Review* 58 (March 1968):1-17; Allan H. Meltzer, "Monetary and Other Explanations of the Start of the Great Depression," *Journal of Monetary Economics* 2 (1976):455-471; and Harry G. Johnson, "Toward a General Theory of the Balance of Payments," in H. G. Johnson, ed., *International Trade and Economic Growth* (London: Allen & Unwin, 1958).

7. Rudiger Dornbusch, "Real and Monetary Aspects of the Effects of Exchange Rate Changes," in R. Z. Aliber, ed., *National Monetary Policies and the International Financial System* (Chicago: University of Chicago Press, 1974), combines both monetary and real sources of payment imbalances and extends the earlier debates regarding the appropriateness of the elasticity, absorption, or monetary views of payment difficulties. The model employed by Dornbusch is a synthesis and an extension of the work of W. Corden, "The Geometric Representation of Policies to Attain Internal and External Balance," *Review of Economic Studies* 28 (1960):1-22; James E. Meade, "The Case of Variable Exchange Rates," in Warren L. Smith and Ronald L. Teigen, eds., *Readings in Money, National Income and Stabilization Policy* (Homewood, Ill.: Richard D. Irwin,

1975), pp. 505–517; Robert A. Mundell, *Monetary Theory* (Pacific Palisades, Calif.: Goodyear, 1971); T. W. Swan, "Economic Control in a Dependent Economy," *Economic Record* 36 (March 1960):51–66; and T. W. Swan, "Longer-Run Problems of the Balance of Payments," in H. W. Arndt and W. M. Corden, eds., *The Australian Economy: A Volume of Readings* (Melbourne: Cheshire Press, 1963), pp. 384–389, specifying the features of "dependent economy" including the distinction between traded and nontraded goods. Dornbusch focuses exclusively on the effects of devaluation. The burden of his observations pertain to the interdependence of influences on a country's international payments position and, by extension, the expected effects of alternative policies.

8. Organization for Economic Cooperation and Development, "The International Transmission of Inflation," *OECD Economic Outlook,* special section (July 1973):81–96.

9. Helmut Frisch, "Inflation Theory 1963–1975: A 'Second Generation' Survey," *Journal of Economic Literature* 15 (December 1977):1289–1317.

10. Grant B. Taplin, "Models of World Trade," *IMF Staff Papers* 14 (November 1967):433–455.

11. Edward E. Leamer and Robert M. Stern, *Quantitative International Economics* (Boston: Allyn & Bacon, 1970).

12. Herbert B. Woolley, *Measuring Transactions Between World Areas* (New York: National Bureau of Economic Research, Studies in International Economic Relations, 1965) constructed such tables for 1950–1954, which required the verification of data from both importer and exporter for each transaction. W. Beckerman, "The World Trade Multiplier and the Stability of World Trade, 1938 to 1953," *Econometrica* 24 (1956):239–252, computed ratios of j's imports from i to j's total exports, with the purpose of identifying shifts in world trade form 1938 to 1953. This type of trade matrix makes it possible to examine comprehensively the nature and consequences of changes in market shares.

13. Uses of the trade matrix approach with greater emphasis on prediction have subsequently been presented by Jan Tinbergen, *Shaping the World Economy: Suggestions for an International Economic Policy* (New York: The Twentieth Century Fund, 1962); and Pentti Poyhonen, "A Tentative Model for the Volume of Trade Between Countries," *Weltwirtschaftliches Archiv*, band 15 (1963):93– 99. This type of model specifies the value of trade as a function of national income and of geographical distance. Income is an indicator of supply potential (for the exporter) and of market size and demand (for the importer). Tinbergen also includes continuity and trade-preference membership variables. Further extension of this model incorporates population of both importer and exporter as an added indication of market size [Hans Linneman, *An Econometric Study of International Trade Flows* (Amsterdam: North-Holland Publishing Co., 1966)]. Variations on this type of model have introduced prices as a means of examining the balance of payments implications of trade [J. Waelbroeck, "la demande extérieure et l'évolution des exportations belges," *Cahiers Économiques de Bruxelles* 15 (1962):397–412]. A successful synthesis is in Simon Kuznets, "Quantitative Aspects of the Economic Growth of Nations: Level and Structure of Foreign Trade: Comparison for Recent Years," *Economic Development and*

Cultural Change 13, part 2 (October 1964):1–106.

14. I. Richard Savage and Karl W. Deutsch, "A Statistical Model of the Gross Analysis of Transaction Flows," *Econometrica* 28 (1960):551–572.

15. L. A. Metzler, "A Multiple-Region Theory of Income and Trade," *Econometrica* 18 (1950):329–354.

16. Hans Neisser and Franco Modigliani, *National Incomes and International Trade: A Quantitative Analysis* (Urbana: University of Illinois Press, 1953).

17. J. J. Polak, *An International Economic System* (London: G. Allen & Unwin, 1954).

18. Rudolf R. Rhomberg, "A Short-term World Trade Model," (Paper presented at the First World Congress of the Econometric Society, Rome, 9–14, September 1945), summarized in *Econometrica* 34 (1966):90–91.

19. For example, Metzler, "A Multiple-Region Theory," specifies imports as a function of incomes. The patterns of trade, therefore, are dependent on the levels and change in levels of national income. The earlier Neisser and Modigliani model specifies imports and exports separately, each determined by the influence of income, prices, and capital flows. Polak, *International Economic System,* also views imports as a function of income. The implications of relations of this type were explored intensively for their insights and policy implications.

20. Much of this work is reported in Lawrence R. Klein and Vincent Su, "Protectionism: An Analysis from Project LINK," *Journal of Policy Modeling* 1 (1979):5–35. National models for thirteen advanced industrial countries have been developed, with similar analytical structures. This research effort tied country-specific econometric models into one overall system. There are also the models developed at the World Bank that are still regarded as experimental in nature but further develop the lines of world trade reviewed in Taplin, "Models of World Trade."

21. John E. Roemer, "The Effect of Sphere of Influence and Economic Distance on the Commodity Composition of Trade in Manufactures," *Review of Economics and Statistics* 59 (August 1977):318–327.

22. Ibid., p. 318.

23. Ibid., p. 327.

24. Charles P. Kindleberger, *Foreign Trade and the National Economy* (New Haven, Conn.: Yale University Press, 1964).

25. Albert O. Hirschman, *National Power and the Structure of Foreign Trade* (Berkeley: University of California Press, 1945).

26. Examples of such work include Michael Michaely, *Concentration in International Trade* (Amsterdam: North-Holland Publishing Co., 1962); James Caporaso, "Methodological Issues in the Measurement of Inequality, Dependence, and Exploitation," in Steven J. Rosen and James R. Kurth, eds., *Testing Theories of Economic Imperialism* (Lexington, Mass.: D. C. Heath & Co., 1974), pp. 87–115; and Raymond Duvall, Bruce Russett, Steven Jackson, Duncan Snidal, and David Sylvan, "A Formal Model of 'Dependencia' Theory: Structure, Measurement, and Some Preliminary Data" (Prepared for delivery at the Edinburgh IPSA Congress, August 1976).

27. David Ricardo, "The Principles of Political Economy and Taxation," vol.

1 in P. Sraffa, ed., *The Works and Correspondence of David Ricardo* (Cambridge: Cambridge University Press, 1962).

28. The political analysis was done by T. Baumgartner and T. R. Burns, "The Structuring of International Economic Relations," *International Studies Quarterly* 19 (June 1975):126–159. The economic analysis was done by S. Sideri, *Trade and Power: Informal Colonialism in Anglo-Portuguese Relations* (Rotterdam, Netherlands: Rotterdam University Press, 1970).

29. Richard S. Eckaus, "Is the IMF Guilty of Malpractice?" *Institutional Investor* 11 (September 1977):13–14.

30. See, for example, Douglas A. Hibbs, *Mass Political Violence: A Cross-National Causal Analysis* (New York: John Wiley & Sons, 1973); and Douglas A. Hibbs, *Economic Interest and the Politics of Macroeconomic Policy* (Cambridge, Mass.: Center for International Studies, M.I.T., January 1976).

31. David Hume, "Of the Balance of Trade," vol. 1 in *Essays Moral, Political and Literary* (London: Longmans Green, 1898), pp. 330–345.

32. Robert Gilpin, *U.S. Power and the Multinational Corporation: The Political Economy of Foreign Direct Investment* (New York: Basic Books, 1975).

33. Examples include Quincy Wright, *A Study of War,* 2nd ed. (Chicago: University of Chicago Press, 1965); and E. H. Carr, *The Twenty Years' Crisis, 1919–1939* (London: MacMillan, 1946).

34. Hans J. Morgenthau, *Politics Among Nations: The Struggle for Power and Peace,* 4th ed. (New York: Alfred A. Knopf, 1966), pp. 28–29.

35. Francis W. Hoole and Dina A. Zinnes, eds., *Quantitative International Politics: An Appraisal* (New York: Praeger Publishers, 1976).

36. Examples of the postbehavioral work include Robert C. North, *The World That Could Be* (Stanford, Calif.: The Portable Stanford, 1976); and Hayward R. Alker and Cheryl Christensen, "From Causal Modelling to Artificial Intelligence: The Evolution of a UN Peace-Making Simulation," in J. A. LaPonce and P. Smoker, eds., *Experimentation and Simulation in Political Science* (Toronto: University of Toronto Press, 1972), pp. 177–224.

37. The neo-mercantilist approach includes the following works: Gilpin, *U.S. Power and the Multinational Corporation*; Susan Strange, *Sterling and British Policy* (London: Oxford University Press, 1971); and Stephen D. Krasner, *Defending the National Interest: Raw Materials Investments and U.S. Foreign Policy* (Princeton, N.J.: Princeton University Press, 1978).

38. Integrationist works include: Ernst B. Haas, *Beyond the Nation-State: Functionalism and International Organization* (Stanford, Calif.: Stanford University Press, 1964); David Mitrany, *The Functional Theory of Politics* (New York: St. Martin's Press, 1975); and Karl W. Deutsch et al., *Political Community and the North Atlantic Area* (Princeton, N.J.: Princeton University Press, 1957).

39. Works in the interdependence field include: Hayward R. Alker, "A Methodology for Design Research on Interdependence Alternatives," *International Organization* 31 (Winter 1977):29–63; Hayward R. Alker and Nazli Choucri, *Analyzing Global Interdependence: Methodological Perspectives and Research Implications,* vol. 3 (Cambridge, Mass.: Center for International Studies,

M.I.T., 1974); Richard N. Cooper, *The Economics of Interdependence: Economy Policy in the Atlantic Community* (New York: McGraw-Hill Book Co., 1968); and Robert O. Keohane and Joseph S. Nye, Jr., *Power and Interdependence* (Boston: Little, Brown and Co., 1977).

40. Nazli Choucri (with Vincent Ferraro), *International Politics of Energy Interdependence* (Lexington, Mass.: Lexington Books, 1976). As pointed out by Alexander L. George in a personal communication, the term "constraint" includes variables that prevent a nation from behaving as it wishes, as well as factors that motivate a nation to behave in a certain way. Both usages are intended here.

41. Savage and Deutsch, "Analysis of Transaction Flows."

42. Choucri, *Energy Interdependence*.

43. The interdependence orientation is also responsible for the recent concern in political science for "eco-politics" and efforts to incorporate environmental constraints on the analysis of relations among nations [Dennis Clark Pirages, ed., *The Sustainable Society* (New York: Praeger Publishers, 1977); and Walt Anderson, ed., *Politics and Environment: A Reader in Ecological Crisis,* 2nd ed. (Pacific Palisades, Calif.: Goodyear, 1975)]. A schematic outline for such an orientation places emphasis on population, resources, and technology as three characteristics of state capability that determine the range of possible behaviors; see Nazli Choucri (with the assistance of James P. Bennet), "Population, Resources, Technology: Political Implications of the Environmental Crisis," in David A. Kay and Eugene B. Skolnikoff, eds., *World Eco-Crisis: International Organizations in Response* (Madison: University of Wisconsin Press, 1972), pp. 9–46. The debt of the "eco-politics" version of interdependence theory is to the earlier work of Sprout; see Harold Sprout and Margaret Sprout, *Foundations of International Politics* (Princeton, N.J.: Van Nostrand, 1962) and their recent restatement, i.e., Harold Sprout and Margaret Sprout, *Toward a Politics of the Planet Earth* (New York: Van Nostrand Reinhold Co., 1971). Another theoretical offshoot of the interdependence theories is more clearly related to aspects of economic theory, namely, that which focuses on multinational corporations and seeks to deduce their international political implications. See, for instance, Theodore H. Moran, *Multinational Corporations and the Politics of Interdependence: Copper in Chile* (Princeton, N.J.: Princeton University Press, 1974); Thomas J. Biersteker, *Distortion or Development? Contending Perspectives on the Multinational Corporation* (Cambridge, Mass.: M.I.T. Press, 1979); and Vincent A. Ferraro, "The Political Dynamics of International Resource Cartels: Case Studies of Petroleum and Copper" (Ph.D. diss. M.I.T., 1976). Primarily, the focus is on corporate influence, or degree of control, over political processes and political outcomes in their "host" countries, but not on the elements inducing changes in relations. The literature is descriptive rather than theoretical or predictive.

44. See, for example, Fernando Henrique Cardoso and Enzo Faletto, *Dependency and Development in Latin America* (Berkeley: University of California Press, 1979); Susanne Bodenheimer, "Dependency and Imperialism: The Roots of Latin American Underdevelopment," *Politics and Society* 1 (1971):327–359; Samir Amin, *Accumulation on a World Scale* (New York: Monthly Review,

1974); and Arghiri Emmanuel, *Unequal Exchange* (New York: Monthy Review, 1972).

45. Recent, more rigorous extensions include the works of Johan Galtung, "A Structural Theory of Imperialism," *Journal of Peace Research* 2 (1971):81–118; and James A. Caporaso, "Dependence, Dependency, and Power in the Global System: A Structural and Behavioral Analysis," *International Organization* 32 (Winter 1978):13–44.

46. Emmanuel, *Unequal Exchange.*

47. Duvall et al., "A Formal Model."

48. Hirschman, *National Power.*

49. Gilpin, *U.S. Power and the Multinational Corporation.*

50. International political position is meant to include capability as well as "power." See Hayward R. Alker, "On Political Capabilities in a Schedule Sense: Measuring Power, Integration, and Development," in Hayward R. Alker, Karl W. Deutsch, and Antoine H. Stoetzel, eds., *Mathematical Approaches to Politics* (Amsterdam: Elsevier, 1973), pp. 307–373.

51. C. Fred Bergsten, *The Dilemmas of the Dollar: The Economics and Politics of United States International Monetary Policy* (New York: New York University Press, 1975).

52. Ibid.; see also Eckaus, "Is the IMF Guilty of Malpractice?"

53. Analysts of international relations rarely, if ever, refer to a country's international trade, payments, or financial manifestations of overall national power in world politics. The few exceptions in the literature treat military and economic factors as two distinct dimensions of national power. For an exception, see Klaus Knorr, *Power of Nations: The Political Economy of International Relations* (New York: Basic Books, 1975).

54. Charles P. Kindleberger, "U.S. Foreign Economic Policy, 1776–1976," *Foreign Affairs* 55 (January 1977):395–417.

55. Nazli Choucri and Robert C. North, *Nations in Conflict: National Growth in International Violence* (San Francisco: W. H. Freeman and Co., 1975).

56. This is only partly consistent with Robert O. Keohane, "The Theory of Hegemonic Stability and Changes in International Economic Regimes, 1967–1977" in this volume.

57. The convention of using annual intervals in international analysis research conflicts with the economists' convention of employing quarterly data, clearly because of the differences in the data base employed and in the problems addressed. But in each case the characteristics of the data, not of the underlying theory, determine the choice of time frame and intervals. See Nazli Choucri "Forecasting in International Relations: Problems and Prospects," *International Interactions* 1 (1974):63–86.

58. The term "multilevel" should not be confused with "multivariate." A multivariate model is very simply one that includes more than one variable. However, a multilevel model implies not only a multivariate model, but one in which certain variables (or sets of variables) in the model are asymmetrically related. See Thomas Baumgartner, Thomas Burns, L. David Meeker, and Bradford Wild,

"Open Systems and Multi-Level Processes: Implications for Social Research," *International Journal of General Systems* 3 (1976):25–42.

59. J. David Singer, "The Level-of-Analysis Problem in International Relations," in Klaus Knorr and Sidney Verba, eds., *The International System: Theoretical Essays* (Princeton, N.J.: Princeton University Press, 1961), pp. 77–92.

6

ROBERT O. KEOHANE

The Theory of Hegemonic Stability and Changes in International Economic Regimes, 1967-1977

Background

In 1967 the world capitalist system, led by the United States, appeared to be working smoothly. Europe and Japan had recovered impressively from World War II and during the 1960s the United States had been enjoying strong, sustained economic growth as well. Both unemployment and inflation in seven major industrialized countries stood at an average of only 2.8 percent. International trade had been growing even faster than output, which was expanding at about 5 percent annually; and direct investment abroad was increasing at an even faster rate.[1] The Kennedy round of trade talks was successfully completed in June 1967; in the same month, the threat of an oil embargo by Arab countries in the wake of an Israeli-Arab war had been laughed off by the Western industrialized states. Fixed exchange rates prevailed; gold could still be obtained from the United States in exchange for dollars; and a prospective "international money," Special Drawing Rights (SDRs), was created in 1967 under the auspices of the International Monetary Fund (IMF). The United States, "astride the world like a colossus," felt confident enough of its power and position to deploy half a million men to settle the affairs of Vietnam. U.S. power and dynamism constituted the problem or the promise; "the American challenge" was global. Conservative and radical commentators alike regarded U.S. dominance as the central reality of contemporary world politics, although they differed as to whether its implications were benign or malign.[2]

A decade later the situation was very different. Unemployment rates in the West had almost doubled while inflation rates had increased almost threefold. Surplus capacity had appeared in the steel, textiles, and shipbuilding industries, and was feared in others.[3] Confidence that Keynesian policies could ensure uninterrupted growth had been undermined if not shattered. Meanwhile, the United States had been defeated in Vietnam and no longer seemed to have either the capability or inclination to extend its military domination to the far corners of the world. The inability of the United States to prevent or counteract the oil price increases of 1973–1974 seemed to symbolize the drastic changes that had taken place.

The decade after 1967 therefore provides an appropriate historical context for exploring recent developments in the world's political economy, and for testing some explanations of change.

What changes are observed, and how can they be accounted for in a politically sophisticated way? As the question suggests, this chapter has both a descriptive and an explanatory aspect. Descriptively, it examines changes between 1967 and 1977 in three issue areas: trade in manufactured goods, international monetary relations, and petroleum trade. The focus in each issue area is on the character of its *international regime* — that is, with the norms, rules, and procedures that guide the behavior of states and other important actors.[4] In each issue area an international regime can be identified as of 1967; and in each area identifiable changes in that regime took place during the following decade. These changes in regimes constitute the dependent variable of this study.

The explanatory portion of this chapter attempts to test a theory of "hegemonic stability," which posits that changes in the relative power resources available to major states will explain changes in international regimes. Specifically, it holds that hegemonic structures of power, dominated by a single country, are most conducive to the development of strong international regimes whose rules are relatively precise and well obeyed. According to the theory, the decline of hegemonic structures of power can be expected to presage a decline in the strength of corresponding international economic regimes.

It is necessary to explain more fully what is meant in this chapter by an "international regime," and to specify the criteria used here for the selection of a theory to account for regime change. The major changes that took place in each of the three regimes during the decade after 1967 will be briefly described before turning to the problem of explanation.

The Concept of International Regime

The concept of international regime can be relatively narrow and precise or quite elastic. Regimes in the narrow sense are defined by explicit rules, usually agreed to by governments at international conferences and often associated with formal international organizations. The International Telecommunications Union, for instance, supervises rules governing radio broadcasting. International commodity agreements have sometimes been characterized by explicit agreements about international price maintenance arrangements. The international monetary regime agreed to at Bretton Woods, which came fully into force at the end of 1958, was characterized by explicit rules mandating pegged exchange rates and procedures for consultation if exchange rates were to be changed. With some exceptions these rules were respected by governments during the early- to mid-1960s. The nondiscriminatory reciprocal trade regime of the General Agreement on Tariffs and Trade (GATT) contains rules about which governmental measures affecting trade are permitted, and which are prohibited, by international agreement. Each successive trade negotiation adds to the list of rules, although some of the old rules have decayed over time.

The definition of regime employed in this chapter, however, is more elastic than this relatively precise and rule-oriented version. The focus is less on institutionalization and rule development than on patterns of regularized cooperative behavior in world politics. Therefore this chapter includes as regimes those arrangements for issue areas that embody implicit rules and norms insofar as they actually guide behavior of important actors in a particular issue area. The distinction between explicit and implicit rules is less important than the distinction between strong regimes — in which predictable, orderly behavior takes place according to a set of standards understood by participants — and weak ones — in which rules are interpreted differently or broken by participants. Explicit regimes may be stronger than implicit ones, but this is not always the case, as indicated by the weakness of the international monetary regime between 1971 and 1976 despite the fact that the rules of Bretton Woods still remained nominally in force.

By this definition, there have not only been international regimes for money and trade during the postwar period, but there has also been an international regime governing the production for export, and the pricing, of oil. In 1967 this regime was dominated by the major international oil companies and their home governments, and the norms emphasized maintaining cooperation among the companies (through a variety of joint agreements, especially with respect to production), acting to maintain barriers to entry by new producers, limiting price competition (with increasing difficulty as the industry became somewhat less concentrated), and refraining from competing with one another vis à vis the host governments, in order to avoid bidding up the price of concessions or the host governments' share of the profits.[5] In 1977 the regime for oil was quite different: its norms had been developed by oil-producing governments largely within the framework of the Organization of Petroleum Exporting Countries (OPEC), with the strongest norm being the injunction not to sell oil so far, or so massively, below the official OPEC price that the cartel structure would be threatened. For both 1967 and 1977 operative norms can be identified and therefore it can be asserted that an international regime existed, although patterns of behavior may have been more orderly and predictable in 1967 than in 1977.

The concept of international regime enables a coherent analysis of changes in world politics. Rather than on an explanation of particular events, in which idiosyncratic and frequently random factors have played a role, the focus is on a pattern of events—not on particular bargaining outcomes but on what a pattern of bargaining outcomes reveals about implicit norms and rules in world politics. Fragments of political behavior take on additional meaning when thought of in terms of regimes: they are part of a larger mosaic, a context within which they become intelligible.[6] In this larger mosaic, accidental factors and improbable events become less important, since the focus is on a pattern of behavior and overall trends rather than on one particular event or another. Having identified the international regime and described how it has changed, we can then proceed to the second, more difficult analytical task—to account for these changes in terms of deeper political and economic forces. Describing changes in regimes provides interpretive richness for the analysis of political behavior; attempts to explain these changes may lead to insights about causal patterns.

The emphasis in the study of international regimes has usually been on their creation—how and under what conditions they developed. Here, however, stress must necessarily be placed on the dis-integration of international regimes. Can their collapse in theoretically interesting ways be explained? For policymakers, periods of stress are threatening and difficult; for students of world politics, however, they provide opportunities for insights into change.

Explaining Changes in International Regimes

This chapter attempts to account for changes in international regimes over time. It therefore poses different questions from those of the literature on comparative foreign policy, particularly comparative foreign economic policy, which seeks to account for cross-national variation in policy historically as well as at similar points in time.[7] Assuming that such policy variation exists without trying to explain it, we focus here on the international regimes that result from political bargaining among governments.

Changes in international economic regimes could in principle be explained by either domestic or international developments or by some combination of the two. Shifts in the policies or constitutional status of national governments can be extremely important — elections, coups d'état, and social revolutions may change the orientation of major states toward the world economy and therefore affect international economic regimes. The coming to power of fascist regimes in Italy, Japan, and Germany during the interwar period certainly helped (along with other factors) to push the world toward autarchic and semiautarchic arrangements during the 1930s. The Iranian revolution of 1978–1979 has exerted significant effects, at least in the short run, on the international petroleum regime; and there is little doubt that a nationalist-fundamentalist revolution or coup in Saudi Arabia would have more profound and far-reaching implications.

From a theoretical standpoint, however, explanations of regime change based on domestic politics would encounter serious problems. So many potentially important causal factors become potentially important that one can no longer construct a parsimonious model that facilitates interpretation and anticipation (if not prediction) of events. Sickness or assassination of a ruler, the revival of fundamentalist values, or failure in war can lead to changes in national policies affecting international regimes. Since many of these phenomena represent unique events involving large elements of chance they cannot be intelligently incorporated into a theory. In principle, therefore, it is impossible to obtain a complete theory of international economic regime without developing an integrated theory of national and international politics.

The search for theoretical completeness would therefore lead to descriptive anarchy: investigation of domestic political reasons for international regime change could easily lead to an increasingly diffuse set of ad hoc observations about particular cases. The result would be a theoretical inductivism in which "additional variables" were added to the account at will. If we wish to build theory, it makes more sense to proceed in the opposite way, by constructing a relatively parsimonious theory that purports to explain relevant phenomena through the use of propositions linking a small number of variables to one another. Such a theory will not account perfectly for the observed changes — after all, the independent variables will not include the personalities of either a de Gaulle or an Ayatollah Khomeini — but it should correctly explain tendencies and directions of change. Whether it does so — not whether it accounts for every perturbation or crisis — is the test of its theoretical adequacy.[8]

A parsimonious theory of international regime change has recently been developed by a number of authors, notably Charles Kindleberger, Robert Gilpin, and Stephen Krasner. According to this theory, strong international economic regimes depend on hegemonic power. Fragmentation of power between competing countries leads to fragmentation of the international economic regime; concentration of power contributes to stability.[9] Hegemonic powers have the capabilities to maintain international regimes that they favor. They may use coercion to enforce adherence to rules; or they may rely largely on positive sanctions — the provision of benefits to those who cooperate. Both hegemonic powers and the smaller states may have incentives to collaborate in maintaining a regime — the hegemonic power gains the ability to shape and dominate its international environment, while providing a sufficient flow of benefits to small and middle powers to persuade them to acquiesce. Some international regimes can be seen partially as collective goods, whose benefits (such as stable money) can be consumed by all participants without detracting from others' enjoyment of them. Insofar as this is the case, economic theory leads us to expect that extremely large, dominant countries will be particularly willing to provide these goods, while relatively small participants will attempt to secure "free rides" by avoiding proportionate shares of payment. International systems with highly skewed distributions of capabilities will therefore tend to be more amply supplied with such collective goods than systems characterized by equality among actors.[10]

The particular concern of this chapter is the erosion of international economic regimes. The hegemonic stability theory seeks sources of erosion in changes in the relative capabilities of states. As the distribution of tangible resources, especially economic resources, becomes more equal, international regimes should weaken. One reason for this is that the capabilities of the hegemonial power will decline — it will become less capable of enforcing rules against unwilling participants, and it will have fewer resources with which to entice or bribe other states into remaining within the confines of the regime. Yet the incentives facing governments will also change. As the hegemonial state's margin of resource superiority over its partners declines, the costs of leadership will become more burdensome. Enforcement of rules will be more difficult and side payments will seem less justifiable. Should other states — now increasingly strong economic rivals — not have to contribute their "fair shares" to the collective enterprise? The hegemon (or former hegemon) is likely to seek to place additional burdens on its allies. At the same time, the incentives of the formerly subordinate secondary states will change. They will not only become more capable of reducing their support for the regime; they may acquire new interests in doing so. On the one hand, they will perceive the possibility of rising above their subordinate status, and they may even glimpse the prospect of reshaping the international regime in order better to suit their own interests. On the other hand, they may begin to worry that their efforts (and those of others) in chipping away at the hegemonial power and its regime may be too successful — that the regime itself may collapse. This fear, however, may lead them to take further action to hedge their bets, reducing their reliance on the hegemonial regime and perhaps attempting to set up alternative arrangements of their own.

As applied to the last century and a half, this theory — which will be referred to as the "hegemonic stability" theory — does well at identifying apparently necessary conditions for strong international economic regimes, but poorly at establishing sufficient conditions. International economic regimes have been most orderly and predictable where there was a single hegemonic state in the world system: Britain during the mid-nineteenth century in trade and until 1914 in international financial affairs; the United States after 1945. Yet although tangible U.S. power resources were large during the interwar period, international economic regimes were anything but orderly. High inequality of capabilities was not, therefore, a sufficient condition for strong international regimes; there was in the case of the United States a lag between its attainment of capabilities and its acquisition of a willingness to exert leadership, or of a taste for domination depending on point of view.[11]

The concern here is not with the validity of the hegemonic stability theory throughout the last 150 years, but with its ability to account for changes in international economic regimes during the decade between 1967 and 1977. Since the United States remained active during those years as the leading capitalist country, the problem of "leadership lag" does not exist, which raises difficulties for the interpretation of the interwar period. Thus the theory should apply to the 1967–1977 period. Insofar as "potential economic power" (Krasner's term) became more equally distributed — reducing the share of the United States — during the 1960s and early to mid-1970s, U.S.-created and U.S.-centered international economic regimes should also have suffered erosion or decline.

The hegemonic stability thesis is a power-as-resources theory, which attempts to link tangible state capabilities (conceptualized as "power resources") to behavior. In its simplest form, it is what James G. March calls a "basic force model" in which outcomes reflect the potential power (tangible and known capabilities) of actors. Basic force models typically fail to predict accurately particular political outcomes, in part because differential opportunity costs often lead competing actors to use different proportions of their potential power. Yet they offer clearer and more easily interpretable explanations than "force activation models," which incorporate assumptions about differential exercise of power.[12] Regarding tendencies rather than particular decisions, they are especially useful in establishing a baseline, a measure of what can be accounted for by the very parsimonious theory that tangible resources are directly related to outcomes, in this case to the nature of international regimes. The hegemonic stability theory, which is systemic and parsimonious, therefore seems to constitute a useful starting point for analysis, on the assumption that it is valuable to see how much can be learned from simple explanations before proceeding to more complex theoretical formulations.

Ultimately, it will be necessary to integrate systemic analysis with explanations at the level of foreign policy. Domestic forces help to explain changes in the international political structure; changes in the international political structure affect domestic institutions and preferences.[13] This chapter focuses only on one part of the overall research problem: the relationship between international structure and international regimes. It examines to what extent changes in recent international economic regimes can be accounted for by changes in international power distributions within the relevant issue areas.

Changes in International Economic Regimes, 1967–1977

The dependent variable in this analysis is international regime change between 1967 and 1977 in three issue areas: international monetary relations, trade in manufactured goods, and the production and sale of petroleum. These are not the only important areas of international economic activity — for example, foreign investment is not included — but they are among the most important.[14] Descriptive contentions about international regime change in the three chosen areas are that (1) all three international regimes existing in 1967 became weaker during the subsequent decade; (2) this weakening was most pronounced in the petroleum area and in monetary relations, where the old norms were destroyed and very different practices emerged — it was less sudden and less decisive in the field of trade; and (3) in the areas of trade and money, the dominant political coalitions supporting the regime remained largely the same, although in money certain countries (especially Saudi Arabia) were added to the inner "club," whereas in the petroleum issue area, power shifted decisively from multinational oil companies and governments of major industrialized countries to producing governments. Taking all three dimensions into account, it is clear that regime change was most pronounced during the decade in oil and least pronounced in trade in manufactured goods, with the international monetary regime occupying an intermediate position.

These descriptive contentions will now be briefly documented and then interpreted, inquiring about the extent to which the hegemonic stability theory accounts for these changes in international economic regimes.

The international trade regime of the General Agreement on Tariffs and Trade was premised on the principles of reciprocity, liberalization, and nondiscrimination. Partly as a result of its success, world trade had increased since 1950 at a much more rapid rate than world production. Furthermore, tariff liberalization was continuing: in mid-1967 the Kennedy round was successfully completed, substantially reducing tariffs on a wide range of industrial products. Yet despite its obvious successes, the GATT trade regime in 1967 was already showing signs of stress. The reciprocity and nondiscrimination provisions of GATT were already breaking down. Tolerance for illegal trade restrictions had grown, few formal complaints were being processed, and by 1967 GATT did not even require states maintaining illegal quantitative restrictions to obtain formal waivers of the rules. The "general breakdown in GATT legal affairs" had gone very far indeed, largely as a result of toleration of illegal restrictions such as the variable levy of the European Economic Community (EEC), EEC association agreements, and export subsidies.[15] In addition, nontariff barriers, which were not dealt with effectively by GATT codes, were becoming more important. The trade regime in 1967 was thus strongest in the area of tariff liberalization, but less effective on nontariff barriers or in dealing with discrimination.

In the decade ending in 1967 the international monetary regime was explicit, formally institutionalized, and highly stable. Governments belonging to the International Monetary Fund were to maintain official par values for their currencies, which could be changed only to correct a "fundamental disequilibrium" and only in consultation with the IMF. During these nine years, the rules were largely followed; parity changes for major currencies were few and minor.[16] In response to large U.S. deficits in its overall liquidity balance of payments, the U.S. government introduced an Interest Equalization Tax in 1963 and voluntary capital controls in 1965; in addition, a variety of ingenious if somewhat ephemeral expedients had been devised, both to improve official U.S. balance of payments statements and to provide for cooperative actions by central banks or treasuries to counteract the effects of destabilizing capital flows. Until November 1967 even British devaluation (seen by many as imminent in 1964) had been avoided. Nevertheless, as in trade, signs of weakness in the system were apparent. U.S. deficits had to a limited extent already undermined confidence in the dollar; and the United States was fighting a costly war in Vietnam which it was attempting to finance without tax increases at home. Consequentially, inflation was increasing in the United States.[17]

The international regime for oil was not explicitly defined by intergovernmental agreement in 1967. There was no global international organization supervising the energy regime. Yet, as mentioned above, the governing arrangements for international oil production and trade were rather clear. With the support of their home governments, the major international oil companies cooperated to control production and, within limits, price. The companies were unpopular in the host countries, and these host country governments put the companies on the defensive on particular issues, seeking increased revenue or increased control. However, as Turner puts it, "the critical fact is that the companies did not really lose control of their relationship with host governments until the 1970s, when the concessionary system finally came close to being swept away. The long preceding decade of the 1960s had seen only minimal improvement for the host governments in the terms under which the majors did business with them."[18] The companies retained superior financial resources and capabilities in production, transportation, and marketing that the countries could not attain. Furthermore, the companies possessed superior information: "Whatever the weakness of company defences which is apparent in retrospect, the host governments did not realize it at the time. Their knowledge of the complexities of the industry was scanty, their experience of serious bargaining with the companies was limited and their awe of the companies was great."[19]

In addition, and perhaps most important, the feudal and semifeudal elites that controlled many oil-producing countries until the end of the 1960s were more often concerned with their personal and family interests than with modernization or national interests on a larger scale.

Although the U.S. government did not participate directly in oil production or trade, it was the most influential actor in the system. The United States had moved decisively during and after World War II to ensure that U.S. companies would continue to control Saudi Arabian oil.[20] Later, when the Anglo-Iranian Oil Company became unwelcome as sole concessionaire in Iran, the United States sponsored an arrangement by which U.S. firms received 40 percent of the consortium established in the wake of the U.S.-sponsored coup that overthrew Premier Mossadegh and restored the shah to his throne.[21] U.S. tax policy was changed in 1950 to permit U.S. oil companies to increase payments to producing governments without sacrificing profits, thus solidifying the U.S. position in the Middle East and Venezuela.[22] The United States had provided military aid and political support to the rulers of Saudi Arabia and Iran, maintaining close relations with them throughout the first two postwar decades (except for the Mossadegh period in Iran). And in case of trouble—as in 1956–1957—the United States was willing to use its own reserves to supply Europe with petroleum.[23] The governing arrangements for oil thus reflected the U.S. government's interests in an ample supply of oil at stable or declining prices, close political ties with conservative Middle Eastern governments, and profits for U.S.-based multinational companies.

The international economic regime of 1977 looked very different. Least affected was the trade regime, although even here important changes had taken place. Between 1967 and 1977, nontariff barriers to trade continued to proliferate, and the principle of nondiscrimination was further undermined. Restrictions on textile imports from less developed countries, originally limited to cotton textiles, were extended to woolen and manmade fabrics in 1974.[24] Nontariff barriers affecting world steel trade in the early 1970s included import licensing, foreign exchange restrictions, quotas, export limitations, domestic-biased procurement, subsidies, import surcharges, and antidumping measures.[25] During the 1970s, "voluntary" export restraints, which had covered about one-eighth of U.S. imports in 1971, were further extended.[26] In late 1977, the United States devised a "trigger price system" to help protect the U.S. steel industry from low-priced imports. Contemporaneously, the European Economic Community launched an ambitious program to protect and rationalize some of its basic industries afflicted with surplus but relatively inefficient capacity, such as steel and shipbuilding. On the basis of a general survey, the GATT secretariat estimated tentatively in 1977 that import restrictions introduced or seriously threatened by industrially advanced countries since 1974 would affect 3–5 percent of world trade—$30 to $50 billion. The stresses on the international trade system, according to the director-general of GATT, "have now become such that they seriously threaten the whole fabric of postwar cooperation in international trade policy."[27]

Nevertheless, the weakening of some aspects of the international trade regime had not led, by the end of 1977, to reductions in trade or to trade wars; in fact, after a 4 percent decline in 1975, the volume of world trade rose 11 percent in 1976 and 4 percent in 1977.[28] Furthermore, by 1977 the Tokyo round of trade negotiations was well underway; in 1979 agreement was reached on trade liberalizing measures that not only would (if put into effect) reduce tariffs on industrial products, but that would also limit or prohibit a wide range on nontariff barriers, including export subsidies, national preferences on government procurement, and excessively complex import licensing procedures.[29] The weakening of elements of the old regime was therefore accompanied both by expanding trade (although at a lower rate than before 1973) and by efforts to strengthen the rules in a variety of areas.

By 1977 the international monetary regime had changed much more dramatically. The pegged-rate regime devised at Bretton Woods had collapsed in 1971, and its jerry-built successor had failed in 1973. Since then, major currencies had been floating against one another, their values affected both by market forces and frequently extensive governmental intervention. In 1976 international agreement was reached on amendments to the Articles of Agreement of the International Monetary Fund, yet this did not return the world to stable international exchange rates or multilateral rule making but merely provided for vaguely defined "multilateral surveillance" of floating exchange rates. Exchange rates have fluctuated quite sharply at times, and have certainly been more unpredictable than they were in the 1960s. Substantial secular changes have also taken place; nominal effective exchange rates on 15 May 1978, as a percentage of the rates prevailing in March 1973, ranged from 58.6 for Italy to 130.0 for Germany and 154.2 for Switzerland.[30]

In the oil area, the rules of the old regime were shattered between 1967 and 1977, as power shifted dramatically from the multinational oil companies and home governments (especially the United States and Britain), on the one hand, to producing countries' governments, on the other. The latter, organized since 1960 in the Organization of Petroleum Exporting Countries, secured a substantial price rise in negotiations at Teheran in 1971, then virtually quadrupled prices without negotiation after the Yom Kippur War of October 1973. Despite some blustering and various vague threats the United States could do little directly about this, although high rates of inflation in industrial countries and the decline of the dollar in 1977 helped to reduce substantially the real price of oil between 1974 and 1977.[31] By 1977 the United States had apparently conceded control of the regime for oil pricing and production to OPEC, and particularly to its key member, Saudi Arabia. OPEC made the rules in 1977, influenced (but not controlled) by the United States. Only in case of a crippling supply embargo would the United States be likely to act. The United States was still, with its military and economic strength, an influential actor, but it was no longer dominant.

Reviewing this evidence about three international economic regimes supports the generalizations offered earlier. Although all three old regimes became weaker during the decade, this was most pronounced for oil and money, least for trade. In oil, furthermore, dominant coalitions changed as well, so that by 1977 the regime that existed, dominated by OPEC countries, was essentially a *new regime*. The old petroleum regime had disappeared. By contrast, the 1977 trade regime was still a recognizable version of the regime existing in 1967; and the international monetary regime of 1977, although vastly different than in 1967, retained the same core of supportive states along with the same international organization, the IMF, as its monitoring agent. Since the rules had changed, the function of the IMF had also changed; but it persisted as an element, as well as a symbol, of continuity. In the oil area, the emergence of the International Energy Agency (IEA) after the oil embargo symbolized discontinuity: only after losing control of the pricing-production regime did it become necessary for the industrialized countries to construct their own formal international organization.

The Theory of Hegemonic Stability and International Regime Change

It should be apparent from the above account that a theory purporting to explain international economic regime change between 1967 and 1977 faces two tasks: first, to account for the *general pattern* of increasing weakness, and second, to explain why the oil regime experienced the most serious changes, followed by money and trade. Furthermore, the hegemonic stability theory must show not only a correspondence between patterns of regime change and changes in tangible power resources, but it must be possible to provide at least a plausible account of how those resource changes could have caused the regime changes that we observe.

The most parsimonious version of a hegemonic stability theory would be that changes in the *overall* international economic structure account for the changes in international regimes that we have described. Under this interpretation, a decline in U.S. economic power (as measured crudely by gross domestic product) would be held responsible for changes in international economic regimes. Power in this view would be seen as a fungible set of tangible economic resources that can be used for a variety of purposes in world politics.

There are conceptual as well as empirical problems with this parsimonious overall structure theory. The notion that power resources are fungible—that they can be allocated to issues as policymakers choose, without losing efficacy — is not very plausible in world political economy. As David Baldwin has recently argued, this theory fails to specify the context within which specific resources may be useful: "What functions as a power resource in one policy-contingency framework may be irrelevant in another. The only way to determine whether something is a power resource or not is to place it in the context of a real or hypothetical policy-contingency framework."[32] A second problem with the overall structure version of the hegemonic stability thesis is itself contextual: since we have to account not only for the general pattern of increasing weakness but also for differential pattens by issue area, focusing on a single independent variable will clearly not suffice. Changes in the overall U.S. economic position will clearly not explain different patterns of regime change in different issue areas.

Table 6.1 indicates the gross domestic product of the United States and the five other major market economy countries. As the last column indicates, the U.S. share of gross domestic product (GDP) of all five countries fell between 1960 and 1975 from about two-thirds to about one-half of the total five-country GDP. This is consistent with the hegemonic stability thesis, although one can question whether such a moderate decline (leaving the United States more than triple the economic size of its nearest competitor) accounts very convincingly for the regime changes that have been observed.

To explain different patterns of regime change in different issue areas, a differentiated, issue-specific version of the hegemonic stability thesis has greater value than the overall structure version. According to this view, declines in resources available to the United States for use in a given issue area should be closely related to the weakening of the international regime (*circa* 1967) in that area. Specifically, the least evidence of

TABLE 6.1
Distribution of Overall Economic Resources Among the Five Major
Market-Economy Countries, 1960-1975
(Gross Domestic Product in Billions of Current U.S. Dollars)

Year	United States	Germany	Britain	France	Japan	U.S. as Percent of Top Five Countries
1960	507	72	71	61	43	67
1963	594	95	85	83	68	64
1970	981	185	122	141	197	60
1975	1526	419	229	335	491	51

Source: United Nations Statistical Yearbook, 1977, pp. 742-744.
Last column calculated from these figures.

structural change should be found in the trade area, an intermediate amount in international monetary relations, and the most in petroleum. This correspondence between changes in the independent and dependent variables would lend support to the theory. To establish the theory of a firmer basis, however, it would be necessary to develop a plausible causal argument based on the hegemonic stability theory for the issue areas and regimes under scrutiny here.

Table 6.2 summarizes the evidence about changes in the distribution of economic power resources in the areas of trade, money, and petroleum. For trade and money the same comparative measures are used, similar to those used in Table 6.1: the U.S. proportion of resources is compared to that of the top five market-economy countries taken as a group. This measure can be justified on the grounds that only Germany, Britain, France and Japan were strong enough during this period to consider challenging the United States or attempting to thwart it in significant ways; they are the potential rivals against whom it is significant to measure U.S. resources. The measures have to be somewhat different for petroleum. The relevant resources here appear to be U.S. imports vs. excess production capacity (since in 1956–1957 and 1967 the United States helped to maintain the existing regime by shipping oil to Europe from its own wells), and oil imports as a percentage of energy supply, giving a measure of relative U.S. and European dependence on imports.[33]

None of these measures of "economic power" is perfect; indeed, they are quite crude. Often the composition of exports, for instance, may be as important as the amount; and the balance of trade may in some cases weigh as heavily as the combination of imports and exports. Probably most deficient is the monetary measure, since reserves are not necessarily an indication of a country's *net* position. Measures of the U.S. net liquidity position, however, would also show a sharp decline.[34]

The figures on economic resources provide prima facie support for the hegemonic stability thesis. The U.S. proportion of trade, for the top five market-economy countries, fell only slightly between 1960 and 1975 — much less than its proportion of gross domestic product, reflecting the rapid increases during these years in U.S. trade as a proportion of total product. As we saw, the international trade regime — already under pressure in 1967 — changed less in the subsequent decade than the regimes for money and oil. U.S. financial resources in the form of reserves fell sharply, reflecting the shift from U.S. dominance in 1960 to the struggles over exchange rates of the 1970s. In view of the continued ability of the United States to finance its deficits with newly printed dollars and treasury bills rather than with reserves, Table 6.2B should not be overinterpreted: it does *not* mean that Germany was "twice as powerful as the

TABLE 6.2
Distribution of Economic Resources, by Issue Area, Among the Five Major
Market-Economy Countries, 1960-1975

A. Trade Resources (exports plus imports as percentage of world trade)

Year	United States	Germany	Britain	France	Japan	U.S. as Percent of Top Five Countries
1960	13.4	8.1	8.7	4.9	3.3	35
1965	14.4	9.4	8.0	5.7	4.2	35
1970	15.0	11.0	6.9	6.3	6.2	33
1975	13.0	10.0	5.8	6.4	6.6	31

Source: Kenneth N. Waltz, Theory of International Politics (Reading, Mass.:
Addison-Wesley, 1979), Appendix Table IV, p. 215.
Last column calculated from these figures.

B. Monetary Resources (reserves as percentage of world reserves)

Year	United States	Germany	Britain	France	Japan	U.S. as Percent of Top Five Countries
1960	32.4	11.8	6.2	3.8	3.3	56
1965	21.8	10.5	4.2	9.0	3.0	45
1970	15.5	10.7	3.0	5.3	5.2	39
1975	7.0	13.6	2.4	5.5	5.6	21

Source: Calculated from International Financial Statistics (Washington:
IMF), Volume XXXI-5 (May, 1978), 1978 Supplement, pp. 34-35.
Last column calculated from these percentages.

United States" in the monetary area by 1975. Yet it does, as indicated
above, signal a very strong shift in the resource situation of the United
States. Finally, the petroleum figures — especially in Table 6.2, C-1 — are
dramatic: the United States went from a large positive position in 1956
and a small positive position in 1967 to a very large petroleum deficit by
1973. The hegemonic stability theory accurately predicts from this data
that U.S. power in the oil area and the stability of the old international
oil regime would decline sharply during the 1970s.

These findings lend plausibility to the hegemonic stability theory by
not disconfirming its predictions. They do not, however, establish its
validity, even for this limited set of issues over one decade. It is also
necessary, before concluding that the theory accounts for the observed
changes, to see whether plausible causal sequences can be constructed

Table 6.2 (cont.)

C. Petroleum Resources

1. United States imports and excess production capacity in three crisis years

Year	U.S. Oil Imports as Percent of Oil Consumption	U.S. Excess Production Capacity as Percent of Oil Consumption	Net U.S. Position
1956	11	25	+14
1967	19	25	+6
1973	35	10	-25

Source: Joel Darmstadter and Hans H. Landsberg, "The Economic Background," in Raymond Vernon, ed., The Oil Crisis, special issue of Daedalus, Fall, 1975 (pp. 30-31).

2. Oil Imports as percentage of energy supply

Year	United States	Western Europe	Japan	Ratio of U.S. to European Dependence
1967	9	50	62	.18
1970	10	57	73	.18
1973	17	60	80	.28
1976	20	54	74	.37

Source: Kenneth N. Waltz, Theory of International Politics (Reading, Mass.: Addison-Wesley, 1979), Appendix Table X, p. 221.
Last column calculated from these figures.

linking shifts in the international distribution of power to changes in international regimes. The following sections of this paper therefore consider the most plausible and well-founded particular accounts of changes in our three issue areas, to see whether the causal arguments in these accounts are consistent with the hegemonic stability theory. The ensuing discussion begins with oil, since it fits the theory so well, and then addresses the more difficult cases.

Interpreting Changes in the Petroleum Regime

The transformation in oil politics between 1967 and 1977 resulted from a change in the hegemonic coalition making the rules and supporting the regime: OPEC countries, particularly Saudi Arabia, replaced the Western powers, led by the United States. OPEC members had previously lacked the ability to capture monopolistic profits by forming a producers' cartel. In part, this reflected low self-confidence. Poor communications and a low level of information about one another also played a role, although both were already being corrected by greater elite sophistication and more intensive contacts among OPEC members. Yet OPEC's impotence was also a result, in the 1950s and 1960s, of overwhelming U.S. power. Until the huge asymmetry between U.S. power and that of the OPEC members was reduced or reversed, massive changes in the implicit regime could not be expected to occur. Without these changes, neither foolish U.S. tactics nor an Israeli-Arab war could have led to the price rises observed in February 1971, or October–December 1973.[35]

U.S. military power vis-à-vis Middle Eastern members of OPEC was lower in the late 1960s and early 1970s than it had been before the entry of Russia into the Middle East in 1955; but it is not clear that U.S. military power declined dramatically between 1967 and the oil crisis of 1973. Yet fundamental shifts in available petroleum supplies were taking place. When previous oil crises had threatened in the wake of Arab-Israeli wars in 1956 and 1967, the United States was able to compensate by increasing domestic production, since about 25 percent of its oil-producing capacity was not being used prior to each crisis. In 1973 U.S. spare capacity had declined to about 10 percent of the total. In 1956 U.S. imports were only about 11 percent of consumption, mostly from Venezuela and Canada; in 1967 they constituted 19 percent; but by 1973 they amounted to over 35 percent, a substantial proportion of which came from the Middle East. U.S. proved reserves had fallen from 18.2 to 6.4 percent of world proved reserves.[36] In the earlier situations, the United States could be "part of the solution"; in 1973, it was "part of the problem." Its fundamental petroleum resource base had been greatly weakened.

The hegemonic stability model leads us to expect a change in international petroleum arrangements during the mid-1970s: The dominance of the United States and other industrialized countries was increasingly being undermined, as OPEC members gained potential power resources at their expense. What the Yom Kippur War did was to make the Arab members of OPEC willing to take greater risks. When their actions succeeded in quadrupling the price of oil almost overnight, mutual confidence rose that members of the cartel who cut back production would not be "double-crossed" by other producers, but would rather benefit from the externalities (high prices as a result of supply shortages) created by others' similar actions. Calculations about externalities became positive and risks fell. A self-reinforcing cycle of underlying resource strength leading to success, to increased incentives to cooperate, and to greater strength was launched.

Interpreting Changes in the International Monetary Regime

The breakdown of the Bretton Woods pegged-rate monetary system is usually attributed by economists principally to two factors. First is the inherent instability of a gold-exchange standard, which Benjamin J. Cohen describes, with reference to the 1960s, as follows:

> A gold-exchange standard is built on the illusion of convertibility of its fiduciary element into gold at a fixed price. The Bretton Woods system, though, was relying on deficits in the U.S. balance of payments to avert a world liquidity shortage. Already, America's "overhang" of overseas liabilities to private and official foreigners was growing larger than its gold stock at home. The progressive deterioration of the U.S. net reserve position, therefore, was bound in time to undermine global confidence in the dollar's continued convertibility. In effect, governments were caught on the horns of a dilemma. To forestall speculation against the dollar, U.S. deficits would have to cease. But this would confront governments with the liquidity problem. To forestall the liquidity problem, U.S. deficits would have to continue. But this would confront governments with the confidence problem. Governments could not have their cake and eat it too.[37]

This situation would have made the international monetary system of the 1960s quite delicate under the best of circumstances. As a response to it during the 1960s, negotiations took place to create Special Drawing Rights, designed to provide a source of international liquidity to serve in lieu of dollars when the U.S. deficit came to an end. Whether this reform would have been effective, however, is unclear because the conditions that it was meant to deal with never came into being. Rather than eliminating its deficit, the United States let its balance of payments on current account deteriorate sharply in the last half of the 1960s, as a result of increased military spending to fight the Vietnam War, coupled with a large fiscal deficit, excess demand in the United States, and the inflationary momentum that resulted. When U.S. monetary policy turned from restriction to ease in 1970, in reaction to a recession, huge capital outflows took place. The U.S. decision of August 1971 to suspend the convertibility of the dollar into gold and thus to force a change in the Bretton Woods regime followed. An agreement reached in December 1971 to restore fixed exchange rates collapsed under the pressure of monetary expansion in the United States and abroad and large continuing U.S. deficits, which reached a total (on an official settlements basis) of over $50 billion during the years 1970-1973.[38]

As this account suggests, the collapse of the international monetary regime in 1971-1973 was in part a result of the inherent instability of gold-exchange systems; but the proximate cause was U.S. economic policy, devised in response to the exigencies of fighting an unpopular and costly war in Vietnam. The hegemonic stability theory does not account for either the long-run entropy of regimes resting on both gold and foreign exchange or policy failures by the U.S. government. Yet in at least a narrow sense the theory is consistent with events: the Bretton Woods regime collapsed only after U.S. reserves had fallen sharply, which contributed to the difficulty of maintaining the value of the dollar at the old exchange rates.

The hegemonic stability theory is thus not disconfirmed by the monetary case. For several reasons, however, it functions as a highly unsatisfactory explanation of regime change in the monetary area. In the first place, the resources that were most important to the United States to maintain the regime were not tangible resources (emphasized by the theory) but the symbolic resources that go under the name of "confidence" in discussion of international financial affairs. U.S. reserves were less important than confidence in U.S. policy: as a reserve-currency country, the United States could generate more international money (dollars), as long as holders of dollars believed that the dollar would retain value compared to alternative assets, such as other currencies or gold. By 1970-1971, however, confidence in U.S. economic policy, and hence in the dollar, had become severely undermined, and after August 1971 became impossible to restore.

The second major problem with the hegemonic stability theory's explanation of the monetary case is that it focuses on a variable—U.S. resources in the monetary area—which was itself largely a result of U.S. policy. The theory, as indicated earlier, is systemic: but the most important sources of change (*reflected* in resource shifts) lay within the U.S. polity. To some extent, of course, this was true in the oil areas as well, since the United States could have conserved its oil resources during the 1950s and 1960s; but it is particularly important in monetary politics, since confidence depended on evaluations of U.S.-policy and expectations about it. Perceptions of U.S. economic policy as inflationary thus translated directly into loss of intangible U.S. resources (confidence on the part of foreigners) through changes in the expectations of holders, or potential holders, of dollars.

The final problem with the explanation offered by the hegemonic stability theory is that it does not capture the *dual* nature of the U.S. power position in 1971. On the one hand, as we have seen, the U.S. position was eroding. Yet to a considerable extent the scope of U.S. weakness was the *result* of the rules of the old regime: within these rules the United States, not being able to force creditor nations such as Germany and Japan to revalue their currencies, thus was in the position of having to defend the dollar by a variety of short-term expedients. Only by breaking the rules explicitly—by suspending convertibility of the dollar into gold —could the United States transform the bargaining position and make its creditors offer concessions of their own. As Henry Aubrey had pointed out in 1969, "surely a creditor's influence over the United States rests on American willingness to play the game according to the old concepts and rules. If the United States ever seriously decided to challenge them, the game would take a very different course."[39] The United States thus had a strong political incentive to smash the old regime, and it also had the political power to do so. Once the regime had been destroyed, other governments had to heed U.S. wishes, since the active participation of the United States was the sine qua non of a viable international monetary regime.

As we have seen, the hegemonic stability theory is helpful in accounting for the collapse of the Bretton Woods regime, and its proposition linking potential power resources to regime outcomes is not disconfirmed by events. Yet the causal sequences that it suggests are not adequate; one has to take into account the symbolic nature of power resources, direct effects of U.S. policy, and the dual nature of the U.S. power position in 1971.

On the basis of the hegemonic stability theory, one would predict that the major financial powers would have had great difficulty reconstructing the international monetary regime after the events of 1971. Yet the theory's precise prediction would have been ambiguous. As Table 6.1 indicates, in the early 1970s the gross domestic product of the United States still exceeded the combined total of the four next largest market-economy countries. Unilateral U.S. actions, furthermore, had strengthened the U.S. position and made its weak official reserve position less relevant. Thus there was some reason to believe that it might have been possible to reconstruct a stable international monetary regime under U.S. leadership in 1971.

This, of course, failed to occur. The exchange rates established at the Smithsonian Institution in December 1971 collapsed within fifteen months. The United States was no more willing after 1971 to play a responsible, constrained international role than it had been during the six years before the destruction of the Bretton Woods regime. Indeed, the

U.S. monetary expansion of 1972, which helped to secure Richard Nixon's reelection, implied a decision by the administration to abandon that role.[40] Had its own economic policies been tailored to international demands, the United States could probably in 1971 have resumed leadership of a reconstructed international monetary system; but the United States did not have sufficient power to compel others to accept a regime in which only it would have monetary autonomy. Between 1971 and 1976, the United States was the most influential actor in international monetary negotiations, and secured a weak flexible exchange rate regime that was closer to its own preferences than to those of its partners; but given its own penchant for monetary autonomy, it could not construct a strong, stable new regime.

Interpreting Changes in the International Trade Regime

As has been seen, changes in the trade regime between 1967 and 1977 were broadly consistent with changes in potential power resources in the issue area. Power resources (as measured by shares of world trade among the industrialized countries) changed less in trade than in money or oil; and the regime changed less as well. So once again, the hegemonic stability theory is not disconfirmed.

The causal argument of the hegemonic stability theory, however, implies that the changes we do observe in trade (which are less than those in money and oil but are by no means insignificant) should be ascribable to changes in international political structure. Yet this does not appear to be the case. Protectionism is largely a grass-roots phenomenon, reflecting the desire of individuals for economic security and stability and of privileged groups for higher incomes than they would command in a free market. Adam Smith excoriated guilds for protecting the wages of their members at the expense of society (although to the advantage, he thought, of the towns).[41] Officials of the GATT now criticize labor unions and inefficient industries for seeking similar protection and attempt to refute their arguments that such actions would increase national as well as group income. Most governments of advanced capitalist states show little enthusiasm for protectionist policies, but have been increasingly goaded into them by domestic interests.

A recent GATT study identifies as a key source of protectionism "structural weaknesses and maladjustments" in the countries of the Organization for Economic Cooperation and Development (OECD). Its authors focus particularly on the recent tendency in Europe for wages to rise at similar rates across sectors, regardless of labor productivity. Yet industries that are old in one country, faced by dynamic, low-cost competitors from abroad, can only adjust effectively either by paying lower wages than higher-productivity industries or by reducing employment: "To maintain *both* the wage differential and the absolute size of employment in the industry, protection is necessary." Yet the workers affected and their political leaders may prevent steps to widen wage differentials or to reduce employment. This resistance to change leads both to inflation and to pressures for protection. According to this view, governments share the responsibility for inflation and protectionism insofar as they tolerate and accommodate these pressures.[42]

It may be true that for reasons internal to advanced industrial societies — or to certain societies, since some seem to be affected more than others — people of these countries are more resistant to adjustment than they once were.[43] This may not just be a problem of the masses. More emphasis could be placed on insufficient levels of research and development by governments and firms, thus contributing to failure to innovate; or one could attempt to account for stagnation by reference to managerial inadequacy on the part of leaders of established oligopolistic industries.[44] In either case, however, explanations from domestic politics or political culture would appear necessary to account for changes in international regimes. Shifts in preference functions — from profit maximization to the quiet life, as Charles Kindleberger has put it — are not accounted for by the hegemonic stability model.[45]

Most explanations of increased protectionism also focus on the recession of the 1970s and the rise of manufactured exports from less developed countries. Between the end of 1973 and the end of 1977, rates of growth in industrial production lagged throughout the OECD area, and in Western Europe and Japan industrial production hardly grew at all. Unemployment rates in Europe in 1977 were three times as high as average unemployment rates between 1957 and 1973. At the same time, recessionary pressure was accentuated by the rapid growth of exports of manufactured goods from developing countries, which increased by about 150 percent in volume terms between 1970 and 1977, while manufacturing output in the developed market economy countries increased by only about 30 percent. Although developing countries still account for barely more than 10 percent of the combined manufacturing output of developing countries and developed market economy countries, that proportion has been rising and in some sectors (textiles; processed food, drink, and tobacco; and clothing, leather, and footwear) it exceeds or approaches 20 percent.[46] Some recent restrictive measures, particularly the progressive tightening of export restraints on textiles, reflect these pressures from dynamic developing country exporters.

To some extent, difficulties in maintaining liberal trade among the OECD countries do reflect erosion of U.S. hegemony, although this is more pronounced as compared with the 1950s than with the late 1960s. In the 1950s the United States was willing to open its markets to Japanese goods in order to integrate Japan into the world economic system, even when most European states refused to do so promptly or fully. This has been much less the case in recent years. Until the European Common Market came into existence, the United States dominated trade negotiations; but since the EEC has been active, it has successfully demanded numerous exceptions to GATT rules. Relative equality in trade-related power resources between the EEC and the United States seems to have been a necessary, if not sufficient, condition for this shift.[47]

On the whole, the hegemonic stability theory does not explain recent changes in international trade regimes as well as it explains changes in money or oil. The theory is not disconfirmed by the trade evidence, and correctly anticipates less regime change in trade than in money or oil; but it is also not very helpful in interpreting the changes that we do observe. Most major forces affecting the trade regime have little to do with the decline of U.S. power. For an adequate explanation of changes in trade, domestic political and economic patterns, and the strategies of domestic political actors, would have to be taken into account.

Hegemonic Stability and Complex Interdependence: A Conclusion

A structural approach to international regime change, differentiated by issue area, takes us some distance toward a sophisticated understanding of recent changes in the international politics of oil, money, and trade. Eroding U.S. hegemony helps to account for political reversals in petroleum politics, to a lesser extent for the disintegration of the Bretton Woods international monetary regime, and to a still lesser extent for the continuing decay of the GATT-based trade regime.

Table 6.3 summarizes the results of the analysis. There is a definite correspondence between the expectations of a hegemonic stability theory and the evidence presented here. Changes in tangible power resources by issue area and changes in regimes tend to go together. In terms of causal analysis, however, the results are more mixed. In the petroleum area a plausible and compelling argument links changes in potential economic power resources directly with outcomes. With some significant caveats and qualifications, this is also true in international monetary politics; but

TABLE 6.3
Hegemonic Stability and International Economic Regimes,
1966-1977: An Analytical Summary

	Issue Areas		
	Oil	Money	Trade
Correspondence Between Changes in Power Resources and Changes in International Regimes:			
Extent of change in tangible power resources, 1965-1975 (rank orders)	1	2	3
Extent of change in regime, 1967-1977 (rank orders)	1	2	3
Causal Links:			
Plausibility of causal argument linking tangible resource changes to changes in the regime	high	medium	low

in trade, the observed changes do not seem causally related to shifts in international political structure.

On the basis of this evidence, we should be cautious about putting the hegemonic stability theory forward as a powerful explanation of events. It is clearly useful as a first step; to ignore its congruence with reality, and its considerable explanatory power, would be foolish. Nevertheless, it carries with it the conceptual difficulties and ambiguities characteristic of power analysis. Power is viewed in terms of resources; if the theory is to be operationalized, these resources have to be tangible. Gross domestic product, oil import dependence, international monetary reserves, and share of world trade are crude indicators of power in this sense. Less tangible resources such as confidence (in oneself or in a currency) or political position relative to other actors are not taken into account. Yet these sources of influence would seem to be conceptually as close to what is meant by "power resources" as are the more tangible and measurable factors listed above. Tangible resource models, therefore, are inherently crude and can hardly serve as more than first-cut approximations — very rough models that indicate the range of possible behavior or the probable path of change, rather than offering precise predictions.

The version of the hegemonic stability theory that best explains international economic regime change between 1967 and 1977 is an "issue structure" rather than "overall structure" model.[48] That is, changes in power resources specific to particular issue areas are used to explain regime change. Issue structure models such as this one assume the separateness of issue areas in world politics; yet functional linkages exist between issue areas, and bargaining linkages are often drawn by policymakers between issue areas that are not functionally linked. The decline in the value of the dollar from 1971–1973, after the conclusion of the Teheran Agreements in February 1971, contributed strongly to dissatisfaction by OPEC states with oil prices, since it adversely affected their share of the rewards.[49] Sudden oil price rises had a major impact on the international financial system during 1974; if floating exchange rates had not already been in place, they would almost certainly have had to be implemented. And the inflationary effects of monetary disorder and oil price rises, as well as the recessionary effects of those price increases, certainly had an impact on the international trade regime, although the effects are more difficult to trace.

The existence of interissue linkages limits the explanatory power of issue structure models. To solve this problem would require a strong and sophisticated theory of linkage, which would indicate under what conditions linkages between issue areas would be important and what their impact on outcomes would be.[50] No issue-specific explanation of events can be completely satisfactory in a world of multiple issues linked in a variety of ways.

Despite all the limitations on power structure analysis, beginning with it has the great advantage of setting up some very general predictions based on a theory that requires only small amounts of information. A remarkable portion of the observed changes rely only on this parsimonious, indeed almost simple-minded, theory. Furthermore, its very inadequacies indicate where other explanations and other levels of analysis must be considered. Having examined the explanatory strengths and weaknesses of a hegemonic stability theory, we understand better what puzzles remain to be solved by investigating other systemic theories or by focusing on domestic politics and its relationship to foreign economic policy. Beginning with a simple, international-level theory clarifies the issues. It helps to bring some analytical rigor and order into the analysis of international economic regimes. Without employing a structural model as a starting point, it is difficult to progress beyond potentially rich but analytically unsatisfactory description, which allows recognition of complexity to become a veil hiding our ignorance of the forces producing change in world political economy. To limit ambitions to such description would be a premature confession of failure.

Acknowledgments

I have benefited from comments by numerous colleagues on earlier drafts of this chapter. I am particularly obliged for extensive comments to Benjamin J. Cohen, Peter J. Katzenstein, Stephen D. Krasner, and David Laitin; and to three graduate students at Stanford University, Vinod Aggarwal, Linda Cahn, and David Yoffie. My greatest debt is to Alexander George, who went beyond an editor's call of duty by thoroughly pointing out the lacunae and non sequiturs in two earlier drafts. The first draft of this chapter was written when I was a fellow at the Center for Advanced Study in the Behavioral Sciences. There I benefited from the research assistance of Shannon Salmon and from research support from the German Marshall Fund of the United States and the National Science Foundation, the latter through a grant to the Center for Advanced Study (BNS 76-22943).

Notes

1. For figures relating to these points, see Paul McCracken et al., *Towards Full Employment and Price Stability* (Paris: Organization for Economic Co-operation and Development, 1977), esp. pp. 41–42. Cited below as "McCracken Report."

2. See, for instance, George Liska, *Imperial America: The International Politics of Primacy,* no. 2 (Washington, D.C.: Johns Hopkins Studies in International Affairs, 1967); J. J. Servan-Schreiber, *The American Challenge,* trans. Ronald Steel (New York: Avon Books, 1969); and Harry Magdoff, *The Age of Imperialism* (New York: Monthly Review Press, 1969).

3. Susan Strange, "The Management of Surplus Capacity," *International Organization* 33 (Summer 1979).

4. For a similar earlier definition, see Robert O. Keohane and Joseph S. Nye, Jr., *Power and Interdependence: World Politics in Transition* (Boston: Little, Brown and Co., 1977), p. 19–22.

5. Edith T. Penrose, *The Large International Firm in Developing Countries: The International Petroleum Industry* (Cambridge, Mass.: M.I.T. Press, 1968), pp. 150–165, 183–197; and Morris A. Adelman, *The World Petroleum Market* (Baltimore, Md.: Johns Hopkins University Press, 1971), pp. 78–100.

6. This way of thinking about international regimes was suggested by the work of Clifford Geertz, especially his essay, "Thick Description: Toward an Interpretive Theory of Culture," in Clifford Geertz, *The Interpretation of Cultures* (New York: Basic Books, 1973). Geertz, however, is principally concerned with meaning and symbolism, whereas the explanatory theory tested in this paper emphasizes tangible power resources. Thus, apart from the suggestiveness of

Geertz's concept of culture for the concept of regime, this chapter has little in common with Geertz's mode of analysis.

7. See especially Peter J. Katzenstein, ed., *Between Power and Plenty: Foreign Economic Policies of Advanced Industrial States* (Madison: University of Wisconsin Press, 1978). As noted in the text, the dependent variable of this study is national political strategy, not change in international regimes.

8. For a lucid discussion of these issues, see Kenneth N. Waltz, *Theory of International Politics* (Reading, Mass: Addison-Wesley Publishing Co., 1979), chap. 1.

9. For analysis along these lines, see the following: Charles P. Kindleberger, *The World in Depression, 1929–1939* (Berkeley: University of California Press, 1974); Robert Gilpin, *U.S. Power and the Multinational Corporation* (New York: Basic Books, 1975); and Stephen D. Krasner, "State Power and the Structure of International Trade," *World Politics* 28 (April 1976):317–347.

10. Kindleberger relies most heavily on the theory of collective goods. See his "Systems of International Economic Organization," in David P. Calleo, ed., *Money and the Coming World Order* (New York: New York University Press for the Lehrman Institute, 1976), pp. 19–20; and Kindleberger, *The World in Depression*, chap. 14. It is necessary to be cautious in viewing international regimes as "collective goods," since in many cases rivalry may exist (everyone may benefit from stable money but not everyone can benefit noncompetitively from an open U.S. market for imported electronic products) and countries can be excluded from many international regimes (as the debate over whether to give most-favored-nation status to the Soviet Union illustrates). On the provision of collective goods, a useful article is Mancur Olson, Jr., and Richard Zeckhauser, "An Economic Theory of Alliances," *Review of Economics and Statistics* 48 (1966): 266–279, reprinted in Bruce Russett, ed., *Economic Theories of International Politics* (Chicago: Markham Publishing Co., 1968). See also John Gerard Ruggie, "Collective Goods and Future International Collaboration," *American Political Science Review* 66 (September 1972):874–893.

11. Both Krasner, "State Power," and Kindleberger, *World In Depression,* make this admission. The hegemonic stability theory is criticized by David P. Calleo in his concluding essay in Benjamin Rowland, ed., *Balance of Power or Hegemony: the Interwar Monetary System* (New York: New York University Press, published for the Lehrman Institute, 1976). Calleo dislikes hegemony and seems reluctant to admit its association with economic order; he therefore seeks both to reinterpret the pre-1914 period as not "imperial," and to characterize the bloc system of the 1930s as having "worked relatively well." Harold van B. Cleveland and Benjamin Rowland make better differentiated arguments in the same volume that critique or qualify the hegemonic stability thesis.

12. The problem with "force activation models" is that such models can "save" virtually any hypothesis, since one can always think of reasons, after the fact, why an actor may not have used all available potential power. See James G. March, "The Power of Power," in David Easton, ed., *Varieties of Political Theory* (New York: Prentice-Hall, 1966), esp. pp. 54–61. See also John C. Harsanyi, "Measurement of Social Power, Opportunity Costs, and the Theory of

Two-Person Bargaining Games," *Behavioral Science* 7 (1962):67–80.

13. Peter A. Gourevitch, "The Second Image Reversed," *International Organization* 32 (Autumn 1978):881–912.

14. Recent work on foreign investment indicates that international regimes in this area have also changed since 1967. See Stephen D. Krasner, *Defending the National Interest: Raw Materials Investment and U.S. Foreign Policy* (Princeton, N.J.: Princeton University Press, 1978); and Charles Lipson, *Standing Guard: The Protection of Foreign Investment* (Berkeley: University of California Press, forthcoming).

15. Robert E. Hudec, *The GATT Legal System and World Trade Diplomacy* (New York: Praeger Publishers, 1975), p. 256. See also Gardner C. Patterson, *Discrimination in International Trade* (Princeton, N.J.: Princeton University Press, 1965).

16. For good discussions, see Benjamin J. Cohen, *Organizing the World's Money: The Political Economy of International Monetary Relations* (New York: Basic Books, 1977); C. Fred Bergsten, *Dilemmas of the Dollar* (New York: New York University Press, 1975); Alfred E. Eckes, Jr., *A Search for Solvency: Bretton Woods and the International Monetary System, 1941–1971* (Austin: University of Texas Press, 1975); and Fred Hirsch, *Money International* (London: Penguin Press, 1967).

17. Harold T. Shapiro, "Inflation in the United States," in Lawrence B. Krause and Walter S. Salant, eds., *Worldwide Inflation: Theory and Recent Experience* (Washington, D.C.: Brookings Institution, 1977).

18. Louis Turner, *Oil Companies in the International System* (London: George Allen & Unwin for the Royal Institute of International Affairs, 1978), p. 70.

19. Ibid., pp. 94–95.

20. Gabriel Kolko, *The Politics of War: 1943–45* (New York: Vintage Books, 1968), pp. 294–307; Krasner, *Defending the National Interest,* pp. 190–205; Herbert Feis, *Petroleum and American Foreign Policy* (Stanford, Calif.: Food Research Institute, Stanford University, March 1944); Herbert Feis, *Seen From E.A.: Three International Episodes* (New York: Alfred A. Knopf, 1947), pp. 104ff.; and Benjamin Shwadran, *The Middle East, Oil and the Great Powers* (New York: Praeger Publishers, 1955), pp. 302–309. See also *Foreign Relations of the United States* (Washington, D.C.: U.S. Government Printing Office, 1943 and 1944), vol. 4, pp. 941–948; vol. 3, pp. 94–111.

21. See Krasner, *Defending the National Interest,* pp. 119–128; Joyce and Gabriel Kolko, *The Limits of Power: The World and American Foreign Policy, 1946–1954* (New York: Harper & Row, 1972), pp. 413–420; John M. Blair, *The Control of Oil* (New York: Pantheon Books, 1976), pp. 43–47, 78–80; U.S., Congress, Senate, Committee on Foreign Relations, Subcommittee on Multinational Corporations, *The International Petroleum Cartel, The Iranian Consortium and U.S. National Security,* Committee Print, 93d Cong., 2d sess., 21 February 1974.

22. U.S., Congress, Senate, Committee on Foreign Relations, Subcommittee on Multinational Corporations, *Multinational Corporations and United States*

Foreign Policy, Part 4, Hearings, 93d Cong., 2d sess. 30 January 1974, pp. 84–110. See also Glenn P. Jenkins and Brian D. Wright, "Taxation of Income of Multinational Corporations: The Case of the United States Petroleum Industry," *Review of Economics and Statistics* 17 (February 1975); and Krasner, *Defending the National Interest,* pp. 205–213.

23. U.S., Congress, Senate, Committee on the Judiciary and on Interior and Insular Affairs, *Emergency Oil Lift Program,* Hearings, 85th Cong., 1st sess., February 1957; OECD, *Europe's Need for Oil: Implications and Lessons of the Suez Crisis* (Paris, 1958); and News Conference of President Eisenhower, 6 February 1957 (*Public Papers of the President,* 1957), p. 124.

24. This was accomplished by the Arrangement Regarding International Trade in Textiles, known as the "Multifiber Agreement," or MFA. For the text, see "Arrangement Regarding International Trade in Textiles" (GATT publication, 1974). UNCTAD has commented on implementation of the agreement in "International Trade in Textiles," Report by UNCTAD secretariat, 12 May 1977.

25. Craig R. MacPhee, *Restrictions on International Trade in Steel* (Lexington, Mass.: Lexington Books, 1974).

26. C. Fred Bergsten, "On the Non-Equivalence of Import Quotas and 'Voluntary' Export Restraints," in C. Fred Bergsten, ed., *Toward a New World Trade Policy: The Maidenhead Papers* (Lexington, Mass.: Lexington Books, 1975).

27. *IMF Survey,* 12 December 1977, p. 373.

28. *IMF Survey,* 20 March 1978, p. 81; and 18 September 1978, p. 285.

29. *New York Times,* 12 April 1979.

30. Morgan Guaranty Trust Company, *World Financial Markets,* May 1978.

31. On the basis of an index with 1974 as 100, OPEC's terms of trade had declined by 1977 to 91.0 (and by 1978 to 81.0). In 1977 this reflected import prices that were 25 percent higher, compared with oil prices that had only increased by 14 percent. Morgan Guaranty Trust Company, *World Financial Markets,* December 1978.

32. As an argument against the overall structural version of a hegemonic stability theory, this is convincing, since it is hard to see how undifferentiated economic power resources (as measured by gross domestic product) would be equally efficacious in a variety of issue areas. As a general criticism of much international relations literature, the criticism is too harsh. Those who use the notion of undifferentiated power in world politics have rather clear assumptions about the nature of world politics, which help to set (admittedly broad) scope conditions on their generalizations. For what these authors regard as the essential core of world politics (adversary relations among competitive states), aggregate economic resources, and the military capabilities for which economic resources are essential preconditions, play an extremely large role. For the quotation in the text and the policy-contingency argument, see David A. Baldwin, "Power Analysis and World Politics: New Trends vs. Old Tendencies," *World Politics* (January 1979):165. For a carefully worked-out overall structure argument, see Waltz, *Theory of International Politics.*

33. Since excess U.S. capacity fell between 1967 and 1976, the figures in Table

6.2, part C-2, actually understate the increase in U.S. dependence on foreign oil during that nine-year period. In 1967 the United States could have withstood a complete embargo quite comfortably (apart from any obligations or desire it might have had to export oil), simply by increasing production from shut-in wells. In a sense, then, its real energy dependence increased from zero to 20 percent during the 1967–1976 period.

34. U.S. liquid liabilities to all foreigners began to exceed reserve assets in 1959 (not alarming for a country acting in many ways like a bank), and had reached five times reserve assets by 1971. *The United States in the Changing World Economy,* statistical background material (Washington, D.C.: U.S. Government Printing Office, 1971), chart 53, p. 40. However, total U.S. assets abroad remained about 50 percent higher than foreign assets in the United States in 1975 [*International Economic Report of the President* (January 1977), p. 161].

35. For discussions of U.S. tactics at Teheran in 1971, see Henry M. Schuler, "The International Oil Negotiations," in I. William Zartman, ed., *The 50% Solution* (New York: Doubleday & Co., 1976), pp. 124–207; John M. Blair, *The Control of Oil,* pp. 223–227; and Edith T. Penrose, "The Development of Crisis," in Raymond Vernon, ed., *The Oil Crisis,* special issue of *Daedalus* (Fall 1975):39–57. *The Oil Crisis* also contains a number of accounts of other aspects of the events in 1973–1974.

36. Joel Darmstadter and Hans H. Landsberg, "The Economic Background," in Raymond Vernon, ed., *The Oil Crisis,* special issue of *Daedalus* (Fall 1975):30–32.

37. Benjamin J. Cohen, *Organizing the World's Money,* p. 99.

38. "McCracken Report," pp. 52–56; charts 14B (p. 83) and 12 (p. 71). See also Cohen, *Organizing the World's Money,* pp. 103–104.

39. Henry Aubrey, "Behind the Veil of International Money," *Princeton Essays in International Finance,* no. 71 (January 1969):9.

40. For a discussion of President Nixon's manipulation of U.S. monetary policy for electoral purposes in 1971–1972, see Edward R. Tufte, *Political Control of the Economy* (Princeton, N.J.: Princeton University Press, 1978), pp. 45–55.

41. Adam Smith, *An Inquiry into the Nature and Causes of the Wealth of Nations,* book 1, part 2, chap. 10, (Chicago: University of Chicago Press, 1976), pp. 132ff.

42. Richard Blackhurst, Nicolas Marian, and Jan Tumlir, *Trade Liberalization, Protectionism and Interdependence,* GATT Studies in International Trade, no. 5 (Geneva: GATT, November 1977), esp. pp. 44–52. For a discussion along similar lines, see the "McCracken Report," esp. chaps. 5, 8.

43. William Diebold, Jr., "Adaptation to Structural Change," *International Affairs* (October 1978).

44. The emphasis on innovation and technological development is suggested by Schumpeter's theory of economic development and has been the subject of substantial recent comment in the business press in the United States. See Joseph A. Schumpeter, *The Theory of Economic Development: An Inquiry into Profits,*

Capital, Credit Interest and the Business Cycle, translated from the German by Redvers Opie, 1934 (Cambridge, Mass.: Harvard University Press, 1951); and Schumpeter, *Business Cycles* 2 vols., (New York: McGraw-Hill Book Co., 1939). A critique of attempts to attribute Britain's poor economic performance in the last quarter of the nineteenth century to low-quality managerial and entrepreneurial skills can be found in Donald N. McCloskey, *Economic Maturity and Entrepreneurial Decline: British Iron and Steel, 1870–1913* (Cambridge, Mass.: Harvard University Press, 1973).

45. Kindleberger, *Economic Response,* chap. 7.

46. For the figures, see United Nations Conference on Trade and Development, *Review of Recent Trends and Developments in Trade in Manufactures and Semi-Manufactures,* Report by the secretariat, 21 March 1978, chart 1, p. 4 and chart 3, p. 24.

47. On discrimination against Japan, see Gardner C. Patterson, *Discrimination in International Trade* chap. 6, pp. 271–322; on the EEC and the United States in trade negotiations, see Robert E. Hudec, *The GATT Legal System and World Trade Diplomacy.*

48. The distinction between "issue structure" and "overall structure" models is drawn in Keohane and Nye, *Power and Interdependence,* chap. 3.

49. Edith T. Penrose, "The Development of Crisis," in Vernon, ed., *The Oil Crisis,* pp. 39–58.

50. Kenneth A. Oye has made some useful distinctions that may help to contribute to such a theory. See "Towards Disentangling Linkage: Issue Interdependence and Regime Change," mimeo (Berkeley, Calif.: Institute of International Studies, April 1979).

7

P. TERRENCE HOPMANN
TIMOTHY D. KING

From Cold War to Détente:
The Role of the Cuban Missile Crisis and
the Partial Nuclear Test Ban Treaty

Introduction

The period from the Cuban missile crisis of October 1962 to the signing of the Partial Nuclear Test Ban Treaty in July 1963 reflected a fundamental shift in the overall relations between the two major protagonists of the postwar period, the United States and the Soviet Union. The Cuban missile crisis was in many respects a culmination of the cold war tensions that had been building in a steady, though uneven, progression since the end of World War II. By bringing the world to the threshold of nuclear war, the likelihood of which President Kennedy estimated as between one in three and one in two,[1] the crisis spurred a reconsideration of those cold war policies that brought the world so close to nuclear destruction. It also provided an incentive for policymakers to develop innovative solutions to those problems that were perceived to be root causes of the crisis, including the Soviet-U.S. arms race. Although measures to limit the arms race had been discussed for almost a decade, no concrete results had been achieved prior to the outbreak of the Cuban missile crisis. However, only ten months after the crisis was resolved, the stalemate which had characterized all previous arms control negotiations was broken with the signing of the Partial Nuclear Test Ban Treaty.

This treaty did not abolish nuclear testing altogether, as the superpowers continued underground testing while other nuclear powers such as France and the People's Republic of China refused to sign the agreement. Nevertheless, President Kennedy saw this treaty as the first step to "reduce tension, to slow down the perilous arms race and to check the world's slide toward final annihilation."[2] In the span of ten months Soviet-U.S. relations moved from the most dangerous event in the postwar period to perhaps the most hopeful.

The dramatic changes during this period prompted many analysts — including Roger Hilsman on the U.S. side[3] and Sivachev and Yakovlev of the USSR[4] — to conclude that these events were closely related. The purpose of this chapter is to explore the impact of these events on Soviet-U.S. relations. Two substantive questions will be addressed. First, what was the nature of the connection, if any, between the Cuban missile crisis of 1962 and the attainment of the Partial Nuclear Test Ban Treaty in July 1963? Second, beyond any short-term impact, did the events prove to be a watershed in relations as President Kennedy had so clearly hoped? In short, the objective is to identify both short-term and long-term changes in Soviet-U.S. relations as a result of the crisis in Cuba over the emplacement of Soviet missiles. As North suggests:

> Given a particular environmental event, we want to know in the short run what types of behavioral outputs we can expect from various nation-states, and we want to try to account for such outputs when they occur. For the longer run, we want to know which of the more stable elements — relatively constant in the short run — are likely to change and how and why.[5]

In addition to these substantive considerations, this chapter explores the utility of several methodological procedures for evaluating the effects of these events. Specifically, a system known as Bargaining Process Analysis (BPA) is employed to analyze changes in the verbatim texts of the test ban negotiations and an events data procedure is used to measure changes in the level of cooperation and conflict between the United States and the Soviet Union during the twenty-two-year period from 1952 through 1973. These procedures can determine whether there were changes in Soviet-U.S. interactions as a result of these events as well as some important aspects of the nature of those changes. In the quantitative analyses, however, the focus is not simply on regularities in behavior over time but rather on crucial changes and turning points that might indicate transformations in the system of interactions between the two major powers of the postwar period.

In order to avoid a problem — "that unique events having system-changing consequences are averaged out in the pool of typical behaviors or statistical trends,"[6] — some procedures of quasi-experimental design will be used to explore the particular effects of the Cuban missile crisis, treating it as if it were an experimental intervention in a series of ongoing events. In these procedures particular attention will be focused on the catalytic role of this crisis, not only in leading the world to the brink of nuclear war but also in laying the foundations for the subsequent period of Soviet-U.S. détente.

The Post–World War II Period: From Cold War to Détente

Postwar Soviet-U.S. relations have been dominated by cold war politics, including strong ideological opposition between the two super-powers and direct conflicts of interest in areas such as Europe, the Middle East, and other parts of the Third World. Major elements of this cold war are still present in relations between these two global powers. However, a growing awareness of the mutual dangers inherent in nuclear warfare has led the two antagonists to modify the fundamental nature of their relationship and to seek more cooperative patterns of behavior. In this section, how the Cuban missile crisis of 1962 and the Partial Nuclear Test Ban Treaty of 1963 contributed to this fundamental change from cold war to détente will be examined.[7]

Research Methodology

The Quasi-Experimental Design

Since the purpose of this chapter is to evaluate the impact of the Cuban missile crisis of 1962 on both the short- and long-term changes in the international system, a procedure known as the quasi-experimental design has been selected as the basis for the analysis. In the absence of a true experiment this procedure enables the researcher to evaluate the impact of a critical set of events upon an ongoing process, roughly analogous to the pretest/posttest design in experimental research.[8] One aim in this research is to observe whether or not the occurrence of the Cuban missile crisis in the midst of a series of ongoing events made any significant changes in the patterns of those events. The concern here is with both the short-term impact of the crisis upon the nuclear test ban negotiations which were going on at that time, and the impact on the overall long-term trends in political relations between the United States and the Soviet Union. Caporaso notes that there are two questions involved in the evaluation of this impact: "Did a nonrandom change occur in the vicinity of the experiment? Is this change attributable to the occurrence of the experimental event?"[9]

The first question will be answered through the use of statistical techniques to determine whether there were significant changes in the trends and relationships among variables in the aftermath of the Cuban crisis. There are several kinds of changes which can be observed here. First, there can be changes in the overall magnitude or level of intensity in the variables. Thus the hypothesis is that the average level of conflict in Soviet-U.S. relations would be lower after than before the Cuban crisis and that there would be more convergent, "softer" behaviors within the test ban negotiations after the crisis of October 1962. A second kind of change is in the trend lines in the aftermath of this intervening event, especially in the slope of a least squares regression line. Thus an increasing rate of cooperative interactions both in the test ban negotiations and in overall events following the Cuban missile crisis would be predicted. Third, changes in the relationships among variables as a result of this intervention may be identified. For example, the reciprocity in Soviet-U.S. interactions before and after the Cuban missile crisis may be examined to determine if there was a greater correlation in their behaviors in the wake of this major event.

The statistical procedure used to determine the significance of these changes is based on the dummy variable strategy suggested by Gujarti and recently employed by Hoole in the analysis of international organizations.[10] This procedure uses a regression equation of the following form:

$$Y_t = a + b_1 X_t + b_2 D_t + b_3 (X_t \cdot D_t) + e_t \qquad (1)$$

where Y_t refers to the dependent variable, i.e., the behavior in which the change is evaluated; X_t refers to the independent variable, either time or some other variable whose relationship to Y_t is evaluated; D_t is a dummy variable with value 0 for all events leading up to and including the Cuban missile crisis and 1 for all subsequent events; a refers to the intercept; b represents all fixed coefficients; and e is an error term that accounts for factors not included in the equation. The level of contribution of the dummy variable, D_t, to the overall linear regression equation thus becomes an indicator of the impact of the intervening event on the relationships among other variables.

The second question noted by Caporaso about the interpretation of quasi-experimental results is somewhat more complex and subjective. Whether the change, if one is found, is or is not attributable to the occurrence of the "experimental" event, in this case the Cuban missile crisis, must be determined. Historical analysis is relied upon in order to exclude other major events which might have accounted for such changes. Of course, in a complex international system where many changes occur at the same time it is impossible to completely eliminate extraneous causes of these changes.

The Quantitative Indicators

In order to perform the statistical tests required for the quasi-experimental design, it is necessary to collect quantitative data to measure the processes for which the evaluation of changing patterns of interaction is proposed. Here the interest is in the impact of the Cuban missile crisis on both short-term changes, namely the bargaining within the nuclear test ban negotiations, and long-term changes, specifically the overall political interactions between the United States and the Soviet Union from 1952 through 1973.

A procedure called Bargaining Process Analysis[11] was employed to evaluate changes in the negotiations leading up to the Partial Nuclear Test Ban Treaty of 1963. This procedure entails a systematic content analysis of the verbatim transcripts of these negotiations in order to quantify factors such as substantive moves, bargaining strategies, and attitudes involved in the negotiations. This procedure was applied to all speeches by representatives of the United States and the Soviet Union within the Eighteen Nation Disarmament Conference (ENDC) and its subcommittee on the test ban in which the subject of a test ban agreement was discussed. This included a total of 112 documents beginning on 21 March 1962 and culminating on 17 June 1963. These sessions were divided into sixteen equal periods of seven sessions each; some of the sixteen periods span only a few weeks whereas others span several months. The precise dates and session numbers of each of the sixteen periods are reported in Table 7.1. In addition, for some analyses a seventeenth period was added, based on reports from the major secondary sources about the occurrences at the secret trilateral meetings in Moscow, 15–25 July 1963, at which the final Partial Nuclear Test Ban Treaty was drafted. Since no verbatim transcripts of this conference are publicly available, secondary sources had to be used for this analysis.[12] The entire set of seventeen periods was then divided for purposes of the quasi-experimental design. The first ten of these periods, from 21 March 1962 through 1 November 1962, come before or during the Cuban missile crisis, whereas the final seven periods beginning on 6 November 1962 and concluding with the signing of the treaty on 25 July 1963 occurred after the crisis events.

The BPA system is intended to measure change in the bargaining process in each of the negotiating sessions. In this system, statements made by the representatives of the United States and the Soviet Union were placed into a series of categories which focus on various behaviors undertaken by negotiators as they engage in the process of bargaining. Statements were not assigned to various categories simply on the basis of

TABLE 7.1
Changes in National Negotiating Position of the United States and the
Soviet Union in the Partial Test Ban Negotiations, 1962-1963

Period and Date	United States*	Soviet Union*
1) Mar. 21-Apr. 3, 1962	+4	-27
2) Apr. 4-Apr. 13, 1962	0	+6
3) Apr. 16-Apr. 25, 1962	0	+49
4) Apr. 26-May 11, 1962	0	0
5) May 15-June 6, 1962	+16	0
6) June 6-Aug. 14, 1962	+24	-12
7) Aug. 15-Aug. 29, 1962	+32	-18
8) Aug. 31-Sept. 18, 1962	0	0
9) Sept.20-Oct. 11, 1962	0	0
10) Oct. 16-Nov. 1, 1962	0	0
Average before and during Cuban missile crisis, October 1962	+7.60	-0.20
11) Nov. 6-Dec. 3, 1962	+14	+20
12) Dec. 4-Dec. 11, 1962	-6	+23
13) Dec. 13, 1962-Feb. 18, 1963	+7	+26
14) Feb. 20-Mar. 8, 1963	+13	-3
15) Mar. 11-Apr. 1, 1963	-7	0
16) Apr. 8-June 17, 1963	+6	-20
17) July 15-July 25, 1963	+40	+84
Average after Cuban missile crisis, October 1962	+9.57	+18.57
Overall average	+8.41	+7.53
Overall standard deviation	13.24	27.09

* These data are scaled scores on position changes, based on the cumulative
total scores for each period of seven ENDC sessions in which the test ban
issue was discussed, except for period 17 which includes the secret negotiations of the final treaty text in Moscow. The scale ranges from (+) to
indicate positive movement to (-) indicating negative movement, that is,
moves towards stalemate or away from agreement. There is no predetermined
upper or lower limit on this scale. Details of the scaling process are
described in the text.

formalistic observations of discrete behaviors. Rather the role of each statement within the overall context of the negotiations was considered. To assist in making these judgmental codings, not only were the entire verbatim transcripts of these negotiations read several times, but also the considerable secondary literature on the test ban negotiations was read, including several accounts by participants in these negotiations.[13] Background interviews also were conducted with a number of participants.

The BPA system, then, is composed of numerous categories of bargaining behavior. Although many analyses can be made of all of these behaviors, this study focused on a few basic dimensions of behavior that have yielded interesting results in past research using this procedure. The most significant dimension involves substantive movement or position change, with behavior either tending towards a convergence or divergence of positions. This overall dimension is composed of a number of subcomponents, which tend to relate to one another in different and complex ways. Nevertheless, this dimension produces the best general indicator of the contribution of each party towards agreement or stalemate within negotiations. These changes also have been weighted, as indicated below, to reflect an estimate of the overall importance of each kind of move in either contributing to or detracting from agreement. Furthermore, some moves were rated as "minor," meaning that they were either judged to be of only technical significance or introduced largely for purposes of propaganda or generating other side effects; such moves were given only half of the value normally assigned to each category. The two categories, and the eight components included in them, with the weighting score for each, are as follows:

1. Positive Position Changes (Convergence):
   a. Initiation of new proposals: weight $= +3$
   b. Accommodation or concession to a position favored by the other side: weight $= +10$
   c. Acceptance of an initiation or accommodation presented by the other side: weight $= +6$
   d. Promises of contingent reward or removal of a punishment: weight $= +6$
2. Negative Position Change (Divergence or Stalemate):
   a. Commitments to prior positions: weight $= -3$
   b. Retractions of previous initiations or accommodations: weight $= -10$
   c. Rejection of an initiation or accommodation presented by the other side: weight $= -6$

   d. Threats of contingent punishments or removal of a reward: weight = -6

   Thus the content analysis procedure yielded weighted totals of these position changes based on the sum of all positive and negative changes in each of the seventeen periods of the negotiations. This made it possible to chart the progress of the test ban negotiations towards agreement or, conversely, tendencies towards stalemate or even movement away from agreement from 21 March 1962 through the conclusion of the Partial Nuclear Test Ban Treaty on 25 July 1963. These data are reported in Table 7.1.

   Several other variables were also analyzed because of their importance in affecting the "atmosphere" of the negotiations. These variables, listed below, deal particularly with the style of argumentation or debate employed by the negotiators as well as the emotional overtones of the negotiations.

   1. *Self-presentation* refers to arguments made in support of one's own position in the negotiations, as well as clarifications of that position.
   2. *Attacking arguments* refer to negative statements and arguments made about the position of the other party in the negotiations.
   3. *Problem solving* refers to the process in which a negotiator tries to explore innovative alternatives in a noncommital fashion in the search for possible solutions to outstanding problems.
   4. *Positive and negative affect* treat the emotional side of the negotiations, including affect directed towards oneself and towards other parties in the negotiations.

   Each occurrence of these behaviors was recorded, and the frequency of these behaviors over each set of seventeen sessions was calculated. Since the raw frequency of these behaviors may in part be a function of the length of each session, for some analyses the frequency was divided by the total number of interactions for each country in each period. This then gave an indication of the percentage of the total interactions composed of each particular category of behavior.

   In summary, the BPA system provided a rich set of data about the test ban negotiations, aggregated into seventeen periods for purposes of analysis. Thus, positive and negative changes in the positions of the United States and the Soviet Union during the course of these negotiations, as well as changes in a number of other important dimensions of negotiating behavior, could be charted. Of course, any simple coding process of the type employed in this research fails to take adequate account of many of the subtle moves within negotiations, which may not be well represented on such simple dimensions. In interpreting the results, however, some of these important considerations will be taken into account.[14]

The second set of analyses focused on the long-term trends in Soviet-U.S. political interactions. In this case, "events data" were employed to scale major actions between these two countries along a continuum ranging from conflict to cooperation. Specifically, a thirty-point scale was used, with values ranging from one for highest cooperation to thirty for most intense conflict.[15] Two sources were used to identify the events, including one Western source, *Keesing's Contemporary Archives,* and one Soviet source, *The New Times.* All events in which the United States was the actor and the Soviet Union was the target, and vice versa, were taken from these sources during the period from 1952 through 1973, including eleven years before and after the Cuban missile crisis. A total of 808 actions were included in the data set, comprising 351 actions by the United States towards the Soviet Union and 457 in the opposite direction.

These actions were then scaled on the thirty-point continuum by three graduate student judges specializing in international politics. A deck of thirty "marker cards" was used as a guide for identifying the approximate point on this scale where each event appropriately belonged. Judges were instructed to use the "marker" deck as a general guide to suggest the range of events encompassed within the conflict-cooperation dimension; on the other hand, they were instructed not to look for matches between events and marker cards in terms of the content of specific events. The judges were aware of the identity of the nations in these events, and they coded the events in chronological order. Although some bias may be removed by disguising the actors and randomizing the order of events, this procedure also entails a substantial loss of information about the context for each individual event. In this procedure, the judges were able to bring context to bear in scaling these events, based both on other events scaled previously and on their general knowledge of the history of this period. Although this might permit some bias to enter the coding process, especially since all judges were Americans, this procedure also enhances the validity of the results substantially in comparison with the use of "blind" events. Intercoder reliability coefficients were computed on the basis of a sample of 10 percent of the events, with the composite reliability for the three judges reaching a respectable level of 0.87. Given this high reliability coefficient, the average of the three ratings by each of the judges was employed as the value assigned to each dyadic action.

Events were then summed within the six-month periods from January

TABLE 7.2
Soviet-American Interactions on Conflict/Cooperation Continuum (30 = highest
conflict; 1 = highest cooperation) from 1952-1973

6-Month Period	U.S. to U.S.S.R.			U.S.S.R. to U.S.		
	Conflict/ Cooperation Score	Standard Deviation	Range	Conflict/ Cooperation Score	Standard Deviation	Range
Jan.-June 1952	13.3	2.3	11-17	13.7	2.3	11-17
July-Dec. 1952	16.0	2.6	13-20	16.8	3.4	11-24
Jan.-June 1953	12.8	3.0	9-16	12.0	3.6	9-19
July-Dec. 1953	14.5	4.2	10-20	14.8	4.0	10-20
Jan.-June 1954	11.1	2.5	9-15	10.5	1.9	9-15
July-Dec. 1954	16.0	4.0	10-20	14.6	3.9	9-24
Jan.-June 1955	11.8	3.0	9-16	12.5	3.0	9-17
July-Dec. 1955	12.1	2.9	9-15	11.0	2.3	9-14
Jan.-June 1956	11.2	2.9	8-15	13.1	4.1	8-19
July-Dec. 1956	14.8	1.3	12-16	13.1	3.3	9-19
Jan.-June 1957	15.7	3.1	9-19	14.9	3.5	9-19
July-Dec. 1957	14.0	3.7	10-19	14.3	3.4	10-19
Jan.-June 1958	12.9	3.0	9-19	13.3	3.7	9-21
July-Dec. 1958	12.3	3.0	9-17	13.6	3.2	9-20
Jan.-June 1959	14.6	2.9	11-18	13.3	3.0	10-18
July-Dec. 1959	10.6	2.3	9-16	11.0	3.0	9-17
Jan.-June 1960	15.4	1.5	13-18	16.9	3.8	13-24
July-Dec. 1960	17.5	1.2	14-19	18.1	1.8	12-20
Jan.-June 1961	11.5	3.0	9-18	12.8	4.0	9-21
July-Dec. 1961	14.3	3.2	10-18	13.8	3.6	10-19
Jan.-June 1962	11.3	2.1	9-15	12.3	2.7	9-16
July-Dec. 1962	15.8	6.2	10-25	15.2	3.7	10-24
Average 1952-1962	13.6	2.0	8-25	13.7	1.9	8-24

through June and from July through December for each of the twenty-two years between 1952 and 1973. The average score on the thirty-point continuum for each of the forty-four six-month periods is reported for each nation as actor in Table 7.2, as well as the standard deviation and range for the events in each period. Throughout the entire period, the most cooperative events were at level eight on the scale, while the most conflictual events reached level twenty-five. The most conflictual event was the following: "October 22, 1962: Kennedy announces a naval quarantine of Cuba to prevent military shipments from the USSR from reaching Cuba." Many events were scored at level eight on the cooperative end of the continuum. The following is one example: "May 26, 1972: A treaty on the Limitation of Anti-Ballistic Missile Systems between the US and the USSR is signed by Nixon and Brezhnev in Moscow."

TABLE 7.2 (cont.)

6-Month Period	U.S. to U.S.S.R.			U.S.S.R. to U.S.		
	Conflict/ Cooperation Score	Standard Deviation	Range	Conflict/ Cooperation Score	Standard Deviation	Range
Jan.-June 1963	11.0	2.1	9-15	11.2	2.3	9-16
July-Dec. 1963	10.6	3.1	8-17	10-5	3.6	8-16
Jan.-June 1964	11.9	5.1	9-23	13.9	5.6	9-23
July-Dec. 1964	9.8	1.0	9-12	11.5	3.3	9-18
Jan.-June 1965	10.0	0.0	10-10	18.6	0.9	18-20
July-Dec. 1965	no events			no events		
Jan.-June 1966	13.0	0.0	13-13	16.3	2.9	13-18
July-Dec. 1966	9.8	0.8	9-11	15.4	5.6	9-21
Jan.-June 1967	10.0	0.7	9-11	10.7	1.2	10-12
July-Dec. 1967	11.0	0.0	11-11	16.0	0.0	16-16
Jan.-June 1968	9.0	0.0	9-9	15.1	3.6	9-20
July-Dec. 1968	10.2	2.2	9-14	10.2	1.9	9-14
Jan.-June 1969	9.8	0.8	9-11	9.3	0.6	9-10
July-Dec. 1969	10.0	0.0	10-10	11.3	2.5	10-15
Jan.-June 1970	9.5	0.7	9-10	9.5	0.7	9-10
July-Dec. 1970	9.3	3.3	9-15	12.0	3.2	9-17
Jan.-June 1971	10.6	1.3	9-12	9.7	0.6	9-10
July-Dec. 1971	9.0	0.0	9-9	9.0	0.0	9-9
Jan.-June 1972	8.3	0.5	8-9	8.0	0.0	8-8
July-Dec. 1972	9.1	0.9	8-11	8.9	0.4	8-9
Jan.-June 1973	8.6	0.5	8-9	8.6	0.5	8-9
July-Dec. 1973	11.6	2.1	8-18	10.9	1.9	8-14
Average 1963-1973	10.1	1.1	8-23	11.7	3.0	8.23
Overall average 1952-1973	11.9	2.4	8-25	12.7	2.7	8-24

Therefore, the events scaled along this dimension should give a general indication of variation over time in the level of conflict and cooperation involved in the behaviors of the United States and the Soviet Union towards one another throughout this important historical period. For purposes of the analyses making use of the quasi-experimental design, these events were divided at the midpoint between 1962 and 1963, reflecting the changes from the Cuban missile crisis in the last half of 1962 to the Partial Nuclear Test Ban Treaty negotiated successfully in 1963. These data thus provided the foundation for the quantitative analyses of the effects of these two important events on the long-term course of Soviet-U.S. relations during the postwar period. The subsequent analyses will focus not only on the substantive changes in Soviet-U.S. relations during this period but also on the utility of these methodological procedures for revealing these changes.

The Results: The Effects of the Cuban Missile Crisis on Soviet-U.S. Relations

Effects of the Cuban Missile Crisis on the Nuclear Test Ban Negotiations

The first analyses focus on the impact of the Cuban missile crisis on the nuclear test ban negotiations. The Partial Nuclear Test Ban Treaty emerged in July 1963 from the negotiations in the Eighteen Nation Disarmament Conference which had been dealing with that issue since its inception in March 1962. Six months after the opening of the ENDC, at a time when some of the differences between the two superpowers seemed to be narrowing, the Cuban missile crisis occurred. The purpose here is to evaluate the effects of this abrupt event upon the course of these negotiations.

First, the effects of these events on the substantive movement of the United States and the Soviet Union during the seventeen periods into which the test ban negotiations have been divided will be examined. The patterns of this position change are revealed in Table 7.1, which summarizes the scaled data on changes in the negotiating positions of the United States and the Soviet Union. The overall average scores for the two major powers were almost the same ($+8.41$ for the United States and $+7.53$ for the Soviet Union), but the different standard deviations (13.24 for the United States and 27.09 for the Soviet Union) indicated that there was considerably greater variability in the negotiating behavior of the Soviet Union over the course of these negotiations.

The correlations between time and the position changes of the two superpowers are weakly positive and none of the relationships reached the 0.10 level of statistical significance. As stated in Table 7.1, while both countries made significant positive moves in the Moscow Conference (period 17), the trends prior to that conference were somewhat inconsistent. The United States made many positive moves in the months immediately preceding the Cuban missile crisis (periods 5 through 7), especially in new proposals, which the United States and the United Kingdom tabled in August 1962. However, the U.S. position changes became much less positive and occasionally even negative in the periods after the crisis and prior to the Moscow meeting. The Soviet pattern was even more inconsistent. They started off with negative moves at the opening of the ENDC, and then they proceeded to make significant forward steps in period 3. However, the positive Western moves in periods 5 through 7 were met with a negative response. After the Cuban crisis the overall pattern of Soviet behavior became much more positive, with a series of concessions and new proposals in periods 11 through 13. However, the Soviet position toughened just prior to the opening of the Moscow Conference, at which the USSR made substantial concessions in order to reach eventual agreement. Once again, none of the overall trends reached statistical significance.

In addition to examining trends in negotiating behavior over time, the reciprocity between the United States and the Soviet Union in their negotiating behaviors has been noted. Reciprocity refers here to situations in which the two nations appeared to be responding roughly "in kind" to the behavior of their negotiation partners. As an indicator of reciprocity, the correlations between the position changes of the two parties have been examined. Positive correlations would tend to suggest that there is reciprocity, in the sense that the negotiation behavior of each nation tended to change at the same time and in roughly the same direction as the other; since simultaneous correlations are used here, it cannot be determined who was responding to whom, but merely that the behaviors of the two sides tended to be reciprocal. Low correlations would tend to indicate the absence of such reciprocity. Negative correlations would generally suggest that there was negative reciprocity and exploitation present, in which the positive moves of one side were met by an increased toughening of the position of the other party.[16]

The correlations between the position changes of the two countries suggest that the Cuban missile crisis exerted an interesting effect on negotiating reciprocity. Throughout the negotiations there was a weak but insignificant positive correlation ($r = 0.26$, $p = 0.16$) between the behaviors of the two countries. However, there is a very substantial difference in the correlations before and after the missile crisis. Through the beginning of November 1962 there was a negative relationship ($r = -0.44$, $p = 0.10$) between the movements of the two countries. However, in the aftermath of the Cuban crisis, this relationship became quite positive ($r = 0.72$, $p = 0.03$). Therefore, the changes in Soviet and U.S. positions in the early phases of the negotiation tended to be largely exploitative. For example, positive Soviet moves in period 3 (the last half of April 1962) were met with an unchanging behavior on the part of the United States. Furthermore, positive U.S. moves in periods 5 through 7 (the end of May through August 1962) were met with intransigence by the Soviet Union. This relationship was clearly reversed after the Cuban missile crisis, when U.S. and Soviet movements became more positively reciprocal. Since much literature on negotiation has suggested that such reciprocity is conducive to the attainment of agreement,[17] it seems likely that this post-Cuban-crisis trend may have been an important factor in contributing to the successful outcome in the summer of 1963. After the Cuban crisis there appeared to be a greater effort by the two superpowers to coordinate their mutual behaviors and to respond in a reciprocal way, in both forward movement and intransigence, to one another's changes in behavior. This may well have been one of the most significant effects of the Cuban missile crisis upon these negotiations.

Table 7.3 reports on a before-and-after analysis of these negotiations, employing the Mann-Whitney U-Test to evaluate differences in the levels of negotiating behaviors in the two broad periods of this study. Looking first at position changes, the U.S. actions towards the Soviet Union were only slightly more positive after the events in Cuba than before. As noted

TABLE 7.3
Scores of Negotiating Behaviors by the United States and the Soviet Union in the Test Ban Negotiations Before and After the Cuban Missile Crisis; Significance of Before and After Differences Computed Using a Mann-Whitney U-Test

Negotiating Behavior	Time Period	U.S. to U.S.S.R.	U.S.S.R. to U.S.
Position change (average change on position per period; see Table 1 data)	before Cuban crisis	+7.60	-0.20
	after Cuban crisis	+9.57	+18.57
	significance of difference (Mann-Whitney U-Test)	U = 32	U = 23.5
Attacking arguments (average frequency per period)	before Cuban crisis	66.8	95.0
	after Cuban crisis	41.5	51.0
	significance of difference (Mann-Whitney U-Test)	U = 14*	U = 12.5*
Self Presentation (average frequency per period)	before Cuban crisis	108.5	56.7
	after Cuban crisis	78.8	51.5
	significance of difference (Mann-Whitney U-Test)	U = 21.5	U = 27
Affect towards other (average percent positive)	before Cuban crisis	7.18%	1.75%
	after Cuban crisis	16.20%	1.52%
	significance of difference (Mann-Whitney U-Test)	U = 8**	U = 30

* Difference is significant, with the probability of a Type I error being less than .05.

** Difference is significant, with the probability of a Type I error being less than .01.

previously, this is largely due to the positive initiatives which the United States made during the summer of 1962. This difference did not approach statistical significance using the Mann-Whitney U-Test. A comparison of the means of Soviet behaviors indicates a much more positive movement after the Cuban crisis than before. However, since such a large amount of this behavior occurred in the final period, the difference between the two periods was not significant using the Mann-Whitney U-Test, which takes account solely of the rank-ordering and not the magnitude of the data. Therefore, with the exception of the sudden leap to agreement at the Moscow Conference, in which the Soviet Union largely accepted the positive moves made by the United States and the United Kingdom the preceding August, there was little noticeable difference in the patterns of substantive movements before and after the Cuban missile crisis.

Also some of the other bargaining behaviors which might have influenced changes in the substantive positions were noted. First, attacking arguments refers to arguments that each side advanced against the positions of the other. The data in Table 7.3 reveal that both the United States and the Soviet Union substantially lowered the levels of attacking arguments after the missile crisis in comparison with the earlier periods. The U-scores for both countries' actions towards the other on this dimension were significant at better than the 0.05 level. Second, self-presentation refers to arguments presented by each country in defense of its own position. In this case, the data did not reveal any significant differences between the two periods. Third, the percentage of positive affect relative to total affect that each country expressed towards the other was noted. In the case of the United States, the percentage of positive affect, though low throughout the negotiations, increased significantly after the Cuban missile crisis ($U = 8$, $p < 0.01$). On the other hand, Soviet positive affect towards the United States remained very low throughout the entire negotiations.

The examination also included the changes in the reciprocity between the United States and the Soviet Union in the two categories of negotiating behavior that showed significant differences, employing an analysis similar to that discussed above for the variable of substantive movement. First, there was substantial reciprocity between the United States and the Soviet Union in the use of attacking arguments, with the highest levels ($r = 0.87$, $p = 0.01$) being reached after the Cuban crisis. This means that attacking arguments not only declined throughout the course of the negotiations, but also both countries tended to reduce the frequency of these generally antagonistic debating processes in tandem.

Second, the results presented in Table 7.4 regarding the positive affect expressed by each country towards the other reveal a pattern which is quite similar to that for the position change variable. In this instance the overall positive correlation was quite weak between the two parties for the entire negotiation ($r = 0.15$, $p = 0.25$). However, the correlation changed from an inverse one ($r = -0.31$, $p = 0.38$) before the Cuban crisis to a strong positive one ($r = 0.76$, $p = 0.08$) after the crisis. In the case of the responsiveness of Soviet affective behavior to the expressions of affect directed towards it, the dummy variable reached significance ($r = 0.50$, $p = 0.03$), thus indicating that the change between the two periods was statistically significant. On the other hand, U.S. expressions of affective behavior towards the Soviet Union did not change significantly between the two periods, as indicated by the relatively weak contribution of the dummy variable in the multiple regression equation reported in Part B of Table 7.4.

TABLE 7.4
Soviet and American Positive Affect Towards the Other During the Test Ban Negotiations, 1962-1963: Multiple Regressions and Correlations

A. U.S.S.R. Towards U.S.

Overall R^2:　　　　　　　　　　　　　R^2 = .67　　　　p = .08
　Individual components:
　　positive affect of U.S.　　　　r = .15　　　p = .25
　　dummy　　　　　　　　　　　　r = .50　　　p = .03

Correlations before and after
Cuban missile crisis: positive affect of U.S.

　　before:　　　　　　　　　　　　r = -.31　　　p = .38

　　after:　　　　　　　　　　　　　r = .76　　　p = .08

B. U.S. Towards U.S.S.R.

Overall R^2:　　　　　　　　　　　　　R^2 = .39　　　p = .34
　Individual components:
　　positive affect of U.S.S.R.　　r = .15　　　p = .25
　　dummy　　　　　　　　　　　　r = .24　　　p = .18

Correlations before and after
Cuban missile crisis: Positive affect of U.S.S.R.*

　　before:　　　　　　　　　　　　r = -.31　　　p = .38

　　after:　　　　　　　　　　　　　r = .76　　　p = .08

Key: R^2 = squared multiple regression coefficient; r = Pearson Product Moment Correlation; p = probability of a Type 1 error.

  * These correlations are identical to those reported in Part A because they are the same bivariate correlation, with the independent and dependent variables inverted.

In summarizing the short-term effects of the Cuban missile crisis upon the Partial Nuclear Test Ban Treaty negotiations, several findings stand out. First, there was generally more positive movement, especially by the Soviet Union, after the Cuban crisis than before it. Second, attacking arguments presented by both nations tended to be reduced after the Cuban crisis in a mutually reciprocal fashion. Third, positive affect expressed by the United States towards the Soviet Union was greater in the post-Cuban-crisis period. Fourth, and perhaps most significantly, reciprocity in negotiating behavior between the two competing nations tended to increase substantially after the events of October 1962. This was evident in substantive position changes, in the presentation of attacking arguments, and in mutual positive affect. In short, the negotiations seemed to be making little progress prior to the Cuban missile crisis, and the mutual behaviors of the two principal antagonists were out of synchronization. By contrast, after the events in Cuba brought the world to the brink of nuclear war, there were mutually reciprocal increases in positive position changes and in positive affect, accompanied by a reciprocal decline in the use of attacking arguments within the negotiations. This does not necessarily mean, however, that the agreement was attained through a smooth progression of mutual convergence; on the contrary, the major changes made in the final Moscow negotiations were indicative of a sudden jump to agreement. Nevertheless, this leap to a final solution may have been substantially aided by the high levels of responsiveness established between the two major powers after the Cuban missile crisis, making possible not only the attainment of the Partial Nuclear Test Ban Treaty but also the opening of an era of Soviet-U.S. détente.

Effects of the Cuban Missile Crisis on Soviet-U.S. Interactions, 1952–1973

An examination of the long-term effects of these events in Cuba and the agreement upon a Partial Nuclear Test Ban Treaty upon the overall nature of Soviet-U.S. interactions follows. In particular, whether the effects of the Cuban missile crisis were simply short term, affecting only such immediate events as the negotiations on the test ban issue, or whether these effects were felt significantly in subsequent interactions will be determined. For this purpose, major events or actions by the United States and the Soviet Union towards one another during a twenty-two-year period from 1952 through 1973 have been analyzed. These data, coded on a scale ranging from one (greatest cooperation) to thirty (highest conflict), are averaged for six-month periods, and these averages are reported in Table 7.2. The summaries at the bottom of Table 7.2

report on the average levels of intensity on this conflict/cooperation continuum for the entire twenty-two-year period; furthermore, averages for the two subperiods before and including the Cuban missile crisis (1952–1962) and including the Partial Nuclear Test Ban Treaty and subsequent events (1963–1973) are also reported at the appropriate points in this table. The differences between these two subperiods for each nation's actions towards the other are then tested, using the Mann-Whitney U-Test. The results clearly indicate that the level of conflict in Soviet-U.S. relations was less intense in the decade after this crucial turning point than in the decade which preceded it. Although the overall magnitude in the level of conflict did not drop very much, the periods since 1963 tended to be characterized by higher levels of cooperation.

Table 7.5 reports the results of multiple regression analyses of these data, with the behavior of each nation towards the other as the dependent variable. First, look at the regression equation in which the independent variables included the passage of time and a dummy variable that marked the breakpoint between 1962 and 1963. For the United States, the overall equation produced a multiple R of 0.75, significant at better than the 0.001 level. The negative correlation between the passage of

TABLE 7.5
Analysis of Soviet-U.S. Interaction on Conflict/Cooperation Scale
(30 = highest conflict; 1 = highest cooperation), 1952-1973

	Soviet Union		United States	
A. Multiple Regression Analysis, 1952-1973: Dependent Variable = Conflict/Cooperation Intensity; Independent Variables = Time + Dummy (1952-1962 = 0, 1963-1973 = 1)				
Multiple R: time + dummy	R = .45	p = .01	R = .75	p = .001
(time alone)	r = -.45	p = .09	r = -.69	p = .39
(dummy alone)	r = -.37	p = .86	r = -.74	p = .008
B. Pearson Product Moment Correlations Between Time and Conflict/Cooperation Scores with Breakpoint Between 1962 and 1963				
Before and during Cuban missile crisis, 1952-1962	r = .14	p = .26	r = .05	p = .42
After Cuban missile crisis, 1963-1973	r = -.55	p = .005	r = -.47	p = .02
Overall, 1952-1973	r = -.45	p = .001	r = -.69	p = .001

Key: R = Multiple Regression Coefficient; r = Pearson Product Moment Correlation; p = probability of Type 1 error.

time and the intensity of conflict indicates that conflict declined over this period, although this relationship did not make a significant overall contribution to the regression equation ($r = -0.69$, $p = 0.39$). However, the dummy variable did make a significant contribution to the equation ($r = -0.74$, $p = 0.008$), suggesting that the nature of the relationship between U.S. behavior towards the Soviet Union and time changed substantially after the Cuban crisis of 1962. The specific nature of this change is also indicated in Part B of Table 7.5, showing the separate trends from the periods 1952–1962 and 1962–1973. These data indicate that there was virtually no correlation between the passage of time and changes in the level of U.S. behavior towards the Soviet Union prior to 1963 ($r = 0.05$, $p = 0.42$). This trend changed substantially after 1962. The data in Table 7.5, Part B, for the 1963–1973 time period indicate that the correlation between time and conflict intensity became quite negative ($r = -0.47$, $p = 0.02$). This indicates that in general the level of cooperation in U.S. actions toward the Soviet Union grew fairly steadily throughout the period from 1963 through 1973.

In summary, the decade prior to the Cuban missile crisis was characterized by a generally flat trend in U.S. conflictual and cooperative behaviors towards the Soviet Union, although there were numerous ups and downs around the overall trend line. On the other hand, after the Cuban missile crisis there developed a pattern of much greater and more consistent cooperativeness on the part of the United States. The dummy variable in the multiple regression equation reported in Table 7.5 was highly significant, indicating the magnitude of this change in the trend line. Not only did the trend line change, but also, as the data reported in Table 7.4 indicate, the average level of cooperation was considerably higher in the second subperiod than in the first. There was a rather abrupt decline in U.S. conflict behavior towards the Soviet Union almost immediately after the Cuban missile crisis. In general, U.S. behavior towards the Soviet Union seems to have been significantly influenced by the events in Cuba in 1962 and by the signing of the Partial Nuclear Test Ban Treaty in 1963.

Turning next to the behavior of the Soviet Union towards the United States, a different but interesting pattern emerges. In Table 7.5, the multiple R for the equation in which Soviet behavior was the dependent variable was also significant ($R = 0.45$, $p = 0.01$). However, in contrast to the U.S. case, the passage of time was the most significant factor accounting for this ($r = -0.45$, $p = 0.09$), while the dummy variable which divided the period between 1962 and 1963 was not at all significant. The data for the Soviet Union (Table 7.4), when subjected to a separate least squares regression analysis for the 1952–1962 and

1963–1973 periods, indicate that the dummy was not significant, primarily due to a series of highly conflictual behaviors which continued more or less unabated through the first half of 1968. Most of these were due to Soviet criticism of the role of the United States in Vietnam through the years of greatest escalation, lessening after President Johnson's decision in early 1968 not to seek reelection. Conversely, since the United States did not view the Soviet Union as a major actor in the Vietnam conflict, these negative behaviors were generally not reciprocated by the United States. Indeed, when the overall period is broken in two after 1966 instead of after 1962, then quite different results appear. Table 7.6 reports on the results when this breakpoint was employed for the dummy variable in the multiple regression equations. In this case the multiple R for the Soviet Union reached a higher level (R = 0.55, p = 0.001), and the dummy variable was significant (r = − 0.55, p = 0.02). Thus, for the Soviet behaviors towards the United States, the major turning point seemed to come after the conflict escalation in Vietnam rather than after the crisis in Cuba.

Nevertheless, referring to the data about Soviet behavior in Part B of Table 7.4, and using the 1962–1963 period as the breakpoint for our analysis, an interesting pattern appears. During the period 1952–1962,

TABLE 7.6
Analysis of Soviet-American Interactions on Conflict/Cooperation Scale
(30 = highest conflict; 1 = highest cooperation), 1952-1973 With Breakpoint
Between 1966 and 1967

	Soviet Union		United States	
A. Multiple Regression Analysis, 1952-1973: Dependent Variable = Conflict/ Cooperation Intensity; Independent Variables = Time + Dummy (1952-1966 = 0, 1967-1973 = 1)				
Multiple R: time + dummy	R = .55	p = .001	R = .70	p = .001
(time alone)	r = -.45	p = .99	r = -.69	p = .01
(dummy alone)	r = -.55	p = .02	r = -.64	p = .21
B. Pearson Product Moment Correlations Between Time and Conflict/Cooperation Scores with Breakpoint Between 1966 and 1967				
1952-1966	r = .16	p = .20	r = -.39	p = .02
1967-1973	r = -.60	p = .01	r = -.20	p = .25
Overall, 1952-1973	r = -.45	p = .001	r = -.69	p = .001

Key: R = Multiple Regression Coefficient; r = Pearson Product Moment Correlation; p = probability of Type 1 error.

there was a very modest increase in Soviet conflict towards the United States ($r = 0.14$, $p = 0.26$), though this fell short of statistical significance. By contrast, in the post-Cuban-crisis period there was a significant decline in Soviet conflictual behavior ($r = -0.55$, $p = 0.005$). The correlation between conflict and the passage of time reported in Part B of Table 7.5 indicated a significant decline over this period from 1963 through 1973 ($r = -0.55$, $p = 0.005$). Thus, although the dummy variable indicated that a more significant turning point occurred between 1966 and 1967 rather than between 1962 and 1963, these data still do indicate some substantially different trends after the Cuban missile crisis than were evidenced before; however, the effects of the Cuban missile crisis and the test ban treaty were confounded by the impact of the escalating conflict in Vietnam.

Finally, we may examine the correlations between Soviet and U.S. behaviors throughout this period in order to determine the extent of mutual reciprocity in their relationship. For the twenty-two-year period the correlations were significantly positive ($r = 0.65$, $p = 0.001$), suggesting that there was generally a high level of reciprocity in the actions between these two countries. Somewhat surprisingly, however, this was accounted for most by a high positive relationship in the period prior to and including the Cuban missile crisis ($r = 0.86$, $p = 0.001$), which fell off somewhat during the period from 1963 through 1973 ($r = 0.46$, $p = 0.02$). Nevertheless, there was a positive responsiveness between the two superpowers throughout this period, although it was greater during the periods of higher conflict than during the more cooperative period after 1963. Thus responsiveness does not appear to be a feature exclusively associated with détente; indeed, in this case it was clearly associated with rising tensions as well as with their reduction.

Conclusions: Some Lessons About the Relationship Between Crises and Détente

This chapter has explored changes in the international system during the period from 1952 through 1973, bringing to bear some quantitative data to evaluate the extent and nature of some of these changes. The results have demonstrated rather clearly that Soviet-U.S. relations have undergone some significant changes during this period, and that the events surrounding the Cuban missile crisis and the signing of the Partial Nuclear Test Ban Treaty were important turning points for this relationship. Furthermore, it has demonstrated the utility of procedures such as Bargaining Process Analysis to evelute changes within test ban negotiations and events data procedure for exploring long-term trends in super-power interactions.

Undoubtedly the changes in the bilateral linkages between the two superpowers were influenced by many factors, especially by the effects of the relationships between each of the superpowers and other actors within the international system. Thus the growing conflict between the Soviet Union and the People's Republic of China, the loosening of some of the U.S. ties with Western European allies, and the rise of a bloc of nonaligned actors in the international system all affected the structure of postwar international relations. Nevertheless, perhaps the most significant change in postwar relations occurred in the interactions between the United States and the Soviet Union, as their interactions turned from a general pattern of conflict known as the "cold war" towards a relaxation of tensions known as détente or peaceful coexistence.

This analysis has indicated that the Cuban missile crisis exerted some important short- and long-term effects on the behaviors of the two super-powers. While no single event could have accounted for changes in their patterns of interactions alone, this one event did seem to have important catalytic effects. In searching for short-term influences, the impact of these events on the ongoing negotiations in the ENDC on the issue of banning nuclear testing was investigated. Here some significant effects were identified. Perhaps most importantly, the behaviors of the United States and the Soviet Union within these negotiations became more sym-metrical and reciprocal in the aftermath of the Cuban missile crisis. Thus each nation tended to respond to the behaviors of the other in a more or less tit-for-tat fashion. Furthermore, this positive reciprocity in the after-math of the Cuban crisis included a general mutual increase in positive affect expressed toward one another, in a reduction of attacking arguments, and in forward movement in positions on the issues under negotiation. Thus a stalemate in these negotiations was broken in the summer of 1963 that enabled the two superpowers to conclude the first in a series of arms control agreements through which they attempted to place some mutual restraints on the arms race.

In order to examine the long-term effects of the Cuban missile crisis, Soviet and U.S. actions towards one another during the period 1952–1973 were analyzed, measuring their behaviors along a con-flict/cooperation continuum. In the case of the United States, the Cuban crisis had an immediate and direct effect on behavior towards the Soviets. Beginning in 1963 there was a sudden increase in U.S. cooperative behaviors towards the Soviet Union. Furthermore, the trend in U.S. behavior changed from an almost flat pattern to one of significantly decreasing conflict. Overall, the magnitude of U.S. conflict behavior after the Cuban crisis was significantly less than it was before. In the case of Soviet behaviors, the effects of the Cuban crisis were confounded by the Vietnam War. Therefore, the Soviets continued to express some substantial hostility towards the United States through the first half of 1968, due largely to their intense criticism of U.S. involvement in Vietnam. On the other hand, the post-Cuban-crisis trend for Soviet actions showed a significant increase in cooperation for the period from 1963 through 1973, in contrast to a weak trend of increasing conflict in the eleven years leading up to the crisis. Furthermore, overall levels of Soviet conflict were less intense in the post-Cuban-crisis period than in the period which preceded these events.

In general, it can be concluded that the Cuban missile crisis did exert substantial short- and long-term effects on the behaviors of the United States and the Soviet Union towards one another. Although the Vietnam War seems to have delayed this effect for the Soviets, during the remainder of the decade that followed the Cuban crisis the overall trend towards détente continued to grow in relations between the superpowers. The irony of this relationship is that the basis for Soviet-U.S. cooperation seems to have come significantly from the logical consequences of their own competition, namely the threat of nuclear war. Indeed, it took an immediate and direct confrontation with nuclear holocaust to remind the leaders and peoples of these two nations of the logical consequence of their conflict, enabling them to pull back and seek ways to resolve their most serious disputes. Since that time both superpowers have endeavored to make this new relationship mutually profitable through a series of agreements on cultural exchanges, increased trade, arms control, and other measures. All of this was designed to make the process of détente irreversible.

Yet ironically all of this might not have been achieved so rapidly had it not been for the close brush with nuclear confrontation in the Caribbean. Perhaps this irony also contains a warning. If cooperation in the nuclear age is largely dependent upon the mutual threat of annihilation, then when that threat recedes, the resultant cooperation may wane. Although the trends after 1973 were not examined here, other research using similar data suggests that there was a marked slowing of the détente process and even some increasing Soviet-U.S. conflict in the last half of the decade of the 1970s.[18] Perhaps this lost momentum for the détente process was partially a result of the distance which separated the new generation of leadership from the most intense days of the cold war when nuclear war seemed like a more concrete possibility. The ultimate paradox of this relationship, then, would occur if the world must once again experience a renewal of the cold war, and perhaps even experience another major crisis like that in Cuba, in order to get the détente process "back on track." Unless the world's leaders can find other bases upon which to construct the détente process besides this mutual threat, then détente contains within itself the seeds of its own destruction. The very success of détente, by reducing the threat of nuclear war, removes from center stage the very basis upon which détente is built, namely the threat of war.

Surely crises like that which occurred in Cuba in October 1962 are a dangerous mechanism for reinforcing the détente process. There is no guarantee that the world will be as lucky in emerging from future crises as it was in the aftermath of the events in the Caribbean in the fall of 1962. For détente to succeed in the long run, therefore, it is imperative that more effort be made to construct it on a firmer basis than just the mutual fear of nuclear war. This fear can provide the impetus to seek out new, more positive measures designed to broaden the base of cooperation. Then, as John F. Kennedy noted after the signing of the Partial Nuclear Test Ban Treaty, we may reinvigorate the effort to "get back from the shadows of war and seek out the way of peace."

Acknowledgments

The authors are grateful for the generous support of the Quigley Center of International Studies at the University of Minnesota, especially for a bequest from the estate of Morton Berland. Timothy King is also grateful for the support of the John Parker Compton Fellowship Program at the Center of International Studies, Woodrow Wilson School of Public and International Affairs, Princeton University. The authors profited greatly from the comments on a preliminary draft by the three editors of this volume, Alexander George, Ole Holsti, and Randolph Siverson.

Notes

1. Theodore Sorenson, *Kennedy* (New York: Harper & Row, 1965), p. 705.

2. "Text of President's Remarks on Test Ban Treaty," *New York Times,* 27 July 1963, p. 2.

3. Roger Hilsman, *To Move A Nation* (New York: Dell Publishing Co., 1967), pp. 228–229.

4. Nikolai V. Sivachev and Nikolai N. Yaklovlev, *Russia and the United States,* trans. Olga Adler Titelbaum (Chicago: University of Chicago Press, 1979), pp. 245–246.

5. Robert C. North, "The Behavior of Nation-States: Problems of Conflict and Integration," in Morton Kaplan, ed., *New Approaches to International Relations* (New York: St. Martin's Press, 1968), p. 304.

6. K. J. Holsti, "Retreat from Utopia: International Relations Theory, 1945–70," *Canadian Journal of Political Science* 4:2 (June 1971):165.

7. Space limitations preclude a discussion of Soviet-U.S. relations leading to the missile crisis and the test ban treaty. The interested reader might wish to consult one of the many works on the subject; for example, Walter LeFeber, *America, Russia, and the Cold War, 1945–1975* (New York: John Wiley & Sons, 1976).

8. Donald T. Campbell and Julian C. Stanley, *Experimental and Quasi-Experimental Designs for Research* (Skokie, Ill.: Rand McNally & Co., 1963), p. 37.

9. James A. Caporaso, "Quasi-Experimental Approaches to Social Science: Perspectives and Problems," in James A. Caporaso and Leslie L. Roos, Jr., eds., *Quasi-Experimental Approaches: Testing Theory and Evaluating Policy* (Evanston, Ill.: Northwestern University Press, 1973), p. 19.

10. Damodar Gujarti, "Use of Dummy Variables in Testing Equality Between Sets of Coefficients in Two Linear Regressions: A Note," *The American Statistician* 24:1 (1970):50–52; and Damodar Gujarti, "Use of Dummy Variables in Linear Regressions: A Generalization," *The American Statistician* 24:5 (1970):18–22. Cited in Francis W. Hoole, "Evaluating the Impact of International Organizations," *International Organization* 31:3 (1977):554.

11. Charles Walcott and P. Terrence Hopmann, "Interaction Analysis and Bargaining Behavior," in Robert T. Golembiewski, ed., *The Small Group in Political Science: The Last Two Decades of Development* (Athens: University of Georgia Press, 1978), pp. 251–261.

12. The most relevant sources include: Harold Jacobson and Eric Stein, *Diplomats, Scientists, and Politicians: The United States and the Nuclear Test Ban Negotiations* (Ann Arbor: University of Michigan Press, 1966); Arthur Dean, *Test Ban and Disarmament: The Path of Negotiation* (New York: Harper & Row, 1966); and David E. Mark, *Die Einstellung der Kernwaffenversuche: Probleme und Ergebnisse der bisherigen Verhandlungen* (Frankfurt/M.: Alfred Melzner Verlag, 1965).

13. Jacobson and Stein, *Diplomats, Scientists, and Politicians;* Dean, *Test Ban and Disarmament;* and Mark, *Die Einstellung der Kernwaffenversuche.*

14. A more detailed analysis of the bargaining processes within the test ban negotiations may be found in P. Terrence Hopmann, Timothy D. King, and Charles Walcott, *Bargaining in International Arms Control Negotiations* (forthcoming).

15. Lincoln E. Moses, Richard A. Brody, Ole R. Holsti, Joseph B. Kadane, and Jeffrey S. Milstein, "Scaling Data on Inter-Nation Action," *Science* 156 (26 May 1967):1054–1059.

16. For a different approach to measuring reciprocity in East-West relations see William A. Gamson and Andre Modigliani, *Untangling the Cold War: A Strategy for Testing Rival Theories* (Boston: Little, Brown and Co., 1971).

Although their approach has considerable advantage in searching for specific interaction patterns in sequences of related events, it is extremely complex to operationalize and leaves considerable room for error. Our more straightforward approach aggregates all types of behavior within a given time period and simply looks for correlation in the overall behavior of all types within those given time periods. Some appreciation of subtleties of individual sequences of events is no doubt lost by our procedure, but it nevertheless supplies a simple and direct indicator of the extent to which the behaviors of the two superpowers tended to "mirror" one another over time.

17. See, for example, from the experimental literature, Warner Wilson, "Reciprocation and Other Techniques for Inducing Cooperation in Prisoner's Dilemma Case," *Journal of Conflict Resolution* 15:2 (1971):167–196; from research on the test ban negotiations this point is made in P. Terrence Hopmann and Theresa C. Smith, "An Application of a Richardson Process Model: Soviet-American Interactions in the Test Ban Negotiations, 1962–63," in I. William Zartman, ed., *The Negotiation Process: Theories and Applications* (Beverly Hills, Calif.: Sage Publications, 1978), pp. 149–174; see also Daniel Druckman, *Human Factors in International Negotiations: Social-Psychological Aspects of International Conflict* (Beverly Hills, Calif.: Sage Publications, 1973), pp. 28–30.

18. See P. Terrence Hopmann, "Détente and Security in Europe: The Vienna Force Reduction Negotiations" (Paper presented at the 11th World Congress of the International Political Science Association, Moscow, USSR, 12–18 August 1979). Using data on Soviet-U.S. interactions scaled on the same scale as in the present chapter during the period from 1 September 1973 through 31 December 1978, broken down by four-month periods, the author found the following correlations between the passage of time and increasing conflict: U.S. behaviors: $r = 0.49$, $p = 0.03$; Soviet behaviors: $r = 0.73$, $p = 0.001$. Thus the behaviors of both countries became significantly more conflictual during this period, reversing the prior trend towards increasing cooperation reported here.

8

**CHARLES F. HERMANN
ROBERT E. MASON**

Identifying Behavioral Attributes of Events That Trigger International Crises

Introduction

History records the ceaseless process of political system formation, development, and transformation. Whether one examines the Chou dynasty, the Greek city-state system, the Concert of Europe, or the post–World War II bipolar system, the existence of potent elements of system change can always be found. A simple fourfold classification of system transformations distinguishes between gradual and abrupt changes and between intended and unintended ones. Gradual transformations in political systems may result from movement in other systems such as resource, technological, or population shifts which have effects on political systems over a protracted period. Sudden political upheavals often result from collective violence such as revolution or war. Revolutions and wars for at least some parties are intended change agents; natural disasters, economic breakdowns, and, for many, wars[1] and revolutions are unintended agents of system transformation.

Although dreamers, philosophers, and would-be rulers often conceive of transformed national or global political systems, humans historically have not been very effective at controlling the process of system transformation. Napoleon, Marx, Jefferson, Lenin, Hitler, and their associates, for example, did not foresee the shape of the structures that actually emerged from the activity they promoted as agents of change. Perhaps few of them would be pleased with the results. The discrepancy between intended effects and experienced results has always led many humans to stress stability as a basic value of statecraft and to shun any changes that are not incremental. These individuals and groups must always contend with others who look at the social, political, and economic injustices of the present system or the projected disasters that await it unless changes are made. Such people urge that humankind endeavor to introduce controlled system transformation to achieve a better world. Presently there is widespread popular and scholarly interest in controlled system change on a global level and at the same time despair of governments as a means for realizing such change.

Despite the differences among individuals and groups on the most desirable ratio of system stability to system change, there should be relatively broad agreement that abrupt, unintended system transformations are the least preferred mode of system transformation. Abrupt and unintended agents of change include international crises, which have been variously defined. They have been described specifically in terms of "a set of events which raises the impact of destabilizing forces in the general international system or any of its subsystems substantially above 'normal.'"[2] Alternatively, they have been viewed as a sequence of interactions in which one party issues a challenge to one or more others that leads to "the perception of a dangerously high probability of war."[3] Still others have emphasized properties of transitory situations such as high threat to major values, short time for decision, and surprise or the lack of anticipation.[4] Despite the variety of definitions flowing from different research questions, most agree that such episodes are abrupt and unintended (at least for some parties at the outset and perhaps for all in the eventual outcomes). Some analysts have noted the positive benefits of crises and the tendency of some leaders to create them deliberately.[5] Such observations do not alter the conclusion that the parties to a crisis can lose control of the process (noted by some as a defining characteristic) and the results can be unattractive for and unanticipated by virtually all parties. In sum, international crises are a poor device for controlled and predictable system change.

If that assumption is accepted, then the tasks are to avoid international crises whenever possible and to minimize the inability of parties to control them should they occur. The ability to forecast crises and the conditions likely to precipitate them becomes a part of the strategy for both advertence and control. This chapter explores one approach to short-term forecasts of international political crises.

The Immediate Beginnings of Crises

How do crises between nations begin? Are they the culmination of a gradual spiral of escalating tension and hostility between adversaries as in the situation prior to the Arab-Israeli War of 1967? Or are they the product of a single dramatic event that suddenly bursts upon one or more governments as illustrated by the situation that faced the Israeli government with the 1976 hijacking to Entebbe, Uganda, of the jet carrying passengers from Tel Aviv? Both orientations have been used in previous research. In the various studies of the outbreak of World War I conducted by those who have been associated with Professor Robert North at Stanford, the gradual escalation between parties has been traced as an important antecedent to the crisis.[6] Using the same historical episode as his example, Russett describes the decisive turning point as: "The moment when those controlling the foreign policy of a state realize that something is going wrong and is likely to involve their state in war. While the awareness may exist to some degree for a very long period before the *key event*, there is usually a point which can be identified as signalling a sharp increase in the awareness of danger."[7]

The investigator's definition of crisis as well as the purpose of the research could affect the choice of interpretation. Alternatively, one might adopt a rather inclusive definition of international crises maintaining the distinction between those with a gradual buildup and those that appear abruptly without any prior warning. Even if one includes as part of the class of situations to be studied as crises those that emerge after a relatively protracted exchange, it may be reasonable to search for some critical event that crystallizes the evolving relationship as a crisis. This chapter will offer a definition of crisis that encompasses both abrupt outbreaks and gradual buildups, and will search in both types for a crisis precipitating event that triggers the onset of a crisis for at least one of the parties.

In crises that result from the actions of human actors (as compared to those that might result from acts of nature), one actor or a coalition of actors will precipitate an event (or perhaps several events in close temporal sequence) that by its properties increases the likelihood of precipitating a crisis, as defined, for the recipient(s). If the properties of the class of events that have an increased probability of triggering crises can be determined, then this information can be used to create short-term forecasts of crises.

The properties of an event can be determined by a careful observer of international relations, even though a state of crisis for a set of policymakers depends on the perceptions of the event by the recipients. The impact of a signal or stimulus depends on the meaning given to it by its recipients and the possibilities of misperception of the actor's intended message are often substantial.[8] At least three factors, however, increase the capacity of a careful observer to estimate the manner in which a recipient will interpret a crisis precipitating event. First, certain properties of an event are less susceptible to varying interpretation than others. A declaration that "this place is on fire" is less likely to be misunderstood

than a statement that "I am uneasy about the present situation." Some of
these unambiguous qualities mark crisis precipitating events. Second, the
foreign ministries of governments appear to be populated by individuals
who are part of an international network or subculture of diplomats and
other internationally experienced persons who have acquired shared
meanings for a variety of behaviors and terms to a greater degree than
most other individuals in their respective societies. (Of course, this does
not preclude deliberate attempts at maintaining ambiguity in interstate
communication.) Third, the observer can examine the context and prior
activities of the parties to a potential crisis to minimize misinterpretation.
Regrettably, indicators of contextuality are not included among actors in
this study. However, these important dimensions of context are expected
to be introduced in future research to sharpen the accuracy of this procedure.

The conceptualization underlying this study assumes that an acting
government initiates some observable behavior intended to influence
some external recipient. If the behavior is interpreted by the recipient to
involve high threat and short time, then a crisis exists for it.

International exchanges often involve multiple actors or recipients;[9]
initially that complication can be ignored. At some point, the authoritative policymakers or their representatives in the initiating country
reach a decision to take some form of action directed at one or more
recipients and intended to influence their behavior. Assuming the decision to engage in an influence attempt is not totally obstructed in the implementation process, this single political level decision is manifested as
an event consisting of one or a series of activities — all flowing in a
relatively short period of time. The event may be a verbal message or a
nonverbal physical deed or a combination of both.[10]

Whatever its character, the event is the observable trace of a decision
to engage in an influence attempt having at least one recipient that is outside its political jurisdiction. By definition, events are capable of being
observed if one is at the right place at the right time. Unfortunately,
governments often attempt to deny observers who are not part of their
implementative process access to the necessary place at the right time that
would enable them to identify some events. To the extent such secrecy
succeeds, errors in the present estimating procedure will result. The
significance of that problem could be explored empirically. When an
event is detected by the recipient, it is interpreted as a "definition of the
situation." By identifying certain properties of events, one can infer
when the recipient will likely define a situation as creating high threat
and short time, i.e., a crisis. The transmission of the actor's decision to
the recipient by means of the event occurs in a particular context that

helps to anticipate how the event will be defined.

This chapter examines some characteristics of foreign policy events that, if present, are hypothesized to increase the probability of a subsequent international crisis. The suggested properties for anticipating crises will be tested, by determining which foreign policy events initiated by various governments between 1959 and 1968 had the stipulated properties and whether those that did were promptly followed by crises. Independent means will be used to establish whether a crisis, as defined, occurred. Which properties, if any, are the best predictors of crises will then be determined.

Definitions of Crisis and Relevant Event Properties

Crisis is defined as a situation that the relevant decisionmakers interpret as (1) constituting a high threat to values they regard as important to their regime or country, and (2) presenting a relatively short period of time (a few days at most) for decision before the situation evolves further in a way that is unfavorable from the perspective of those policymakers. For an international crisis, the relevant decisionmakers must regard the source of the threat to be one or more entities existing outside the political jurisdiction of their government. Notice that it is irrelevant for this analysis whether the affected decisionmakers elect to call the situation a crisis, as long as it has these two defining characteristics.

Situations perceived by decisionmakers as having these characteristics will result in decision processes and actions significantly different from those that would result if either or both characteristics were absent.[11] A third crisis characteristic employed in the research just cited—surprise or an absence of prior awareness on the part of the relevant decisionmakers—has been deleted in the present research for two reasons. First, previous empirical research failed to establish surprise as generating a measurable result either as a separate main effect or in interaction with the other two dimensions.[12] Second, we want to include both crises that occur suddenly without warning and those that result from an escalatory spiral.

Crisis precipitating events are those characterized by certain properties, each of which can be regarded as one end or an extreme value of a continuum or dimension. The hypothesis is that the more of eight selected properties an event has, the more it is likely to trigger a crisis.

Both dimensions and their values have been constructed from variables in the CREON (Comparative Research on the Events of Nations) data set, which at the time of this analysis consists of over 12,000 separate foreign policy events for thirty-six nations. The events have been coded from an uncollapsed version of *Deadline Data on World Affairs,*[13] for one randomly selected quarter of each year in the decade 1959–1968. The operational procedure used for each of the eight properties is described more fully in other works.[14]

The key to our interpretation of crisis precipitating events is the presence of a high degree of obstruction of one or more goals judged by the observer to be basic to the regime or nation. If the event jeopardizes a valued goal, then the recipient decisionmakers are likely to perceive threat to their basic values. The continuum of goal obstruction ranges from events posing no obstacle to valued goals to those involving complete future denial of the goal. Notice the requirement that the obstruction either has not yet occurred (is intended) or is reversible; otherwise there would only be the perception of punishment, not threat. The degree of perceived threat can be expected to vary with the completeness of the obstacle to goal realization and with the credibility of the source to carry out the obstruction. The first three event properties described below are concerned with the basic requirement of intended goal obstruction.

Anticipated Desirability-Undesirability

For the anticipated desirability-undesirability dimension the observer must determine the extent to which the recipient(s) will find the event a relatively more or less attractive occurrence. At one extreme on this continuum are events that are greeted by the recipient with great enthusiasm. Recipients are expected to regard events at the other end of the dimension with great displeasure. To capture this dimension with the CREON data, coders were asked to judge each event on a three-point rating scale — one extreme value of which was "anticipated undesirability by the recipient" — the property here associated with the triggering of a crisis.

Presence/Absence of Physical Assault

The physical assault dimension concerns the actor's use of physical efforts against the recipient or its possessions, either forcibly controlling or destroying the goal object or similarly controlling or destroying the humans necessary for its continued or greater realization. Ignoring the complicating factor of context, it may be generally true that the use of physical force constitutes one of the most complete means of obstructing any goal. Whereas the first dimension (anticipated undesirability-desirability) attempted to estimate only whether some goal obstruction might occur, this one poses a more severe indicator that goals will be obstructed.

To capture this dimension with the CREON data, each event was checked to see if it had been coded as having involved either "force" or "seize." These two nominal categories are part of a larger set in the World Event/Interaction Survey (WEIS) coding system.[15]

Instrumentalities

The third dimension, instrumentalities, introduces the means or skills and resources used to execute the event, including diplomatic, military, and other instrumentalities. Just as physical assault is regarded as a crisis precipitating property, intended goal obstruction is assumed to be more likely if military instruments are included in the mix of skills and resources used to implement the actor's decision. A historical review suggests that increased military preparedness, alerts, maneuvers, mobilizations, and so on have been associated with the onset of an international crisis.

Affect

This dimension refers to the feelings, ranging from friendliness to hostility, that policymakers express toward the policies, actions, or government of another nation. Such feelings have both direction and intensity. Direction indicates whether the feeling expressed is positive (friendly) or negative (hostile), while intensity suggests the degree of feeling that is expressed (mild or strong).

Governments that perceive themselves facing an international crisis normally find that they are the recipients of others' negative affect. Expression of the actor's hostile feeling reduces the ability of the recipient to interpret any obstructive behavior as inadvertent or unintended. The explicit communication of displeasure combined with the activity that blocks one or more of the recipient's important goals heightens the likelihood of perceived threat. Affect is measured along a seven-point scale, from $+3$ through 0 to -3, with $+3$ indicating strong positive affect and -3 indicating strong negative affect (the assumed crisis triggering property).

External Consequentiality

By the external consequentiality dimension is meant the potential impact of a foreign policy behavior on other national governments. What is the likelihood that a specific foreign policy action will generate attention and activity in the governments of other nations? A high degree of external consequentiality is important for any signal in which one actor attempts to communicate to others. It is analogous to the old joke about first hitting a mule with a 2 × 4 board in order to get its attention. By designing an event with a high degree of consequentiality, the actor is assuring that his action will be noticed — the recipients, finding it difficult to ignore the action, are forced into an occasion for decision. When combined with the other properties in this group, high external consequentiality is assumed to make the recognition of a crisis by the recipients less avoidable.

External consequentiality is measured on a scale from 0 to 1.00 with 1.00 representing actions which have the greatest impact on the governments of other nations. A number of characteristics are used to construct the scale, including the previous incidence of the event and the nature of the prior relationship between the actor and recipients.

Specificity

The specificity dimension describes the amount of information an actor provides to the recipient of his behavior about the actor's future expectations: To what extent does the action contain information about what the actor intends to do or desires some external entity to do? Put another way, specificity is defined as the part of a recipient's uncertainty that is under the control of the initiating actor's signal or event.

To increase the credibility of a threat, an actor will attempt to increase the recipient's certainty of the intended goal obstruction and the action required to avoid that outcome. The CREON data contains a series of items that seek to establish whether the actor is specific with respect to five areas: (1) the problem, (2) the addressee, (3) the kinds of resources used, (4) the amount of resources used, and (5) the time frame. Crisis precipitating events are expected to be specific on all or nearly all five areas.

Commitment

The commitment continuum measures the extent to which an event involves the present or future allocation of tangible resources. Resources are allocated by the use or transfer of goods, services, or capital, or by the generation of expectations concerning their future use that limit the freedom of national decisionmakers.

When resources are committed in support of a government's expression of hostility toward another, the recipient is likely to increase its estimate that the acting government is prepared to follow up on its displeasure. Thus, high commitment becomes important for establishing the credibility of intended goal obstruction and should be associated with crisis triggering events.

In the CREON Project commitment is measured along an eleven-point scale ranging from least (1) to most extensive (11) commitment.

Implementation Time

The implementation time dimension of an event concerns an estimate of the amount of time the acting government will require for executing the action once a decision has been reached and a strategy for its realization established. A diplomatic conversation can be conducted in minutes or hours, but the administration of a technical assistance program may take months or years to complete.

If the actor's event requires extensive time for completion, then the recipient has more time to make a response and search for some alternative means of goal realization other than the one being obstructed by the actor. Protracted execution time may cause the actor to lose his will to complete the event, an occurrence that can be abetted by the recipient and third parties who have more time to develop counterpressures when the actor's event unfolds gradually. The credibility of the complete fulfillment of the triggering event is eroded. Thus, we would expect events precipitating a crisis for the recipient to have relatively short implementation times.

For the CREON variable, "Time Required for Execution of Action," the coder estimates the amount of time the behaviors of the type initiated by the actor normally require for full implementation on an ordinal scale consisting of minutes/hours, days, weeks, months, or years.

Table 8.1 summarizes the dimensions that have been described and the extreme values of each that are hypothesized to be associated with events that precipitate crises. It is expected that a crisis is most likely to follow the initiation of an event by an actor that is a clear, recognizable, hostile behavior that credibly intends to obstruct the recipient's goals. A series of specificity variables designed to monitor different aspects of the event estimate clarity. A complex indicator called external consequentiality determines if the event has qualities that make it likely to be recognized. The expression of negative effect represents hostility. Both commitment and implementation time judge credibility. Finally, anticipated undesirability is first used as a general measure to calculate intent to obstruct goals; the kind of instrumentality employed and whether the event involves physical assault are more rigorous indicators.

TABLE 8.1
Dimensions and Variables Used in Constructing Crisis Precipitating
Properties

Dimension Name	CREON Variable (s)[a]	Specified Value for Crisis Precipitating Property
Anticipated desirability-undesirability	CREON Variable 33 (3 point rating scale)	undesired by recipient
Presence/absence of physical assault	CREON Variable 28 (2 of 35 revised WEIS categories)	"force" or "seize" categories
Instrumentality	Modified CREON Variable 35[b] (1 of 6 skill/resource categories)	military instrumentality
Affect	Modified CREON Variables 38 & 39[c] (7 point scale from -3 to +3)	strong negative affect
External consequentiality	Constructed CREON Scale[d] (range from 0.0 to 1.00)	highly consequential
Specificity	CREON Variables 40, 41, 42, 43, 44 (separate nominal variables)	each aspect of event coded as specific
Commitment	Constructed CREON Scale[e] (11 point scale)	high commitment
Implementation time	CREON Variable 54 (5 point rating scale)	short time (minutes/ hours or days)

[a]CREON variable numbers refer to the numbered descriptions in the appendix of Hermann, et al. (1973).

[b]The nominal categories for instrumentalities have been slightly revised from the description given in Hermann, et al. (1973). The changes are described in Hermann (1974).

[c]The affect score has been expanded to a more differentiated scale as reported in Hutchins (1974).

[d]External consequentiality is a scale that has been constructed by using information from various CREON variables. For its development see East and Hermann (1974).

[e]Commitment is a scale that has been constructed by using information from various CREON variables. For its development see Callahan and Swanson (1974).

Selecting the International Crises

The CREON data set was used to identify events having one or more of the stipulated characteristics; then it was determined whether they were soon followed by a crisis for the recipient of those signals. The results can take one of several forms. One possibility is that events with these properties were seldom followed by crises. Another is that the events with these properties did precede most crises; they also appeared prior to many other situations that were not crises. In that case, the ability of the stipulated class of events to discriminate crises from noncrises would be inadequate to serve any forecasting purpose. A third outcome is that events with the designated properties or some subset of them were found to be antecedents of crises but of very few other situations.

To undertake the analysis we needed a means of determining the occurrence of international crises during the decade 1959–1968 (the period of the CREON data). Several efforts have been made to construct post–World War II inventories of international crises. Although the authors of these inventories have not necessarily used the present definition of crisis, the identified lists are a first approximation of international crises that occurred from 1959 to 1968.[16] Three inventories have been most helpful. A list prepared by Phillips and Moore enumerates international crises for the entire time period covered in the CREON data.[17] A list of both internal and external political conflicts between 1944 and 1966 by Cady and Prince[18] did not provide exactly the focus required by the present study but could be used selectively for our purposes. A short compilation by Callahan focuses exclusively on international crises.[19] Table 8.2 lists the resulting thirty-nine crises that appeared on either the Phillips-Moore or the combined Cady-Prince and Callahan lists, and which also conform to our definition of a crisis (e.g., presenting decisionmakers with high threat and short time).

The CREON data cannot be searched for crisis precipitating events related to all thirty-nine crises contained on the independently established lists. One limitation stems from the requirement that the crises had to begin during the quarter of each year for which data were collected. The fourth column of Table 8.2 indicates that twenty-two of the thirty-nine crises began in quarters not included in the CREON sample.

Moreover, we can establish precipitating events only for the thirty-six countries that are included as actors in the CREON data set. As the fifth column of Table 8.2 reveals, seventeen of the thirty-nine could not be ex-

TABLE 8.2
International Crises and Their Coverage in CREON Data

| | Inventory Source | | Included in Analysis | Reason for Exclusion | |
Candidate Crisis/Conflict	Phillips-Moore	Cady-Prince Plus Callahan		Begins Outside Time Period	Precipitator Not CREON Actor
China/India, 1959		X	no	X	X
Dominican Republic, 1959	X		no	X	X
Haiti/Cuba, 1959	X		no	X	X
Panama/Cuba, 1959	X		no	X	X
China/Nepal, 1960	X	X	yes		
Congo, 1961	X		no		
Kuwait/Iraq, 1961	X	X	no	X	X
Bay of Pigs, 1961	X	X	no	X	X
India/Portugal, 1961	X	X	no	X	
Berlin Wall, 1961	X	X	no	X	
Cuba, 1962	X	X	yes		
India/China, 1962	X	X	yes		
Taiwan Straits, 1962	X		no	X	
Yemen, 1963-69	X	X	no		X
Haiti/Dominican Republic, 1963	X		no	X	X

	(1)	(2)	(3)	yes/no	(5)	(6)	(7)	(8)	(9)
Kenya/Somalia, 1963	X	X		no				X	X
Berlin, 1963	X	X		no	X	X		X	X
Algeria/Morocco, 1963	X	X	X	no	X	X	X	X	
Malaysia, 1963	X	X	X	no					
Cyprus, 1963-64	X	X	X	yes					
Somalia/Ethiopia, 1964	X	X		no				X	X
Malaysia, 1964	X	X		no					
North Vietnam, 1964-68	X	X	X	yes					
India/China, 1965	X	X		no	X	X			
Kashmir, 1965	X	X	X	no					
Jordan/Syria, 1965	X	X		no	X	X		X	X
Rhodesia, 1966	X	X		no	X	X			
Sino/Soviet, 1967	X	X	X	yes					
Arab/Israeli, 1967	X	X	X	no	X	X	X	X	X
Cyprus, 1967	X	X	X	no	X	X	X	X	X
Hong Kong, 1967	X	X	X	no	X	X	X		
Israel/Jordan, 1968	X	X	X	no	X	X	X		
Pueblo, 1968	X	X	X	no	X	X			
Czechoslovakia, 1968	X	X	X	no	X	X			
Israel/Syria, 1962			X	no					
Israel/Syria, 1964			X	no					
Afghanistan/Pakistan, 1964			X	no				X	
Cambodia/S. Vietnam, 1964			X	no				X	X
Haiti/Dominican Republic, 1964			X	no				X	

amined because the data did not contain relevant actors.

Together these two constraints reduced to six the number of situations independently identified as crises:[20]

China/Nepal	1960	Cyprus	1963–1964
Cuba	1962	North Vietnam	1964–1968
India/China	1962	Arab/Israel	1967

Even the casual reader will discover several problems with this list of six crises. First, the starting dates for the crises are extremely important to the analysis, yet they are difficult to establish with confidence. As displayed in Table 8.2, the original sources normally reported only the year (not the day and month) and in several instances the initially assigned dates covered several years. One or more crises, under our requirements of threat and short decision time, were difficult to establish with the time period originally assigned by the independent source. For example, the North Vietnamese conflict listed for the years 1964–1968 was disaggregated into at least three events prior to the beginning of the crisis. As a result of these considerations, fourteen situations will be the basis for an initial test of our stipulated properties for estimating events that precipitate crises.

> India enters a crisis on 20 October 1959 as a result of China's actions (1959 border clash)
>
> China enters a crisis on 20 October 1959 as a result of India's actions (1959 border clash)
>
> Nepal enters a crisis on 28 June 1962 as a result of China's actions (1962 border clash)
>
> India enters a crisis on 11 October 1962 as a result of China's actions (1962 border clash)
>
> China enters a crisis on 11 October 1962 as a result of India's actions (1962 border clash)
>
> United States enters a crisis on 16 October 1962 as a result of discovering Soviet missiles in Cuba (1962 missile crisis)
>
> USSR enters a crisis on 22 October 1962 as a result of U.S. action (Blockade in Cuban missile crisis)
>
> North Vietnam enters a crisis on 5 August 1964 as a result of U.S. action (Bombing in response to Gulf of Tonkin)

Greece enters a crisis on 8 August 1964 as a result of Turkey's actions (Turkey bombs Greek Cypriot positions)

North Vietnam enters a crisis on 7 February 1965 as a result of U.S. actions (Beginning of U.S. sustained bombing of the North)

Israel enters a crisis on 22 May 1967 as a result of Egypt's actions (Egypt closes Gulf of Aqaba)

Israel enters a crisis on 5 June 1967 as a result of Egypt's actions (1967 Arab-Israeli War)

Egypt enters a crisis on 5 June 1967 as a result of Israel's actions (1967 Arab-Israeli War)

North Vietnam enters a crisis on 20 April 1967 as a result of U.S. actions. (U.S. initial bombing of Hanoi and Haiphong)

Results and Conclusions

A total of 11,962 events in the CREON data were searched to determine if they possessed any of the crisis precipitating properties. In an initial experiment the highest possible scale values for high commitment, high specificity, and high external consequentiality were too severe a threshold and eliminated many events that appeared relevant to the identified crises. Accordingly, slightly lower values were used, but still in the direction of the extreme value or property presented earlier.

The recipients in the fourteen crises established in the previous section were national governments. In the CREON data, however, recipients may be international governmental organizations as well as subunits within a nation (both governmental and private) including specific individuals. Therefore, it was necessary to add a ninth property to the eight crisis precipitating ones; namely, that the addressee of the action be a national government.

Each of the properties was used as a screen through which all CREON events were filtered. Not all the properties proved equally useful in creating the class of events hypothesized to precipitate crises. As Table 8.3 shows, the data set could most rapidly be reduced by first applying the physical assault category, which by itself eliminated all but 146 of the events. By next using the high external consequentiality variable, the remaining events were reduced to 70, of which 10 involved only nonnational government recipients. The property that required all crisis

TABLE 8.3
Sequential Application of Properties in Creating
Set of Crisis Precipitating Events

Property	Events Remaining in Set*
Physical assault present	146
High external consequentiality	70
Nation as recipient	60
Negative affect	54
Short implementation time	52
Military instrumentality	52
High specificity	52
Anticipated undesirability	52
High commitment	52

The total number of events in this version of CREON data set before any
were eliminated by specified properties was 11,962

precipitating events to have strong negative affect was applied next and it
reduced the set from 60 to 54 events. Another property, short implementation time, eliminated 2 additional events. None of the remaining four
stipulated properties — military instruments, high specificity, anticipated
undesirability, or high commitment — reduced the remaining set of 52
events.

How many of the fifty-two events pertained to the fourteen crises identified as falling within the domain of the CREON data? Forty (77 percent) concerned one of the fourteen crises. Furthermore, twelve of the
fourteen crises had at least one of the events with the crisis precipitating
properties that occurred on the day estimated that the recipient entered a
state of crisis (Table 8.4). Of the forty events, twelve occurred on or
before the specified dates for the beginning of the crises; another three
are dated as having transpired within twenty-four hours of the designated onset of the crisis. (Given the difficulty of pinpointing the starting
point of a crisis, some variability in the dating of events should probably
be considered.) The remaining twenty-five events took place in a matter
of days after the initiation of the crises.

Twelve events (23 percent) assumed to precipitate crises were unrelated
to any of the fourteen crises. Ten of these concerned the Vietnam War
and several may very well flag events that some analysts might designate
as crises. For example, one event referred to the first air strikes by the
United States in the demilitarized zone (DMZ), and four others referred
to incidents along the Cambodian border. Unrelated to Vietnam were the

TABLE 8.4
Distribution of Crisis Precipitating Events for Crises

Crisis	Day Crisis Began	Day + 1	Day + 2	Total
1959 China/India	1			1
1959 India/China	1			1
1960 China/Nepal	1			1
1962 China/India	1		5	6
1962 India/China	1		4	5
1962 U.S.S.R./U.S.	0			0
1962 U.S./U.S.S.R.	1	1		2
1964 U.S./North Vietnam	1			1
1964 Turkey/Greece	1	2		3
1965 U.S./North Vietnam	1		11	12
1967 Egypt/Israel (Gulf)	1			1
1967 Israel/Egypt (War)	0			0
1967 Egypt/Israel (War)	1			1
1967 U.S./North Vietnam	1		5	6
Total crisis precipitating events	12	3	25	40
Total events not applicable to any of 13 designated crises				12
Total events having properties assumed to precipitate a crisis				52

Chinese shelling of Quemoy and Matsu in May 1959 and again a month later upon President Eisenhower's arrival in Taiwan.

In forming conclusions about this study, it should be recalled that neither the event data nor the variables designating event properties were originally designed for the purposes of this research. Furthermore, it is evident that a comprehensive, independent inventory of international crises covering the entire time period and employing a standard definition of crisis and techniques of dating was missing. Whether or not correction of these limitations would alter the results is uncertain, but their absence could affect the interpretation of these results.

If the proposed procedures do have merit, two modifications would undoubtedly improve their effectiveness. The first would be to develop some indicators of context that could be used in conjuction with crisis precipitating properties. As McClelland observed: "The type of act perceived to have been the immediate cause of an acute crisis does not 'communicate' the same way at all times. The immediate 'logic of the situation' and the timing of events seem crucial."[21] It should be possible to construct some background indicators concerning the condition of particular governments and the state of relations between governments against which specific events could be more readily interpreted. Choucri notes that on a thirteen-point tension scale contemporary relations between Canada and the United States might range normally between 2 and 5, whereas those between Israel and the Arab states might be closer to 11 or 12. Thus, "If the United States–Canada interactions were to jump to a mean of 8 on a 13-point conflict scale the implications would be quite different than if Arab/Israeli interactions were to converge around a mean of 8."[22] A background conflict scale of the kind Azar[23] has been developing could establish a baseline to serve as a contextuality indicator for interpreting crisis precipitating events.

A second change would be the use of multiple sources for event collection, including sources from the nations to be monitored. The stipulated properties described in this chapter could be equally well applied to official governmental cable traffic and related materials, if available to the analyst.

Finally, the proposed configuration of crisis precipitating properties may have placed too heavy an emphasis on military factors (i.e., physical assault and military instruments). Such concentration might be less appropriate in the future than in the examined decade of 1959–1968.

But why should anyone—in government or elsewhere—consider adopting a procedure such as this one even if improved and demonstrated to be relatively dependable? For one thing it proposes the possibility of identifying a class of events that may precede the occurrence of a crisis. As Wilbert Moore commented in a discussion of scientific forecasting: "Although single political events are sometimes very important, the best we can hope to do is predict the probability of a class of events."[24] With further development, these procedures might provide a probability estimate of a certain class of events (crises) based on a combination of contextual indicators and properties of other prior classes of events.

The lead time between the triggering event and the onset of the crisis is short indeed. In every case, the crisis precipitating event occurred on the same day as we stipulated the recipient to be in crisis. The introduction of other event properties and contextual variables might improve the lead time. But what if they do not? Such a system would be of little use to recipients of such events as a means of anticipating crises. An acting government might be unaware that its own behaviors contained elements tending toward crisis, but those circumstances would seem infrequent. Perhaps the primary beneficiaries of such a system would be third parties who are not at the outset among either the initiators or the recipients of the crisis. Evidence from the study of past crises suggests that third parties have sometimes been slow to recognize crises that subsequently spread and engulfed them. Not only would an early warning available to third parties enable them to take prompt steps to reduce the enlargement of the confrontation, it would also give them more time to introduce mediating capabilities.

Beyond the prospects of the immediate technique for forecasting explored in the preceding pages is the larger issue with which this chapter began — the role of international crises as agents of system change. The world will certainly continue to experience international crises. Their potential for system disruption will increase if better means for dealing with them are not devised. Crises of the future are likely to be more complex and diverse than those faced by political leaders during the past few generations. The number and variety of interactional actors is expanding. The means of destruction available to humans continue to become more deadly, diverse, and widely distributed. The real gap between haves and have nots is increasing on a number of dimensions at the same time that global communications enhance everyone's awareness of the discrepancies. The growing complexity of social systems and their technological supports makes them more susceptible to accidental or deliberate disruption at a very large number of points. Heightened interdependence not only between social systems but between different types of systems makes breakdowns in one likely to affect others.

For all these reasons, crises are likely to become even more potent agents of system change and transformation in the coming decades. If humankind desires to assume a more active role in shaping a planned future, part of the task must be to gain greater control over abrupt, unintended change agents. Better understanding of the phenomena called crises and means of forecasting them are a necessary part of this undertaking.

Acknowledgments

This research was conducted under a contract with the Office of Naval Research for the Advanced Research Projects Agency (Contract No. N00014-75-C-0765). The views expressed are exclusively those of the authors. An earlier version of this paper was presented at the 18th Annual Meeting of the International Studies Association in St. Louis, Missouri, 16–20 March 1977. The authors gratefully acknowledge the helpful comments of the contractor, participants on the ISA panel, and Ole Holsti.

Notes

1. For a further discussion, see Chapter 9.
2. Oran R. Young, *The Intermediaries* (Princeton, N.J.: Princeton University Press, 1967).
3. Glenn H. Snyder and Paul Diesing, *Conflict Among Nations* (Princeton, N.J.: Princeton University Press, 1977).
4. See, for example, Charles F. Hermann, "International Crisis as a Situational Variable," in *International Politics and Foreign Policy,* ed. James N. Rosenau (New York: Free Press, 1969).
5. See, for example, Thomas W. Milburn, "The Management of Crisis," in *International Crises: Insights from Behavioral Research,* ed. Charles F. Hermann (New York: Free Press, 1972).
6. See, for example, Robert C. North, Richard Brody, and Ole R. Holsti, "Some Empirical Data on the Conflict Spiral," *Peace Research Society Papers* 1 (Chicago Conference, 1963); Ole R. Holsti, Robert C. North, and Richard A. Brody, "Perception and Action in the 1914 Crisis," in *Quantitative International Politics: Insights and Evidence,* ed. J. David Singer (New York: Free Press, 1968); and Dina A. Zinnes, "The Expression and Perception of Hostility in Pre-War Crisis: 1914," in *Quantitative International Politics.*
7. Bruce M. Russett, "Cause, Surprise, and No Escape," *The Journal of Politics* 24:1 (1972):3–22, emphasis in original.
8. We agree in this assertion with, among others, Robert C. North, Ole R. Holsti, M. George Zaninovich, and Dina A. Zinnes, *Content Analysis* (Evanston, Ill.: Northwestern University Press, 1963), see esp. Appendixes A, B; and Robert Jervis, *Perception and Misperception in International Politics* (Princeton, N.J.: Princeton University Press, 1976).
9. The CREON Project, from which the data used in this research are drawn, makes the distinction between the direct target of an event (the receiver of a communication), and the indirect object of that event (the entity that the actor is attempting to influence). The target and object may be the same but need not be. For the purposes of this initial inquiry, we are combining targets and objects under the term "recipients." It is possible that an actor creates a crisis for an entity that is not an identifiable recipient in the way we have used the term. For the moment we have no way of specifying such nonrecipient potential subjects for crisis.
10. The combination of physical deeds and verbal behavior is illustrated by the concept of coercive diplomacy advanced by Alexander L. George, David K. Hall, and William E. Simons, *The Limits of Coercive Diplomacy* (Boston: Little, Brown and Co., 1971). It entails the incorporation of physical deeds in signaling activities.
11. Hermann, "International Crisis"; Charles F. Hermann, ed., *International Crises: Insights from Behavioral Research,* (New York: Free Press, 1972); Linda P. Brady, "Bureaucratic Politics and Situational Constraints in Foreign Policy" (Paper presented at the American Political Science Association meetings, Chicago, 29 August–2 September 1974); Linda P. Brady, "Threat, Decision Time,

and Awareness: The Impact of Situational Variables on Foreign Policy Behavior" (Ph.D. diss., Ohio State University, 1974); Thomas L. Brewer, *Foreign Policy Situations: American Elite Response to Variations in Threat, Time, and Surprise* (Beverly Hills, Calif.: Sage Publications, 1972); and Michael Brecher, "Toward a Theory of International Crisis Behavior," *International Studies Quarterly* 21 (1971):39–74.

12. One may attribute part of the difficulty to the inadequate conceptualization and operationalization of the concept of surprise in our previous research. For example, one might wish to distinguish between such features as the familiarity of a problem (i.e., whether more or less similar problems have been experienced in the past) and the extent to which the present problem was anticipated (i.e., whether the urgent problem was expected before it occurred). These conceptual distinctions have been confounded in the past. The difficulty has been aggravated by the absence of good indicators of surprise in event data descriptions and relatively unsophisticated questionnaire items.

13. By an "uncollapsed" version of *Deadline Data,* we mean that none of the index cards on which the material is displayed have been discarded. The producer of this reference service instructs subscribers to eliminate many of the older file cards and replace them with newly provided summary cards that greatly telescope prior events into a much shorter list that retains only those events that the *Deadline Data* editors regard as most significant in view of subsequent developments. This process maintains the file at a fixed size by constantly collapsing the number of older entries. The procedure significantly reduces the utility of the reference for longitudinal analysis. Regrettably, most libraries follow the producer's instructions and, even more regrettably, most of the studies using *Deadline Data* have used this truncated version.

14. Charles F. Hermann et al., *CREON: A Foreign Affairs Data Set* (Beverly Hills, Calif.: Sage Publications, 1973); and Patrick T. Callahan, Linda P. Brady, and Margaret G. Hermann, eds., *Events, Behaviors, and Policies* (Columbus: Ohio State University Press, forthcoming).

15. Charles A. McClelland and Gary D. Hoggard, "Conflict Patterns in the Interactions Among Nations," in James N. Rosenau, ed., *International Politics and Foreign Policy,* rev. ed. (New York: Free Press, 1969).

16. Two other inventories considered for this chapter were a list of "imperialist wars" enumerated by official sources of the People's Republic of China and an inventory of local wars by a noted Hungarian social scientist, Istvan Kende, "Twenty-five Years of Local Wars," *Journal of Peace Research* 7:1 (1971):5–22. Although these inventories would have greatly expanded the international flavor of research, neither list added any new crises that were not already contained in the other inventories and that also met the additional requirements of the CREON data to be discussed in the text. A third inventory, Leo Hazelwood et al., "Planning for Problems in Crisis Management," *International Studies Quarterly* 21:1 (1977):75–106, prepared for CACI, Inc., was also considered for this chapter. However, this inventory listed only crises involving the United States, and therefore was of limited use for this research.

17. Warren R. Phillips and James A. Moore, "U.S. Policy Positions and Actions in Crises," [Paper presented at the 13th North American Peace Science Conference, Peace Science Society (International), Cambridge, Mass., 10–12 November 1975].

18. Richard Cady and William Prince, *Political Conflicts, 1944–1946* (Ann Arbor: Social Science Division, Bendix Corporation, 1974).

19. Patrick T. Callahan, "Third Party Responses Behavior in Foreign Policy," (Ph.D. diss., Ohio State University, 1974).

20. The nation whose action is assumed to trigger the crises (e.g., China in the first item) must be one of the actor nations for which events were cited in the CREON data set. We do not assume that the designated actor is the only entity responsible for creating the crisis for the other nation or that it is necessarily the ultimate source of the situation. For the purpose of this analysis, however, it is the CREON actor whose behaviors prior to the crisis were searched for actions manifesting the postulated crisis precipitating properties.

A technical appendix prepared for this study is available from the authors. It presents the case for assigning the specific dates (day and month) used to fix the beginning of each crisis. It also summarizes the evidence the authors used to determine that each selected situation created a situation of high threat and short decision time for the recipient nation and thus conform to our stipulated definition. A copy of the appendix may be obtained by writing: Charles F. Hermann, Mershon Center, The Ohio State University, 199 W. Tenth Avenue, Columbus, Ohio 43201.

21. McClelland and Hoggard, "Conflict Patterns."

22. Nazli Choucri, "Forecasting and International Relations: Problems and Prospects," *International Interactions* 1:2 (1974):63–86.

23. Edward E. Azar, "Behavioral Forecasts and Policy-Making: An Events Data Approach," in Charles W. Kegley et al., eds., *International Events and the Comparative Analysis of Foreign Policy* (Columbia: University of South Carolina Press, 1975).

24. Wilbert E. Moore et al., "The Nature and Limitations of Forecasting," *Daedalus* 96:3 (1967):939–947.

9

RANDOLPH M. SIVERSON

War and Change
in the International System

Although students of international relations analyze many phenomena, perhaps none has been of such central, enduring interest as warfare among nations. A large, extensive literature exists on this subject, much of which specifically attempts to explain the occurrence of war. Within this literature one particularly prominent theme seeks to link the structure of the international system to the amount of war the system experiences. It is asserted, for example, by Waltz that a bipolar system will experience less war than a multipolar system; but Deutsch and Singer, on the other hand, argue that the multipolar system is more congenial to international stability, i.e., the absence of war, or at least major war.[1] There are, of course, numerous variations on this theme, but there is little escape from its enduring persistence. Despite the various manners in which the conceptualization is put forward, the almost single-minded focus has been on the propensity for war in various types of systems. In contrast, however, the equally important problem of the consequences of war for system change until recently has been addressed only in passing rather than in systematic comparative studies.

This relative lack of attention to war as an agent of system change— and for that matter the entire subject of system change itself—may be related to the tendency for studies of the international system to focus on the equilibrium behavior of particular, named systems (e.g., the balance of power). This tendency may derive from the fact that many of the mainly conceptual renditions of the international system are based upon general systems theory, which has as one of its main axioms the process of homeostasis or system maintenance. Kaplan's early and influential *System and Process in International Politics* is a case in point.[2] Kaplan devotes his attention almost exclusively to the statics of international politics. His well-known rules are rules of system maintenance, and wars are engaged in to maintain the system, be it balance of power, loose bipolar, or tight bipolar.[3] This tendency to study statics is also true of Rosecrance's *Action and Reaction in International Politics,* although to a lesser extent.[4] Rosecrance, while preoccupied with system maintenance, does recognize that when variety cannot be reduced by the regulatory capacity of the system, change will take place. Moreover, Rosecrance explicitly notes that wars may have a function in system transformation, and in later research, Denton reports findings concerning the coincidence of peaks of war in the international system at about the time Rosecrance argued a system transformation was taking place.[5] Despite such recognition and repeated assertions throughout the literature that wars can cause change or even transformation in a system, an explicit understanding of how and why such changes take place is still lacking. For example, World Wars I and II frequently are alleged to have transformed the international system, but what was it that they altered to cause this transformation?

This question cannot be answered without reference to some view of what constitutes the international system. At once one may begin with a statement that the international system, like all other systems, consists of a set of objects, in this case nations, interacting with each other in an environment. While such a view is useful, it does not adequately distinguish what it is about this system that is political. Insofar as conceptions of the international system are structural, it is important to note that one factor which is either implicitly or explicitly important in many of these is the distribution of military power among the nations in the system.[6] This power distribution results in a structure which influences not only the security levels of the nations, but also shapes the pattern of interaction and bargaining among nations in the security issue area and frequently in other areas as well.[7] While the international system is often discussed in terms of types (i.e., bipolar or multipolar), it is not always useful to view the structures within these types as static. Rather, a dynamic view of the international system, such as that offered by North, sees the structure of the system as changing through time as the power relationships of the nations vary.[8] But wars, with their ability to alter the distribution of power in the international system with great rapidity, offer dramatic alterations in these smooth patterns. Frequently, the alterations are confined to one locality of the system and may have an impact upon only a few of the nations, but the consequences may be dramatic for the manner in which those nations endeavor to maintain their national security. Much less frequently, the shift may involve many nations and hence result in abrupt changes throughout the entire system of nations.

Organski and Kugler, however, cast some doubt on the proposition that wars bring about change in the international system.[9] Following

Organski's well-known view that the distribution of economic capability among nations is one of the basic components of national power,[10] Organski and Kugler use a time series of economic data on thirty-two participants in World Wars I and II to find that international war has only a slight impact upon the economic performance of winning and neutral nations. Moreover, although losing nations are set back a substantial amount in their immediate postwar economic performance, within the span of fifteen to twenty years they are able to regain what was lost. A conclusion reached from these data is that nations "return to levels of national capabilities they would reasonably expect hold had there been no war."[11] Moreover, in advancing a somewhat more general conclusion than that based strictly on the economic data, Organski and Kugler assert that "the outcomes of war, insofar as international power is concerned, make no difference."[12] Although this conclusion is followed by qualifying language, particularly with regard to the possibility that winners may occupy, exploit, and repress losers, it is clearly their view that "soon [after the war] the power distribution in the system returns to levels anticipated had the war not occurred."[13] Consequently, one is asked to accept the conclusion that the distribution of world political power in 1965 (twenty years after the end of World War II) is pretty much what it would have been without the war (with the exception — not insignificantly — of several Eastern European nations).

Not only are the data advanced by Organski and Kugler on this "phoenix factor" persuasive, but the *economic* growth of Germany and Japan in the years since 1945 offers salient, readily recognizable examples of exactly what they argue. Those cases are familiar and probably unarguable.[14] It is not clear, however, whether such individual postwar recoveries have been the general pattern. There are numerous cases of nations which have gone into decline as political powers after losing a war; consider, for example, the instances of Spain after 1588 and the defeat of the Spanish Armada,[15] the Netherlands after the Treaty of Breda in 1667 ended the Dutch Wars,[16] and Austria after 1918. Moreover, one may question whether the economic recoveries of Japan and *West* Germany have been projected into the international political arena as they were before World War II.

Further, it is in some respects also difficult to accept the implications of their argument for the international system. For example, consider the instance of World War II, which has been almost universally viewed as a system-transforming event. How can we reconcile the data so clearly presented by Organski and Kugler with the widely held perception that the shape of world politics was rapidly transformed by that upheaval? The answer lies in the fact that both views are correct. Organski and

Kugler's data indicate that nations do rise from the ashes. They are not alone in this belief.[17] However, by almost any set of calculations there has been a massive reshuffling of the global power distribution since the onset of World War II. The problem of squaring Organski and Kugler's data with current interpretations of the international system lies in the fact that their data measure only the dimension of national productivity, when in fact power may be understood and measured in other ways as well, ways which may be more in accord with widely shared perceptions of the distribution of political power.

Although Organski and Kugler may be correct about the possible existence of a phoenix factor, the recovery of the gross national product (GNP) to levels that would have existed had the war not occurred is not *sufficient* grounds for concluding that the "power distribution in the system returns to levels anticipated had the war not occurred."[18] A somewhat more comprehensive approach to this problem is taken here to support the argument that wars do in fact produce changes in the international system through a number of complex and often interrelated processes, *some* of which are economic.

The basic premise of this chapter is in some respects not unlike that of Organski and Kugler. The overall productive capacity of a nation, typically measured by GNP, is critically important in establishing the *possibility* of a nation's international power. However, nations do not use their productive capacities in identical manners. In some respects this is the result of resource endowments. But for the present purpose what is important is the willingness and ability of national elites to direct their nation's productive capacity or existing power capabilities into influencing the behavior of other nations in the issue area of national security. The argument of this chapter is that as a consequence of war national elites may find their nation's productive capacities changed and may further gain or lose control of these. Moreover, as a consequence of war, the issues over which the elites wish to use power may be correspondingly altered.[19] As nations lose military capability, they will in general lose the ability to protect themselves and suffer a corresponding loss of position in the international system.

As part of a preliminary effort to evaluate the impact of war on nations and consequently on the international system, the extent to which wars have produced changes within several aspects of elite choice and elite stability will be examined. Additionally, since the distribution of military resources is deemed to be of critical import in determining the structure of the international system, an effort will be made toward evaluating the impact of war on this distribution. Finally, an effort will be made to link the structure of the system with the relations and interactions among nations.

War and National Power

National Choices

Since wars involve costs for nations, the postwar consequences of these costs may have profound implications for the way in which elites are able to control resources and the direction in which they attempt to use those they do control. There are three basic effects which can be traced to war participation: (1) alteration of elite attitudes about the efficacy of force, (2) internal political instability, resulting in loss of control, and (3) regime change, resulting in a basic restructuring of the manner in which an elite approaches the existing distribution of values in the international system.

For some nations war participation is so costly in terms of human or economic resources that its leadership is reluctant to enter into conflicts or conflict-preparatory behaviors in the future. Shortly after the termination of U.S. participation in the Vietnam War, U.S. decisionmakers were faced with the possibility of becoming involved in another distant war in Angola. In the ensuing debate over the issue of potential U.S. involvement in Angola one of the frequently asserted points against action was the "lessons of Vietnam." Systematic data on this point may be found in Chapter 11 by Holsti and Rosenau in which it is shown that one effect of the Vietnam War on U.S. attitudes has been the breakdown of consensus on cold war axioms favoring intervention. One of Holsti and Rosenau's questionnaire items specifically refers to Angola, and the results indicate a clear unwillingness on the part of the leaders in the sample to pursue intervention. Moreover, Vietnam may have produced more general consequences than simply restraining action in Vietnam, for as Holsti argues the consensus supporting a centralist coalition that favored a globalist U.S. foreign policy "became just another in the long list of Vietnam casualties."[20]

This pattern of behavior is not unique to the United States. Consider British behavior in the period 1935–1939 when they were confronted with the rise of Hitler and Mussolini. Could the policy of appeasement – admittedly aimed at avoiding war – have had any of its roots in the memories British and French decisionmakers had of the slaughter of World War I? While no systematic data are available on this point, the following statement to the House of Commons by Prime Minister Neville Chamberlain is illustrative of how a belief system may be affected by war:

> When I think of four terrible years and I think of the 7,000,000 young men who were cut off in their prime, the 13,000,000 who were maimed and mutilated, the misery and the suffering of the mothers and fathers, the sons and daughters, and the relatives and friends of those who were killed and wounded, then I am bound to say again what I have said before, and what I say now not only to you, but to all the world—in war, whichever side may call itself victor, there are no winners, but all are losers. It is these thoughts which have made me feel that it was my prime duty to strain every nerve to avoid a repetition of the Great War in Europe.[21]

There is a second possible impact of war on a nation's decisionmaking elites. It is sometimes the case that either the cost of war participation or the event subsequent to the outcome will result in the removal of a government or a regime. If one uses the Singer-Small list of wars between 1815 and 1965, then by reference to Banks's *Cross-Polity Time-Series Data* and Langer's *Encyclopedia of World History* one may observe the relationship between war participation and postwar governmental survival.[22] Such a procedure indicates that within three years of the end of a nation's war participation, 45 of 184 war participants experienced a nonconstitutional change of government. Additionally, if these data are divided into winners and losers (according to the decision of Singer and Small), the chances of a nonconstitutional change for losers are more than twice those of winners, as Table 9.1 illustrates. Finally, what about the impact of the size of the war? Do big wars produce greater change

TABLE 9.1
Non-Constitutional Change of Government and
Nation's Position in Outcome of War, 1815-1965

		Non-Constitutional Change of Government	
		Yes	No
Nation's outcome	winner (N = 114)	20 (17.5%)	94 (82.4%)
	loser (N = 70)	25 (35.7%)	45 (64.3%)

TABLE 9.2
Non-Constitutional Change of Government and
Nation's Position in Outcome of War, WW I and II

		Non-Constitutional Change of Government	
		Yes	No
Nation's outcome	winner (N=30)	6 (20.0%)	24 (80.0%)
	loser (N=11)	10 (90.9%)	1 (9.1%)

than small wars? Table 9.2 indicates the relationship between a nation's position in the war outcome and change of government for the two largest wars in the Singer-Small data set, World Wars I and II. As it may be seen, only one loser in these two wars (Finland) was able to maintain its government intact; all the others were changed in various nonconstitutional ways.

While these changes in themselves may reflect instability and bring about conditions in which elites are not fully able to control the resources of the nation in order to exercise power internationally, it is not the mere change of government which has had the most profound restructuring impact, but the change of complete regimes. In the nineteenth century regime changes were relatively infrequent, but did occur and were sometimes associated with warfare. The fall of the liberal government in Spain in 1823 was the consequence of that nation's war with France, and the abdication of Napoleon III and emergence of the Third Republic were the direct result of the Franco-Prussian War. These changes, however, pale in comparison to those which took place in the aftermaths of World Wars I and II. Of the nations defeated in either of these two wars only one (again, Finland) escaped without a major change of regime. In World War I the Ottoman, German, Austro-Hungarian, and Russian empires were dismembered and each nation's regime was drastically reconstituted. World War II brought about drastic changes in the forms of government of Japan, Italy, and Germany. Further, changes of regime were not limited to the losers. Italy, which had been on the winning side in World War I, found itself in 1919 loaded with debt, a high cost of living, and substantial political unrest, all in large part connected to participation in the war. These factors eventually brought about the fall of the Facta government and the installation of Mussolini's dictator-ship.

The change of these regimes is important not simply because it in-dicates instability, but because the elites brought to power in some of those nations (most notably in Italy, the Soviet Union, and eventually Germany) by the short- and long-range consequences of World War I did not accept the prevailing international order and sought to disrupt and restructure it.

Changes in the Distribution of Power

One of the fundamental conclusions reached by Organski and Kugler is that wars do not change the distribution of power beyond what it would have been without the war. Their data, however, do not address this point directly since the issue of distribution is not explicitly in-vestigated. Instead they assume that because levels of GNP regain the losses caused by the war that power is distributed as it would have been. Such an approach is certainly not irrelevant, but it does tend to neglect particular aspects of the distribution of international power which may be critical to the international political system. For example, it is not unreasonable to argue that there are particular uses for GNP which will produce more power than others. Whether GNP itself or some of these alternative uses of it are the most appropriate indicator depends, in part, upon the conceptualization one has of the international system and political bargaining in that system.

Basic to many conceptions of international politics is the notion of in-ternational anarchy. Under the conditions of anarchy, in which a nation must rely upon itself (and whatever friends it may be able to find) in order to defend its interests — the most basic of which is survival — the ac-quisition of the means of defense may be thought of as a critical element in that nation's power. While wealth, as expressed in GNP, may provide the capacity or capability for acquiring the military goods necessary for defending a nation and its interests, it is by no means clear in this concep-tualization that GNP should be equated with power. The reason for this is that GNP may be used to provide a variety of diverse goods and ser-vices for a nation. It can be used, in the classic choice posed by Joseph Goebbels, to provide either guns or butter. In examining the distribution of power in the international system, therefore, it may be useful to ex-plore the extent to which wars brought about redistributions of power when that power is viewed as a consequence of military effort such as, for example, military spending.

Prior to World War II the great powers of the world, as defined by

TABLE 9.3
Military Expenditures of the Great Powers in Current Dollars, 1937 and 1976

	1937*		1976**	
	Amount (in millions)	Percent of Great Power Total	Amount (in millions)	Percent of Great Power Total
United States	992	6.9	91,000	29.4
Great Britain	1,263	8.8	12,600	4.1
France	909	6.4	14,200	4.6
Japan	1,130	7.9	5,070	1.6
Germany	4,000	28.0	20,290+	6.6
Italy	870	6.1	4,980	1.6
Soviet Union	5,026	35.2	127,000	41.0
China	95	.7	34,400	11.1
Total	14,285	100	209,540	100

* <u>Source:</u> Quincy Wright, <u>A Study of War</u> (Chicago, University of Chicago Press, 1965, second edition), pp. 670-72.

** <u>Source:</u> United States Arms and Disarmament Agency, <u>World Military Expenditures and Arms Transfers, 1967-1976</u> (Washington: U.S. Arms Control and Disarmament Agency, 1978), pp. 28-32.

+ The 1976 data for Germany are the sum of East and West German military expenditures.

Singer and Small, were Great Britain, France, Japan, the Soviet Union, Germany, the United States, and Italy.[23] For comparative purposes, China will also be included in this group. Table 9.3 reports the 1937 and 1976 military expenditures for each of these nations. The 1937 figures indicate substantial concentrations of military spending in Germany and the Soviet Union with lower amounts being spent in Great Britain, France, Italy, Japan, and the United States. China hardly enters the picture in 1937 in terms of spending. In 1976, the pattern is drastically altered. The Soviet Union still retains a leading position as a military spender, but the United States and China have greatly increased their percentage of great power military expenditures. Germany (which in 1976 represents a *sum* of expenditures of both East and West Germany), Italy, and Japan have lost large amounts of their shares, while France and Great Britain have lost less, but still significant, shares of military power. It may be observed that the military expenditures of Japan and the two Germanys have been increasing through time, but the point is that thirty years after the end of World War II, these actors fell from positions of great power to clients of the United States. Moreover, if it appears incongruous to include China as a power in 1937, it is equally so to include Italy today.

Clearly, the implication of these data is that there has been a massive redistribution of power in the international system between 1937 and 1976. As Modelski has shown, the concentration of this military power in the United States and the Soviet Union took place at the end of World War II and has persisted since.[24] It is, of course, the case that the USA-USSR share of world military expenditures has declined since the 1950s, but it is also true that this relative decline is based upon the recovery of nations defeated in World War II as well as the very heavy spending by Third World nations on military equipment, much of which they acquire from the United States or the Soviet Union. In several respects such a decline is more apparent than real. While data on expenditures indicate current spending they do not fully reveal the "capital stock" of the nation's weapons or the types of weapons being acquired. For example, the United States and the Soviet Union expend very substantial amounts of their military funds on regional and intercontinental nuclear weapons and delivery systems.

Not only can wars dramatically alter the military expenditure distribution of groups of nations, but they may cause equally rapid shifts in the basic territorial nature of the national unit. Such changes can have profound consequences not only for the nation, but also for the distribution of power in the system. Consider, for example, the case of Austria-Hungary. Organski and Kugler do not include Austria-Hungary in their sample of nations because of its troubled post–World War I performance. They accurately describe the plight of Austria in this period: "Austria-Hungary was dismembered after World War I; the economic depression was particularly acute; there was civil war; and finally, Austria was absorbed into the Third Reich."[25] Are we to presume that the transformation of Austria-Hungary's international position was not without its consequences for European politics? As Chatterjee describes it, Austria moved from the core of European politics to the periphery, but could offer a significant augmentation to German power once absorbed.[26]

Just as this sudden waning of a nation's position may have important consequences for the distribution of power, so can the rapid growth of a nation. The unification of Italy in 1860, as a consequence of several wars, transformed a group of small, relatively weak nations from the prey of France and Austria to a major power whose existence altered the calculations of the other actors with regard to southern Europe and the Mediterranean. Moreover, it allowed Italy to gather sufficient resources to begin colonial expansion in Africa.

An even clearer case of war transforming an important portion of the international system may be found in the final unification of Germany as one outcome of the Franco-Prussian War in 1870. As described by Smoke, the alterations in the balance of power brought about by this war were profound and far reaching.

> What had previously been the North German Confederation was joined with the southern states to become the German Reich, constructed substantially according to Prussian design, and the King of Prussia became the kaiser. Among other consequences, creation of the empire completed the upset of the European balance of power begun earlier, for where there had been a multitude of competing states, there now was just one—one, furthermore, that clearly was the strongest military power on the Continent. The leaders of Austria-Hungary . . . finally abandoned their centuries-old interest and involvements in Germany, and directed their ambitions into the Balkans, a shift that contributed greatly to the cataclysm a generation later. And for the first time in the modern age, the French found themselves faced with a great power of the first rank on their very doorstep, a fact which was to define the core problem of the international politics of Europe for the next seventy-five years.[27]

The Consequences of Power Change

The Aggregation of Power

Theorists of the international system usually posit a relationship between the structure of the system and the interaction of states. As Snyder and Diesing point out, however, alliances are frequently subsumed within the conception of a system's structure when for analytical purposes it is most useful to view them as *relations* that are influenced by the system's structure but constituting a separate class. As Snyder and Diesing argue, if such a distinction is not drawn "the effects of structure upon relations are simply lost from view."[28] Adhering to the view that alliances are influenced by structure but do not themselves define the structure prevents the mistaken comparison of the supposed "bipolar" system of 1914 with the actual bipolar system that followed 1945. If this argument is correct, then changes in the distribution of military capability, a structural variable, should produce roughly similar changes in alliance patterns.

The point may be taken somewhat further. While alliances may function as many goals for decisionmakers, national security is surely chief among them. An alliance between two nations is an arrangement wherein each party expects to gain security. Nonetheless, to the extent that these nations enjoy differential military capability they will be able to furnish

differential amounts of security to each other. Consequently, powerful
nations are able to provide more protection for their allies than weak nations and should, other things being equal, be more in demand as alliance
partners. Following this logic, powerful nations should have a larger
number of alliances than weak nations. Moreover, to the extent that
military capabilities shift as the result of a war, a roughly corresponding
shift should be expected in alliance patterns.

Has the concentration of power in the United States and the Soviet
Union in the post–World War II era, as shown in Table 9.3, had an impact upon the structure of alliances of the international system? One may
observe the extent to which pre- and post–World War II alliance configurations reflect similar or dissimilar behaviors. Since the period
following the end of World War II has seen a rapid increase in the
number of nations—a not insignificant alteration of the system although
only partly related to the war—we will focus only on the alliance patterns
of the great powers as given above in Table 9.3. Table 9.4 displays for
each power the number of alliances it entered into within the period
1919–1939 and 1945–1965.[29]

The pre- and post–World War II levels of alliance participation reveal
very strong differences. The United States, which between 1919 and 1939
had entered into only one alliance, was a member of seven in the postwar
era. China follows the same pattern. Germany,[30] Italy, and France all
lost their positions as leaders in alliance participation and lost them
rather dramatically. Italy, for example, participated in 14 alliances in the
pre–World War II period, but only one in the most recent postwar
period. Similarly, Germany, which had ten alliances between 1919 and

TABLE 9.4
Great Power Alliance Participation, 1919-1939 and 1945-1965

	1919-1939		1945-1965	
	Number of Alliances	Percent of Great Power Total	Number of Alliances	Percent of Great Power Total
United States	1	1.7	7	19.4
Great Britain	5	8.5	7	19.4
France	11	18.6	4	11.1
Japan	2	3.4	0	0
Germany	10	16.9	2	5.1
Italy	14	23.7	1	2.8
Soviet Union	15	25.4	8	22.2
China	1	1.7	7	19.4
Total	59	99.9	36	99.4

Source: Alan Sabrosky, "The War-Time Reliability of Interstate Alliances,"
mimeo, 1975.

1939 (and nine of these were created between 1933 and 1939), was a partner in only two in the latter period (this reflects one alliance each for East and West Germany). Overall, the data in this table portray a rather abrupt shift in the alliance participation of the major powers.

In general, the shifts reflected in Table 9.4 parallel the changes in military expenditures shown in Table 9.3. For both the United States and China percentage shares of military expenditures and number of alliances increase dramatically, while Italy, France, and Germany drop in these areas to a substantial degree. Two anomalous cases are Great Britain and the Soviet Union. Although in the pre-World War II period the Soviet Union was the leading military spender and had the largest number of alliances, its number of alliances declined in the postwar period despite the continuing high level of military spending. The Soviet decline, however, is only in terms of actual number. As a percentage of all alliances those of the Soviet Union remain fairly constant, dropping from 25.4 percent of the prewar alliances to 22.85 percent in the post–World War II era. Moreover, while the Soviet's prewar alliances were all composed of two nations only (and in several of these the Soviets were by no means the dominant power), the postwar pattern includes at least one alliance (the Warsaw Pact) in which the Soviets are highly dominant, for reasons in large part related to World War II, as Organski and Kugler point out. The British pattern is slightly different, and a structural analysis would reveal that whereas Great Britain was independent in its pre-World War II alliances, in the post–World War II era it was incorporated as a senior partner in several alliances dominated by the United States.

There is another difference in alliance patterns before and after World War II. In a paper investigating the processes through which alliances are formed, Siverson and Duncan found that the processes of alliance formation were characterized by heterogeneity in the period 1919–1939 and contagion in the years 1945–1965.[31] The substantive interpretation of these processes leads to the conclusion that in the interwar years a relatively small number of actors were highly alliance prone, while in the post–World War II period, numerous nations were active and the formation of one alliance increased the probability of other alliances. In this latter period it was noted that with the general exception of several large alliances in the Third World, the contagious alliance activity centered around the two poles of the cold war.

The Structure of Trade

The data above indicate that World War II produced changes in both the structure of the international system and the relationships among many of its major power members. From this it should follow that changes took place in the pattern of interaction among the members of the system. There are, of course, many interaction areas in which these changes should have occurred, and, in fact, many of these changes are manifestly obvious, such as the emergence of the cold war. One area in which less obvious changes have taken place is in the area of trade. Chapter 6 by Keohane outlines the growth of the U.S.-dominated international economic regime following the end of World War II. Notwithstanding the international economic centrality of this, at least as important from a political vantage point is the economic consolidation of Western Europe and the economic domination of Eastern Europe by the Soviet Union.

Available evidence indicates that there are widespread changes in the patterns of trade in post–World War II Western Europe. For example, two observers of these changes note the following alterations in Franco-German trade before and after World War II: "Whereas in 1938 the French traded with the Germans in volumes 27 percent lower than would be expected under the RA null model, by 1951 they were trading with the Germans in volumes 93 percent greater than expected—a remarkable restructuring of economic relationships."[32]

Such alterations, moreover, were not limited to winner-loser partnerships, but were more general throughout Western Europe. While France and the Netherlands, for example, were economically isolated from each other in the years prior to World War II, by 1948 these nations were trading with each other "in volumes 50 percent greater than null expectations."[33] Additionally, the post–World War II period saw increased trade between Scandinavia and its southern neighbors. Alker and Puchala conclude by indentifying World War II as a major factor in producing the observed alterations: "These changes in trading relationships between 1928 and 1951 appear to reflect major European political realignment brought about by the conclusion of World War II and subsequent American foreign policy."[34] Although there appears to have been unrecognized methodological problems with the null model Alker and Puchala used to draw these conclusions, Chadwick and Deutsch, in removing these impediments, reached essentially the same conclusions regarding the course of European economic partnership, although the patterns are not so pronounced as in the earlier studies.[35]

More dramatic changes may be seen in the trading patterns of the Eastern European nations with the Soviet Union. The data given by Chadwick and Deutsch show the sharpest increases within the COMECON nations.[36] The data in Table 9.5 display the 1936 and 1973 trading patterns of six East European nations with the Soviet Union. The top

TABLE 9.5
Trade of East European Nations with the Soviet Union, 1936 and 1973

	1936*	1973**
Percentage of Total Imports from Soviet Union:		
Czechoslovakia	<1	31.1
Poland	1.53	25.1
Romania	<1	20.3
Yugoslavia	1.06	10.1
Bulgaria	<1	51.2
Hungary	<1	33.8
Percentage of Total Exports to Soviet Union:		
Czechoslovakia	2.67	31.6
Poland	<1	33.1
Romania	<1	22.4
Yugoslavia	<1	15.9
Bulgaria	<1	54.5
Hungary	<1	33.3

* Source: John Paxton (ed.), The Statesman's Yearbook, London: Macmillan, 1937.
** Source: United Nations, Yearbook of Industrial Statistics, United Nations Publishing Service: New York, 1978.

half of the table indicates very substantial shifts in the percentage of the nations' imports coming from the Soviet Union. In every case the 1936 import percentages from the Soviet Union are very low — in fact, remarkably low considering the geographical proximity of many of these nations to the USSR. However, in the post–World War II era the percentage of imports these nations receive from the USSR is vastly higher, even in the case of Yugoslavia which is not tied to the Soviet Union as are the others. The picture with regard to exports is quite similar with very low export percentages in 1936 and much higher percentages in 1973. It is also noteworthy that in 1973 the Soviet Union was the largest importer from and exporter to these nations.

Shifts of this magnitude obviously reflect a major restructuring of international economic activity. While the United States does not dominate its Western European trading partners as the Soviet Union does in Eastern Europe, it is clear that the end of World War II did bring about some major shifts in economic activity. In large part these were brought about by the combination of a weakened British economy and a strengthened U.S. economy. The British economy was not weakened so much by the actual destruction of the war as by the huge external debts that built up in buying war material. A graphic picture of the development of Great Britain's war-related external debt is given by Millward:

> United Kingdom exports to India fell from 34 million in 1939 to 18 million in 1943, while military orders and expenditures in India shot upwards. India's real trade balance with the United Kingdom became a favorable one, and the rapid inflation there increased the cost of exports and of military supplies to the United Kingdom, exaggerating this swing in the trade balance. . . . Therefore, it was possible for Britain to pay for supply by piling up post-war claims against balances kept in London for use after the war. The Indian government insisted on using these sterling balances to buy out British investments in India. But in spite of the systematic sale of these investments, the sterling balance of the Indian government still rose from £259 million in the middle of 1943 to £1,321 million at the end of 1945.[37]

Lend-lease had a similar impact upon the British economic position in the United States. It is ironic that in fighting primarily to defend its European interests the British created the conditions for the "purchase" of their critical strategic resources.

Conclusion

There remains, however, one vexing but important question which this chapter has not raised. International war is a fairly frequent event; in fact, by Singer and Small's data set, the period between 1815 and 1965 averaged 0.33 international wars per year, and if one did not use Singer and Small's restrictive criteria many more conflicts could be included as wars. Yet given the frequency of war it is not evident that the international system changed in proportion to the amount of war that took place. Why did some wars change the international system and others not?

From the power-centered perspective of this chapter the answer that emerges to this question is that wars will change the system in proportion to the changes produced in power relationships. That is a straightforward deterministic answer, and yet it clearly begs the question, for now it must be asked why some wars have a greater impact upon the power structure than others. Although no data on this particular point are presented here, several plausible hypotheses are briefly discussed. Within the idea of a power structure is the implicit assumption that power is differentially—i.e., unequally—distributed. If one simply dichotomizes nations as being either major or minor powers, then the power status of the belligerents on the two sides of a war may be characterized as being either major-major, major-minor or minor-minor.[38] Given the assumption that power is the most important element in structuring the international system, the logical consequence of this typology is that major-major wars would have the greatest impact upon the system's processes, while the other types would have far less impact.

One may also judge that the size of a war is likely to have an effect on the structure of the international system. The greater the number of belligerents in a war, the greater the number of nations likely to be affected. Through time there has been considerable variation in the size of wars. While the most common war is dyadic, wars of much larger size are obviously present. Recent research indicates that the growth of wars in size is influenced by a probabilistic process of infectious contagion,[39] and subseqsuent research indicates that the presence of alliances may have an impact upon the tendency for wars to expand.[40] From this one may hypothesize that large wars among major powers will produce the greatest amount of change in the international system and that small wars among minor powers will produce the least. Giving an exact or even ordinal ranking to the other types of wars is somewhat more difficult, except to enter the tentative suggestion that the power status of the combatants may be more potent in producing change since it is in the view of many that power is the most important element in structuring the system.

Acknowledgments

The author wishes to express his appreciation to Alexander L. George, Ole R. Holsti, Francis Hoole, and Michael Sullivan for their comments on earlier versions of this paper and to Michael Tennefoss for his assistance in gathering the data.

Notes

1. Kenneth Waltz, "International Structure, National Force and the Balance of World Power," *Journal of International Affairs* 21:2 (1967):215–231; Karl W. Deutsch and J. David Singer, "Multipolar Power Systems and International Stability," *World Politics* 16 (April 1964):390–406. For another view of the relationship between systemic type and the occurrence of war, see Richard Rosecrance, "Bipolarity, Multipolarity and the Future," *The Journal of Conflict Resolution* 10 (September 1966):314–327.

2. Morton A. Kaplan, *System and Process in International Politics* (New York: John Wiley & Sons, 1957).

3. Ibid.; for the respective discussions see pp. 23, 38, 44.

4. Richard N. Rosecrance, *Action and Reaction in International Politics*

(Boston: Little, Brown and Co., 1963).

5. Frank Denton, "Some Regularities in International Conflict," *Background* 9 (February 1966):283–296. For recent research that attempts to model some of these regularities, see William Davis, George Duncan, and Randolph Siverson, "The Dynamics of Warfare, 1815–1965," *American Journal of Political Science* 22 (November 1978):772–792.

6. For examples, see Glenn Snyder and Paul Diesing, *Conflict Among Nations* (Princeton, N.J.: Princeton University Press, 1977); A.F.K. Organski, *World Politics,* 2d ed. (New York: Alfred A. Knopf, 1958); Waltz, "International Structure"; and Raymond F. Hopkins and Richard W. Mansbach, *Structure and Process in International Politics* (New York: Harper & Row, 1973).

7. J. David Singer, "Internation Influence: A Formal Model," *American Political Science Review* 58 (June 1963):420–430.

8. Robert C. North, "Some Paradoxes of War and Peace," *Peace Science Society (International) Papers* (1975).

9. A.F.K. Organski and Jacek Kugler, "The Costs of Major Wars," *American Political Science Review* 71 (September 1977):1347–1366.

10. Organski, *World Politics,* pp. 207–215.

11. Organski and Kugler, "Costs of Major Wars," p. 1359.

12. Ibid., p. 1365.

13. Ibid.

14. One might nonetheless suggest that to some extent the economic recoveries of Germany, Japan, and Italy were assisted by U.S. protection under which they were not required to invest in defense in the years immediately following World War II. Hence scarce resources might be used to render greater economic growth by investing in more productive capacity at an early point. In addition, the United States also furnished substantial protection for emerging international trade. On the cost of protecting trade, see Frederic C. Lane, *Venice and History* (Baltimore, Md.: Johns Hopkins University Press, 1966), pp. 373–382.

15. J. H. Elliott, *Imperial Spain* (New York: Mentor, 1966).

16. Charles Wilson, *Profit and Power: A Study of England and the Dutch Wars* (London: Longmans, Green and Co., 1957).

17. Allan S. Millward, *War, Economy and Society, 1939–1945* (London: Penguin, 1977).

18. Organski and Kugler, "Costs of Major Wars," p. 1365.

19. Rosecrance, *Action and Reaction.*

20. Ole R. Holsti, "The Three Headed Eagle: The United States and System Change," *International Studies Quarterly* 23 (September 1979).

21. Duncan Keith Shaw, *Prime Minister Neville Chamberlain* (London: Wells Gardner Darton, n.d.), pp. 111–112.

22. J. David Singer and Melvin Small, *The Wages of War* (New York: John Wiley & Sons, 1972); Arthur S. Banks, *The Cross-Polity Time Series Data* (Cambridge, Mass.: M.I.T. Press, 1971); and William Langer, ed., *An Encyclopedia of World History* (Boston: Houghton Mifflin Co., 1960).

23. Singer and Small, *Wages of War,* p. 23.

24. George Modelski, *World Power Concentrations Typology, Data, Explanatory Framework* (Morristown: General Learning Press, 1974).

25. Organski and Kugler, "Costs of Major Wars," p. 1354.

26. Partha Chatterjee, *Arms, Alliances and Stability* (New York: Wiley-Halstead, 1975).

27. Richard Smoke, *War: Controlling Escalation* (Cambridge, Mass.: Harvard University Press, 1977), p. 472.

28. Snyder and Diesing, *Conflict Among Nations*.

29. A few words of clarification are in order with regard to the delineation of these periods. In the period 1919–1939 no alliances are included that were signed within three months of the outbreak of World War II; hence only half of 1939 is actually included. In the period 1945–1965 no alliances are included that were undertaken before the surrender of Japan, so only a quarter of 1945 is included. The data are drawn from Alan Sabrosky, "The War-time Reliability of Interstate Alliances," mimeo (1975).

30. The post–World War II alliance data for Germany include alliances for both East and West Germany.

31. Randolph M. Siverson and George T. Duncan, "Stochastic Models of International Alliance Initiation, 1815–1965," in Dina Zinnes and John Gillespie, eds., *Mathematical Models in International Relations* (New York: Praeger Publishers, 1976), pp. 110–131.

32. Hayward Alker and Donald Puchala, "Trends in Economic Partnership: The North Atlantic Area, 1928–1963," in J. David Singer, ed., *Quantitative International Politics* (New York: Free Press, 1968), pp. 287–316. The RA null model is a mathematical model representing what would happen under conditions of random behavior. In fact, as in many models of randomness, what is usually most interesting are the deviations from randomness. For the derivation of the model, see I. Richard Savage and Karl W. Deutsch, "A Statistical Model of the Gross Analysis of Transaction Flows," *Econometrica* 28 (July 1960):551–572. Some problems have been found in the model. Their nature and a method to repair them are given in Richard Chadwick and Karl W. Deutsch, "International Trade and Economic Integration: Further Developments in Trade Matrix Analysis," *Comparative Political Studies* 6 (April 1973):84–122.

33. Alker and Puchala, "Trends in Economic Partnership," p. 305.

34. Ibid., emphasis deleted.

35. Chadwick and Deutsch, "International Trade."

36. Ibid.

37. Millward, *War, Economy and Society,* pp. 349–50.

38. This characterization, of course, represents a slightly oversimplified view of war coalitions. It is certainly the case that numerous coalitions have consisted of major and minor powers. At the present time, however, it does not appear to be advantageous to further divide these types rather than simply classifying a major-minor coalition as being a major power type for purposes of initial presentation.

39. Davis, Duncan, and Siverson, "Dynamics of Warfare."

40. Randolph M. Siverson and Joel King, "Alliances and the Expansion of War, 1815–1965," in J. David Singer and Michael Wallace, eds., *To Augur Well: The Design and Use of Early Warning Indicators in Interstate Conflict* (Beverly Hills, Calif.: Sage Publications, 1979).

PART 3

Constraints upon Change
in the International System

10

ALEXANDER L. GEORGE

Domestic Constraints on Regime Change in U.S. Foreign Policy: The Need for Policy Legitimacy

> *The acid test of a policy . . . is its ability to obtain domestic support. This has two aspects: the problem of legitimizing a policy within the governmental apparatus . . . and that of harmonizing it with the national experience.*
>
> —Henry Kissinger, *A World Restored,* p. 327

The study of change in the international system must include, of course, attention to the efforts of national actors to create new regimes or to modify existing ones. This chapter focusses upon the role of domestic constraints on the ability of governments to pursue goals of this kind in their foreign policy. The primary objective of the chapter will be to develop an analytical framework suitable for this purpose. The framework will be applied to an analysis of two historical cases in which the United States has attempted to develop a cooperative U.S.-Soviet relationship: first, Franklin D. Roosevelt's effort during World War II to develop a postwar international security system based on cooperation with the Soviet Union; second, the Nixon-Kissinger détente policy of attempting to develop a more constructive relationship with the Soviet Union.

The analysis of these historical cases will be selective and provisional; it is designed to illustrate the utility of the framework for assessing the impact of domestic constraints rather than to produce a definitive scholarly interpretation. For this reason documentation will be minimal.[1]

The Problem of Democratic Control of Foreign Policy

No one who reviews the history of U.S. foreign policy since the end of

World War II can fail to be impressed with the importance of domestic constraints in the shaping and conduct of that policy. Democratic control of foreign policy is of course indispensable in the U.S. political system. But the forces of public opinion, Congress, the media, and powerful interest groups often make themselves felt in ways that seriously complicate the ability of the president and his advisers to pursue long-range foreign policy objectives in a coherent, consistent manner. It is not surprising that presidents have reacted to these domestic pressures at times by trying to manipulate and control public opinion — as well as to inform and educate the public as best they can.

While efforts to manipulate public opinion cannot be condoned, nonetheless this unhappy experience does point to a fundamental problem that Roosevelt and every president since has faced. This is the problem of obtaining enough legitimacy for his policy towards the Soviet Union in the eyes of Congress and public opinion so that the forces of democratic control and domestic pressures do not hobble him and prevent him from conducting a coherent, consistent, and reasonably effective long-range policy.

To be able to do so, the president must achieve a fundamental and stable national consensus, one that encompasses enough members of his own administration, of Congress and of the interested public. It is contended here that such a consensus can *not* be achieved and maintained simply by the president adhering scrupulously to constitutional-legal requirements for the conduct of foreign policy, *or* by his following the customary norms for consultation of Congress, *or* by conducting an "open" foreign policy that avoids undue secrecy and deceptive practices, *or* by attempting to play the role of broker mediating and balancing the competing demands and claims on foreign policy advanced by the numerous domestic interest groups.

Neither can the president develop such a consensus merely by invoking the "national interest" nor the requirements of "national security." In principle, of course, the criterion of "national interest" should assist the policymaker to cut through the complex, multivalued nature of foreign policy issues and to improve his judgment of the relative importance of different objectives. In practice, however, "national interest" has become so elastic and ambiguous a concept that its role as a guide to foreign policy is highly problematical and controversial. Most thoughtful observers of U.S. foreign policy have long since concluded that the "national interest" concept unfortunately lends itself more readily to being used by our leaders as political rhetoric for *justifying* their decisions and gaining support rather than as an exact, well-defined criterion that enables them to determine what actions and decisions to take. It is symptomatic of the deep crisis of U.S. foreign policy in the past decade that large elements of the public and of Congress are no longer persuaded that foreign policy actions are appropriate merely by the president's invocation of the symbol of "national interest." These skeptical sectors of the public and of Congress have come to view "the national interest" phrase as part of the shopworn political rhetoric that every administration in recent times has employed in order to justify questionable or arbitrary policies and decisions.

If "national interest" does not endow policy with legitimacy, what about a "bipartisan" foreign policy—is not that the way in which a basic consensus on foreign policy can be achieved in a democracy such as the United States? There have been times, it is true, when policy legitimacy has been associated with a bipartisan foreign policy, but it is important not to confuse cause and effect. Bipartisanship is the result, not the cause, of policy legitimacy. If enough members of both parties do not share a sense of the legitimacy of a particular foreign policy, calls for a bipartisan policy and appeals that politics should stop at the water's edge will have little effect, except in crisis situations.

How, then, can a broad and stable consensus on behalf of a long-range foreign policy be achieved? The concept of "policy legitimacy" is relevant and useful in this context.[2] A president can achieve legitimacy for his policy only if he succeeds in convincing enough members of his administration, Congress, and the public that he indeed does have a policy and that it is soundly conceived. This requires two things: first, he must convince them that the objectives and goals of his policy are desirable and worth pursuing—in other words, that his policy is consistent with fundamental national values and contributes to their enhancement. This is the *normative* or moral component of policy legitimacy.

Second, the president must convince people that he knows how to achieve these desirable long-range objectives. In other words, he must convince them that he understands other national actors and the evolving world situation well enough to enable him to influence the course of events in the desired direction with the means and resources at his disposal. This is the *cognitive* (or knowledge) basis for policy legitimacy.

Thus, policy legitimacy has both a normative-moral component and a cognitive basis. The normative component establishes the *desirability* of the policy; the cognitive component its *feasibility*.

Policy legitimacy is invaluable for the conduct of a long-range foreign policy. If the president gains this kind of understanding and acceptance of his effort to create a new international regime, then the day-to-day actions he takes on behalf of it will become less vulnerable to the many pressures and constraints the various manifestations of "democratic control" would otherwise impose on his ability to pursue that policy in a coherent, consistent manner. In the absence of the fundamental consensus that policy legitimacy creates it becomes necessary for the president to justify each action to implement the long-range policy on its own merits rather than as part of a larger policy design and strategy. The necessity for ad hoc day-to-day building of consensus under these circumstances makes it virtually impossible for the president to conduct a long-range foreign policy in a coherent, effective manner.

Thus far we have identified the requirements for policy legitimacy in very general terms. In fact, however, the specific operational requirements of normative and cognitive legitimacy will be affected by the marked differences in level of interest and sophistication among individuals and groups. Policy legitimacy must encompass a variety of individuals and groups. Foremost among them are the president and his top foreign policy advisers and officials. It is difficult to imagine them pursuing foreign policy goals that they do not regard as possessing normative and cognitive legitimacy. The bases for their beliefs, however, will not necessarily be communicated fully to all other political actors. In general, as one moves from the highest level of policymaking to the mass public, one expects to find a considerable simplification of the set of assertions and beliefs that lend support to the legitimacy of foreign policy. (This important refinement of the analytical framework will not be developed further here since it will not be utilized in the case studies that follow.)

The "Architecture" of Foreign Policy

It was noted that in order to establish cognitive legitimacy for his policy a president must be able to plausibly claim that he and his advisers possess the relevant knowledge and competence needed to choose correct policies and carry out them out effectively. Upon closer examination it is seen that the knowledge evoked in support of a policy consists of several sets of beliefs, each of which supports a different component of the policy in question. It is useful, therefore, to refine the analytical framework that we have presented thus far in order to understand better the policymaker's task of developing policy legitimacy.

Foreign policy that aims at establishing a new international system or regime generally has an internal structure—a set of interrelated components. These are (1) the *design-objective* of the policy; (2) the *strategy* employed to achieve it; and (3) the *tactics* utilized in implementing that strategy. The choice of each of these components of the policy must be supported by claims that it is grounded in relevant knowledge. A set of plausible cognitive beliefs must support each of these three components of the policy if it is to acquire what we have been calling "cognitive legitimacy."

By taking the internal structure of policy explicitly into account we add a useful dimension to the concept of policy legitimacy. Now the cognitive component of policy legitimacy is analytically differentiated in a way that permits a more refined understanding of the task of achieving and maintaining policy legitimacy. The analytical structure of the problem of achieving cognitive legitimacy is depicted in Figure 10.1.

By differentiating in this manner the *functional role* that different cognitive assertions and beliefs play in supporting different parts of the internal structure or "architecture" of a policy, the investigator is in a position to do a number of useful things. First, he can understand better the nature of the task a policymaker faces in attempting to achieve legitimacy for his policy. Thus in order for the policymaker himself to believe that his policy is feasible and to argue this plausibly to others, he has to articulate a set of cognitive beliefs about other national actors whose behavior he seeks to influence and about causal relationships in the issue-area in question that will lend support not only to his choice of

FIGURE 10.1
The Problem of Cognitive Legitimacy: The "Internal Structure" of Foreign Policy and Supporting Cognitive Assertions and Beliefs

The "Internal Structure" of Foreign Policy	Supporting Cognitive Assertions and Beliefs
Choice of (1) Design-objective	a,b,c...n
Choice of (2) Strategy	a,b,c...n
Choice of (3) Tactics	a,b,c...n

the design-objectives of that policy but also to the strategy and tactics that he employs on its behalf.

Second, the specification of beliefs supporting the internal structure of a complex foreign policy enables the analyst, either at that time or later, to compare these beliefs with the state of scholarly knowledge on these matters. This permits a sharper, better focussed evaluation of the validity of the cognitive premises on which different components of a given foreign policy are based.

Third, by keeping in mind the differentiated functional role of cognitive premises the investigator can more easily refine the description and explanation of pressures for changes in foreign policy that are brought about by interpretations of events that are held to challenge the validity of some of these cognitive premises.

Roosevelt's "Great Design," Strategy, and Tactics

We shall now utilize the analytical framework outlined above to describe the substance of Roosevelt's postwar policy and to indicate how domestic opinion—and the related need for achieving as much policy legitimacy as possible—constrained Roosevelt's policy choices and his ability to achieve them.

We shall consider first Roosevelt's design-objective for a postwar security system, what he himself called his Great Design.

To begin with, the very close connection between Roosevelt's wartime policy and his postwar plans should be recalled. Both were quite self-consciously based on Roosevelt's perception—widely shared by his generation—of the "lessons of the past," more specifically the explanations attributed to the various failures of policy after World War I that had led to the rise of totalitarianism and to World War II.[3] Thus, in contrast to the way in which World War I had ended, Roosevelt believed it to be essential this time to completely defeat, disarm, and occupy those aggressor nations that had started World War II. It was also necessary in Roosevelt's view to promote national self-determination more effectively and to prevent future depressions. But above all Roosevelt's planning was dominated by the belief that it was necessary to forestall the possibility that once the war was over the United States would once again return to an isolationist foreign policy as it had after World War I.

Thus the postwar objective to which Roosevelt gave the highest priority was to ensure and to legitimize an *internationalist* U.S. postwar foreign policy. He wanted the United States to participate fully and, in fact, to take the lead in efforts to create a workable postwar security system.

To gain public support for his war objectives and to prepare the ground for an internationalist foreign policy thereafter, Roosevelt invoked the nation's traditional idealist impulses and principles. They were written into the Atlantic Charter that he and Churchill agreed to in August 1941 (even before the United States formally entered the conflict), and to which the Russians gave qualified support later.

Thus the principles of the Atlantic Charter provided *normative* legitimacy for Roosevelt's war arms and his hopes for peace. Among the traditional ideals that Roosevelt invoked, one in particular is of interest here. This was the principle of self-determination and independence for all nations. It was this aspect of the normative legitimacy for his policies that was to severely complicate Roosevelt's problems with U.S. public opinion — and President Harry S Truman's problems later on — when he had to deal with the Russians on matters of territorial settlements and control over Eastern Europe. (We shall return to this later.)

Isolationism had been strong in the United States in the 1930s *before* Pearl Harbor. But once the United States got into the war, U.S. opinion developed strong support for the idea that it should not return to an isolationist position. This shift in public opinion was helpful to Roosevelt's postwar plans, but only up to a point, for, in fact, those who opposed a return to isolationism were sharply divided over what type of internationalist policy the United States should pursue after the war. Woodrow Wilson's concept of collective security was revived and its supporters, strong in numbers and influence, wanted the United States to take the lead in establishing a new and stronger League of Nations.

Roosevelt himself, however, rejected this idealist approach as impractical and inadequate. He favored an approach that would take power realities into account. In his view it was important that the great powers use their military resources to preserve the peace. This would provide a more reliable way than a league for dealing with any new aggressive states that might emerge after the war. Roosevelt also wanted to establish a more effective postwar system than a new league could provide for preventing dangerous rivalries and conflicts from erupting among Britain, Russia, and the United States once the common enemy had been defeated. But Roosevelt did not wish to risk a battle with the Wilsonian idealists, and so he did not publicly articulate his disagreement with their views. Instead he attempted, with partial success, to use their internationalist viewpoint to help legitimate his own quite different version of an internationalist postwar policy.

Roosevelt's thinking about the requirements of a postwar security system was deeply influenced by his awareness of the situation that would confront the peacemakers once the war against the enemy powers was successfully concluded. The defeat of Nazi Germany and its allies would create an important power vacuum in Central Europe. The question of who and what would fill this vacuum would pose the most serious implications for the vital interests of both the Soviets and the Western powers. If the two sides could not cooperate fairly quickly in finding a mutually acceptable approach for dealing with the vacuum in Europe, then they would inevitably enter into the sharpest competition for control of Central Europe.

The resulting dangers to the peace, it could be foreseen, could be dealt with only within the framework of the existing alliance between the Western powers and the Soviet Union. There would be no other international forums or institutions to bring into play to regulate competition among the victorious powers over Central Europe. Whatever semblance of an international system that had existed in the period between the two world wars had collapsed. What is more, the military alliance between the Western powers and the Soviet Union had been forced on them by circumstances—the common danger of defeat and domination by Nazi Germany and its allies. Once the enemy powers were defeated, all of the long-standing differences in ideology and the historic lack of trust and mutual suspiciousness between the West and the Soviet Union would have an opportunity to emerge once again.

Roosevelt was aware that once the wartime alliance achieved its purpose of defeating Hitler, there would remain only victors and vanquished and no international system that could provide an institutionalized structure and procedures by means of which the Western powers and the Russians could work out a solution to the power vacuum in the center of Europe. Roosevelt, then, was faced with two important and difficult postwar tasks: the need to create the beginnings of a new international system and the necessity of finding a way to prevent dangerous competition to fill the vacuum in Central Europe.

What were the various possibilities available for dealing with these closely related tasks? One possibility was to try to recreate a new balance-of-power system. But the question was what kind of a balance-of-power system? The history of the last few centuries had seen several significantly different variants of a balance-of-power system.

Roosevelt rejected the kind of balance-of-power system marked by a great deal of competition and conflict among the major powers—the kind of system that had existed during the eighteenth century that had failed to deter Napoleon from attempting to achieve hegemony and that had also failed for a number of years to form the kind of coalition needed to bring him down. In Roosevelt's view a highly competitive balance-of-power system of this type for the postwar period would be neither desirable nor feasible. Britain would be too weak by itself to provide a military counterweight to Russia on the European continent. The United States, even with its enormous military power, would not want to or be able to bolster England for the purpose of balancing Soviet pressure in Europe. It must be remembered that Roosevelt operated on the premise — which seemed completely justified at the time — that U.S. public opinion would not tolerate leaving large U.S. military forces in Europe very long once the war ended. So the grim prospect Roosevelt had to contend with, and to avoid if possible, was that the Soviet Union could end up dominating Europe unless the Russians could be brought into a different kind of balance-of-power system.

One way to avoid this dilemma, of course, would have been for the United States and Britain to forego the war objective of inflicting total defeat on Germany and Italy and to settle instead for a negotiated, compromise peace with Hitler and Mussolini. But it was most unlikely that this alternative could be made acceptable to U.S. (or British) public opinion. Besides, since the Russians too could have played this game, it would have quickly led to a race between the Western powers and the Russians to see who could first make a separate peace with Hitler in order to bring Germany in on its side of the newly emerging balance of power.

Possibly there was another way of avoiding the dangers that a power vacuum in Europe would pose to a new balance-of-power system. These dangers might be minimized or avoided if the Western powers and the Soviet Union got together and worked out a political division of Europe before the total defeat and occupation of Germany and Italy. But it is difficult to imagine how a political division of Europe between the Russians and the West could be successfully implemented during or immediately after the war, or be made acceptable to the U.S. people. If the thought occurred to Roosevelt, there is little indication that he regarded it as at all a feasible or desirable option. The most that could be done, and was done, was to agree on zones of occupation into which the military forces of the Soviet Union, Britain, and the United States would regroup after the defeat of Nazi Germany. This agreement on military zones of occupation reduced the immediate danger of conflict but it was neither intended nor expected to eventuate in a political division of Europe; it was *not* part of a "spheres of influence" agreement at that time even though spheres of influence would emerge later on, based on the occupation zones.

There was still another possibility. If a complete division of Europe between the Western powers and the Soviet Union was deemed impractical or undesirable, the two sides might at least agree to grant each other spheres of influence in *parts* of Europe, with Germany itself being placed under their joint military occupation. Something of the kind—a partial spheres-of-influence agreement covering Rumania, Hungary, Bulgaria, Italy, Greece, and Yugoslavia—was proposed by Churchill to Stalin at their private meeting in Moscow in October 1944 and accepted by Stalin. But Roosevelt, although initially sympathetic, felt he could not approve such an arrangement.

Roosevelt rejected the model of a highly competitive balance-of-power system and also the idea of attempting to reduce its conflict potential by creating spheres of influence for several reasons. First of all, he doubted—and in this he was undoubtedly right—that U.S. public opinion would agree to U.S. participation in such arrangements, given its historic antipathy to the European balance-of-power system. Besides, for Roosevelt to endorse or participate in a spheres-of-influence agreement would have directly contradicted the principles of self-determination and independence that he had written into the Atlantic Charter. That declaration was the major statement of allied war arms and a major means by which Roosevelt had secured public support for an internationalist postwar foreign policy. For this reason, while Roosevelt was indeed prepared to accept predominant Soviet influence in Eastern Europe, such an outcome had to be legitimized through procedures consistent with the Atlantic Charter.

Besides, Roosevelt did not believe that a competitive balance-of-power system, even one moderated by spheres of influence in Europe, would eliminate rivalry for very long. Any such arrangements would prove to be unstable and the world would soon become divided into two armed camps—a Western democratic one and a Soviet-led one. An arms race would ensue which at best would result in a dangerous armed truce, and at worst it would lead to another world war. In brief, Roosevelt foresaw the possibility that something like the cold war would emerge—that is, unless some alternative could be devised.

The only alternative, as Roosevelt saw it, was a version of the balance of power modeled on some aspects of the Concert System set up by the European powers in 1815 after defeating Napoleon. To this end Roosevelt hoped that the unity and cooperation of the Allies could be maintained after the defeat of the totalitarian states. This was the option Roosevelt favored from an early stage in the war. He called it his Great Design, and he succeeded in getting Churchill and Stalin to agree to it and to cooperate in trying to bring it about.

The Great Design called for the establishment of a postwar security system in which the United States, Great Britain, the Soviet Union — and hopefully eventually China — would form a consortium of overwhelming power with which to keep the peace. These major powers, forming an executive committee, would consult and cooperate with each other to meet any threat to the peace, either from the defeated powers or any others that might arise to threaten the peace. These four powers would have a virtual monopoly of military power; all other states would be prevented from having military forces that could pose a serious threat to others. Quite appropriately, Roosevelt called this concept the "Four Policemen." It must be noted that such a system would have violated the principle of the sovereign equality of all states, great or small, and hence it could not be reconciled with the Atlantic Charter.

Turning now to Roosevelt's "Grand Strategy" for achieving his Great Design, the first thing to be noted is that it called for the United States, Great Britain, and the Soviet Union to work out mutually acceptable settlements of the important territorial issues and political problems in Europe. These settlements would be reached through joint consultation and agreement; in other words, through a system of *collective* decision-making, not unilateral action by either side. In this respect Roosevelt's Great Design was influenced by the recollection that in 1815, after the European powers finally succeeded in defeating Napoleon, they then formed a Concert System which relied upon frequent meetings of foreign ministers to make joint decisions with regard to keeping the peace, dealing with any threats to it, and resolving any disagreements that might arise among themselves.

Instead of a new balance-of-power system, therefore, Roosevelt sought to create a new Concert System that would maintain the unity and effective cooperation of the victorious allies after the war as well. And instead of secret agreements and spheres of influence, he hoped that new governments would emerge in the occupied states of Europe through procedures and policies that were consistent with the principle of national self-determination and independence.

To this fundamental strategic concept Roosevelt added other elements: reliance on high-level personal diplomacy, confidence-building measures, and conciliation and appeasement of the Soviet Union's legitimate security needs.

As for Roosevelt's *tactics,* the emphasis was on the need to minimize conflict and disagreement in day-to-day relations, the importance of leaning over backwards not to give offense, and the avoidance of behavior that might be interpreted by the Soviets as indicating hostility or lack of sympathy.

Particularly at the level of tactics, but to some extent also at the level of strategy, there were some alternatives to the choices Roosevelt made. Generally speaking, the choice of a design-objective—a particular Grand Design for policy—does of course constrain the choice of strategy; and the choice of a particular strategy constrains in turn the choice of tactics. One strategy may be more appropriate for pursuing a given design-objective than another, and one set of tactics may be more effective than another. These choices of strategy and tactics are likely to be influenced by the policymaker's beliefs as to the relative efficacy of alternative strategies and tactics. It is entirely possible, therefore, as experience accumulates in attempting to achieve a long-range design-objective, that policymakers will be led to question their initial choice of tactics and/or strategy but without questioning—initially at least—the correctness and legitimacy of the design-objective itself.

We have now identified Roosevelt's Grand Design, his Grand Strategy, and his tactics. *Each of them was supported by a set of cognitive beliefs having to do with the characteristics of the Soviets.* These beliefs constituted the knowledge base on which Roosevelt could draw in attempting to gain cognitive legitimacy for his overall postwar plans from members of his administration, Congress, and the public. From available historical materials it is relatively easy to identify the various cognitive beliefs about the Soviets that supported each component of the overall policy.[4]

How well founded were these beliefs about the Soviets on which Roosevelt's postwar policy rested? It must be recognized that the exigencies and pressures of the wartime situation—the need to get along with the Russians in order to ensure the defeat of the enemy powers—no doubt powerfully motivated Roosevelt to develop a somewhat benign, optimistic image of the Soviets. But was that image therefore naive? Was it simply wishful thinking to believe that the Soviets might participate in a cooperative postwar system of some kind?

Roosevelt's hopes and beliefs regarding the Soviets cannot be dismissed so easily as naive. The content of some of Roosevelt's policies and his judgment of the Soviet Union were indeed criticized by some persons at the time. But suffice it to say that the naivete regarding the Soviet Union that Roosevelt has been charged with was much more apparent *after* the failure of his hopes for postwar cooperation with the Russians than before. During the war itself, while Roosevelt was alive, and even for a while thereafter, many specialists on the Soviet Union (for example, Charles Bohlen) and other foreign policy experts were not at all sure that his policy would fail. Many of the beliefs about the Soviet Union that supported Roosevelt's Grand Design enjoyed a considerable measure of plausibility and support. His policies and the beliefs that supported them were not a hasty improvisation but reflected careful deliberation on his part and on the part of quite a few advisers. Even skeptics about the Soviet Union thought that there was a chance that Soviet leaders would cooperate, out of self-interest, with Roosevelt's Grand Design. The generally successful wartime collaboration with the Soviets reinforced these hopes, and they were further strengthened by Roosevelt's assessment of Stalin's postwar intentions and the general endorsement he obtained from Stalin of the concept of a cooperative postwar security system.

It should be noted, further, that despite his generally optimistic personality and outlook, Roosevelt did not hide from himself or others close to him that his image of the Soviets might prove to be defective and that his hopes for postwar cooperation might eventually prove to be unfounded. He realized, in other words, that he was taking a calculated risk and he remained sensitive to any Soviet actions that threatened the success of his postwar plans or appeared to call into question the validity of the premises on which it was based. Roosevelt was also quick to undertake remedial measures to bring Stalin back into line whenever necessary.

Domestic Constraints Affecting the Implementation of Roosevelt's Postwar Policies

In addition to the constraints already noted on Roosevelt's choice of a "realist"-oriented postwar security system, domestic pressures also hampered his effort to secure and maintain strong legitimacy for his policy. Although he strongly favored the Four Policemen concept, Roosevelt was most cautious in publicizing it. He did not seriously attempt to inform and educate public opinion on the matter because he feared that such an effort would shatter the domestic consensus for an internationalist postwar foreign policy. Roosevelt felt he had to blur the difference between his realistic approach to power and security, and the Wilsonian idealists' desire for a system of collective security based on the creation of another, stronger League of Nations. Roosevelt did speak about his Four Policemen concept privately with a number of influential opinion leaders. But when he attempted to float a trial balloon to publicize the idea in an interview with a journalist,[5] it triggered a sharply negative reaction at home from the idealists. As a result Roosevelt backed away from further efforts to educate public opinion in order to gain understanding and legitimacy for his Four Policemen concept.

From an early stage in World War II Roosevelt had strongly opposed setting up a new League of Nations after the war. He felt that the task of enforcing the peace would have to be left to the Four Policemen for a number of years. However, once again to avoid political troubles at home, Roosevelt bowed to the pressure of the idealists who wanted the United Nations set up before the war was over. Roosevelt therefore acquiesced when Secretary of State Cordell Hull, who himself was closely identified with the Wilsonian idealists, gradually transformed the Four Policemen idea into what became the Security Council of the United Nations. Roosevelt consoled himself with the thought that it was not the early establishment of the United Nations and the format of the Security Council that were critical but rather that the United States and the Soviet Union should preserve a friendly and cooperative relationship, and that they should settle all important issues between them outside the Security Council and work together to maintain peace.

Roosevelt, as suggested earlier, could not approve an old-fashioned spheres-of-influence arrangement in Europe. He feared that it would be perceived by U.S. opinion as another example of how the cynical, immoral European powers periodically got together to make secret agreements to divide up the spoils at the expense of weaker states; and hence as a violation of the principle of national self-determination and independence. Such a development in U.S. opinion, Roosevelt foresaw, could jeopardize his postwar plans right from the beginning. But at the same time Roosevelt recognized that the Soviet Union's legitimate security needs in Eastern Europe would have to be satisfied. Since the Red Army was occupying Eastern Europe and would likely move into Central Europe as well, the Soviet Union could do as it wished there in any case. The United States would not employ force or threats of force to prevent or to dissuade the Soviets from creating friendly regimes and making territorial changes in Eastern Europe. This was understood and accepted even by those of Roosevelt's advisers — including Soviet experts in the State Department — who were most negative in their view of Soviet communism.[6]

From the standpoint of maintaining the U.S. public's support for his postwar policy it was terribly important for Roosevelt, first, that the Soviet Union should define its security needs in Eastern Europe in *minimal* terms, and second, that it should go about securing friendly regimes in Eastern Europe in ways that the United States and Britain could agree to and that would not flagrantly conflict with the principles of the Atlantic Charter. What was at stake for Roosevelt was the legitimacy in the eyes of the U.S. public of his entire plan for a postwar security system based on cooperation with the Soviet Union. If Soviet behavior in Eastern Europe was seen by the U.S. public as flagrantly conflicting with the principle of national self-determination and independence, it would create the image of an expansionist Soviet Union—one that could not be trusted.

Roosevelt hoped—perhaps somewhat naively—that the potential conflict between the Soviet Union's security requirements and the principles of the Atlantic Charter could be avoided or minimized in a number of ways. During the war he attempted to persuade Stalin that the complete defeat and disarming of Germany and the arrangements being made to weaken and control postwar Germany would do more to guarantee Soviet security than would Soviet territorial gains and the imposition of tight-fisted Soviet control over Eastern Europe.

Roosevelt also attempted to get Stalin to understand the difficulties with U.S. public opinion that would be created should the Soviet Union fail to cooperate in working out territorial settlements and political arrangements in Eastern Europe that did not flagrantly conflict with the commitment to uphold the principle of national self-determination and independence. In effect, Roosevelt was pleading for Stalin to show self-restraint; he hoped that Stalin would cooperate at least to the extent of providing a "cosmetic" facade to the creation of pro-Soviet regimes in Poland and other Eastern European countries. Stalin in fact *was* disposed to cooperate. Cosmetic solutions were in fact patched up several times. Thus Roosevelt and most of his advisers thought they had achieved that goal at the Yalta Conference in early 1945. But their optimism was quickly shaken by new difficulties with the Russians over interpretation of the Yalta agreements regarding Poland. Within a few months of becoming president, Truman, too, succeeded in patching up the disagreement over Poland, but once the war was over distrust of Soviet intentions mounted in Congress and among the public. People increasingly interpreted Soviet behavior in Eastern Europe as a harbinger of more ambitious expansionist aims, and it became more difficult to arrest the drift into the cold war.

Roosevelt died before these developments made themselves felt so acutely as to force major changes in his policy towards the Soviet Union. Among the many disadvantages Truman labored under in his effort to make a success of Roosevelt's policy was the reassertion by Congress, once the war ended in the summer of 1945, of its role in foreign policy. Truman was genuinely committed to trying to achieve Roosevelt's Great Design—that is, as best he could, given the fact that Roosevelt never took Truman into his confidence and also given the fact that Roosevelt's advisers had various opinions as to how best to deal with the Russians.

Pressures and circumstances of this kind hampered Truman's ability to continue efforts to make Roosevelt's policy succeed, though he certainly tried to do so for a while; eventually, however, Truman was led to move step by step away from that policy to the policy of containment and balance of power associated with the cold war. But only gradually and, it should be noted, with considerable reluctance did Truman replace the image of the Soviets that supported Roosevelt's postwar policy with the quite different set of beliefs about the Soviet Union associated with the cold war.

Several hypotheses help to explain why the transition to containment and cold war was slow and difficult. First, as already noted, the exigencies and situational pressures of the wartime situation provided strong, indeed compelling, incentives for giving credence to evidence that supported the benign, optimistic image of the Soviets. And the generally successful wartime collaboration with the Soviets reinforced hopes that this image was sound and would prove to be stable. But to recognize this fact is by no means to imply that Roosevelt and, later, Truman were engaged in biased information processing of incoming data on Soviet behavior in order to confirm an existing optimistic image of the Russians. Rather the record shows that incoming information of new Soviet actions was interpreted sometimes as undermining some of the optimistic beliefs on which Roosevelt's policy rested but at other times as reinforcing them, so that there were ups and downs rather than a straight-line, steady erosion of the optimistic image of the Soviets.

A second hypothesis helping to account for the gradualness of the transition to the cold war is to be found in the very nature of policy legitimacy. Once a foreign policy is established and achieves a degree of policy legitimacy — both normative and cognitive legitimacy — in the eyes of top policymakers themselves and enough other influential political actors, it is difficult for policymakers to contemplate replacing that policy with one that is radically different. An entirely new foreign policy will require new normative and/or cognitive legitimation. The uncertainty and expected difficulty of achieving adequate legitimation for a different policy reduces incentives for engaging in policy innovation and strengthens incentives to "save" the existing policy if only via modifications at the margins. *Substantial* erosion in public support for the existing policy and/or effective political pressure by influential critics would appear to be a necessary condition for overcoming the momentum of an established policy and for motivating top policymakers to address seriously the need for a basic overhauling of existing policy.

What this suggests, more specifically in the case at hand, is that disavowal of Roosevelt's policy of cooperation with the Soviet Union

carried with it the risk of undermining the basic legitimation of *any* internationalist foreign policy, thereby encouraging a return to isolationism.
The two alternative "realist" internationalist foreign policies which
Roosevelt had rejected had, as noted earlier, severe disadvantages with
regard to public acceptability. In the end Truman rejected both the
spheres-of-influence and balance-of-power alternatives, choosing instead
a somewhat vaguely defined "containment" strategy which he coupled
with support for the United Nations. (That the containment strategy and
the ensuing cold war could take on some of the characteristics of a
balance-of-power system—though bipolar rather than multipolar as in
the eighteenth and nineteenth centuries—and eventually lead to a de
facto spheres-of-influence arrangement was not clearly foreseen.)

The transition from Roosevelt's policy to containment and the cold
war was, as noted earlier, a gradual one. Its relationship to the architecture of Roosevelt's policy is of particular interest. Thus, the change
started at the level of tactics, worked upwards to strategy, and finally extended to the level of design-objectives.

Dissatisfaction with the way in which Roosevelt's policy was working
emerged quite early, well before his death, and it focussed initially and
for some time on the tactics that were being employed. The "kid gloves"
treatment of the Russians was rejected as counter-productive by
some advisers and officials, among them Averell Harriman, who was
to become particularly influential with Truman's administration. It is
true that Truman, quite soon after replacing Roosevelt, adopted a "get
tough" approach to the Russians. But as John Gaddis[7] and others have
noted, "getting tough" was initially meant to apply only to a change in
tactics in dealing with the Russians. This tactical innovation was to remain for some months part of an effort not to change Roosevelt's Great
Design and his strategy but to achieve them more effectively.[8]

In effect, Truman *improvised* an alternative to Roosevelt's Great
Design over a period of time, working as it were from the bottom
up—from tactics to strategy to design-objectives—rather than, deduc-
tively, as Roosevelt had done, from design-objectives to strategy to tactics.[9]

As it evolved, the new cold war policy encountered serious difficulties
in its ability to gain acceptance both from the standpoint of desirability
and feasibility. In striving to attain policy legitimacy with Congress and
the public for its cold war policies the Truman administration was led
into a considerable rhetorical oversimplification and exaggeration of the
Soviet threat, one that rested on a new "devil image" of the Soviets and a
new premise to the effect that the U.S.-Soviet conflict was a zero-sum
contest. The struggle to maintain policy legitimacy for the cold war led in

time to considerable rigidification in the supporting beliefs and an unwillingness of U.S. policymakers to subject them to continual testing that
stands in sharp contrast to Roosevelt's and Truman's initial willingness to
reassess the policy premises of the earlier policy on the basis of new information.

By way of conclusion, several points emerge from this analysis of the
difficulties Roosevelt experienced in his efforts to obtain policy
legitimacy for his postwar plans. First, U.S. isolationist sentiment was
not powerful enough, once the United States got into the war, to prevent
or hamper Roosevelt's ability to commit the country to an internationalist postwar policy. Roosevelt, however, was definitely hampered in
pursuing the particular internationalist security plan that he favored by
the strong idealist wing of the prointernationalist forces in the United
States. The idealists felt that World War II provided a second chance to
realize Woodrow Wilson's shattered dreams for collective security
through a strong League of Nations. Roosevelt, on the other hand,
believed this idealist approach to postwar security was naive and that it
would not be effective. But, in order not to jeopardize domestic support
for the war and in order not to risk shattering the internationalist coalition that favored U.S. participation in some kind of postwar security
system, Roosevelt shied away from trying to educate public opinion to
understand and support his hard-boiled realist approach. Roosevelt felt
he could not afford a direct confrontation with the Wilsonian idealists.
To consolidate opinion behind U.S. war aims he issued the Atlantic
Charter, which restated the country's historic idealist aspirations for national self-determination and equality of nations. And to avoid divisive
controversy with the idealists, Roosevelt gradually diluted and modified
his Four Policemen concept for postwar security and accepted instead
the creation of the United Nations organization much earlier than he had
thought desirable.

Thus, Roosevelt did secure normative legitimation for an internationalist postwar foreign policy. *But* the means he employed for this
purpose—the principles embodied in the Atlantic Charter—severely
hampered his ability to design and pursue the particular kind of postwar
security system he favored. One is struck, therefore, by the fundamental
internal policy contradiction that plagued Roosevelt's efforts to put his
Great Design for postwar cooperation with the Soviet Union into practice. For, in fact, the very national values and aspirations that he
appealed to effectively to secure normative legitimation for an internationalist foreign policy served at the same time to impose severe constraints on the strategic flexibility he needed in order to deal with Eastern
European issues.

Roosevelt's Grand Strategy called for accommodating the security needs of the Soviet Union in Eastern Europe; but the moral legitimation of his overall policy stood in the way. Roosevelt—and Truman later—found it very difficult to work out arrangements in Eastern Europe that would at the same time satisfy the Russians and not alienate idealist U.S. opinion that thought that thereby the principles of national self-determination and independence were being jeopardized. Roosevelt, and for a while Truman as well, continued to try to patch up arrangements in Eastern Europe (even "cosmetic" solutions) that would be acceptable to both Russian leaders and U.S. idealists. Their efforts eventually failed as time ran out; the U.S. image of the Soviets hardened and Truman began to improvise an alternative policy toward the Soviets.

The lesson that emerges from this experience is that a foreign policy is vulnerable if, as in this case, the means employed to secure normative legitimation of the policy at home conflict with the requirements of the grand strategy for achieving the design-objectives of that policy.

The Nixon-Kissinger Effort to Secure Policy Legitimacy for the Détente Policy

We turn now to our second case study, which we shall deal with even more briefly since it is more recent in time and there is less historical data and scholarship on which to draw. After many years of the cold war it is not surprising that the détente policy should be particularly difficult to legitimate well enough to provide U.S. policymakers with a stable, fundamental national consensus to enable them to pursue the difficult long-range objectives of détente in a consistent, coherent manner. Such legitimacy as détente enjoyed was brittle to begin with. Moreover, some of the means Nixon and Kissinger employed to strengthen public support for the détente process, even though successful in the short-run, as will be noted, entailed special risks. For a variety of reasons, such legitimacy and support as Nixon and Kissinger managed to acquire for the more ambitious of their détente objectives eroded badly well before the end of the two Nixon-Ford administrations.

An answer to the question of why the détente policy was difficult to legitimate and why such legitimacy as it acquired eroded so badly suggests itself if we compare its complex objectives and strategy with the stark simplicity of the cold war. During the cold war the U.S. objective was simply to contain the Soviet Union, without World War III, until some day hopefully the force of Soviet ideology and the forward thrust of Soviet foreign policy would moderate and spend themselves. By way of strategy, the United States relied heavily on deterrence to achieve this long-range objective.

Détente policy, on the other hand, was more ambitious in its objectives and more complicated in its strategy. It aimed at persuading the Russians to mend their ways and to enter into a new "constructive relationship" with the United States. This was what might be called the long-range "grand design-objective" of Nixon's détente policy. The development of a new constructive relationship between the two super nuclear powers was to serve as the foundation for a new international system — what Nixon vaguely referred to as "a stable structure of peace." Admittedly, as many commentators noted, what Nixon and Kissinger had in mind in these respects was not clearly conceptualized or spelled out, but it is clear that their détente policy did include the creation of a new U.S.-Soviet regime (or regimes) for security and economic issue areas. In other words, as with Roosevelt's postwar plans, détente too had a long-range system-creating objective which required the development of a friendly, cooperative relationship between the two powers. And, once again as in the case of Roosevelt's policy, the image of the Soviets that underlay the détente policy was that of a limited adversary, not that of an implacably hostile foe as in the cold war image of the Soviets.

The cold war had been easier to legitimate domestically in the United States because it rested on a simple negative stereotype — a devil image of the Soviet leaders. Détente policy, on the other hand, had the more difficult task of getting people to view the Soviets as a limited adversary; but just what that was — neither friend nor foe, something in between — was not easy for many people to understand.

The Grand Strategy for achieving the long-range objectives of détente combined the use of deterrence strategy — a holdover from the cold war era — with various measures of conciliation-accommodation; in other words, a carrot and stick approach. The conciliation-accommodation component of deterrence strategy recalled important aspects of Roosevelt's strategy for winning the Soviet leaders over to cooperation in his postwar security system, but some of the underlying cognitive beliefs were different.

The conciliation-accommodation component of détente strategy consisted of various activities that were supposed to weave an increasingly complex and tighter web of incentives and penalties into the evolving U.S.-Soviet relationship. To this end Nixon and Kissinger held out to the Soviets the prospect of a variety of important benefits from détente:

1. Nixon and Kissinger attempted to turn to account Moscow's interest in trade, access to Western credits, grain, and technology.

2. They also indulged the Soviet Union's desire for enhanced international status and recognition as a superpower equal to the United States.

3. They held out the possibility of agreeing to the Soviets' long-standing desire for formal recognition of the territorial changes in Eastern Europe and of the dominant position the Soviet Union had acquired in Eastern Europe.

4. They hoped to further entangle the Soviets in their "web of incentives" and penalties by concluding a détente with Communist China. This, they expected, would strike fear into the hearts of Soviet leaders and motivate them to adopt more moderate and cooperative policies toward the United States.

5. Last but not least in importance, Nixon and Kissinger's web of incentives included negotiations for limiting the arms race and the danger of war.

The strategy of creating a web of incentives had as one of its underlying cognitive premises the belief that it would give the Soviets a strong and continuing stake in the détente process which would lead them to act with restraint in the Third World lest they jeopardize its benefits. As one writer aptly put it, "the strategy was to evolve détente into a new form of containment of the Soviet Union—or, better still, *self-containment* on the part of the Russians."[10]

The Nixon-Kissinger strategy included other means as well to promote a new U.S.-Soviet regime of a more constructive kind. Thus, U.S. leaders urged upon the Russians the necessity of adhering to a new set of norms and rules of conduct for restraining competition and conflict between the two superpowers throughout the world. (The underlying cognitive premise was that a set of norms of sufficient relevance and specificity could be formulated over time, that Soviet and U.S. leaders would not merely pay lip-service to them but also come to constrain their behavior accordingly in order to avoid conflict and promote the longer-range goals and benefits of détente.) These efforts to formulate a set of norms, encouraged by Soviet leaders, culminated in the Basic Principles Agreement signed by Nixon and Brezhnev at their summit meeting in May 1972. This document, which Kissinger heralded at the time as marking the end of the cold war, laid out general rules of conduct: Both governments agreed to cooperate to prevent "the development of situations capable of causing a dangerous exacerbation of their relations," and the possibility of wars into which they might be drawn; to forego efforts to obtain "unilateral advantage" at each other's expense; and to exercise mutual restraint in their relations. Cooperation to prevent the onset of dangerous crises into which they might be drawn was further emphasized in the Agreement on the Prevention of Nuclear War that the two leaders signed the following year. (The multilateral Helsinki Agreement of 1975, it may be noted, also included general crisis-prevention principles.)

This strategy was increasingly denigrated by U.S. critics of détente who questioned its underlying premise and doubted its practicality. They argued that the Nixon administration was giving Moscow many tangible benefits in return for vague promises of good behavior, and that it could offer no more than pious and naive hopes that the Soviets could be bribed into limiting their ambitions and their meddling in the Third World.

What this criticism overlooked was that Nixon and Kissinger did not rely solely on offering bribes and rewards for good behavior. In fact, as already noted, their strategy for inducing restraint on Soviet behavior relied upon continued use of deterrence threats, as necessary, as well as positive incentives. If and when the Soviets did not act with restraint in the Third World, Nixon and Kissinger believed and often insisted that the United States must react firmly. And there were quite a few occasions when the Nixon-Ford administrations attempted to do so—i.e., in response to the Syrian tank invasion of Jordan in September 1970, in the Indian-Pakistani war in December 1971, in the case of the construction of a possible Soviet submarine base in Cuba in late 1970, in the Arab-Israeli War of 1973, and in Angola in 1975. In other words, when the "self-containment" Kissinger hoped to induce in Soviet leaders via the détente strategy did not suffice, he felt it was necessary to reinforce it with measures of the kind associated with traditional containment policy and deterrence strategy.

At first glance the strategy of rewards and punishments employed by Nixon and Kissinger bears a striking resemblance to what psychologists call "behavior modification." The Nixon administration in fact was using a carrot-and-stick policy in its effort to induce Soviet leaders to modify certain of their foreign policy behaviors and to resocialize them into new patterns of behavior that would be more consistent with the objectives and modalities of a new regime in U.S.-Soviet relations.

Several questions can be raised about the validity of the cognitive premises that underlay this strategy. In the first place, the effort to resocialize Russian leaders appears to have violated two basic principles of behavior modification. This technique works best when the therapist singles out *specific* items of behavior that are to be changed and indicates the *specific* approved behaviors that are to replace them. Nixon and Kissinger, however, described the behaviors to be eliminated from Soviet foreign policy in general terms and used generalities also to identify the hoped-for changes in Soviet behavior (as in the general principles contained in the Basic Principles Agreement).

Another important principle of behavior modification not sufficiently adhered to in détente strategy has to do with the timing of the reward to the subject. Just when the therapist rewards the subject may be critical in influencing him to modify a particular behavior in the desired direction. In behavior modification a reward is supposed to come *after* the subject behaves as desired; the function of the reward is to reinforce the new behavior. But Kissinger often gave benefits to the Soviets beforehand, i.e., as a bribe to induce Soviet leaders to behave in a generally desired direction.

In any case, whether or not Kissinger applied behavior modification principles correctly in his strategy, what he was trying to accomplish was very ambitious, and this raises another question regarding the feasibility of the strategy and whether still other premises on which it was based were justified. The strategy assumed that the rewards and punishments available to U.S. leaders for modifying Soviet behavior were sufficiently potent for the purpose. But this premise may be questioned. Rather, as some critics of détente held, it may be that Kissinger overestimated the leverage available to him for accomplishing so difficult and ambitious an objective. Perhaps it was overly optimistic to believe — and dangerous to encourage the U.S. public to believe, so as to gain legitimacy for the policy — that the web of incentives and penalties realistically available to the Nixon administration would suffice to create a stake in détente so valuable to Soviet leaders that they would give up opportunities to display their increased power and their efforts to extend their influence in the world. Interestingly, this was among the aspects of détente policy that was most sharply challenged by critics in levying the charge that Kissinger had "oversold" détente.

The legitimacy of détente strategy suffered also because its implementation confused the public. It was perhaps predictable that many members of Congress and the public would fail to grasp the subtleties of a strategy that combined deterrence threats and penalties with efforts at conciliation and bestowal of benefits. If the Soviets behaved so badly on some occasions so as to warrant threats or penalties, why then reward them in other respects? Should there not be more explicit *quid pro quos* whereby the Soviets would give up something concrete for each benefit we gave them? Criticism of this kind not only eroded the legitimacy of détente policy; it brought increasing pressure to bear on the administration to abandon or at least make significant changes in the strategy employed. The domestic politics of détente within the United States, magnified by Reagan's unexpectedly strong challenge in the Republican

presidential primaries, forced the Ford administration to drive harder
bargains with Moscow and to apply more exacting standards for acceptable agreements. (And this constraint has applied equally thus far to
President Carter's approach to the Soviets.)

But perhaps the worst consequence of the way in which Kissinger applied the complex strategy of conciliation and deterrence was that it
tended over time to polarize U.S. public opinion. Both the anti-Soviet
hawks and the antiwar doves in this country became dissatisfied with the
détente policy for different reasons. And with the passage of time both
hawk and dove critics of the détente policy became stronger politically.
Thus, when Kissinger bestowed benefits on the Soviets, the anti-Soviet
hawks protested. And whenever Kissinger confronted the Soviets—as in
the Arab-Israeli War of 1973 and over Angola—the doves sounded the
alarm that the administration was about to start down the slippery slope
into another Vietnam.

As a result, Kissinger found himself caught in an increasingly severe
whiplash between hawk and dove critics of his policy. Those members of
Congress and the public who did understand and sympathize with the in-
tricate logic and rationale of the dual strategy of conciliation and deterrence, and who made up the centrist constituency whose support Kissinger so badly needed to maintain the momentum of the détente process,
were gradually neutralized by the growing strength and louder voices of
hawk and dove critics.

Kissinger's difficulties with his hawkish critics were compounded by
other adverse developments that he was unable to control and to which
he inadvertently contributed on occasion. These developments included
the Soviet leaders' repeated insistence—in part no doubt to quiet the opposition to détente from their own hawks—that détente did not mean
that they were betraying their communist ideology and would forego
support for "national liberation" movements. U.S. hawks interpreted
such Soviet statements as exposing the fallacy of the cognitive premises
on which were based Kissinger's aspirations for developing a new constructive relationship with the Soviets. Soviet insistence on defining
détente in terms of their own concept of "peaceful coexistence" also
revived concern over Soviet intentions. And this concern over the premises of the détente policy was much strengthened by the continuing
buildup of Soviet strategic and other military capabilities coupled with
the failure of the Strategic Arms Limitations Talks (SALT) negotiations
to limit the arms race. Thus the question of Soviet intentions, which has
periodically agitated American foreign policy experts and public opinion
since the end of World War II, emerged once again as a highly salient
and controversial issue.

Uneasiness about Kissinger's conduct of détente strategy was aggra-

vated by the way in which he sometimes expressed his views about growing Soviet power and influence in the world. Kissinger's statements sometimes included unfortunate innuendos to the effect that the Soviet Union
was now the ascendant power and the United States a descending power.
This theme was implicit rather than explicit in what Kissinger said, but it
struck a highly sensitive chord among Americans who were suffering the
many evidences of the decline of U.S. power and hegemony. Kissinger
was charged with holding a Spenglerian view of the decline of the West,
which of course he denied. But more than one critic detected evidences of
pessimism in some of Kissinger's philosophical reflections on the state of
the world with regard to the possibility that the West's will to resist expansion of Soviet power and influence was on the decline.

The attribution of such beliefs and predispositions to Kissinger made it
all the more plausible to charge him with pursuing détente in a one-sided
way, as if he were driven by the feeling that it was imperative for the
United States to work out the best deal possible with its mighty adversary
before the West grew even weaker. In this regard, Kissinger's critics felt
that he was underestimating the Soviet Union's economic and political
weaknesses, its problems with its Eastern European client states and with
Communist parties in the West, and the fact that the Soviet system was
not really an appealing model for many developing countries.

For all of these reasons the legitimacy of the détente policy eroded
badly, a development that enormously strengthened those various domestic constraints associated with "democratic control" of foreign policy
mentioned at the beginning of this chapter. As a result, Kissinger's ability
to conduct a coherent, effective foreign policy on behalf of the laudable
objectives of détente was shattered well before the end of the Ford
administration. With the erosion of the stable domestic consensus on
behalf of détente, Kissinger could no longer count on minimal public acceptance of the variety of actions that implementation of his détente
strategy required. Not only was he no longer given the benefit of the
doubt, some of his activities engendered suspicion that they were designed to serve his personal interests or the political fortunes of his
administration. His secretive approach to decisionmaking and his
diplomatic style did much, of course, to enhance the distrust.

No doubt Kissinger believed that his détente policy fell victim to the
public's impatience for quick results and its unreasonable demands for
frequent concrete indications that the policy was succeeding. Kissinger
might complain with some justification that critics of détente were not
justified in expecting that each transaction with the Soviets should give
reciprocal advantages to each side; or that the balance sheet should show
a profit every month.

Given the ambitious character of the détente objective which required resocialization of Soviet leaders and their acceptance of the norms of a new regime in U.S.-Soviet relations, it would be only reasonable to assume that considerable time and repeated efforts would be needed to accomplish that goal. In the meantime, before Dr. Kissinger's behavior modification therapy took full effect, one had to expect that the Soviets would occasionally misbehave. But if so, then how could one evaluate whether the strategy was succeeding? Kissinger's critics pointed to instances of Soviet meddling in Third Areas as evidence of the failure and unsound character of the strategy. Kissinger himself could only retort that Soviet behavior would have been perhaps even more aggressive and the confrontations more dangerous had it not been for détente. Neither side could prove its case; but the possibility must be entertained that the critics pronounced the strategy of inducing self-restraints in Soviet foreign policy a failure prematurely.

Public Opinion and the Problem of Evaluating Foreign Policy

Any complex long-range foreign policy such as Roosevelt's Grand Design or the Nixon-Kissinger détente policy needs considerable time to achieve its objectives. Such politics cannot be achieved overnight: one summit meeting between the heads of state will not do it; neither will one overall agreement or one decisive action. Nor can one even expect steady progress toward the long-range objective. It is more reasonable to expect occasional ups and downs.

Any long-range policy needs to be evaluated along the way. We expect a president and his administration to engage in objective, well-informed evaluations of the policies they are pursuing. Policy evaluation of Roosevelt's approach to the Russians — and of Nixon's détente policy — involve questions such as the following: Is the long-range concept of a "cooperative" U.S.-Soviet relationship clearly enough defined — that is, does the administration have a clear enough notion of what it is striving to accomplish? Is the *general strategy* the administration is employing to achieve that long-range objective a sound one; and is the strategy working well enough or does it need to be changed in some way? Are the day-to-day *tactics* that are being utilized to implement that strategy well conceived? Are they working or do they need to be changed?

These questions associated with policy evaluation, it may be noted, have to do with the "cognitive legitimacy" of a policy — i.e., the basis for the president's claim that he knows what he is doing; that he understands well enough the nature of the opponent and the forces at work in the world situation, and that he knows how to use the means available to him in order to achieve the long-range objectives of his policy.

The evaluation of an ongoing policy is difficult to begin with from a purely intellectual and analytical standpoint. It is all the more difficult if the monitoring and evaluation of a current policy is unduly influenced by the play of domestic politics.

A president who pursues a long-range foreign policy in a democracy such as ours runs into some formidable problems. In the absence of policy legitimacy the character of U.S. politics, the role of the modern mass media in our political life, and the volatile nature of public opinion combine to subject the president's pursuit of long-range foreign policy objectives to constant scrutiny and evaluation. As a result, the president finds himself forced to defend his long-range policy on a month-to-month — if not also a day-to-day — basis. When this happens a shortened and often distorted time perspective is then introduced into the already difficult task of evaluating the policy and the related task of deciding whether changes in strategy and tactics are necessary.

One of the characteristics of the U.S. public is its impatience for quick results and its demand for frequent reassurances that a policy is succeeding. This impatience is often fed by and exploited by the mass media and by political opponents of the administration's policy. The result of these domestic political factors is to complicate the ability of a president to pursue a long-range policy with the patience and persistence that is needed. The play of public opinion and politics can distort the difficult task of evaluating the policy; it can erode its legitimacy; it can force changes in that policy before it has had a chance to prove itself.

Faced with the volatile tendencies of U.S. public opinion, a president and his advisers must attempt to carefully control the public's impatience for quick results. They must also offer meaningful assurances that the cognitive premises of their policy goals and of the strategy and tactics employed on their behalf are being subjected to careful, objective evaluation. They must also control their own tendency to pander to the public's demand for quick, dramatic results as a way of making up for the inadequate legitimacy that their policy enjoys. On this score Kissinger and Nixon can be criticized for having pandered to the public's impatience for quick results and its tendency to be impressed by dramatic achievements of a symbolic rather than substantive import. In the early years of détente, Nixon and Kissinger were able to come up with spectacular events that seemed to offer assurance that détente was working — the trips to Peking, the summits with Soviet leaders in Moscow and Washington, the multitude of agreements.[11] But thereby Nixon and Kissinger helped to create a frame of mind and a set of expectations in the public which worked against them later on when they had no more rabbits to pull out of the hat for the time being. Day-to-day "successes" — whether real successes or contrived public-relations-type successes — are not only a poor substitute for genuine policy legitimacy; they can easily end up helping erode whatever legitimacy has been achieved for a complex, long-range policy such as détente.

Acknowledgments

Research for this chapter was supported by a grant (number SOC 75-14079) from the National Science Foundation and by the Center for Advanced Study in the Behavioral Sciences at which the author was a Fellow in 1976–1977. Parts of the chapter were presented earlier in a paper delivered to the Symposium on U.S. Foreign Policy in the Next Decade at the University of Missouri–Saint Louis, April 1977, and in a paper for a conference on approaches to the study of decisionmaking at the Norwegian Institute of International Affairs, Oslo, Norway, August 1977.

Notes

1. In preparing this interpretative essay the author has relied mostly upon secondary sources describing Roosevelt's plans for a postwar security system and the Nixon-Kissinger détente policy.

Roosevelt's "Great Design" for the postwar period was conveyed by him most explicitly in background interviews with Forrest Davis, who published detailed accounts of Roosevelt's plans and the beliefs supporting them in several articles appearing in the *Saturday Evening Post*: "Roosevelt's World Blueprint," 10 April 1943; "What Really Happened at Teheran — I," 13 May 1944; "What Really Happened at Teheran — II," 20 May 1944. [For background and evidence of Roosevelt's later acknowledgment that Davis's articles accurately reflected his views, see John Lewis Gaddis, *The United States and the Origins of the Cold War* (New York: Columbia University Press, 1972), pp. 6, 153.] Detailed secondary accounts of Roosevelt's thinking and plans are to be found in Willard Range, *Franklin D. Roosevelt's World Order* (Athens: University of Georgia Press, 1959); Roland N. Stromberg, *Collective Security and American Foreign Policy* (New York: Praeger Publishers, 1963), see esp. chap. 8; Robert A. Divine, *Roosevelt and World War II* (Baltimore, Md.: Johns Hopkins University Press, 1969); John Lewis Gaddis, *Origins of the Cold War*; Daniel Yergin, *Shattered Peace* (Boston: Houghton Mifflin Co., 1977), esp. chap. 2; and Robert Garson, "The Atlantic Alliance, Eastern Europe and the Origins of the Cold War: From Pearl Harbor to Yalta," in H. C. Allen and Roger Thompson, eds., *Contrast and Con-*

nection (Columbus: Ohio State University Press, 1976), pp. 296–319.

For various reasons the Nixon-Kissinger policy of détente is more difficult to reconstruct in terms of the analytical framework ("design-objective," "strategy," "tactics") employed in this essay. While Nixon and Kissinger often spoke in general terms regarding their long-range goal of a "new constructive relationship" with the Soviet Union and made cryptic references to a new balance-of-power system, they never disclosed (and perhaps never formulated) a more specific design concept for the international system they hoped to create. The term "détente" itself was a misnomer since, quite obviously, the Nixon administration's objectives and strategy went well beyond securing merely a "relaxation of tensions" (which is the traditional definition of détente) and embraced a willingness to engage in substantial "appeasement" (in the pre-1930s nonpejorative sense of the term) and "accommodation" of the Soviet Union in the interest of inducing and socializing this "revolutionary" power into becoming a responsible member of a new, stable international system.

Perhaps the fullest statement – really, by that time a defense – of the détente policy was provided by Kissinger in his testimony before the U.S. Senate Committee on Foreign Relations, 19 September 1974 ["Détente with the Soviet Union: The Reality of Competition and the Imperative of Cooperation," reprinted in Robert J. Pranger, ed., *Détente and Defense* (Washington, D.C.: American Enterprise Institute for Public Policy Research, 1976), pp. 153–178]. See also earlier statements and speeches by Nixon and Kissinger and, in particular, the annual reports to the nation: Richard M. Nixon, *U.S. Foreign Policy for the 1970's,* (Washington, D.C.: U.S. Government Printing Office, 1970, 1971, 1972, and 1973); see also Helmut Sonnenfeldt, "The Meaning of Détente," *Naval War College Review* 28:1 (Summer 1975).

Among the many published commentaries and critical appraisals of the détente policy, the most useful for present purposes is Stanley Hoffmann, *Primacy or World Order* (New York: McGraw-Hill Book Co., 1978), pp. 33–100, which contains observations regarding the difficulty of gaining legitimacy for the détente policy similar to those offered in the present essay. An important detailed study is the as yet unpublished dissertation by Dan Caldwell, "American-Soviet Détente and the Nixon-Kissinger Grand Design and Grand Strategy" (Ph.D. diss., Department of Political Science, Stanford University, 1978). Among the many other useful commentaries on the Nixon-Kissinger détente policy, see Stephen A. Garrett, "Nixonian Foreign Policy: A New Balance of Power – or a Revived Concert?" *Polity* 8 (Spring 1976); Robert Osgood, ed., *America and the World*, vol. 2, *Retreat from Empire? The First Nixon Administration* (Baltimore, Md.: Johns Hopkins University Press, 1973); and B. Thomas Trout, "Legitimating Containment and Détente: A Comparative Analysis" (Paper presented to the Midwest Political Science Association, Chicago, Ill., 19–21 April 1979).

2. The concept of "policy legitimacy" (versus "regime legitimacy") is discussed in a stimulating and insightful way by B. Thomas Trout, "Rhetoric Revisited: Political Legitimation and the Cold War," *International Studies Quarterly* 19:3 (September 1975).

3. For a fuller account see, for example, John L. Gaddis, *Origins of the Cold War,* chaps. 1, 2.

4. A detailed listing is available from the author upon request.

5. Forrest Davis, "Roosevelt's World Blueprint," *Saturday Evening Post,* 10 April 1943.

6. That the State Department was not an "ideological monolith" in its attitude toward the Soviet Union during and immediately after World War II has been persuasively argued and documented in recent studies. [Cf., for example, Robert L. Messer, "Paths Not Taken: The United States Department of State and Alternatives to Containment, 1945–1946," *Diplomatic History* 1 (Fall 1977).] Moreover, as Eduard Mark demonstrates, Charles Bohlen and other State Department specialists did not operate on the assumption that there was an ineluctable conflict betwen the principle of self-determination in Eastern Europe and legitimate Soviet security interests in that area. Instead, they distinguished between different kinds of spheres of influence, arguing that an "open" (versus an "exclusive") Soviet sphere of influence in Eastern Europe was acceptable to and consistent with U.S. interests. See "Charles E. Bohlen and The Acceptable Limits of Soviet Hegemony in Eastern Europe: A Memorandum of 18 October 1945," *Diplomatic History* 2 (Spring 1979). On this point see also Thomas G. Patterson, *On Every Front: The Making of the Cold War* (New York: W. W. Norton & Co., 1979), chap. 3.

7. Gaddis, *Origins of the Cold War*, pp. 198–205.

8. Important changes in Roosevelt's strategy took place later. They included a shift from appeasement to insistence on *quid pro quos* and, probably of greater significance, a willingness on Truman's part to make important exceptions to Roosevelt's practice of seeking joint decisionmaking among the Great Powers on the major political and territorial questions affecting postwar Europe. Thus Truman, confronted by urgent problems—particularly economic—of governing occupied Germany, which the mechanisms for four-power control could not deal with to his satisfaction, gradually moved toward making unilateral decisions without the Russians and the creation of separate mechanisms for governing the three Western zones of Germany.

9. As John L. Gaddis notes in commenting on Truman's stormy interview with Soviet Foreign Minister Molotov on 23 April 1945, soon after Roosevelt's death— which was perhaps the first example of Truman's new "get tough" tactics: "to view the new President's confrontation with Molotov as the opening move in a well-planned, long-range strategy for dealing with the Soviet Union is to presume a degree of foresight and consistency which simply was not present during the early days of the Truman Administration." (*Origins of the Cold War,* pp. 205–206).

10. Leslie Gelb, "The Kissinger Legacy," *N.Y. Times Magazine*, 31 October 1976, italics supplied.

11. The *timing* of the Nixon-Kissinger "spectaculars" may also have opened them to the criticism that détente moves were being used to gain partisan political advantage. For example, the China trip seemed timed to coincide with the 1972 primaries; the SALT Treaty was advantageously signed during the summer of 1972; and the wheat deal, too, coincided with the 1972 presidential nomination conventions. (Source: Ole R. Holsti in a personal communication.)

11

OLE R. HOLSTI
JAMES N. ROSENAU

Cold War Axioms in
the Post-Vietnam Era

Introduction

The leaders who formulated and implemented U.S. foreign policy during the two decades following World War II had witnessed the bitter consequences of post-Versailles isolationism, of beggar-thy-neighbor international economic policies, of military restraint in the face of rearmament by those committed to destruction of the existing international order, and of efforts to conciliate expansionist dictatorships by offering concessions. That such experiences should have shaped their thinking is neither surprising nor unprecedented in foreign policy decisionmaking.[1] The impact of these events and the "lessons" drawn from them is dramatically evident in memoirs and diaries of many post–World War II foreign policy leaders, as well as in a number of recent studies of postwar diplomacy.

Out of the experiences of this period emerged a series of "lessons of history" or axioms[2] relating to the contemporary international system, the proper role for the United States within it, the nature of adversaries, and the aspirations, strategies, and tactics that should constitute the core of this nation's external relations. Although these guidelines, or what we shall call "cold war axioms," are not unique to this period — some of them can be found in political tracts going as far back as Machiavelli or Kautilya — they represented a rather significant change from the basic premises that had guided external relations during earlier periods in U.S. history.

However, just as experiences before and during World War II gave rise to widely shared beliefs about foreign policy that differed sharply from those of previous eras, U.S. military involvement in Vietnam will perhaps serve as a source of still another set of foreign policy axioms that represents as significant a break from the cold war axioms as the latter did from their predecessors. Vietnam, in other words, may shape the conduct of U.S. foreign policy during the next several decades in the same way that events surrounding World War II did during those decades just passed.

It is not possible to invalidate the alternative hypothesis that, even in the absence of the Vietnam War, the cold war axioms would have come under serious criticism, perhaps even to the point of creating deep fissures within both the public and leadership groups. Several students of foreign policy have commented on an apparently persistent U.S. tendency to swing from periods of isolationism to internationalism and back to isolationism.[3] Theories of generation-long cycles of U.S. orientations toward international affairs thus suggest that by the mid- to late 1960s a mood of retrenchment from expanded global responsibilities would in any case have set in. Perhaps it is significant that in 1964 (about one generation after Pearl Harbor) Barry Goldwater became the first major party presidential nominee since World War II to reject some of these axioms.

But the Vietnam War did happen, and it served as a catalyst for frontal assaults by many leaders on the fundamental premises of U.S. foreign policy. Biographical anecdotes are hardly sufficient to establish even this limited parallel between World War II and the Vietnam War, but they may serve to illustrate the point. Prior to World War II Senator Arthur Vandenberg was a leading spokesman for U.S. isolationism and a not wholly implausible candidate for the Republican presidential nomination. After the Japanese attack that brought the United States into the war, he noted in his diary: "In my own mind, my convictions regarding international cooperation and collective security for peace took firm form on the afternoon of the Pearl Harbor attack. That day ended isolationism for any realist."[4] The disaster in Hawaii was thus of such significance as to reshape Vandenberg's core beliefs about international politics and the proper U.S. response to a rapidly changing world.[5] After World War II, J. William Fulbright was an influential legislative leader whose basic premises were consistent with, and helped to shape, the main contours of a globalist U.S. foreign policy. After escalation of the Vietnam War he became an articulate spokesman for those opposing the U.S. war effort, in the process also rejecting many of the fundamental axioms that had guided his as well as the nation's external policies during the postwar years.

This chapter will explore several related questions in some detail. To what extent has the foreign policy consensus that emerged during the decade following the end of World War II been shattered? Has a new, post-Vietnam consensus emerged among U.S. leaders and, if so, what are its most salient features? Alternatively, do the deep internal divisions that marked the period of active U.S. involvement in Southeast Asia live on as two or more fundamentally divergent sets of beliefs about the international system and this nation's proper role within it? Finally, what implications do the answers to these questions carry for the ability of the United States to carry out a well-defined, overall foreign policy and, more specfically, to pursue basic changes in the international system?

Cold War and Post-Cold War Axioms

Table 11.1 identifies some key elements of the cold war and post-cold war belief system.[6] Even during the chilliest episodes of the cold war it cannot be said that there was an absence of critics in Washington and elsewhere who would take sharp exception to one or more of the eleven propositions listed as cold war axioms in Table 11.1. Henry Wallace, Robert Taft, Herbert Hoover, James Byrnes, Walter Lippmann, George Kennan, and other influential persons at one time or another offered provocative challenges to some of the most important of them. Moreover, these axioms are presented in their most elemental form, without any of the subtle nuances or ceteris paribus clauses that might more accurately reflect the beliefs of any single person. Thus, they represent modal tendencies rather than the verbatim catechism of a homogeneous elite. The eleven counter propositions listed as post-cold war axioms are often attributed to Americans for whom the Vietnam War represented a critical test — and disastrous failure — of the foreign policy beliefs that prevailed during much of the post-World War II period.

These two sets of axioms differ sharply with respect to the nature of the international system, the character and goals of this nation's adversaries, the role of the Third World, the scope and nature of U.S. national interests, and the means by which foreign policy goals can most effectively be pursued. The one depicts a conflictual world in which all issues and conflicts are related to each other, with the result that disturbances in one area will reverberate throughout the system; the United States faces an implacable and united coalition of adversaries led by Peking and Moscow; the Third World plays a crucial role as both the battleground and the prize in the conflict between contending blocs; the United States has global responsibilities to meet any challenges from communism; and military instruments of policy are at least the necessary, if not sufficient, means of securing vital interests.

The post-cold war axioms, on the other hand, portray contemporary international relations quite differently. Within a loosely structured in-

TABLE 11.1
Some "Cold War Axioms" and "Post-Cold War Axioms"

Cold War Axioms	Post-Cold War Axioms
Every nation that falls to communism increases the power of the Communist bloc in its struggle with the Free World	The dominoes are falling. So what?
Peace is indivisible.... Thus any expansion of Communist influence must be resisted	Peace is divisible
Concessions made under pressure constitute appeasement which only whets the appetite of aggressors	While there are important differences between Communist and democratic regimes, the distinction between the Communist bloc and the Free World obfuscates more than it illuminates
The preeminent feature of international politics is conflict between Communism and the Free World	The Soviet Union is an established, status quo-oriented power
Russian intentions toward Western Europe are essentially expansionist. So, too, are Chinese intentions in Asia	Nationalism is stronger than Communism
	Communism is a divided movement

	It is not clear that <u>any</u> development in the Third World would affect the security or vital interests of the United States
The main sources of unrest, disorder, subversion, and civil war in underdeveloped areas is Communist influence and support	
	The United States has neither the power, the responsibility, nor the right to guarantee the defense of the Free World or to serve as the linchpin of international order
Communism is monolithic	
The Third World really matters, because it is the battleground between Communism and the Free World	Opposition to Communism is a misleading guide for U.S. foreign policy
The United States has an obligation to aid any Free People resisting Communism at home or abroad	
The surest simple guide to U.S. interests in foreign policy is opposition to Communism	A number of pressing domestic requirements should have priority over all current issues of foreign affairs
Military strength is the primary route to national security	Increasing military strength will only bring increased national insecurity

Sources: Graham T. Allison, "Cool It: The Foreign Policy of Young America," Foreign Policy, No. 1 (Winter, 1970-71), pp. 150-51; Morton Halperin, Bureaucratic Politics and Foreign Policy (Washington: Brookings Institution, 1974), pp. 11-12; and Michael Roskin, "From Pearl Harbor to Vietnam: Shifting Generational Paradigms and Foreign Policy," Political Science Quarterly, 89 (Fall, 1974), p. 576.

ternational system there exist complex competing interests that do not always find the Western democracies arrayed against the monolithic, Soviet-dominated Communist bloc; the linkages between conflict issues are at best modest, with the consequence that their reverberations may be little more than local in scope; Third World conflicts are more likely to reflect nationalist than communist motivations but, in any case, they rarely pose a serious threat to vital U.S. interests; these interests are sufficiently varied and complex that they cannot adequately be met by employing such simple decision rules as "oppose communism"; and the means by which foreign policy goals can most effectively be pursued are not limited to, or even primarily, military ones.

Embedded within the post–cold war axioms are two somewhat diverging themes. One accepts an active U.S. foreign policy, the imperatives for which derive not from East-West issues but from those either pitting the North versus the South (for example, demands for a new international economic order), or all nations versus nature (for example, some environmental issues). The second view denies the primacy of international concerns and urges that critical domestic problems are addressed and resolved first. Indeed, some assert that an active foreign policy and domestic reforms—if not democratic institutions themselves—are mutually exclusive. The discussion that follows will thus consider not only propositions associated with the cold war, but also both nationalist and internationalist variants of post–cold war axioms.

The Foreign Policy Leadership Survey

Did the Vietnam War represent a watershed in U.S. foreign policy, perhaps analogous to what students of domestic politics have called "critical elections"? To pose the question with reference to the axioms summarized in Table 11.1, did the war in Southeast Asia represent the point at which one paradigm or vision of international relations started a process of irreversible decline that will see its eventual replacement by another? Alternatively the question may be put in the terms suggested by Alexander George's discussion in Chapter 10: To what extent has the "legitimacy" of the "cold war axioms" been eroded?

In order to gain a better understanding of how the Vietnam War has been defined by those presently in leadership positions, as well as by persons who are likely to occupy such roles in the future, an extensive survey of U.S. leaders has been taken. Observations about the impact of the Vietnam War on U.S. foreign policy have been in abundant supply during the past decade. Why, then, pursue the matter by means of a large-scale leadership survey? To acknowledge that for a decade Vietnam dominated many aspects of U.S. life is not to answer all of the significant questions that can be raised about the present and possible future impact of that conflict. For example, most Americans would probably agree with the assertion, "No more Vietnams!" But when asked to be more specific about the policy implications of that slogan, or about the ways in which they would avoid repeating that disastrous experience, a rather wide range of answers could be expected. Because people do indeed "read into history more or less what they want to read," understanding precisely *which* lessons are being drawn from the Vietnam experience, and *by whom*, becomes a complex empirical question.

In order to obtain appropriate evidence on the question, a lengthy questionnaire was mailed to a national leadership sample in February 1976 with a follow-up mailing to nonrespondents two months later. Approximately one-half of the sample was drawn from the most recent edition of *Who's Who in America*. Because that source tends to have rather heavy concentrations of some occupational groups — notably business executives and academics — it concomitantly underrepresents other types of leaders whose views on foreign policy were of interest. To ensure the inclusion of leaders in several other occupations, the remaining half of the sample was drawn from more specialized directories: foreign service officers, labor officials, political leaders, military officers, clergy, foreign affairs experts not presently holding government positions, leaders in the printed and electronic media, and women.[7] Of the 4,290 leaders who received questionnaires, 2,282 — somewhat over 53 percent — completed and returned them.

This chapter, one of a series of reports focusing on the impact of the Vietnam War on the beliefs of U.S. leaders,[8] draws upon data from that survey to address three questions. First, how do U.S. leaders presently assess a series of propositions similar to the axioms that provided the intellectual foundations for much of U.S. foreign policy during the two decades following the end of World War II? Conversely, to what extent have they come to view contemporary international affairs from the perspective described by the "post–cold war axioms"? Second, are divisions among leaders on one axiom or another embedded within and sustained by a network of other, reinforcing ideas about the nature of international relations? Or to pose the question somewhat differently, is it accurate to describe U.S. leaders as divided into two or more groups, each adhering to internally consistent clusters of foreign policy beliefs that have few elements in common with the others? Third, to what extent do cleavages among U.S. leaders fall between rather than across occupations?[9] That is, does occupation serve to attenuate or to magnify and sustain dissensus among Americans in leadership roles?

Cold War and Post-Cold War Axioms

Forty-one propositions were selected from a larger sample of items in the questionnaire because they correspond rather closely to the two sets of axioms described in the previous section. Most of them also focus upon the nature of the international system, adversaries, the proper international role and goals of the United States, and the appropriate instruments for pursuing external goals. To these have been added two items that focus on specific foreign policy undertakings—the appropriate course to be pursued in Angola and in case of another oil embargo[10]— as well as two items that seem especially relevant in the post-Vietnam/Watergate period—the proper role of the president in defining the national interest and of military advice in formulating foreign policy.

The International System

The cold war axioms listed in Table 11.1 depict an international system that is characterized by a tight bipolar structure with cleavages on a single free world–communism axis, and by zero-sum conflicts in which gains for one side constitute an equal loss for the other. However, responses to several questionnaire items that more or less correspond to the cold war axioms reveal considerable ambivalence about the structure and characteristic patterns of relations within the international system (Table 11.2). On the one hand, our respondents indicated very strong support for both the validity of the "domino theory" and for the proposition that failure to honor alliance commitments will result in heavy costs (11.2:A and B).[11] Moreover, over two-thirds of our respondents agreed that communist nations have been encouraged by the outcome in Vietnam to seek other triumphs (11.2:E). On the other hand, substantial if not overwhelming majorities questioned some other core premises of the cold war period; for example, the assumption of a zero-sum relationship between communist gains and the U.S. national interest (11.2:C). Additionally, the proposition that détente is based on false premises received support from less than four respondents in ten (11.2:D).

A mixed pattern also emerges from responses to the first four propositions in Table 11.3. Less than one-third of the respondents believed that present fissures among communist nations are irreparable, but the equation of revolutionary movements in the Third World and international communism was questioned by a substantial majority of the leaders questioned (11.3:A and B).[12] A majority in excess of 60 percent agreed that the United Nations should play a vital role in settling international disputes (11.3:C). However, only one-fourth of the respondents considered strengthening the United Nations to be a "very important" goal for U.S. foreign policy, whereas 30 percent considered that goal to be of no importance (11.3:D).

The picture that emerges from these data, then, is neither unquestioning acceptance nor wholesale rejection of the cold war axioms. Propositions couched as general rules of sound diplomacy—for example, about the importance of honoring alliance commitments—continue to garner substantial support among the leaders in our sample. There appears to be a greater propensity to question axioms that are more specifically concerned with relations between the United States and its adversaries.

Adversaries

Beliefs about the international system are closely related to images of adversaries and their intentions. Cold war beliefs about U.S. opponents centered on the expansionist motivations harbored in Moscow and Peking. During the height of the cold war, assessments of these communist nations typically took one of two forms: (1) they are indistinguishable with respect to powerful and persistent expansionist motivations, or (2) the older Soviet regime has come to play a relatively conservative role in world affairs, whereas the one in Peking is not only inherently expansionist, but it is also recklessly and irrationally so. Thus, U.S. involvement in Vietnam was often justified as an exercise in containing Chinese expansion, and the rhetoric of senior officials in Washington rarely failed to portray the leadership in Peking as aggressive and not altogether predictable with respect to foreign affairs.[13] Other core beliefs about adversaries centered on the monolithic character of the Soviet bloc and the central role of communist influence in disorder and violence within the less developed parts of the world.

An interesting aspect of Table 11.2 is the strikingly different appraisals of Soviet and Chinese foreign policy goals. Skepticism of the Kremlin's purposes abounded among the respondents, more than 80 percent of whom regarded the USSR as expansionist rather than defensive in its foreign policy goals (11.2:F). On the other hand, fewer than 30 percent of the leaders in the sample agreed that Peking is pursuing expansionist ambitions, and less than 7 percent of them expressed strong agreement with that proposition (11.2:G). Perhaps one explanation for the radical shift in leadership views of China is the venerable political adage that "My enemy's enemy is my friend."

Further questions on Soviet-U.S. relations revealed a mixture of

TABLE 11.2
"Cold War Axioms": Responses of 2,282 American Leaders (in percentages*)

	Strongly Agree	Agree Somewhat	Disagree Somewhat	Disagree Strongly	No Opinion	Very Important	Moderately Important	Slightly Important	Not at All Important	Not Sure
A. There is considerable validity to the "domino theory" that when one nation falls to communism, others nearby will soon follow a similar path	25	42	18	14	1					
B. A nation will pay a heavy price if it honors its alliance commitments only selectively	37	43	15	3	3					
C. Any communist victory is a defeat for America's national interest	16	24	36	23	1					
D. The major assumptions of detente have been proven false by the events in Vietnam	11	24	37	17	11					
E. Communist nations have been encouraged to seek triumphs elsewhere as a result in Vietnam	30	39	19	9	3					
F. The Soviet Union is generally expansionist rather than defensive in its foreign policy goals	47	36	11	2	3					
G. China is generally expansionist rather than defensive in its foreign policy goals	7	23	37	25	9					
H. Detente permits the U.S.S.R. to pursue policies that promote rather than restrain conflict	19	38	29	9	6					
I. It is not in our interest to have better relations with the Soviet Union because we are getting less than we are giving to them	9	20	35	35	2					

J. Containing communism (as a foreign policy goal for the United States)	39	42	--	14	5
K. The U.S. should take all steps including the use of force to prevent the spread of communism	9	24	30	35	1
L. The U.S. should never try to get by with half measures; we should apply necessary power if we have it	26	27	24	21	3
M. Rather than simply countering our opponent's thrusts, it is necessary to strike at the heart of the opponent's power	21	25	23	22	9
N. When force is used, military rather than political goals should determine its application	16	20	24	35	5
O. If foreign interventions are undertaken, the necessary force should be applied in a short period of time rather than through a policy of graduated escalation	49	29	8	5	10
P. There is nothing wrong with using the C.I.A. to try to undermine hostile governments	21	30	20	28	1
Q. The U.S. fought with a "no win" approach (as a cause of failure in Vietnam)	46	20	14	18	3
R. The use of American air power was restricted (as a cause of failure in Vietnam)	33	22	20	23	3
S. Insufficient attention was paid to advice from the military (as a cause of failure in Vietnam)	22	21	20	30	8
T. The U.S. should undertake military intervention in the Middle East in case of another oil embargo	6	15	27	49	2

* Excludes those who did not answer or who provided an uncodable response. Owing to rounding error, rows may total slightly more or less than 100 percent.

TABLE 11.3
"Post-Cold War (Internationalist) Axioms": Responses of 2,282 American Leaders (in percentages*)

	Very Important	Moderately Important	Slightly Important	Not at All Important	Not Sure	Strongly Agree	Somewhat Agree	Somewhat Disagree	Strongly Disagree	No Opinion
A. American foreign policy should be based on the premise that the Communist "bloc" is irreparably fragmented						7	25	31	29	7
B. Revolutionary forces in "Third World" countries are usually nationalistic rather than controlled by the U.S.S.R or China						22	39	22	12	5
C. It is vital to enlist the cooperation of the U.N. in settling international disputes						30	33	20	16	2

D. Strengthening the United Nations (as a foreign policy goal for the United States)	25	27	--	30	8
E. Worldwide arms control (as a foreign policy goal for the United States)	66	26	--	5	3
F. Fostering international cooperation to solve common problems, such as food, inflation and energy (as a foreign policy goal for the United States)	70	26	--	3	1
G. Helping to improve the standard of living in less developed countries (as a foreign policy goal for the United States)	38	51	--	9	3
H. Combatting world hunger (as a foreign policy goal for the United States)	50	40	--	7	3
I. Helping solve world inflation (as a foreign policy goal for the United States)	49	42	--	6	3
J. The U.S. should give economic aid to poorer countries even if it means higher prices at home	11	37	32	19	1

* Excludes those who did not answer or who provided an uncodable response. Owing to rounding error, rows may total slightly more or less than 100 percent.

doubts and hopes. On the one hand, a clear majority of respondents questioned Moscow's fidelity to a genuine accommodation between the United States and the Soviet Union; fewer than four respondents in ten disagreed with the proposition that détente permits the USSR to pursue policies that promote rather than restrain international conflict (11.2:H). On the other hand, 70 percent of the leaders in the sample rejected the view that U.S. interests suffer as a consequence of better relations between the two superpowers (11.2:I).

A rather fundamental challenge to the cold war axioms is posed by the suggestion that the real threats to national security may arise from such issues as energy and the environment that have little if anything to do with communism (Table 11.4). By a margin of almost three to one, the respondents expressed some degree of support for the proposition that U.S. preoccupation with Vietnam led to a neglect of the real — and unrelated to communist — threats to national security (11.4:K).

The Role of the United States

The essential premise of the "revolution in U.S. foreign policy" after World War II was a belief that an active U.S. role in world affairs was a necessary, if not sufficient, condition for avoiding another major war. As Alexander George has shown in Chapter 10, Franklin D. Roosevelt's "Grand Design" for the postwar world included membership for this nation in the United Nations and active cooperation by the "Big Four" to ensure peace. With the deterioration of relations between the United States and Great Britain on the one hand, and the Soviet Union on the other, Washington's leadership role came to include a policy of containing Soviet expansion, the first peacetime alliance in U.S. history, and economic and military assistance to allies in Europe and elsewhere. For at least two decades the premises of the Truman Doctrine, the Marshall Plan, and NATO served as the foundations of U.S. external relations; these assumptions and their opposites are summarized in the two columns of Table 11.1 as competing axioms concerning both the degree of U.S. responsibility for free world security and the extent to which that burden is synonymous with opposition to communism.

Responses to several questionnaire items focusing on this nation's general international orientation reflect, once again, considerable ambivalence. Although most respondents agreed that the U.S. economy had been seriously damaged as a consequence of intervention in Vietnam (11.4:J), by a margin of more than three to two they rejected the proposition that the United States should turn away from international concerns to concentrate on domestic problems. Indeed, one respondent in three expressed strong disagreement on this point (11.4:B). However, a slight majority agreed that some scaling down of Washington's leadership role in the world was in order (11.4:A), and two-thirds of the leaders agreed that the best way for the United States to influence domocratic development in the Third World is by solving its own problems (11.4:C).

Asked to assess the importance of "containing communism" as a foreign policy goal for the United States, approximately four respondents in ten replied "very important," an almost equal number checked the "somewhat important" option, and the remainder either dismissed this as a goal of no importance or expressed uncertainty (11.2:J). When faced with the more specific proposition that this nation should take all necessary steps, not excluding the use of force, to prevent the spread of communism, two-thirds of the leaders in the sample demurred (11.2:K). Thus, axioms that had once more or less been beyond debate had become, in the wake of the Vietnam conflict, points of dissensus and controversy.

The post–cold war axioms discussed earlier included the proposition that the real long-term threats to national security arose from problems that have little to do with communism. Consistent with that viewpoint are four further propositions about the importance of international cooperation on economic issues, combating world hunger, coping with global inflation, and improving the standard of living in less developed countries. The first of these was assessed as "very important" by a substantial majority of respondents, the second and third received a similar rating by one-half of the leaders in our sample, but fewer than four in ten attributed the same importance to the fourth of these goals (11.3:F,H,I, and G).

Finally, the respondents were asked about the appropriate ways to cope with the confict in Angola and with any future oil embargo that might be imposed by the petroleum exporting nations of the Middle East. By a margin of more than three to two, they agreed that the United States should avoid involvement in Angola, and an even greater majority rejected the proposition that a military intervention in the Middle East should follow any future oil embargo (11.4:F and 11.2:T). However, only one-sixth of the leaders in our sample agreed that stationing of U.S. technicians in the Sinai, between Egyptian and Israeli forces, was a serious mistake (11.4:G).

On balance, these results appear to indicate support for some retrenchment from the almost limitless global role envisioned, for example, in President Kennedy's inaugural address, but stopping substantially short of a return to isolationism. Even in the wake of the Vietnam experience, U.S. leaders are not prepared to abandon all types of international

TABLE 11.4
"Post-Cold War (Isolationist) Axioms": Responses of 2,282 American Leaders (in percentages*)

	Agree Strongly	Agree Somewhat	Disagree Somewhat	Disagree Strongly	No Opinion	Very Important	Moderately Important	Slightly Important	Not at All Important	Not Sure
A. America's conception of its leadership role in the world must be scaled down	15	41	21	22	1					
B. We shouldn't think so much in international terms but concentrate more on our own national problems	11	26	29	33	1					
C. The best way to encourage democratic development in the "Third World" is for the U.S. to solve its own problems	26	39	20	9	6					
D. Military aid programs will eventually draw the United States into unnecessary wars	10	31	39	17	3					

E. Stationing American troops in other countries encourages them to let us do their fighting for those countries	15	45	28	9	3
F. The U.S. should avoid any involvement in the Angolan civil war	38	24	24	13	2
G. It was a serious mistake to agree to locate American technicians in the Sinai	5	12	38	38	7
H. The conduct of American foreign affairs relies excessively on military advice	20	29	30	18	3
I. Americans have relied too much on Presidents to define the national interest	26	37	26	9	2
J. The foundations of the American economy were seriously damaged by own involvement in Vietnam	33	30	21	15	1
K. The real long-term threats to national security--energy shortages, the environment, etc.--have been neglected as a result of our preoccupation with Vietnam	34	39	17	9	1

* Excludes those who did not answer or who provided an uncodable response. Owing to rounding error, rows may total slightly more or less than 100 percent.

undertakings. To the contrary, there appears to be a fairly widespread recognition that at least certain types of issues cannot effectively be dealt with unilaterally.

Instruments of Foreign Policy

That failure of the Vietnam undertaking, despite a military effort costing some 50 thousand lives and 150 billion dollars, should have given rise to sober second thoughts about the role of military power in contemporary affairs is scarcely surprising. Two-thirds of the respondents rated worldwide arms control as a "very important" foreign policy goal, and another quarter of them checked the "moderately important" option (11.3:E). By a three-to-two margin the leaders in the sample questioned the utility of stationing U.S. troops abroad (11.4:E). A somewhat smaller majority disagreed with the proposition that military aid programs will eventually draw the United States into unnecessary wars (11.4:D). Of the three propositions about restrictions on the military as a factor in the failure of the Vietnam undertaking, none received a "very important" rating by a majority (11.2:Q,R, and S).

Responses to four additional items on military instruments of foreign policy reflect substantial ambivalence among U.S. leaders. On the one hand, an overwhelming majority of them agreed with the proposition that in cases of intervention, force should be applied quickly rather than through a policy of graduated escalation, as was done in Vietnam (11.2:O). On the other hand, the view that military rather than political considerations should govern the employment of force gained the support of fewer than four respondents in ten (11.2:N). Two additional questionnaire items on the uses of military power, both implying criticism of the self-imposed constraints on the conduct of the Vietnam conflict, resulted in an almost even division of the leaders in our sample (11.2:L and M). Ambivalence on these issues is further indicated by the relatively high proportion of respondents marking the "no opinion" option; in two cases, almost 10 percent of those completing the questionnaire did so.

Additional items concerning instruments of foreign policy centered on covert CIA activities against hostile governments and economic assistance to poorer nations. The former issue found the leaders in the sample evenly divided, with almost half of them expressing strong agreement or disagreement (11.2:P). The desirability of foreign aid programs that may contribute to higher prices at home also resulted in an almost equal division of the respondents (11.3:J).

The Conduct of U.S. Foreign Policy

The post-Vietnam debate on U.S. foreign policy has not been limited to the substance or content of policy. Critics at various points on the political spectrum have alleged that there are serious flaws — identified and magnified during the war in Southeast Asia — in the foreign policy process. Two items on the influence of military advice and the influence of the president in defining the national interest are included in Table 11.4.

The proposition that military advice plays an excessive role divided the leaders in the sample exactly down the middle, with one respondent in five expressing strong agreement, and an almost equal number disagreeing strongly (11.4:H). By a margin of better than three to two they agreed that there has been too much reliance on the president to define the national interest (11.4:I).

The picture that emerges from these data is one of declining support for some cold war axioms, but not for others. Conversely, there has been less than a complete embrace for the competing post–cold war axioms. Modal tendencies among respondents can be summarized briefly.

First, the international system is viewed in more multipolar and non-zero-sum terms. Relatively few respondents rejected containment, maintenance of alliance commitments, or the basic reasoning behind the so-called "domino theory." On the other hand, the proposition that any communist victory is a defeat for U.S. national interest received only limited support.

Second, the image of a monolithic adversary has been seriously eroded. Skepticism of Soviet goals, and even of its commitment to a genuine détente, abounds. However, the respondents draw a sharp distinction between the USSR and China in this respect, as well as between Moscow and Peking on the one hand, and revolutionary movements in the Third World on the other. Many of them are not prepared, however, to declare schisms among potential adversaries as a permanent fact of international life.

Third, although there is no evidence of a massive yearning for a return to classical isolationism, many would have this country scale down its role in international affairs. On balance, the respondents seemed to reject sweeping solutions in favor of a more discriminating view of the appropriate U.S. role in the world. Thus, many regarded containment as a very important goal, but such specific undertakings as intervention in Angola or in response to an oil embargo received scant support.

Finally, there is a growing skepticism about the universal value of military instruments of foreign policy. Very substantial numbers — in some cases majorities—expressed agreement with propositions about excessive reliance on military advice in the conduct of foreign affairs and of the adverse consequences of military assistance programs. No doubt these views reflect in part the belief that the agenda of critical international issues is becoming loaded with problems—inflation, energy, food, population, and the like—that lend themselves poorly or not at all to military solutions.

Lacking directly comparable evidence from earlier periods—for example, from 1946, 1956, and 1966—it cannot be stated with complete certitude that the results presented in this section represent a change of dramatic proportions in the beliefs of U.S. leadership. But if other observers are even moderately close to the mark in suggesting that cold war axioms enjoyed widespread support from Americans occupying leadership positions during the two decades prior to the direct U.S. intervention in Vietnam,[14] then these findings would appear to represent a rather marked shift away from a solid consensus.

A New Synthesis or Competing Belief Systems?

The foregoing results reveal a mixed pattern of support for important elements of both the cold war and post-cold war axioms. Thus, what was once accepted as more or less axiomatic about the conduct of U.S. external relations is at least in part the subject of challenge and controversy. Although this finding provides some important insight into the state of leadership thinking in the post-Vietnam era, it does not identify the nature of cleavages and consensus among U.S. leaders. That is, do the findings reported above reflect ambivalence among individual respondents, resulting in support for a mixture of both cold war and post-cold war axioms? An affirmative answer would suggest the emergence, sooner rather than later, of a new consensus on foreign policy, perhaps reflecting a synthesis of the propositions that have been analyzed. Alternatively, will further analysis reveal a rather consistent pattern of cleavages, dividing U.S. leaders into three groups, one adhering to the propositions labelled cold war axioms, the other to each of the two variants of post-cold war axioms? Stated differently, do the data reveal the existence of internally consistent and mutually exclusive systems of beliefs about the conduct of U.S. external relations? Should that be the case, the prospects for any early emergence of a new consensus would be much less sanguine.

In order to answer these questions, correlations among responses to the forty-one questionnaire items were computed. Each of the 190 corre-

TABLE 11.5
"Cold War Axioms": Correlations Among Items in the Responses of 2,282 American Leaders

	T	S	R	Q	P	O	N	M	L	K	J	I	H	G	F	E	D	C	B
A. Domino theory is valid*	33	48	48	50	47	37	34	38	45	49	51	29	39	27	39	40	56	53	34
B. Alliance commitments	15	31	30	33	23	26	19	25	29	28	26	17	24	15	23	21	34	32	
C. Communist victory/ U.S. defeat	32	42	43	39	40	32	31	38	41	57	55	36	40	29	36	42	47		
D. Detente assumptions false	56	44	44	45	40	34	31	37	44	43	44	29	42	26	37	46			
E. Communists encouraged	27	40	38	41	26	31	34	38	37	39	34	46	53	28	30				
F. U.S.S.R. is expansionist	18	29	29	30	30	27	21	26	28	31	37	27	37	24					
G. China is expansionist	15	25	25	25	18	14	20	21	21	24	20	20	24						
H. U.S.S.R. abuses detente	27	40	39	39	33	27	31	37	40	40	33	48							
I. Oppose better U.S.S.R. relations	26	33	29	30	26	27	30	32	35	39	29								
J. Containing communism	30	40	41	37	41	28	26	32	38	60									
K. Force to stop communism	39	45	43	38	46	29	30	39	46										
L. Avoid half measures	36	51	48	53	44	50	43	52											
M. Strike at enemy's power	30	44	46	48	36	45	42												
N. Let military set goals	22	49	42	44	26	36													
O. Oppose gradual escalation	25	40	41	47	34														
P. Approve C.I.A. coups	36	39	39	39															
Q. "No win" approach in Vietnam	29	61	65																
R. Restricted air power	30	64																	
S. Military advice neglected	29																		
T. Middle East intervention																			

Decimals omitted from correlation coefficients.

* Abbreviations of axioms. For full text, refer to Table 11.2. Capital letters in row and column headings correspond to the items in Table 11.2.

lation coefficients among the twenty cold war axioms is positive (Table 11.5). Thus, respondents who accepted one of these propositions were likely to agree with others as well, whereas those who disagreed with them were also prone to doing so across the board. Moreover, correlations reported in Table 11.5 are generally rather high. One hundred thirty-three of the 190 reach at least the 0.30 level, and 67 of them exceed 0.40.

The data also reveal some differences among items. The four propositions related to communism (11.5:C,E,J, and K) have consistently high correlations, as do those concerning the domino theory (11.5:A) and several of the items about the uses of military power (11.5:L–O and Q–S). Thus, these axioms appear to be at the core of what might be described as a "cold war belief system." On the other hand, the question of Chinese foreign policy intentions appears to be a somewhat more peripheral element of that belief system.

The results summarized in Tables 11.6 and 11.7 also indicate consistent patterns within both variants of post–cold war axioms, although the correlation coefficients are, on balance, somewhat lower than those in the previous table. Core beliefs in the internationalist version of the post–cold war axioms are those relating to development and humanitarian issues (11.6:G and H) and to the role of the United Nations (11.6:C and D), whereas beliefs about the permanence of conflict among communist nations (11.6:A) and the nature of Third World revolutionary movements (11.6:B) are more peripheral. Core items among isolationist beliefs are the proposition that the United States should scale down its international leadership role (11.7:A); two others bearing on the performance of the government in Washington — that there is excessive reliance on military advice in the formulation of foreign policy (11.7:H), as well as overdependence on presidential definition of the national interest (11.7:I); and skepticism about military assistance programs (11.7:D).

The previous three tables provide strong testimony to the existence of at least three internally consistent belief systems among U.S. leaders.[15] The cold war and the internationalist version of the post–cold war axioms also tend to be mutually exclusive. All 200 correlations between these items are negative.[16] To be sure, the coefficients for some issues — for example, concerning Chinese foreign policy and the importance of international cooperation on nonsecurity issues — are at best modest, only rarely exceeding the 0.20 level. Nevertheless, the overall pattern clearly identifies a major cleavage among U.S. leaders.

A less consistent pattern emerges from the correlations between the cold war and isolationist axioms. For example, there are only weak correlations between the cold war axioms and propositions relating to the

TABLE 11.6
"Post-Cold War (Internationalist) Axioms": Correlations Among Items in the Responses of 2,282 American Leaders

	J	I	H	G	F	E	D	C	B
A. Communist bloc fragmented*	16	02	07	09	10	08	10	07	30
B. Revolutionaries nationalists	24	11	17	21	19	15	22	19	
C. U.N. role vital	26	16	31	29	30	26	65		
D. Strengthen U.N.	27	24	28	36	35	30			
E. Arms control	18	24	28	24	30				
F. International cooperation	27	28	40	35					
G. LDC standard of living	48	26	59						
H. Combatting world hunger	42	40							
I. Global inflation	19								
J. Economic assistance									

Decimals omitted from correlation coefficients.

* Abbreviations of axioms. For full text, refer to Table 11.3. Capital letters in row and column headings correspond to items in Table 11.3.

TABLE 11.7
"Post-Cold War (Isolationist) Axioms": Correlations Among Items in the Responses of 2,282 American Leaders

	K	J	I	H	G	F	E	D	C	B
A. Scale down U.S. role*	26	23	28	36	16	42	21	34	18	18
B. Primacy of domestic problems	09	10	12	02	21	14	23	20	29	
C. Solve own problems	13	14	14	09	18	17	19	26		
D. Military aid leads to wars	29	25	35	40	30	43	30			
E. Oppose U.S. troops abroad	20	21	22	22	21	21				
F. Avoid Angola involvement	29	24	33	45	21					
G. Oppose technicians in Sinai	13	11	18	13						
H. Excessive military advice	36	28	35							
I. Excessive Presidential role	28	22								
J. Economy damaged by Vietnam	37									
K. Real security threats										

Decimals omitted from correlation coefficients.

* Abbreviations of axioms. For full text, refer to Table 11.4. Capital letters in row and column headings correspond to the items in Table 11.4.

primacy of domestic issues, democratic development in the Third World, and U.S. technicians in the Sinai. In a number of other respects, however, the disagreements are quite sharp. This is notably true of such questions as the U.S. leadership role and the source of threats facing this country, as well as on such specific questions as military assistance programs, military advice, and the wisdom of intervention in Angola.

Given the sharp and consistent differences between the cold war axioms and the two variants of post-cold war beliefs, does it follow that there is a consistent pattern of high agreement among the latter two sets of items? This is not the case. There are some elements in common, notably that there has been excessive dependence upon military advice in the formulation of U.S. foreign policy. But the overall pattern is one of consistently low correlations, only two of which reach the 0.30 level.

These results indicate that a dominant cleavage in U.S. leadership opinion falls along a fault line defined by the cold war versus post-cold war beliefs.[17] The evidence also indicates that there are indeed two variants of the latter that share little other than skepticism about the cold war axioms.

Occupation and Foreign Policy Beliefs

Whether this cleavage also coincides with occupational differences among the respondents remains to be determined. When disaggregated according to occupation, responses to the cold war axioms reveal that the primary sources of variation among the leaders in our sample exist *between* rather than within occupational groups (Table 11.8). Differences for all twenty items exceed even rather stringent statistical standards. The range of responses is especially striking on such issues as the validity of the domino theory, the desirability of using all steps to prevent the spread of communism, the proposition that any communist victory is a defeat for the U.S. national interest, and several items relating to the employment of military power.

Table 11.8 additionally reveals substantial consistency between groups in responses to the twenty axioms. With few exceptions, military officers and business executives were most supportive of these axioms, whereas educators and media leaders (including chief editorial writers and Washington-based correspondents for the printed and electronic media) were consistently among the most critical.[18] They are occasionally joined by foreign service officers on such issues as Chinese foreign policy goals (11.8:G) and the uses of force (11.8:N and O).

In some respects the pattern of responses to both the internationalist

TABLE 11.8
"Cold War Axioms": Responses of 2,282 American Leaders, Classified by Occupation (mean scores)

	All Respondents (2,282)	Military Officers (500)	Business Executives (294)	Lawyers (116)	Clergy (101)	Foreign Service (125)	Labor Officials (74)	Public Officials (110)	Educators (565)	Media Leaders (184)	Others (213)
						Occupations (N)					
A. There is considerable validity to the "domino theory" that when one nation falls to communism, others nearby will soon follow a similar path	0.24	0.56	0.46	0.26	0.29	0.21	0.09	0.19	-0.01	-0.05	0.16
B. A nation will pay a heavy price if it honors its alliance commitments only selectively	0.48	0.70	0.57	0.40	0.56	0.38	0.40	0.44	0.35	0.33	0.40
C. Any communist victory is a defeat for America's national interest	-0.14	0.13	0.05	-0.17	0.03	-0.07	-0.06	-0.18	-0.38	-0.42	-0.22
D. The major assumptions of detente have been proven false by the events in Vietnam	-0.13	0.04	0.05	-0.19	0.11	-0.32	0.11	-0.21	-0.32	-0.33	-0.09
E. Communist nations have been encouraged to seek triumphs elsewhere as a result of Vietnam	0.32	0.60	0.48	0.21	0.45	0.27	0.15	0.26	0.12	0.12	0.21
F. The Soviet Union is generally expansionist rather than defensive in its foreign policy goals	0.58	0.72	0.67	0.57	0.58	0.60	0.57	0.63	0.42	0.54	0.51

G. China is generally expansionist rather than defensive in its foreign policy goals	-0.25	-0.21	-0.10	-0.18	0.01	-0.36	-0.23	-0.23	-0.36	-0.35	-0.25
H. Detente permits the U.S.S.R. to pursue policies that promote rather than restrain conflict	0.15	0.44	0.23	0.14	0.30	-0.05	0.24	0.03	-0.05	0.04	0.07
I. It is not in our best interest to have better relations with the Soviet Union because we are getting less than we are giving to them	-0.33	-0.06	-0.27	-0.34	-0.26	-0.46	0.04	-0.44	-0.50	-0.56	-0.39
J. Containing communism (as a foreign policy goal for the United States)	0.64	0.74	0.75	0.72	0.70	0.70	0.62	0.61	0.51	0.56	0.52
K. The U.S. should take all steps including the use of force to prevent the spread of communism	-0.29	0.09	-0.20	-0.35	-0.22	-0.26	-0.35	-0.34	-0.53	-0.60	-0.43
L. The U.S. should never try to get by with half measures; we should apply necessary power if we have it	0.07	0.55	0.26	0.01	0.05	0.08	-0.11	-0.08	-0.26	-0.40	-0.08
M. Rather than simply countering our opponent's thrusts, it is necessary to strike at the heart of the opponent's power	0.01	0.33	0.21	-0.09	0.14	-0.10	0.11	-0.06	-0.26	-0.25	-0.06
N. When force is used, military rather than political goals should determine its application	-0.21	0.17	-0.08	-0.30	-0.15	-0.40	-0.16	-0.38	-0.46	-0.39	-0.23
O. If foreign interventions are undertaken, the necessary force should be applied in a short period of time rather than through a policy of graduated escalation	0.55	0.82	0.72	0.52	0.60	0.47	0.50	0.49	0.31	0.49	0.47
P. There is nothing wrong with using the C.I.A. to try to undermine hostile governments	-0.02	0.34	0.30	0.08	-0.31	0.02	-0.28	0.09	-0.31	-0.28	-0.22
Q. The U.S. fought with a "no win" approach (as a cause of failure in Vietnam)	0.65	0.90	0.82	0.67	0.70	0.57	0.57	0.56	0.46	0.48	0.59

Table 11.8 (cont.)

	All Respondents (2,282)	Military Officers (500)	Business Executives (294)	Lawyers (116)	Clergy (101)	Foreign Service (125)	Labor Officials (74)	Public Officials (110)	Educators (565)	Media Leaders (184)	Others (213)
						Occupations (N)					
R. The use of American air power was restricted (as a cause of failure in Vietnam)	0.56	0.77	0.70	0.55	0.59	0.50	0.49	0.47	0.39	0.39	0.49
S. Insufficient attention was paid to advice from the military (as a cause of failure in Vietnam)	0.46	0.75	0.55	0.39	0.50	0.32	0.40	0.38	0.28	0.24	0.41
T. The U.S. should undertake military intervention in the Middle East in case of another oil embargo	-0.49	-0.30	-0.27	-0.41	-0.55	-0.60	-0.45	-0.44	-0.65	-0.74	-0.55

Items A-J, K-P and T scored on a scale of 1.00 to -1.00. Items J and Q-S scored on a scale of 1.00 to 0.00.

Differences among occupational groups significant at .001 level, whether computed according to parametric (analysis of variance) or non-parametric (chi-square) statistics, for all items.

and isolationist versions of the post–cold war axioms are the mirror image of those described in Table 11.8. Military officers and business executives were consistently the least prone to accord great importance to such concerns as strengthening international organizations (11.9:C and D) and economic issues (11.9:F–J). Not unexpectedly, educators and media leaders were often at or near the other end of the spectrum. Less predictable is the position of the clergy. Recall that they took a decidedly skeptical view of some propositions—for example, that revolutionary forces in the Third World are nationalistic rather than communist controlled, and that the Communist bloc is irreparably fragmented. The clergy had also been the most inclined to appraise Chinese foreign policy goals as expansionist rather than defensive. In several respects, then, respondents in this group adhered to cold war axioms. Yet in other respects their views did not fit this pattern. By a substantial margin the clergy agreed most strongly that the United Nations has a vital international role, and they attributed the greatest importance to strengthening it. Moreover, the clergy were most inclined to support such foreign policy goals as combating world hunger, improving the standard of living in less developed countries, and fostering international cooperation on common economic problems. On seven of the ten items listed in Table 11.9 the clergy ranked as the group with the highest score.

Military officers and business executives also tended to be the least supportive of the isolationist propositions, although foreign service officers are more often than not also at the low end of the scale. However, the most striking aspect of Table 11.10 is the consistently isolationist stance of labor leaders. Although not notably sanguine about the prospects of better relations between the United States and its adversaries—labor leaders, for example, were among those skeptical about the benefits of détente (11.8:D and H)—respondents in this group generally provided the strongest support for propositions that incorporated a reduced international role for this country. They favored scaling down the U.S. leadership role in the world and greater attention to domestic issues, while also agreeing that military advice and military assistance programs are of dubious value in this nation's foreign policy. Labor leaders were also the only occupational group supporting the proposition that "we shouldn't think so much in international terms but concentrate more on our own problems" (11.10:B). In all, labor leaders provided the strongest group support for ten of the twelve isolationist axioms.[19]

In summary, the data indicate that the cleavages on several foreign policy issues fall between, rather than across, occupational lines. In every case the differences between occupational groups are significant, even when applying the rather stringent criterion that by both parametric and nonparametric methods the differences must be of such a magnitude that

TABLE 11.9
"Post-Cold War (Internationalist) Axioms": Responses of 2,282 American Leaders, Classified by Occupation (mean scores)

	All Respondents (2,282)	Military Officers (500)	Business Executives (294)	Lawyers (116)	Clergy (101)	Foreign Service (125)	Labor Officials (74)	Public Officials (110)	Educators (565)	Media Leaders (184)	Others (213)
A. American foreign policy should be based on the premise that the Communist "bloc" is irreparably fragmented	-0.25	-0.43	-0.42	-0.31	-0.41	-0.22	-0.16	-0.26	-0.05	-0.07	-0.20
B. Revolutionary forces in "Third World" countries are usually nationalistic rather than controlled by the U.S.S.R. or China	0.19	-0.11	-0.03	0.20	-0.05	0.33	0.12	0.32	0.37	0.39	0.27
C. It is vital to enlist the cooperation of the U.N. in settling international disputes	0.20	0.08	0.02	0.12	0.52	0.05	0.43	0.20	0.31	0.24	0.36
D. Strengthening the United Nations (as a foreign policy goal for the United States)	0.47	0.36	0.35	0.44	0.60	0.44	0.58	0.48	0.56	0.51	0.58
E. Worldwide arms control (as a foreign policy goal for the United States)	0.82	0.72	0.87	0.85	0.87	0.78	0.87	0.84	0.87	0.89	0.85
F. Fostering international cooperation to solve common problems, such as food, inflation and energy (as a foreign policy goal for the United States)	0.85	0.79	0.77	0.81	0.93	0.88	0.88	0.83	0.90	0.87	0.89

G. Helping to improve the standard of living in less developed countries (as a foreign policy goal for the United States)	0.65	0.51	0.56	0.62	0.85	0.72	0.72	0.66	0.72	0.75	0.71
H. Combatting world hunger (as a foreign policy goal for the United States)	0.73	0.59	0.65	0.67	0.91	0.77	0.80	0.75	0.78	0.82	0.77
I. Helping solve world inflation (as a foreign policy goal for the United States)	0.73	0.61	0.74	0.73	0.79	0.74	0.76	0.77	0.76	0.79	0.78
J. The U.S. should give economic aid to poorer countries even if it means higher prices at home	-0.05	-0.39	-0.23	-0.12	0.39	0.16	-0.02	-0.06	0.17	0.10	0.03

Items A-C and J scored on a scale of 1.00 to -1.00. Items D-I scored on a scale of 1.00 to 0.00.

Differences among occupational groups significant at .001 level, whether computed according to parametric (analysis of variance) or non-parametric (chi-square) statistics, for all items.

TABLE 11.10
"Post-Cold War (Isolationist) Axioms": Responses of 2,282 American Leaders, Classified by Occupation (mean scores)

	All Respondents (2,282)	Military Officers (500)	Business Executives (294)	Lawyers (116)	Clergy (101)	Foreign Service (125)	Labor Officials (74)	Public Officials (110)	Educators (565)	Media Leaders (184)	Others (213)
						Occupations (N)					
A. America's conception of its leadership role in the world must be scaled down	0.04	-0.29	0.02	0.12	-0.02	0.02	0.19	-0.02	0.26	0.15	0.10
B. We shouldn't think so much in international terms but concentrate more on our own national problems	-0.24	-0.25	-0.07	-0.12	-0.38	-0.36	0.20	-0.23	-0.38	-0.26	-0.10
C. The best way to encourage democratic development in the "Third World" is for the U.S. to solve its own problems	0.27	0.23	0.12	0.30	0.23	0.12	0.53	0.21	0.24	0.28	0.41
D. Military aid programs will eventually draw the United States into unnecessary wars	-0.11	-0.37	-0.17	-0.14	0.07	-0.21	0.13	-0.10	0.01	-0.03	0.11
E. Stationing American troops in other countries encourages them to let us do their fighting for those countries	0.15	-0.04	0.09	0.15	0.14	0.09	0.38	0.20	0.20	0.20	0.25
F. The U.S. should avoid any involvement in the Angolan civil war	0.25	-0.19	0.19	0.30	0.21	0.18	0.47	0.32	0.49	0.51	0.41

G.	It was a serious mistake to agree to locate American technicians in the Sinai	-0.47	-0.57	-0.43	-0.38	-0.38	-0.54	-0.29	-0.47	-0.47	-0.45	-0.40
H.	The conduct of American foreign affairs relies excessively on military advice	0.02	-0.56	-0.10	0.06	0.17	-0.08	0.37	0.17	0.30	0.31	0.30
I.	Americans have relied too much on Presidents to define the national interest	0.22	0.06	0.01	0.21	0.36	0.19	0.54	0.20	0.31	0.36	0.35
J.	The foundations of the American economy were seriously damaged by our involvement in Vietnam	0.22	-0.08	0.27	0.28	0.29	0.10	0.50	0.24	0.40	0.39	0.29
K.	The real long-term threats to national security--energy shortages, the environment, etc.--have been neglected as a result of our preoccupation with Vietnam	0.36	0.15	0.28	0.32	0.32	0.37	0.54	0.47	0.47	0.53	0.48

All items scored on a scale of 1.00 to -1.00.

Differences among occupational groups significant at .001 level, whether computed according to parametric (analysis of variance) or non-parametric (chi-square) statistics, for all items.

they would occur by chance less than once in a thousand times. When combined with the results discussed in the previous section, these findings are not without important implications for the question of consensus, for they suggest that role factors are more likely to sustain than to break down existing systems of beliefs about foreign policy issues.

Conclusion

As the SALT II Treaty was about to be presented to the Senate for ratification, a Carter administration official observed, somewhat wistfully, that, "If Eisenhower was [sic] President, all he'd have to do is say: 'I've read the treaty, I think it's good,' and he'd get a tremendous number of people to follow him."[20] In part this comment acknowledges the high regard with which President Eisenhower's views on military matters were usually received. It also reflects a broader point—that the Carter administration (like the two that preceded it) can no longer count upon a consensus in the Congress and among important elements of U.S. leadership on fundamental questions of foreign and defense policy. A quarter of a century ago, notwithstanding sometimes shrill campaign rhetoric, there was relatively broad agreement about the nature of the international system, the sources of threats to vital U.S. interests, and the appropriate policies to deal with external challenges and opportunities. The premises of such major undertakings as the Truman Doctrine, the Marshall Plan, and the North Atlantic Treaty Organization enjoyed widespread support, or what Alexander George calls "policy legitimacy." This fact had important implications for Washington's efforts to shape a congenial international system for, as George has shown in Chapter 10, there is an intimate relationship between policy legitimacy and a nation's ability to seek changes in the international system. Drawing upon evidence from the Roosevelt and Nixon administrations, he demonstrated both how policy legitimacy served as a necessary condition for system-transforming policies, and how its erosion became a constraint that ultimately prevented these two administrations from pursuing long-range foreign policy objectives.

Policy legitimacy implies a certain degree of consensus on at least the most fundamental beliefs about the nature of the international system, the nation's appropriate international role, and the goals, strategies, and tactics that constitute the core of foreign policy. Given the highly uneven interest in and impact upon foreign policy issues among individuals, it would appear especially important that there be at least a moderate degree of agreement among those holding leadership positions. Pursuing this line of reasoning, the state of leadership thinking on several foreign policy issues during the post–Vietnam period has been assessed. The results suggest, on balance, the absence of consensus on many important questions. By itself, this finding may merely reflect that which is obvious to even the most casual observer: The efforts of neither the Nixon-Ford nor the Carter administrations to reconstruct a foreign policy consensus have been very successful. The further findings that there are both psychological and sociological factors that may sustain rather than break down existing cleavages suggest that efforts to achieve a new consensus may not meet with a great deal of success in the very near future. Stated somewhat differently, in the absence of dramatic or traumatic unifying episodes—for example, another Pearl Harbor—policy legitimacy may prove to be an elusive goal for the near term. To the extent that this prognosis is valid, it suggests that bold American undertakings aimed at achieving fundamental changes in the international system are likely to trigger long and divisive domestic debates. In this respect the divisions on the Panama Canal treaties, the SALT II Treaty, and the establishment of diplomatic relations with China—although all of these undertakings had their genesis in a Republican administration and their consummation in a Democratic one—may be harbingers. Even the anticipation of such confrontations is likely to be an important constraint on the conduct of American foreign policy.

It is, of course, possible that the as-yet-unresolved crisis in Iran or the Soviet invasion of Afghanistan will be the catalyst for creation of a new foreign policy consensus in this country, much as the attack on Pearl Harbor was almost four decades ago. As one senior administration official put it, "In terms of domestic politics, this [Iran] has put an end to the Vietnam syndrome."[21] There is little disagreement about the illegitimacy of taking diplomats hostage but, barring the outbreak of war over Iran, this episode seems as likely to strengthen previously-held convictions as it is to be the crucible from which springs forth a new consensus. Thus, the cold war internationalists will probably emphasize such "lessons of Iran" as: "The United States should use all of its resources to maintain in power such friendly regimes as that of the Shah." The post–cold war internationalists will likely adduce the lesson that this country should never have become so closely aligned with an authoritarian right-wing regime, and the isolationists will probably find in the Iranian crisis confirmation of their basic premise that excessive commitments to and dependence upon other nations will continue to divert our attention from a long agenda of neglected domestic problems. Although Afghanistan has created at least a temporary consensus about the nature of Soviet foreign policy, initial responses by presidential candidates, editorial writers, and pundits indicate anything but agreement concerning the appropriate American response. To the extent that the events in Iran and Afghanistan *do* give rise to any shift of opinion, however, the post–cold war internationalist position is the least likely to gain adherents.

The existence of cleavages such as those described in this chapter does not, of course, reduce the need for a comprehensive long-range policy to guide the more urgent of this nation's external relationships — for example, vis-à-vis the Soviet Union. Nor does it relieve an administration from the responsibility for satisfying both the normative and cognitive components of policy legitimacy. A national catastrophe on the order of a Pearl Harbor may be the midwife of instant foreign policy consensus, but clearly the price is unacceptable. The alternative is the slower process that ultimately depends very heavily on skilled and intelligent leadership in Washington.

Notes

1. Especially valuable discussions of this point may be found in Ernest R. May, *"Lessons" of the Past: The Use and Misuse of History in American Foreign Policy* (New York: Oxford University Press, 1973); and a chapter entitled "How Decision-Makers Learn from History" in Robert Jervis, *Perception and Misperception in International Politics* (Princeton, N.J.: Princeton University Press, 1976).

See also Louis Morton, "Historia Mentem Armet: Lessons of the Past," *World Politics* 12 (January 1960):155–164; J. Lawton Collins, *War in Peacetime: The History and Lessons of Korea* (Boston: Houghton Mifflin Co., 1969); Harvey A. DeWeerd, "Lessons of the Korean War," *Yale Review* 40 (June 1951):592–603; Peter Braestrup, "Limited War and the Lessons of Lebanon," *The Reporter* 20 (30 April 1959):25–27; Harry A. Hadd, "Who's a Rebel? The Lesson Lebanon Taught," *Marine Corps Gazette* 46 (March 1962):25–26; Albert P. Sights, Jr., "Lessons of the Lebanon: A Study in Air Strategy," *Air University Review* 16 (July–August 1965):28–43; Anatole Shub, "Lessons of Czechoslovakia," *Foreign Affairs* 47 (January 1969); Alexander L. George, David K. Hall, and William R. Simons, *The Limits of Coercive Diplomacy* (Boston: Little, Brown and Co., 1971), pp. 211–253; Raymond L. Garthoff, "Negotiating with the Russians: Some Lessons from SALT," *International Security* 1 (Spring 1977):3–24; William H. Chamberlain, "The Lessons of Quemoy," *The New Leader* 41 (15 December 1958); Gerald J. Bender, "Angola, The Cubans, and American Anxieties," *Foreign Policy* 31 (Summer 1978):3–30; and John A. Lauder, "Lessons of the Strategic Bombing Survey for Contemporary Defense Policy," *Orbis* 18 (Fall 1974): 770–790.

2. "Axioms of foreign policy" refer to a set of fundamental principles and assumptions that guide the basic directions of foreign policy. They are thus vir-

tually interchangeable with such terms as "shared images" or "underlying assumptions." The term "axioms of foreign policy" is especially appropriate for our purposes because, as Ernest R. May points out, it is historical experience subjectively interpreted that gives rise to axioms: "While historical experience is the substance of an axiom, it is not the molder. People read into history more or less what they want to read." It is precisely this interest in the posteriori interpretations of the Vietnam conflict, and its meaning for the future conduct of U.S. foreign policy, that were the genesis for the present research project. For further discussions, see Ernest R. May, "The Nature of Foreign Policy: The Calculated Versus the Axiomatic," *Daedalus* 91 (Fall 1962):653–667; Graham T. Allison, "Cool It: The Foreign Policy of Young America," *Foreign Policy* 1 (Winter 1970–1971):144–160; Morton Halperin, *Bureaucratic Politics and Foreign Policy* (Washington, D.C.: Brookings Institution, 1974); Alexander L. George, "The Role of Cognitive Beliefs in the Legitimation of a Long-Range Foreign Policy: The Case of F. D. Roosevelt's Plan for Postwar Cooperation with the Soviet Union" (Paper prepared for the Conference on Approaches to Decision-Making, Oslo, Norway, 9–12 August 1977); B. Thomas Trout, "Rhetoric Revisited: Political Legitimation and The Cold War," *International Studies Quarterly* 19 (September 1975):251–284; and Daniel Yergin, *Shattered Peace: The Origins of the Cold War and the National Security State* (Boston: Houghton Mifflin Co., 1977).

3. See, for example, Frank L. Klingberg, "Historical Alternation of Moods in American Foreign Policy," *World Politics* 4 (January 1952):239–273; and Frank L. Klingberg, "Cyclical Trends in American Foreign Policy Moods and Their Policy Implications," in Charles W. Kegley, Jr., and Patrick J. McGowan, eds., *Challenges to America: United States Foreign Policy in the 1980s, Sage International Yearbook of Foreign Policy Studies* 4 (1979).

4. Arthur H. Vandenberg, Jr., ed., *The Private Papers of Senator Vandenberg* (Boston: Houghton Mifflin Co., 1952), p. 1.

5. For continuities and changes in the beliefs of Vandenberg and Fulbright, see Joel E. Anderson, Jr., *The "Operational Code" Belief System of Senator Arthur Vandenberg: An Application of the George Construct* (Ph.D. diss., University of Michigan, 1973); and Kurt Tweraser, "Changing Patterns of Political Beliefs: The Foreign Policy Operational Codes of J. William Fulbright," *Sage Professional Papers in American Politics,* no. 04–016 (1974).

6. These axioms have been drawn from lists compiled by several other observers of American foreign policy: Allison, "Cool It"; Halperin, *Bureaucratic Politics*; and Michael Roskin, "From Pearl Harbor to Vietnam: Shifting Generational Paradigms and Foreign Policy," *Political Science Quarterly* 89 (Fall 1974):576.

7. A detailed description of sources used to construct the questionnaire and of sampling procedures may be found in an earlier paper, "The Lessons of Vietnam: A Study of American Leadership" (Paper prepared for the 17th Annual Meeting of the International Studies Association, Toronto, Canada, February 1976), Appendixes A, C.

8. Other reports include: "Vietnam Revisited: Beliefs of Foreign Service and Military Officers about the Sources of Failure, Consequences, and 'Lessons' of

the War" (Paper prepared for the 10th Congress of the International Political Science Association, Edinburgh, Scotland, 1976); "The Meaning of Vietnam: Belief Systems of American Leaders," *International Journal* 32 (Summer 1977):452–474; "Vietnam, Consensus, and the Belief Systems of American Leaders," *World Politics* 32 (October 1979); "Does Where You Stand Depend on When You Were Born? The Impact of Generation on Post-Vietnam Foreign Policy Beliefs," *Public Opinion Quarterly* (Spring 1980); and "America's Foreign Policy Agenda: The Post-Vietnam Beliefs of American Leaders," in Kegley and McGowan, eds., *Challenges to America*.

9. The importance of occupation has been established in many other studies, including the 1971–1972 American Leadership Project survey: "Our results have confirmed the importance of current occupational sector as a determinant of attitudes in that it alone is stronger than a variety of background variables." R. Wayne Parsons and Allen H. Barton, "Social Background and Policy Attitudes of American Leaders" (Paper prepared for the 1974 Annual Meeting of the American Political Science Association, Chicago, 1974), p. 30.

10. At the time that the questionnaire was sent out, the issue of military intervention to counter another oil embargo was quite salient. Secretary of State Henry Kissinger had hinted that such a course of action could not be ruled out, and a number of prominent academic observers had proposed that intervention would be both feasible and necessary to avoid the costs of another oil embargo. Robert W. Tucker, "Oil: The Issue of American Intervention," *Commentary* (January 1975):21–31; Tucker, "Further Reflections on Oil and Force," *Commentary* (March 1975):45–56; and Edward Friedland, Paul Seabury, and Aaron Wildavsky, *The Great Detente Disaster: Oil and the Decline of American Foreign Policy* (New York: Basic Books, 1975).

11. In order to facilitate use of the tables, references in the text will identify questionnaire items first by table number and then by the letter preceding the specific item. Thus, (11.2:A) refers to the first item (A) in Table 11.2.

12. A survey conducted by the American Leadership Project in 1971–1972 yielded quite similar responses to the same question: agree strongly (25%), agree with qualifications (52%), disagree with qualifications (16%), and disagree strongly (7%). Allen H. Barton, "Consensus and Conflict Among American Leaders," *Public Opinion Quarterly* 38 (Winter 1974–1975):582. The Barton sample did not include military officers. Another survey, in 1973, of business executives and military officers, also yielded agreement for this proposition among both groups. Business executives: agree strongly (24%), agree with qualifications (50%), disagree with qualifications (20%), and disagree strongly (6%). The comparable figures of the military officers were: 22%–62%–15%–2%. Bruce M. Russett and Elizabeth C. Hanson, *Interest and Ideology* (San Francisco: W. H. Freeman and Co., 1975), pp. 274–275.

13. Recall, for example, arguments by President Lyndon B. Johnson and Secretary of State Dean Rusk about the imperatives of confronting Chinese expansion in Vietnam in order to avoid having to do so later in Honolulu or San Francisco, or by Secretary of Defense Robert McNamara on the role of a limited antiballistic missile defense system.

14. For example, Stanley Hoffmann has described this period in U.S. foreign policy as "the age of consensus." Hoffmann, *Primacy or World Order: American Foreign Policy Since the Cold War* (New York: McGraw-Hill Book Co., 1978).

15. Evidence from other studies also indicates that persons in leadership positions tend to have more structured belief systems. See, for example, Philip E. Converse, "The Nature of Belief Systems in Mass Publics," in David E. Apter, ed., *Ideology and Discontent* (New York: Free Press, 1964), pp. 206-261; and Barton, "Consensus and Conflict."

16. Because of space limitations, tables showing correlations between items in Tables 11.2 and 11.3, Tables 11.2 and 11.4, and Tables 11.3 and 11.4 are not included. They are available upon request from Ole R. Holsti.

17. For further elaboration of these belief systems, see Ole R. Holsti, "The Three-Headed Eagle: The United States and System Change," *International Studies Quarterly* 23 (September 1979):339-359. Evidence of similar cleavages among the public at large may be found in Michael Mandelbaum and William Schneider, "The New Internationalisms: Public Opinion and American Foreign Policy," in Kenneth Oye, Donald Rothchild, and Robert Lieber, *Eagle Entangled: U.S. Foreign Policy in a Complex World* (New York: Longman, 1979).

18. Other studies have also found that media leaders are at the "dovish" end of the scale on foreign policy issues. Barton, "Consensus and Conflict." These results are also quite similar to those of an earlier survey of business and military leaders by Russett and Hanson, *Interest and Ideology*. The post-Vietnam foreign policy views of military officers are also described in Douglas Kinnard, *The War Managers* (Hanover, N.Y.: University Press of New England, 1977). Subjects of the latter survey are general officers who served in Vietnam.

19. The American Leadership Project survey revealed that whereas labor leaders hold views far different from business executives on most domestic questions, these two groups agree on many foreign policy issues. Barton, "Consensus and Conflict," pp. 511-512; and Parsons and Barton, "Social Background," p. 12. Our results indicate that during the five years between the two surveys the views of business executives have remained relatively constant, whereas those of labor leaders have moved sharply toward isolationism.

20. Quoted in Steven B. Roberts, "Arms Pact Friends and Foes Rally for Senate Battle," *New York Times*, 13 April 1979.

21. Hedrick Smith, "Iran Helps U.S. Shed Fears of Intervening Abroad," *New York Times*, 2 December 1979, p. 1.

Index